QGIS 2.8 User Guide

A catalogue record for this book is available from the Hong Kong Public Libraries.

Published in Hong Kong by Samurai Media Limited.

Email: info@samuraimedia.org

ISBN 978-988-8406-22-7

.

.

Contents

## CHAPTER 1

Preamble

This document is the original user guide of the described software QGIS. The software and hardware described in this document are in most cases registered trademarks and are therefore subject to legal requirements. QGIS is subject to the GNU General Public License. Find more information on the QGIS homepage, http://www.qgis.org.

The details, data, and results in this document have been written and verified to the best of the knowledge and responsibility of the authors and editors. Nevertheless, mistakes concerning the content are possible.

Therefore, data are not liable to any duties or guarantees. The authors, editors and publishers do not take any responsibility or liability for failures and their consequences. You are always welcome to report possible mistakes.

This document has been typeset with reStructuredText. It is available as reST source code via github and online as HTML and PDF via http://www.qgis.org/en/docs/. Translated versions of this document can be downloaded in several formats via the documentation area of the QGIS project as well. For more information about contributing to this document and about translating it, please visit http://www.qgis.org/wiki/.

Links in this Document

This document contains internal and external links. Clicking on an internal link moves within the document, while clicking on an external link opens an internet address. In PDF form, internal and external links are shown in blue and are handled by the system browser. In HTML form, the browser displays and handles both identically.

User, Installation and Coding Guide Authors and Editors:

Tara Athan	Radim Blazek	Godofredo Contreras	Otto Dassau	Martin Dobias
Peter Ersts	Anne Ghisla	Stephan Holl	N. Horning	Magnus Homann
Werner Macho	Carson J.Q. Farmer	Tyler Mitchell	K. Koy	Lars Luthman
Claudia A. Engel	Brendan Morely	David Willis	Jürgen E. Fischer	Marco Hugentobler
Larissa Junek	Diethard Jansen	Paolo Corti	Gavin Macaulay	Gary E. Sherman
Tim Sutton	Alex Bruy	Raymond Nijssen	Richard Duivenvoorde	Andreas Neumann
Astrid Emde	Yves Jacolin	Alexandre Neto	Andy Schmid	Hien Tran-Quang

Copyright (c) 2004 - 2014 QGIS Development Team

Internet: http://www.qgis.org

License of this document

Permission is granted to copy, distribute and/or modify this document under the terms of the GNU Free Documentation License, Version 1.3 or any later version published by the Free Software Foundation; with no Invariant Sections, no Front-Cover Texts and no Back-Cover Texts. A copy of the license is included in Appendix *GNU Free Documentation License*.

.

## CHAPTER 2

Conventions

This section describes the uniform styles that will be used throughout this manual.

2.1 GUI Conventions

The GUI convention styles are intended to mimic the appearance of the GUI. In general, a style will reflect the non-hover appearance, so a user can visually scan the GUI to find something that looks like the instruction in the manual.

- Menu Options: *Layer → Add a Raster Layer* or *Settings → Toolbars → Digitizing*

- Tool: Add a Raster Layer

- Button : **[Save as Default]**

- Dialog Box Title: *Layer Properties*

- Tab: *General*

- Checkbox: ☑ *Render*

- Radio Button: ⦿ *Postgis SRID* ◯ *EPSG ID*

- Select a number: `1,00 ◇`

- Select a string: `... ▼`

- Browse for a file: `...`

- Select a color: Border ▬▬▬ ▼

- Slider: ⊙━━━━━━

- Input Text: Display name | lakes.shp|

A shadow indicates a clickable GUI component.

2.2 Text or Keyboard Conventions

This manual also includes styles related to text, keyboard commands and coding to indicate different entities, such as classes or methods. These styles do not correspond to the actual appearance of any text or coding within QGIS.

- Hyperlinks: http://qgis.org

- Keystroke Combinations: Press `Ctrl+B`, meaning press and hold the Ctrl key and then press the B key.

- Name of a File: `lakes.shp`

- Name of a Class: **NewLayer**

- Method: *classFactory*

- Server: *myhost.de*

- User Text: `qgis --help`

Lines of code are indicated by a fixed-width font:

```
PROJCS["NAD_1927_Albers",
  GEOGCS["GCS_North_American_1927",
```

2.3 Platform-specific instructions

GUI sequences and small amounts of text may be formatted inline: Click △ ♯ *File* ✗ *QGIS → Quit to close QGIS*. This indicates that on Linux, Unix and Windows platforms, you should click the File menu first, then Quit, while on Macintosh OS X platforms, you should click the QGIS menu first, then Quit.

Larger amounts of text may be formatted as a list:

- △ Do this

- ♯ Do that

- ✗ Do something else

or as paragraphs:

△ ✗ Do this and this and this. Then do this and this and this, and this and this and this, and this and this and this.

♯ Do that. Then do that and that and that, and that and that and that, and that and that and that, and that and that and that, and that and that and that.

Screenshots that appear throughout the user guide have been created on different platforms; the platform is indicated by the platform-specific icon at the end of the figure caption.

.

## CHAPTER 3

Foreword

Welcome to the wonderful world of Geographical Information Systems (GIS)!

QGIS is an Open Source Geographic Information System. The project was born in May of 2002 and was established as a project on SourceForge in June of the same year. We've worked hard to make GIS software (which is traditionally expensive proprietary software) a viable prospect for anyone with basic access to a personal computer. QGIS currently runs on most Unix platforms, Windows, and OS X. QGIS is developed using the Qt toolkit (http://qt.digia.com) and C++. This means that QGIS feels snappy and has a pleasing, easy-to-use graphical user interface (GUI).

QGIS aims to be a user-friendly GIS, providing common functions and features. The initial goal of the project was to provide a GIS data viewer. QGIS has reached the point in its evolution where it is being used by many for their daily GIS data-viewing needs. QGIS supports a number of raster and vector data formats, with new format support easily added using the plugin architecture.

QGIS is released under the GNU General Public License (GPL). Developing QGIS under this license means that you can inspect and modify the source code, and guarantees that you, our happy user, will always have access to a GIS program that is free of cost and can be freely modified. You should have received a full copy of the license with your copy of QGIS, and you also can find it in Appendix *GNU General Public License*.

Tip: Up-to-date Documentation

The latest version of this document can always be found in the documentation area of the QGIS website at http://www.qgis.org/en/docs/.

.

## CHAPTER 4

Features

QGIS offers many common GIS functionalities provided by core features and plugins. A short summary of six general categories of features and plugins is presented below, followed by first insights into the integrated Python console.

4.1 View data

You can view and overlay vector and raster data in different formats and projections without conversion to an internal or common format. Supported formats include:

- Spatially-enabled tables and views using PostGIS, SpatiaLite and MS SQL Spatial, Oracle Spatial, vector formats supported by the installed OGR library, including ESRI shapefiles, MapInfo, SDTS, GML and many more. See section *Working with Vector Data*.

- Raster and imagery formats supported by the installed GDAL (Geospatial Data Abstraction Library) library, such as GeoTIFF, ERDAS IMG, ArcInfo ASCII GRID, JPEG, PNG and many more. See section *Working with Raster Data*.

- GRASS raster and vector data from GRASS databases (location/mapset). See section *GRASS GIS Integration*.

- Online spatial data served as OGC Web Services, including WMS, WMTS, WCS, WFS, and WFS-T. See section *Working with OGC Data*.

4.2 Explore data and compose maps

You can compose maps and interactively explore spatial data with a friendly GUI. The many helpful tools available in the GUI include:

- QGIS browser
- On-the-fly reprojection
- DB Manager
- Map composer
- Overview panel
- Spatial bookmarks
- Annotation tools
- Identify/select features
- Edit/view/search attributes
- Data-defined feature labeling

- Data-defined vector and raster symbology tools
- Atlas map composition with graticule layers
- North arrow scale bar and copyright label for maps
- Support for saving and restoring projects

4.3 Create, edit, manage and export data

You can create, edit, manage and export vector and raster layers in several formats. QGIS offers the following:

- Digitizing tools for OGR-supported formats and GRASS vector layers
- Ability to create and edit shapefiles and GRASS vector layers
- Georeferencer plugin to geocode images
- GPS tools to import and export GPX format, and convert other GPS formats to GPX or down/upload directly to a GPS unit (On Linux, usb: has been added to list of GPS devices.)
- Support for visualizing and editing OpenStreetMap data
- Ability to create spatial database tables from shapefiles with DB Manager plugin
- Improved handling of spatial database tables
- Tools for managing vector attribute tables
- Option to save screenshots as georeferenced images
- DXF-Export tool with enhanced capabilities to export styles and plugins to perform CAD-like functions

4.4 Analyse data

You can perform spatial data analysis on spatial databases and other OGR- supported formats. QGIS currently offers vector analysis, sampling, geoprocessing, geometry and database management tools. You can also use the integrated GRASS tools, which include the complete GRASS functionality of more than 400 modules. (See section *GRASS GIS Integration*.) Or, you can work with the Processing Plugin, which provides a powerful geospatial analysis framework to call native and third-party algorithms from QGIS, such as GDAL, SAGA, GRASS, fTools and more. (See section *Introduction*.)

4.5 Publish maps on the Internet

QGIS can be used as a WMS, WMTS, WMS-C or WFS and WFS-T client, and as a WMS, WCS or WFS server. (See section *Working with OGC Data*.) Additionally, you can publish your data on the Internet using a webserver with UMN MapServer or GeoServer installed.

4.6 Extend QGIS functionality through plugins

QGIS can be adapted to your special needs with the extensible plugin architecture and libraries that can be used to create plugins. You can even create new applications with C++ or Python!

4.6.1 Core Plugins

Core plugins include:

1. Coordinate Capture (Capture mouse coordinates in different CRSs)

2. DB Manager (Exchange, edit and view layers and tables; execute SQL queries)

3. Dxf2Shp Converter (Convert DXF files to shapefiles)

4. eVIS (Visualize events)

5. fTools (Analyze and manage vector data)

6. GDALTools (Integrate GDAL Tools into QGIS)

7. Georeferencer GDAL (Add projection information to rasters using GDAL)

8. GPS Tools (Load and import GPS data)

9. GRASS (Integrate GRASS GIS)

10. Heatmap (Generate raster heatmaps from point data)

11. Interpolation Plugin (Interpolate based on vertices of a vector layer)

12. Metasearch Catalogue Client

13. Offline Editing (Allow offline editing and synchronizing with databases)

14. Oracle Spatial GeoRaster

15. Processing (formerly SEXTANTE)

16. Raster Terrain Analysis (Analyze raster-based terrain)

17. Road Graph Plugin (Analyze a shortest-path network)

18. Spatial Query Plugin

19. SPIT (Import shapefiles to PostgreSQL/PostGIS)

20. Topology Checker (Find topological errors in vector layers)

21. Zonal Statistics Plugin (Calculate count, sum, and mean of a raster for each polygon of a vector layer)

4.6.2 External Python Plugins

QGIS offers a growing number of external Python plugins that are provided by the community. These plugins reside in the official Plugins Repository and can be easily installed using the Python Plugin Installer. See Section *The Plugins Dialog*.

4.7 Python Console

For scripting, it is possible to take advantage of an integrated Python console, which can be opened from menu: *Plugins → Python Console*. The console opens as a non-modal utility window. For interaction with the QGIS environment, there is the `qgis.utils.iface` variable, which is an instance of `QgsInterface`. This interface allows access to the map canvas, menus, toolbars and other parts of the QGIS application. You can create a script, then drag and drop it into the QGIS window and it will be executed automatically.

For further information about working with the Python console and programming QGIS plugins and applications, please refer to *PyQGIS-Developer-Cookbook*.

4.8 Known Issues

4.8.1 Number of open files limitation

If you are opening a large QGIS project and you are sure that all layers are valid, but some layers are flagged as bad, you are probably faced with this issue. Linux (and other OSs, likewise) has a limit of opened files by process. Resource limits are per-process and inherited. The `ulimit` command, which is a shell built-in, changes the limits only for the current shell process; the new limit will be inherited by any child processes.

You can see all current ulimit info by typing

```
user@host:~$ ulimit -aS
```

You can see the current allowed number of opened files per proccess with the following command on a console

```
user@host:~$ ulimit -Sn
```

To change the limits for an **existing session**, you may be able to use something like

```
user@host:~$ ulimit -Sn #number_of_allowed_open_files
user@host:~$ ulimit -Sn
user@host:~$ qgis
```

To fix it forever

On most Linux systems, resource limits are set on login by the `pam_limits` module according to the settings contained in `/etc/security/limits.conf` or `/etc/security/limits.d/*.conf`. You should be able to edit those files if you have root privilege (also via sudo), but you will need to log in again before any changes take effect.

More info:

http://www.cyberciti.biz/faq/linux-increase-the-maximum-number-of-open-files/ http://linuxaria.com/article/open-files-in-linux?lang=en

.

## CHAPTER 5

What's new in QGIS 2.8

This release contains new features and extends the programmatic interface over previous versions. We recommend that you use this version over previous releases.

This release includes hundreds of bug fixes and many new features and enhancements that will be described in this manual. You may also review the visual changelog at http://qgis.org/en/site/forusers/visualchangelog28/index.html.

5.1 Application

- **Map rotation**: A map rotation can be set in degrees from the status bar
- **Bookmarks**: You can share and transfer your bookmarks
- **Expressions**:
  - when editing attributes in the attribute table or forms, you can now enter expressions directly into spin boxes
  - the expression widget is extended to include a function editor where you are able to create your own Python custom functions in a comfortable way
  - in any spinbox of the style menu you can enter expressions and evaluate them immediately
  - a get and transform geometry function was added for using expressions
  - a comment functionality was inserted if for example you want to work with data defined labeling
- **Joins**: You can specify a custom prefix for joins
- **Layer Legend**: Show rule-based renderer's legend as a tree
- **DB Manager**: Run only the selected part of a SQL query
- **Attribute Table**: support for calculations on selected rows through a 'Update Selected' button
- **Measure Tools**: change measurement units possible

5.2 Data Providers

- **DXF Export tool improvements**: Improved marker symbol export
- **WMS Layers**: Support for contextual WMS legend graphics
- **Temporary Scratch Layers**: It is possible to create empty editable memory layers

5.3 Digitizing

- **Advanced Digitizing**:
    - digitise lines exactly parallel or at right angles, lock lines to specific angles and so on with the advanced digitizing panel (CAD-like features)
    - simplify tool: specify with exact tolerance, simplify multiple features at once ...
- **Snapping Options**: new snapping mode 'Snap to all layers'

5.4 Map Composer

- **Composer GUI improvements**: hide bounding boxes, full screen mode for composer toggle display of panels
- **Grid improvements**: You now have finer control of frame and annotation display
- **Label item margins**: You can now control both horizontal and vertical margins for label items. You can now specify negative margins for label items.
- optionally store layer styles
- **Attribute Table Item**: options 'Current atlas feature' and 'Relation children' in Main properties

5.5 Plugins

- **Python Console**: You can now drag and drop python scripts into the QGIS window

5.6 QGIS Server

- Python plugin support

5.7 Symbology

- live heatmap renderer creates dynamic heatmaps from point layers
- raster image symbol fill type
- more data-defined symbology settings: the data-defined option was moved next to each data definable property
- support for multiple styles per map layer, optionally store layer styles

5.8 User Interface

- **Projection**: Improved/consistent projection selection. All dialogs now use a consistent projection selection widget, which allows for quickly selecting from recently used and standard project/QGIS projections

## CHAPTER 6

Getting Started

This chapter gives a quick overview of installing QGIS, some sample data from the QGIS web page, and running a first and simple session visualizing raster and vector layers.

6.1 Installation

Installation of QGIS is very simple. Standard installer packages are available for MS Windows and Mac OS X. For many flavors of GNU/Linux, binary packages (rpm and deb) or software repositories are provided to add to your installation manager. Get the latest information on binary packages at the QGIS website at http://download.qgis.org.

6.1.1 Installation from source

If you need to build QGIS from source, please refer to the installation instructions. They are distributed with the QGIS source code in a file called INSTALL. You can also find them online at http://htmlpreview.github.io/?https://raw.github.com/qgis/QGIS/master/doc/INSTALL.html

6.1.2 Installation on external media

QGIS allows you to define a --configpath option that overrides the default path for user configuration (e.g., ~/.qgis2 under Linux) and forces **QSettings** to use this directory, too. This allows you to, for instance, carry a QGIS installation on a flash drive together with all plugins and settings. See section *System Menu* for additional information.

6.2 Sample Data

The user guide contains examples based on the QGIS sample dataset.

The Windows installer has an option to download the QGIS sample dataset. If checked, the data will be downloaded to your My Documents folder and placed in a folder called GIS Database. You may use Windows Explorer to move this folder to any convenient location. If you did not select the checkbox to install the sample dataset during the initial QGIS installation, you may do one of the following:

- Use GIS data that you already have

- Download sample data from http://qgis.org/downloads/data/qgis_sample_data.zip

- Uninstall QGIS and reinstall with the data download option checked (only recommended if the above solutions are unsuccessful)

△ X For GNU/Linux and Mac OS X, there are not yet dataset installation packages available as rpm, deb or dmg. To use the sample dataset, download the file qgis_sample_data as a ZIP archive from http://qgis.org/downloads/data and unzip the archive on your system.

The Alaska dataset includes all GIS data that are used for examples and screenshots in the user guide; it also includes a small GRASS database. The projection for the QGIS sample dataset is Alaska Albers Equal Area with units feet. The EPSG code is 2964.

```
PROJCS["Albers Equal Area",
GEOGCS["NAD27",
DATUM["North_American_Datum_1927",
SPHEROID["Clarke 1866",6378206.4,294.978698213898,
AUTHORITY["EPSG","7008"]],
TOWGS84[-3,142,183,0,0,0,0],
AUTHORITY["EPSG","6267"]],
PRIMEM["Greenwich",0,
AUTHORITY["EPSG","8901"]],
UNIT["degree",0.0174532925199433,
AUTHORITY["EPSG","9108"]],
AUTHORITY["EPSG","4267"]],
PROJECTION["Albers_Conic_Equal_Area"],
PARAMETER["standard_parallel_1",55],
PARAMETER["standard_parallel_2",65],
PARAMETER["latitude_of_center",50],
PARAMETER["longitude_of_center",-154],
PARAMETER["false_easting",0],
PARAMETER["false_northing",0],
UNIT["us_survey_feet",0.3048006096012192]]
```

If you intend to use QGIS as a graphical front end for GRASS, you can find a selection of sample locations (e.g., Spearfish or South Dakota) at the official GRASS GIS website, http://grass.osgeo.org/download/sample-data/.

6.3 Sample Session

Now that you have QGIS installed and a sample dataset available, we would like to demonstrate a short and simple QGIS sample session. We will visualize a raster and a vector layer. We will use the `landcover` raster layer, `qgis_sample_data/raster/landcover.img`, and the `lakes` vector layer, `qgis_sample_data/gml/lakes.gml`.

6.3.1 Start QGIS

- Start QGIS by typing "QGIS" at a command prompt, or if using a precompiled binary, by using the Applications menu.

- Start QGIS using the Start menu or desktop shortcut, or double click on a QGIS project file.

- **X** Double click the icon in your Applications folder.

6.3.2 Load raster and vector layers from the sample dataset

1. Click on the   Add Raster Layer icon.

2. Browse to the folder `qgis_sample_data/raster/`, select the ERDAS IMG file `landcover.img` and click [**Open**].

3. If the file is not listed, check if the *Files of type* combo box at the bottom of the dialog is set on the right type, in this case "Erdas Imagine Images (*.img, *.IMG)".

4. Now click on the   Add Vector Layer icon.

5. *File* should be selected as *Source Type* in the new *Add vector layer* dialog. Now click [**Browse**] to select the vector layer.

6. Browse to the folder `qgis_sample_data/gml/`, select 'Geography Markup Language [GML] [OGR] (.gml,.GML)' from the *Filter* ▒▼ combo box, then select the GML file `lakes.gml` and click **[Open]**. In the *Add vector layer* dialog, click **[OK]**. The *Coordinate Reference System Selector* dialog opens with *NAD27 / Alaska Alberts* selected, click **[OK]**.

7. Zoom in a bit to your favorite area with some lakes.

8. Double click the `lakes` layer in the map legend to open the *Properties* dialog.

9. Click on the *Style* tab and select a blue as fill color.

10. Click on the *Labels* tab and check the ▒ *Label this layer with* checkbox to enable labeling. Choose the "NAMES" field as the field containing labels.

11. To improve readability of labels, you can add a white buffer around them by clicking "Buffer" in the list on the left, checking ▒ *Draw text buffer* and choosing 3 as buffer size.

12. Click **[Apply]**. Check if the result looks good, and finally click **[OK]**.

You can see how easy it is to visualize raster and vector layers in QGIS. Let's move on to the sections that follow to learn more about the available functionality, features and settings, and how to use them.

6.4 Starting and Stopping QGIS

In section *Sample Session* you already learned how to start QGIS. We will repeat this here, and you will see that QGIS also provides further command line options.

- 🐧 Assuming that QGIS is installed in the PATH, you can start QGIS by typing `qgis` at a command prompt or by double clicking on the QGIS application link (or shortcut) on the desktop or in the Applications menu.

- ▥ Start QGIS using the Start menu or desktop shortcut, or double click on a QGIS project file.

- **X** Double click the icon in your Applications folder. If you need to start QGIS in a shell, run `/path-to-installation-executable/Contents/MacOS/Qgis`.

To stop QGIS, click the menu option 🐧 ▥ *File* **X** *QGIS* → *Quit*, or use the shortcut `Ctrl+Q`.

6.5 Command Line Options

🐧 QGIS supports a number of options when started from the command line. To get a list of the options, enter `qgis --help` on the command line. The usage statement for QGIS is:

```
qgis --help
QGIS - 2.6.0-Brighton 'Brighton' (exported)
QGIS is a user friendly Open Source Geographic Information System.
Usage: /usr/bin/qgis.bin [OPTION] [FILE]
OPTION:
        [--snapshot filename]   emit snapshot of loaded datasets to given file
        [--width width] width of snapshot to emit
        [--height height]       height of snapshot to emit
        [--lang language]       use language for interface text
        [--project projectfile] load the given QGIS project
        [--extent xmin,ymin,xmax,ymax]   set initial map extent
        [--nologo]      hide splash screen
        [--noplugins]   don't restore plugins on startup
        [--nocustomization]     don't apply GUI customization
        [--customizationfile]   use the given ini file as GUI customization
        [--optionspath path]    use the given QSettings path
        [--configpath path]     use the given path for all user configuration
        [--code path]   run the given python file on load
```

```
[--defaultui]   start by resetting user ui settings to default
[--help]                   this text
```

```
FILE:
  Files specified on the command line can include rasters,
  vectors, and QGIS project files (.qgs):
    1. Rasters - supported formats include GeoTiff, DEM
       and others supported by GDAL
    2. Vectors - supported formats include ESRI Shapefiles
       and others supported by OGR and PostgreSQL layers using
       the PostGIS extension
```

Tip: Example Using command line arguments

You can start QGIS by specifying one or more data files on the command line. For example, assuming you are in the `qgis_sample_data` directory, you could start QGIS with a vector layer and a raster file set to load on startup using the following command: `qgis ./raster/landcover.img ./gml/lakes.gml`

Command line option `--snapshot`

This option allows you to create a snapshot in PNG format from the current view. This comes in handy when you have a lot of projects and want to generate snapshots from your data.

Currently, it generates a PNG file with 800x600 pixels. This can be adjusted using the `--width` and `--height` command line arguments. A filename can be added after `--snapshot`.

Command line option `--lang`

Based on your locale, QGIS selects the correct localization. If you would like to change your language, you can specify a language code. For example, `--lang=it` starts QGIS in italian localization.

Command line option `--project`

Starting QGIS with an existing project file is also possible. Just add the command line option `--project` followed by your project name and QGIS will open with all layers in the given file loaded.

Command line option `--extent`

To start with a specific map extent use this option. You need to add the bounding box of your extent in the following order separated by a comma:

`--extent xmin,ymin,xmax,ymax`

Command line option `--nologo`

This command line argument hides the splash screen when you start QGIS.

Command line option `--noplugins`

If you have trouble at start-up with plugins, you can avoid loading them at start-up with this option. They will still be available from the Plugins Manager afterwards.

Command line option `--customizationfile`

Using this command line argument, you can define a GUI customization file, that will be used at startup.

Command line option `--nocustomization`

Using this command line argument, existing GUI customization will not be applied at startup.

Command line option `--optionspath`

You can have multiple configurations and decide which one to use when starting QGIS with this option. See *Options* to confirm where the operating system saves the settings files. Presently, there is no way to specify a file to write settings to; therefore, you can create a copy of the original settings file and rename it. The option specifies path to directory with settings. For example, to use /path/to/config/QGIS/QGIS2.ini settings file, use option:

```
--optionspath /path/to/config/
```

Command line option `--configpath`

This option is similar to the one above, but furthermore overrides the default path for user configuration (`~/.qgis2`) and forces **QSettings** to use this directory, too. This allows users to, for instance, carry a QGIS installation on a flash drive together with all plugins and settings.

Command line option `--code`

This option can be used to run a given python file directly after QGIS has started.

For example, when you have a python file named `load_alaska.py` with following content:

```
from qgis.utils import iface
raster_file = "/home/gisadmin/Documents/qgis_sample_data/raster/landcover.img"
layer_name = "Alaska"
iface.addRasterLayer(raster_file, layer_name)
```

Assuming you are in the directory where the file `load_alaska.py` is located, you can start QGIS, load the raster file `landcover.img` and give the layer the name 'Alaska' using the following command: `qgis --code load_alaska.py`

6.6 Projects

The state of your QGIS session is considered a project. QGIS works on one project at a time. Settings are considered as being either per-project or as a default for new projects (see section *Options*). QGIS can save the state of your workspace into a project file using the menu options *Project →* 🖫 *Save* or *Project →* 🖫 *Save As...*.

Load saved projects into a QGIS session using *Project →* 📁 *Open...*, *Project → New from template* or *Project → Open Recent →*.

If you wish to clear your session and start fresh, choose *Project →* 🗋 *New*. Either of these menu options will prompt you to save the existing project if changes have been made since it was opened or last saved.

The kinds of information saved in a project file include:

- Layers added
- Which layers can be queried
- Layer properties, including symbolization and styles
- Projection for the map view
- Last viewed extent
- Print Composers
- Print Composer elements with settings
- Print Composer atlas settings
- Digitizing settings
- Table Relations
- Project Macros
- Project default styles
- Plugins settings
- QGIS Server settings from the OWS settings tab in the Project properties
- Queries stored in the DB Manager

The project file is saved in XML format, so it is possible to edit the file outside QGIS if you know what you are doing. The file format has been updated several times compared with earlier QGIS versions. Project files from older QGIS versions may not work properly anymore. To be made aware of this, in the *General* tab under *Settings → Options* you can select:

- ☑ *Prompt to save project and data source changes when required*

- ☑ *Warn when opening a project file saved with an older version of QGIS*

Whenever you save a project in QGIS a backup of the project file is made with the extension ~.

6.7 Output

There are several ways to generate output from your QGIS session. We have discussed one already in section *Projects*, saving as a project file. Here is a sampling of other ways to produce output files:

- Menu option *Project →* 🗔 Save as Image opens a file dialog where you select the name, path and type of image (PNG,JPG and many other formats). A world file with extension PNGW or JPGW saved in the same folder georeferences the image.

- Menu option *Project → DXF Export ...* opens a dialog where you can define the 'Symbology mode', the 'Symbology scale' and vector layers you want to export to DXF. Through the 'Symbology mode' symbols from the original QGIS Symbology can be exported with high fidelity.

- Menu option *Project →* 🗋 *New Print Composer* opens a dialog where you can layout and print the current map canvas (see section *Print Composer*).

## CHAPTER 7

QGIS GUI

When QGIS starts, you are presented with the GUI as shown in the figure (the numbers 1 through 5 in yellow circles are discussed below).

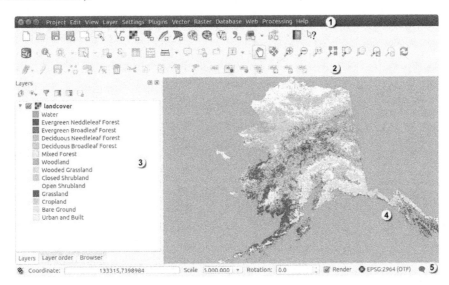

Figure 7.1: QGIS GUI with Alaska sample data

Note: Your window decorations (title bar, etc.) may appear different depending on your operating system and window manager.

The QGIS GUI is divided into five areas:

1. Menu Bar

2. Tool Bar

3. Map Legend

4. Map View

5. Status Bar

These five components of the QGIS interface are described in more detail in the following sections. Two more sections present keyboard shortcuts and context help.

7.1 Menu Bar

The menu bar provides access to various QGIS features using a standard hierarchical menu. The top-level menus and a summary of some of the menu options are listed below, together with the associated icons as they appear on the toolbar, and keyboard shortcuts. The shortcuts presented in this section are the defaults; however, keyboard shortcuts can also be configured manually using the *Configure shortcuts* dialog, opened from *Settings → Configure Shortcuts...*.

Although most menu options have a corresponding tool and vice-versa, the menus are not organized exactly like the toolbars. The toolbar containing the tool is listed after each menu option as a checkbox entry. Some menu options only appear if the corresponding plugin is loaded. For more information about tools and toolbars, see section *Toolbar*.

7.1.1 Project

Menu Option	Shortcut	Reference	Toolbar
New	Ctrl+N	see *Projects*	*Project*
Open	Ctrl+O	see *Projects*	*Project*
New from template →		see *Projects*	*Project*
Open Recent →		see *Projects*	
Save	Ctrl+S	see *Projects*	*Project*
Save As...	Ctrl+Shift+S	see *Projects*	*Project*
Save as Image...		see *Output*	
DXF Export ...		see *Output*	
New Print Composer	Ctrl+P	see *Print Composer*	*Project*
Composer manager ...		see *Print Composer*	*Project*
Print Composers →		see *Print Composer*	
Exit QGIS	Ctrl+Q		

7.1.2 Edit

Menu Option	Shortcut	Reference	Toolbar
Undo	Ctrl+Z	see *Advanced digitizing*	*Advanced Digitizing*
Redo	Ctrl+Shift+Z	see *Advanced digitizing*	*Advanced Digitizing*
Cut Features	Ctrl+X	see *Digitizing an existing layer*	*Digitizing*
Copy Features	Ctrl+C	see *Digitizing an existing layer*	*Digitizing*
Paste Features	Ctrl+V	see *Digitizing an existing layer*	*Digitizing*
Paste features as →		see *Working with the Attribute Table*	
Add Feature	Ctrl+.	see *Digitizing an existing layer*	*Digitizing*
Move Feature(s)		see *Digitizing an existing layer*	*Digitizing*
Delete Selected		see *Digitizing an existing layer*	*Digitizing*
Rotate Feature(s)		see *Advanced digitizing*	*Advanced Digitizing*
Simplify Feature		see *Advanced digitizing*	*Advanced Digitizing*
Add Ring		see *Advanced digitizing*	*Advanced Digitizing*
Add Part		see *Advanced digitizing*	*Advanced Digitizing*
Fill Ring		see *Advanced digitizing*	*Advanced Digitizing*
Delete Ring		see *Advanced digitizing*	*Advanced Digitizing*
Delete Part		see *Advanced digitizing*	*Advanced Digitizing*
Reshape Features		see *Advanced digitizing*	*Advanced Digitizing*
Offset Curve		see *Advanced digitizing*	*Advanced Digitizing*
Split Features		see *Advanced digitizing*	*Advanced Digitizing*
Split Parts		see *Advanced digitizing*	*Advanced Digitizing*
Merge Selected Features		see *Advanced digitizing*	*Advanced Digitizing*
Merge Attr. of Selected Features		see *Advanced digitizing*	*Advanced Digitizing*
Node Tool		see *Digitizing an existing layer*	*Digitizing*
Rotate Point Symbols		see *Advanced digitizing*	*Advanced Digitizing*

After activating ✏ Toggle editing mode for a layer, you will find the Add Feature icon in the *Edit* menu depending on the layer type (point, line or polygon).

7.1.3 Edit (extra)

Menu Option	Shortcut	Reference	Toolbar
Add Feature		see *Digitizing an existing layer*	*Digitizing*
Add Feature		see *Digitizing an existing layer*	*Digitizing*
Add Feature		see *Digitizing an existing layer*	*Digitizing*

7.1.4 View

Menu Option	Shortcut	Reference	Toolbar
Pan Map			Map Navigation
Pan Map to Selection			Map Navigation
Zoom In	Ctrl++		Map Navigation
Zoom Out	Ctrl+-		Map Navigation
Select →		see Select and deselect features	Attributes
Identify Features	Ctrl+Shift+I		Attributes
Measure →		see Measuring	Attributes
Zoom Full	Ctrl+Shift+F		Map Navigation
Zoom To Layer			Map Navigation
Zoom To Selection	Ctrl+J		Map Navigation
Zoom Last			Map Navigation
Zoom Next			Map Navigation
Zoom Actual Size			Map Navigation
Decorations →		see Decorations	
Preview mode →			
Map Tips			Attributes
New Bookmark	Ctrl+B	see Spatial Bookmarks	Attributes
Show Bookmarks	Ctrl+Shift+B	see Spatial Bookmarks	Attributes
Refresh	F5		Map Navigation

7.1.5 Layer

Menu Option	Shortcut	Reference	Toolbar
Create Layer →		see *Creating new Vector layers*	*Manage Layers*
Add Layer →			*Manage Layers*
Embed Layers and Groups ...		see *Nesting Projects*	
Add from Layer Definition File ...			
Copy style		see *Style Menu*	
Paste style		see *Style Menu*	
Open Attribute Table		see *Working with the Attribute Table*	*Attributes*
Toggle Editing		see *Digitizing an existing layer*	*Digitizing*
Save Layer Edits		see *Digitizing an existing layer*	*Digitizing*
Current Edits →		see *Digitizing an existing layer*	*Digitizing*
Save as...			
Save as layer definition file...			
Remove Layer/Group	Ctrl+D		
Duplicate Layers (s)			
Set Scale Visibility of Layers			
Set CRS of Layer(s)	Ctrl+Shift+C		
Set project CRS from Layer			
Properties ...			
Query...			
Labeling			
Add to Overview	Ctrl+Shift+O		*Manage Layers*
Add All To Overview			
Remove All From Overview			
Show All Layers	Ctrl+Shift+U		*Manage Layers*
Hide All Layers	Ctrl+Shift+H		*Manage Layers*
Show selected Layers			
Hide selected Layers			

7.1.6 Settings

Menu Option	Shortcut	Reference	Toolbar
Panels →		see *Panels and Toolbars*	
Toolbars →		see *Panels and Toolbars*	
Toggle Full Screen Mode	F 11		
Project Properties ...	Ctrl+Shift+P	see *Projects*	
Custom CRS ...		see *Custom Coordinate Reference System*	
Style Manager...		see *Presentation*	
Configure shortcuts ...			
Customization ...		see *Customization*	
Options ...		see *Options*	
Snapping Options ...			

7.1.7 Plugins

Menu Option	Shortcut	Reference	Toolbar
⚙ *Manage and Install Plugins ...*		see *The Plugins Dialog*	
Python Console	Ctrl+Alt+P		

When starting QGIS for the first time not all core plugins are loaded.

7.1.8 Vector

Menu Option	Shortcut	Reference	Toolbar
Open Street Map →		see *Loading OpenStreetMap Vectors*	
◢ *Analysis Tools* →		see *fTools Plugin*	
⬇ *Research Tools* →		see *fTools Plugin*	
⚙ *Geoprocessing Tools* →		see *fTools Plugin*	
▽ *Geometry Tools* →		see *fTools Plugin*	
◣ *Data Management Tools* →		see *fTools Plugin*	

When starting QGIS for the first time not all core plugins are loaded.

7.1.9 Raster

Menu Option	Shortcut	Reference	Toolbar
Raster calculator ...		see *Raster Calculator*	

When starting QGIS for the first time not all core plugins are loaded.

7.1.10 Database

Menu Option	Shortcut	Reference	Toolbar
Database →		see *DB Manager Plugin*	*Database*

When starting QGIS for the first time not all core plugins are loaded.

7.1.11 Web

Menu Option	Shortcut	Reference	Toolbar
Metasearch		see *MetaSearch Catalogue Client*	*Web*

When starting QGIS for the first time not all core plugins are loaded.

7.1.12 Processing

Menu Option	Shortcut	Reference	Toolbar
Toolbox		see *The toolbox*	
Graphical Modeler ...		see *The graphical modeler*	
History and log ...		see *The history manager*	
Options ...		see *Configuring the processing framework*	
Results viewer ...		see *Configuring external applications*	
Commander	Ctrl+Alt+M	see *The QGIS Commander*	

When starting QGIS for the first time not all core plugins are loaded.

7.1.13 Help

Menu Option	Shortcut	Reference	Toolbar
Help Contents	F1		*Help*
What's This?	Shift+F1		*Help*
API Documentation			
Need commercial support?			
QGIS Home Page	Ctrl+H		
Check QGIS Version			
About			
QGIS Sponsors			

Please note that for Linux △, the menu bar items listed above are the default ones in the KDE window manager. In GNOME, the *Settings* menu has different content and its items have to be found here:

Custom CRS	*Edit*
Style Manager	*Edit*
Configure Shortcuts	*Edit*
Customization	*Edit*
Options	*Edit*
Snapping Options ...	*Edit*

7.2 Toolbar

The toolbar provides access to most of the same functions as the menus, plus additional tools for interacting with the map. Each toolbar item has pop-up help available. Hold your mouse over the item and a short description of the tool's purpose will be displayed.

Every menu bar can be moved around according to your needs. Additionally, every menu bar can be switched off using your right mouse button context menu, holding the mouse over the toolbars (read also *Panels and Toolbars*).

Tip: Restoring toolbars

If you have accidentally hidden all your toolbars, you can get them back by choosing menu option *Settings* → *Toolbars* →. If a toolbar disappears under Windows, which seems to be a problem in QGIS from time to time, you have to remove key \HKEY_CURRENT_USER\Software\QGIS\qgis\UI\state in the registry. When you restart QGIS, the key is written again with the default state, and all toolbars are visible again.

7.3 Map Legend

The map legend area lists all the layers in the project. The checkbox in each legend entry can be used to show or hide the layer. The Legend toolbar in the map legend are list allow you to **Add group**, **Manage Layer Visibility** of all layers or manage preset layers combination, **Filter Legend by Map Content**, **Expand All** or **Collapse All** and **Remove Layer or Group**. The button allows you to add **Presets** views in the legend. It means that you can choose to display some layer with specific categorization and add this view to the **Presets** list. To add a preset view just click on , choose *Add Preset...* from the drop down menu and give a name to the preset. After that you will see a list with all the presets that you can recall pressing on the button.

All the added presets are also present in the map composer in order to allow you to create a map layout based on your specific views (see *Main properties*).

A layer can be selected and dragged up or down in the legend to change the Z-ordering. Z-ordering means that layers listed nearer the top of the legend are drawn over layers listed lower down in the legend.

Note: This behaviour can be overridden by the 'Layer order' panel.

Layers in the legend window can be organised into groups. There are two ways to do this:

1. Press the icon to add a new group. Type in a name for the group and press Enter. Now click on an existing layer and drag it onto the group.

2. Select some layers, right click in the legend window and choose *Group Selected*. The selected layers will automatically be placed in a new group.

To bring a layer out of a group, you can drag it out, or right click on it and choose *Make to toplevel item*. Groups can also be nested inside other groups.

The checkbox for a group will show or hide all the layers in the group with one click.

The content of the right mouse button context menu depends on whether the selected legend item is a raster or a vector layer. For GRASS vector layers, Toggle editing is not available. See section *Digitizing and editing a GRASS vector layer* for information on editing GRASS vector layers.

Right mouse button menu for raster layers

- *Zoom to Layer*
- *Show in overview*
- *Zoom to Best Scale (100%)*
- *Remove*
- *Duplicate*
- *Set Layer Scale Visibility*
- *Set Layer CRS*
- *Set Project CRS from Layer*
- *Styles* →
- *Save as ...*
- *Save As Layer Definition File ...*
- *Properties*
- *Rename*

Additionally, according to layer position and selection

- *Move to Top-level*

- *Group Selected*

Right mouse button menu for vector layers

- *Zoom to Layer*
- *Show in overview*
- *Remove*
- *Duplicate*
- *Set Layer Scale Visibility*
- *Set Layer CRS*
- *Set Project CRS from Layer*
- *Styles* →
- *Open Attribute Table*
- *Toggle Editing* (not available for GRASS layers)
- *Save As ...*
- *Save As Layer Definition Style*
- *Filter*
- *Show Feature Count*
- *Properties*
- *Rename*

Additionally, according to layer position and selection

- *Move to Top-level*
- *Group Selected*

Right mouse button menu for layer groups

- *Zoom to Group*
- *Remove*
- *Set Group CRS*
- *Rename*
- *Add Group*

It is possible to select more than one layer or group at the same time by holding down the Ctrl key while selecting the layers with the left mouse button. You can then move all selected layers to a new group at the same time.

You may also delete more than one layer or group at once by selecting several layers with the Ctrl key and pressing Ctrl+D afterwards. This way, all selected layers or groups will be removed from the layers list.

7.3.1 Working with the Legend independent layer order

There is a panel that allows you to define an independent drawing order for the map legend. You can activate it in the menu *Settings → Panels → Layer order*. This feature allows you to, for instance, order your layers in order of importance, but still display them in the correct order (see figure_layer_order). Checking the ✔ *Control rendering order* box underneath the list of layers will cause a revert to default behavior.

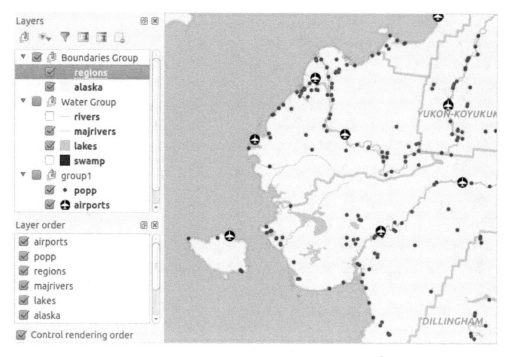

Figure 7.2: Define a legend independent layer order

7.4 Map View

This is the "business end" of QGIS — maps are displayed in this area! The map displayed in this window will depend on the vector and raster layers you have chosen to load (see sections that follow for more information on how to load layers). The map view can be panned, shifting the focus of the map display to another region, and it can be zoomed in and out. Various other operations can be performed on the map as described in the toolbar description above. The map view and the legend are tightly bound to each other — the maps in view reflect changes you make in the legend area.

Tip: Zooming the Map with the Mouse Wheel

You can use the mouse wheel to zoom in and out on the map. Place the mouse cursor inside the map area and roll the wheel forward (away from you) to zoom in and backwards (towards you) to zoom out. The zoom is centered on the mouse cursor position. You can customize the behavior of the mouse wheel zoom using the *Map tools* tab under the *Settings → Options* menu.

Tip: Panning the Map with the Arrow Keys and Space Bar

You can use the arrow keys to pan the map. Place the mouse cursor inside the map area and click on the right arrow key to pan east, left arrow key to pan west, up arrow key to pan north and down arrow key to pan south. You can also pan the map using the space bar or the click on mouse wheel: just move the mouse while holding down space bar or click on mouse wheel.

7.5 Status Bar

The status bar shows you your current position in map coordinates (e.g., meters or decimal degrees) as the mouse pointer is moved across the map view. To the left of the coordinate display in the status bar is a small button that will toggle between showing coordinate position or the view extents of the map view as you pan and zoom in and out.

Next to the coordinate display you will find the scale display. It shows the scale of the map view. If you zoom in or out, QGIS shows you the current scale. There is a scale selector, which allows you to choose between predefined scales from 1:500 to 1:1000000.

To the right of the scale display you can define a current clockwise rotation for your map view in degrees.

A progress bar in the status bar shows the progress of rendering as each layer is drawn to the map view. In some cases, such as the gathering of statistics in raster layers, the progress bar will be used to show the status of lengthy operations.

If a new plugin or a plugin update is available, you will see a message at the far left of the status bar. On the right side of the status bar, there is a small checkbox which can be used to temporarily prevent layers being rendered to the map view (see section *Rendering* below). The icon immediately stops the current map rendering process.

To the right of the render functions, you find the EPSG code of the current project CRS and a projector icon. Clicking on this opens the projection properties for the current project.

Tip: Calculating the Correct Scale of Your Map Canvas

When you start QGIS, the default units are degrees, and this means that QGIS will interpret any coordinate in your layer as specified in degrees. To get correct scale values, you can either change this setting to meters manually in the *General* tab under *Settings → Project Properties*, or you can select a project CRS clicking on the ⊕ Current CRS: icon in the lower right-hand corner of the status bar. In the last case, the units are set to what the project projection specifies (e.g., '+units=m').

General Tools

8.1 Keyboard shortcuts

QGIS provides default keyboard shortcuts for many features. You can find them in section *Menu Bar*. Additionally, the menu option *Settings → Configure Shortcuts..* allows you to change the default keyboard shortcuts and to add new keyboard shortcuts to QGIS features.

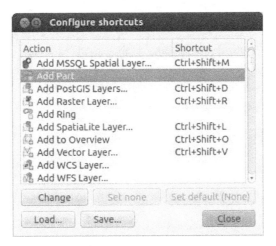

Figure 8.1: Define shortcut options 🐧 (Gnome)

Configuration is very simple. Just select a feature from the list and click on **[Change]**, **[Set none]** or **[Set default]**. Once you have finished your configuration, you can save it as an XML file and load it to another QGIS installation.

8.2 Context help

When you need help on a specific topic, you can access context help via the **[Help]** button available in most dialogs — please note that third-party plugins can point to dedicated web pages.

8.3 Rendering

By default, QGIS renders all visible layers whenever the map canvas is refreshed. The events that trigger a refresh of the map canvas include:

- Adding a layer
- Panning or zooming

- Resizing the QGIS window

- Changing the visibility of a layer or layers

QGIS allows you to control the rendering process in a number of ways.

8.3.1 Scale Dependent Rendering

Scale-dependent rendering allows you to specify the minimum and maximum scales at which a layer will be visible. To set scale-dependent rendering, open the *Properties* dialog by double-clicking on the layer in the legend. On the *General* tab, click on the ☑ *Scale dependent visibility* checkbox to activate the feature, then set the minimum and maximum scale values.

You can determine the scale values by first zooming to the level you want to use and noting the scale value in the QGIS status bar.

8.3.2 Controlling Map Rendering

Map rendering can be controlled in the various ways, as described below.

Suspending Rendering

To suspend rendering, click the ☑ *Render* checkbox in the lower right corner of the status bar. When the ☑ *Render* checkbox is not checked, QGIS does not redraw the canvas in response to any of the events described in section *Rendering*. Examples of when you might want to suspend rendering include:

- Adding many layers and symbolizing them prior to drawing

- Adding one or more large layers and setting scale dependency before drawing

- Adding one or more large layers and zooming to a specific view before drawing

- Any combination of the above

Checking the ☑ *Render* checkbox enables rendering and causes an immediate refresh of the map canvas.

Setting Layer Add Option

You can set an option to always load new layers without drawing them. This means the layer will be added to the map, but its visibility checkbox in the legend will be unchecked by default. To set this option, choose menu option *Settings* → *Options* and click on the *Rendering* tab. Uncheck the ☑ *By default new layers added to the map should be displayed* checkbox. Any layer subsequently added to the map will be off (invisible) by default.

Stopping Rendering

To stop the map drawing, press the ESC key. This will halt the refresh of the map canvas and leave the map partially drawn. It may take a bit of time between pressing ESC and the time the map drawing is halted.

Note: It is currently not possible to stop rendering — this was disabled in the Qt4 port because of User Interface (UI) problems and crashes.

Updating the Map Display During Rendering

You can set an option to update the map display as features are drawn. By default, QGIS does not display any features for a layer until the entire layer has been rendered. To update the display as features are read from the datastore, choose menu option *Settings → Options* and click on the *Rendering* tab. Set the feature count to an appropriate value to update the display during rendering. Setting a value of 0 disables update during drawing (this is the default). Setting a value too low will result in poor performance, as the map canvas is continually updated during the reading of the features. A suggested value to start with is 500.

Influence Rendering Quality

To influence the rendering quality of the map, you have two options. Choose menu option *Settings → Options*, click on the *Rendering* tab and select or deselect following checkboxes:

- ☑ *Make lines appear less jagged at the expense of some drawing performance*

- ☑ *Fix problems with incorrectly filled polygons*

Speed-up rendering

There are two settings that allow you to improve rendering speed. Open the QGIS options dialog using *Settings → Options*, go to the *Rendering* tab and select or deselect the following checkboxes:

- ☑ *Enable back buffer.* This provides better graphics performance at the cost of losing the possibility to cancel rendering and incrementally draw features. If it is unchecked, you can set the *Number of features to draw before updating the display*, otherwise this option is inactive.

- ☑ *Use render caching where possible to speed up redraws*

8.4 Measuring

Measuring works within projected coordinate systems (e.g., UTM) and unprojected data. If the loaded map is defined with a geographic coordinate system (latitude/longitude), the results from line or area measurements will be incorrect. To fix this, you need to set an appropriate map coordinate system (see section *Working with Projections*). All measuring modules also use the snapping settings from the digitizing module. This is useful, if you want to measure along lines or areas in vector layers.

To select a measuring tool, click on ▭ and select the tool you want to use.

8.4.1 Measure length, areas and angles

▭ Measure Line: QGIS is able to measure real distances between given points according to a defined ellipsoid. To configure this, choose menu option *Settings → Options*, click on the *Map tools* tab and select the appropriate ellipsoid. There, you can also define a rubberband color and your preferred measurement units (meters or feet) and angle units (degrees, radians and gon). The tool then allows you to click points on the map. Each segment length, as well as the total, shows up in the measure window. To stop measuring, click your right mouse button. Note that you can interactively change the measurement units in the measurement dialog. It overrides the *Preferred measurement units* in the options. There is an info section in the dialog that shows which CRS settings are being used during measurement calculations.

▭ Measure Area: Areas can also be measured. In the measure window, the accumulated area size appears. In addition, the measuring tool will snap to the currently selected layer, provided that layer has its snapping tolerance set (see section *Setting the Snapping Tolerance and Search Radius*). So, if you want to measure exactly along a

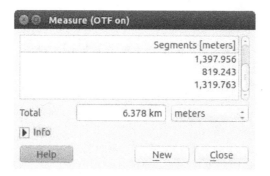

Figure 8.2: Measure Distance 🐧 (Gnome)

line feature, or around a polygon feature, first set its snapping tolerance, then select the layer. Now, when using the measuring tools, each mouse click (within the tolerance setting) will snap to that layer.

Figure 8.3: Measure Area 🐧 (Gnome)

Measure Angle: You can also measure angles. The cursor becomes cross-shaped. Click to draw the first segment of the angle you wish to measure, then move the cursor to draw the desired angle. The measure is displayed in a pop-up dialog.

Figure 8.4: Measure Angle 🐧 (Gnome)

8.4.2 Select and deselect features

The QGIS toolbar provides several tools to select features in the map canvas. To select one or several features, just click on and select your tool:

- Select Single Feature
- Select Features by Rectangle
- Select Features by Polygon
- Select Features by Freehand
- Select Features by Radius

To deselect all selected features click on Deselect features from all layers.

Chapter 8. General Tools

$\mathcal{E}$ Select feature using an expression allow user to select feature using expression dialog. See *Expressions* chapter for some example.

Users can save features selection into a **New Memory Vector Layer** or a **New Vector Layer** using *Edit → Paste Feature as ...* and choose the mode you want.

8.5 Identify features

The Identify tool allows you to interact with the map canvas and get information on features in a pop-up window.

To identify features, use *View → Identify features* or press Ctrl + Shift + I, or click on the   Identify features icon in the toolbar.

If you click on several features, the *Identify results* dialog will list information about all the selected features. The first item is the number of the layer in the list of results, followed by the layer name. Then, its first child will be the name of a field with its value. The first field is the one selected in *Properties → Display*. Finally, all information about the feature is displayed.

This window can be customized to display custom fields, but by default it will display three kinds of information:

- Actions: Actions can be added to the identify feature windows. When clicking on the action label, action will be run. By default, only one action is added, to view feature form for editing.

- Derived: This information is calculated or derived from other information. You can find clicked coordinate, X and Y coordinates, area in map units and perimeter in map units for polygons, length in map units for lines and feature ids.

- Data attributes: This is the list of attribute fields from the data.

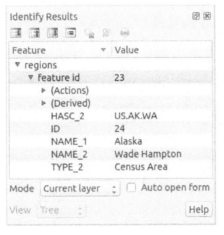

Figure 8.5: Identify feaures dialog (Gnome)

At the top of the window, you have five icons:

- Expand tree
- Collapse tree
- Default behaviour
- Copy attributes
- Print selected HTML response

At the bottom of the window, you have the *Mode* and *View* comboboxes. With the *Mode* combobox you can define the identify mode: 'Current layer', 'Top down, stop at first', 'Top down' and 'Layer selection'. The *View* can be set as 'Tree', 'Table' and 'Graph'.

The identify tool allows you to auto open a form. In this mode you can change the feautures attributes.

Other functions can be found in the context menu of the identified item. For example, from the context menu you can:

- View the feature form
- Zoom to feature
- Copy feature: Copy all feature geometry and attributes
- Toggle feature selection: adds identified feature to selection
- Copy attribute value: Copy only the value of the attribute that you click on
- Copy feature attributes: Copy only attributes
- Clear result: Remove results in the window
- Clear highlights: Remove features highlighted on the map
- Highlight all
- Highlight layer
- Activate layer: Choose a layer to be activated
- Layer properties: Open layer properties window
- Expand all
- Collapse all

8.6 Decorations

The Decorations of QGIS include the Grid, the Copyright Label, the North Arrow and the Scale Bar. They are used to 'decorate' the map by adding cartographic elements.

8.6.1 Grid

 ^Grid^ allows you to add a coordinate grid and coordinate annotations to the map canvas.

1. Select from menu *View → Decorations → Grid*. The dialog starts (see figure_decorations_1).
2. Activate the ☑ *Enable grid* checkbox and set grid definitions according to the layers loaded in the map canvas.
3. Activate the ☑ *Draw annotations* checkbox and set annotation definitions according to the layers loaded in the map canvas.
4. Click **[Apply]** to verify that it looks as expected.
5. Click **[OK]** to close the dialog.

8.6.2 Copyright Label

 ^Copyright label^ adds a copyright label using the text you prefer to the map.

1. Select from menu *View → Decorations → Copyright Label*. The dialog starts (see figure_decorations_2).

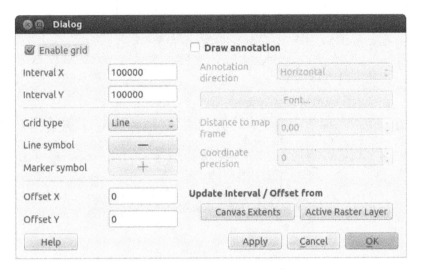

Figure 8.6: The Grid Dialog

Figure 8.7: The Copyright Dialog

2. Enter the text you want to place on the map. You can use HTML as shown in the example.

3. Choose the placement of the label from the *Placement* [...▼] combo box.

4. Make sure the ☑ *Enable Copyright Label* checkbox is checked.

5. Click [**OK**].

In the example above, which is the default, QGIS places a copyright symbol followed by the date in the lower right-hand corner of the map canvas.

8.6.3 North Arrow

A North Arrow places a simple north arrow on the map canvas. At present, there is only one style available. You can adjust the angle of the arrow or let QGIS set the direction automatically. If you choose to let QGIS determine the direction, it makes its best guess as to how the arrow should be oriented. For placement of the arrow, you have four options, corresponding to the four corners of the map canvas.

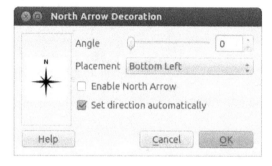

Figure 8.8: The North Arrow Dialog 🐧

8.6.4 Scale Bar

Scale Bar adds a simple scale bar to the map canvas. You can control the style and placement, as well as the labeling of the bar.

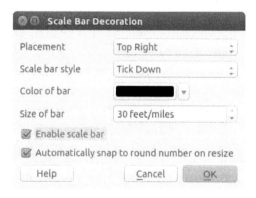

Figure 8.9: The Scale Bar Dialog 🐧

QGIS only supports displaying the scale in the same units as your map frame. So if the units of your layers are in meters, you can't create a scale bar in feet. Likewise, if you are using decimal degrees, you can't create a scale bar to display distance in meters.

To add a scale bar:

1. Select from menu *View → Decorations → Scale Bar*. The dialog starts (see figure_decorations_4).

2. Choose the placement from the *Placement* [...▼] combo box.

3. Choose the style from the *Scale bar style* [...▼] combo box.

4. Select the color for the bar *Color of bar* Border [███████]▼ or use the default black color.

5. Set the size of the bar and its label *Size of bar* [1.00 ↕].

6. Make sure the ☑ *Enable scale bar* checkbox is checked.

7. Optionally, check ☑ *Automatically snap to round number on resize*.

8. Click **[OK]**.

Tip: Settings of Decorations

When you save a `.qgs` project, any changes you have made to Grid, North Arrow, Scale Bar and Copyright will be saved in the project and restored the next time you load the project.

8.7 Annotation Tools

The [T] Text Annotation tool in the attribute toolbar provides the possibility to place formatted text in a balloon on the QGIS map canvas. Use the *Text Annotation* tool and click into the map canvas.

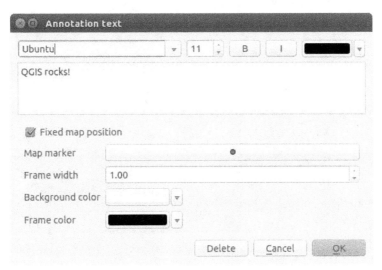

Figure 8.10: Annotation text dialog 🐧

Double clicking on the item opens a dialog with various options. There is the text editor to enter the formatted text and other item settings. For instance, there is the choice of having the item placed on a map position (displayed by a marker symbol) or to have the item on a screen position (not related to the map). The item can be moved by map position (by dragging the map marker) or by moving only the balloon. The icons are part of the GIS theme, and they are used by default in the other themes, too.

The [🖼] Move Annotation tool allows you to move the annotation on the map canvas.

8.7.1 Html annotations

The 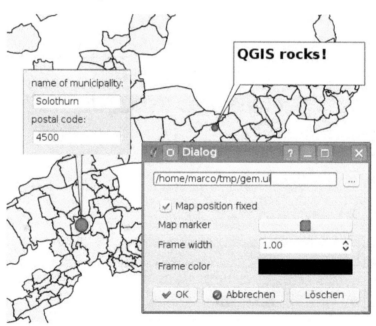 Html Annotation tools in the attribute toolbar provides the possibility to place the content of an html file in a balloon on the QGIS map canvas. Using the *Html Annotation* tool, click into the map canvas and add the path to the html file into the dialog.

8.7.2 SVG annotations

The SVG Annotation tool in the attribute toolbar provides the possibility to place an SVG symbol in a balloon on the QGIS map canvas. Using the *SVG Annotation* tool, click into the map canvas and add the path to the SVG file into the dialog.

8.7.3 Form annotations

Additionally, you can also create your own annotation forms. The Form Annotation tool is useful to display attributes of a vector layer in a customized Qt Designer form (see figure_custom_annotation). This is similar to the designer forms for the *Identify features* tool, but displayed in an annotation item. Also see this video https://www.youtube.com/watch?v=0pDBuSbQ02o from Tim Sutton for more information.

Figure 8.11: Customized qt designer annotation form

Note: If you press `Ctrl+T` while an *Annotation* tool is active (move annotation, text annotation, form annotation), the visibility states of the items are inverted.

8.8 Spatial Bookmarks

Spatial Bookmarks allow you to "bookmark" a geographic location and return to it later.

8.8.1 Creating a Bookmark

To create a bookmark:

1. Zoom or pan to the area of interest.

2. Select the menu option *View → New Bookmark* or press Ctrl-B.

3. Enter a descriptive name for the bookmark (up to 255 characters).

4. Press Enter to add the bookmark or [**Delete**] to remove the bookmark.

Note that you can have multiple bookmarks with the same name.

8.8.2 Working with Bookmarks

To use or manage bookmarks, select the menu option *View → Show Bookmarks*. The *Geospatial Bookmarks* dialog allows you to zoom to or delete a bookmark. You cannot edit the bookmark name or coordinates.

8.8.3 Zooming to a Bookmark

From the *Geospatial Bookmarks* dialog, select the desired bookmark by clicking on it, then click [**Zoom To**]. You can also zoom to a bookmark by double-clicking on it.

8.8.4 Deleting a Bookmark

To delete a bookmark from the *Geospatial Bookmarks* dialog, click on it, then click [**Delete**]. Confirm your choice by clicking [**Yes**], or cancel the delete by clicking [**No**].

8.8.5 Import or export a bookmark

To share or transfer your bookmarks between computers you can use the *Share* pull down menu in the *Geospatial Bookmarks* dialog.

8.9 Nesting Projects

If you want to embed content from other project files into your project, you can choose *Layer → Embed Layers and Groups*.

8.9.1 Embedding layers

The following dialog allows you to embed layers from other projects. Here is a small example:

1. Press [...] to look for another project from the Alaska dataset.

2. Select the project file grassland. You can see the content of the project (see figure_embed_dialog).

3. Press Ctrl and click on the layers grassland and regions. Press [**OK**]. The selected layers are embedded in the map legend and the map view now.

While the embedded layers are editable, you can't change their properties like style and labeling.

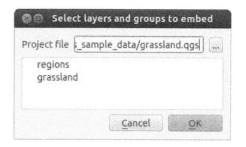

Figure 8.12: Select layers and groups to embed

8.9.2 Removing embedded layers

Right-click on the embedded layer and choose Remove.

.

## CHAPTER 9

QGIS Configuration

QGIS is highly configurable through the *Settings* menu. Choose between Panels, Toolbars, Project Properties, Options and Customization.

Note: QGIS follows desktop guidelines for the location of options and project properties item. Consequently related to the OS you are using, location of some of items described above could be located in the *View* menu (Panels and Toolbars) or in *Project* for Options.

9.1 Panels and Toolbars

In the *Panels*→ menu, you can switch on and off QGIS widgets. The *Toolbars*→ menu provides the possibility to switch on and off icon groups in the QGIS toolbar (see figure_panels_toolbars).

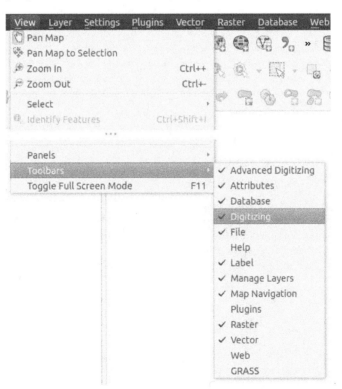

Figure 9.1: The Panels and Toolbars menu

Tip: Activating the QGIS Overview

In QGIS, you can use an overview panel that provides a full extent view of layers added to it. It can be selected under the menu △ *Settings → Panels* or ▦ *View → Panels*. Within the view is a rectangle showing the current map extent. This allows you to quickly determine which area of the map you are currently viewing. Note that labels are not rendered to the map overview even if the layers in the map overview have been set up for labeling. If you click and drag the red rectangle in the overview that shows your current extent, the main map view will update accordingly.

Tip: Show Log Messages

It's possible to track the QGIS messages. You can activate ▦ *Log Messages* in the menu △ *Settings → Panels* or ▦ *View → Panels* and follow the messages that appear in the different tabs during loading and operation.

9.2 Project Properties

In the properties window for the project under △ *Settings → Project Properties* (kde) or △ ▦ *Project → Project Properties* (Gnome), you can set project-specific options. These include:

- In the *General* menu, the project title, selection and background color, layer units, precision, and the option to save relative paths to layers can be defined. If the CRS transformation is on, you can choose an ellipsoid for distance calculations. You can define the canvas units (only used when CRS transformation is disabled) and the precision of decimal places to use. You can also define a project scale list, which overrides the global predefined scales.

- The *CRS* menu enables you to choose the Coordinate Reference System for this project, and to enable on-the-fly re-projection of raster and vector layers when displaying layers from a different CRS.

- With the third *Identify layers* menu, you set (or disable) which layers will respond to the identify tool (see the "Map tools" paragraph from the *Options* section to enable identifying of multiple layers).

- The *Default Styles* menu lets you control how new layers will be drawn when they do not have an existing .qml style defined. You can also set the default transparency level for new layers and whether symbols should have random colours assigned to them. There is also an additional section where you can define specific colors for the running project. You can find the added colors in the drop down menu of the color dialog window present in each renderer.

- The tab *OWS Server* allows you to define information about the QGIS Server WMS and WFS capabilities, extent and CRS restrictions.

- The *Macros* menu is used to edit Python macros for projects. Currently, only three macros are available: openProject(), saveProject() and closeProject().

- The *Relations* menu is used to define 1:n relations. The relations are defined in the project properties dialog. Once relations exist for a layer, a new user interface element in the form view (e.g. when identifying a feature and opening its form) will list the related entities. This provides a powerful way to express e.g. the inspection history on a length of pipeline or road segment. You can find out more about 1:n relations support in Section *Creating one to many relations*.

9.3 Options

✎ Some basic options for QGIS can be selected using the *Options* dialog. Select the menu option *Settings →* ✎ *Options*. The tabs where you can customize your options are described below.

9.3.1 General Menu

Application

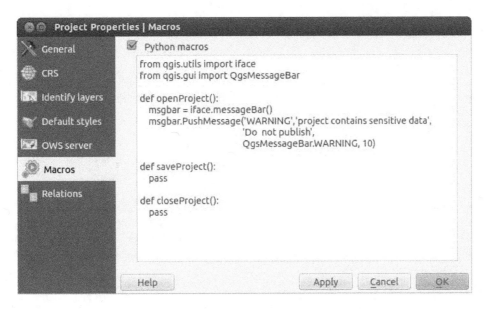

Figure 9.2: Macro settings in QGIS

- Select the *Style (QGIS restart required)* and choose between 'Oxygen','Windows','Motif','CDE', 'Plastique' and 'Cleanlooks' ( ).

- Define the *Icon theme* . Currently only 'default' is possible.

- Define the *Icon size* .

- Define the *Font*. Choose between *Qt default* and a user-defined font.

- Change the *Timeout for timed messages or dialogs* .

- *Hide splash screen at startup*

- *Show tips at startup*

- *Bold group box titles*

- *QGIS-styled group boxes*

- *Use native color chooser dialogs*

- *Use live-updating color chooser dialogs*

- *Custom side bar style*

- *Experimental canvas rotation support (restart required)*

Project files

- *Open project on launch* (choose between 'New', 'Most recent' and 'Specific'). When choosing 'Specific' use the to define a project.

- *Create new project from default project*. You have the possibility to press on *Set current project as default* or on *Reset default*. You can browse through your files and define a directory where you find your user-defined project templates. This will be added to *Project → New From Template*. If you first activate *Create new project from default project* and then save a project in the project templates folder.

- *Prompt to save project and data source changes when required*

- ☑ *Prompt for confirmation when a layer is to be removed*

- ☑ *Warn when opening a project file saved with an older version of QGIS*

- *Enable macros* ⬚▾ . This option was created to handle macros that are written to perform an action on project events. You can choose between 'Never', 'Ask', 'For this session only' and 'Always (not recommended)'.

9.3.2 System Menu

Environment

System environment variables can now be viewed, and many configured, in the **Environment** group (see figure_environment_variables). This is useful for platforms, such as Mac, where a GUI application does not necessarily inherit the user's shell environment. It's also useful for setting and viewing environment variables for the external tool sets controlled by the Processing toolbox (e.g., SAGA, GRASS), and for turning on debugging output for specific sections of the source code.

- ☑ *Use custom variables (restart required - include separators).* You can **[Add]** and **[Remove]** variables. Already-defined environment variables are displayed in *Current environment variables*, and it's possible to filter them by activating ☑ *Show only QGIS-specific variables*.

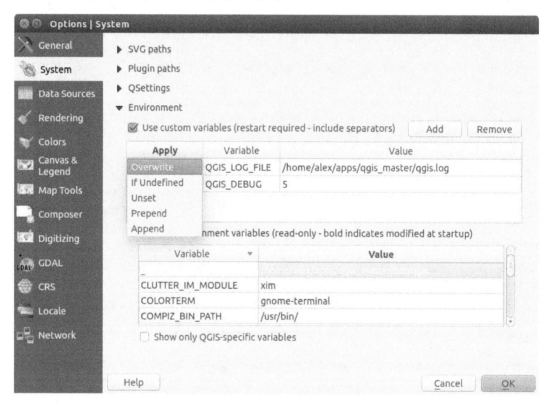

Figure 9.3: System environment variables in QGIS

Plugin paths

[Add] or **[Remove]** *Path(s) to search for additional C++ plugin libraries*

9.3.3 Data Sources Menu

Feature attributes and table

- ☑ *Open attribute table in a dock window (QGIS restart required)*

- ☑ *Copy geometry in WKT representation from attribute table.* When using 🗎 Copy selected rows to clipboard from the *Attribute table* dialog, this has the result that the coordinates of points or vertices are also copied to the clipboard.

- *Attribute table behaviour* ⬚▾ . There are three possibilities: 'Show all features', 'Show selected features' and 'Show features visible on map'.

- *Attribute table row cache* ⬚1,00 ▾ . This row cache makes it possible to save the last loaded N attribute rows so that working with the attribute table will be quicker. The cache will be deleted when closing the attribute table.

- *Representation for NULL values.* Here, you can define a value for data fields containing a NULL value.

Data source handling

- *Scan for valid items in the browser dock* ⬚▾ . You can choose between 'Check extension' and 'Check file contents'.

- *Scan for contents of compressed files (.zip) in browser dock* ⬚▾ . 'No', 'Basic scan' and 'Full scan' are possible.

- *Prompt for raster sublayers when opening.* Some rasters support sublayers — they are called subdatasets in GDAL. An example is netCDF files — if there are many netCDF variables, GDAL sees every variable as a subdataset. The option allows you to control how to deal with sublayers when a file with sublayers is opened. You have the following choices:

  - 'Always': Always ask (if there are existing sublayers)

  - 'If needed': Ask if layer has no bands, but has sublayers

  - 'Never': Never prompt, will not load anything

  - 'Load all': Never prompt, but load all sublayers

- ☑ *Ignore shapefile encoding declaration.* If a shapefile has encoding information, this will be ignored by QGIS.

- ☑ *Add PostGIS layers with double click and select in extended mode*

- ☑ *Add Oracle layers with double click and select in extended mode*

9.3.4 Rendering Menu

Rendering behaviour

- ☑ *By default new layers added to the map should be displayed*

- ☑ *Use render caching where possible to speed up redraws*

- ☑ *Render layers in parallel using many CPU cores*

- ☑ *Max cores to use*

- *Map update interval (default to 250 ms)*

- ☑ *Enable feature simplication by default for newly added layers*

- *Simplification threshold*

- ☑ *Simplify on provider side if possible*

- *Maximum scale at which the layer should be simplified*

Rendering quality

- ☑ *Make lines appear less jagged at the expense of some drawing performance*

Rasters

- With *RGB band selection*, you can define the number for the Red, Green and Blue band.

Contrast enhancement

- *Single band gray* [...▼] . A single band gray can have 'No stretch', 'Stretch to MinMax', 'Stretch and Clip to MinMax' and also 'Clip to MinMax'.

- *Multi band color (byte/band)* [...▼] . Options are 'No stretch', 'Stretch to MinMax', 'Stretch and Clip to MinMax' and 'Clip to MinMax'.

- *Multi band color (>byte/band)* [...▼] . Options are 'No stretch', 'Stretch to MinMax', 'Stretch and Clip to MinMax' and 'Clip to MinMax'.

- *Limits (minimum/maximum)* [...▼] . Options are 'Cumulative pixel count cut', 'Minimum/Maximum', 'Mean +/- standard deviation'.

- *Cumulative pixel count cut limits*

- *Standard deviation multiplier*

Debugging

- ☑ *Map canvas refresh*

9.3.5 Colors Menu

This menu allows you to add some custom color that you can find in each color dialog window of the renderers. You will see a set of predefined colors in the tab: you can delete or edit all of them. Moreover you can add the color you want and perform some copy and paste operations. Finally you can export the color set as a `gpl` file or import them.

9.3.6 Canvas and Legend Menu

Default map appearance (overridden by project properties)

- Define a *Selection color* and a *Background color*.

Layer legend

- *Double click action in legend* [...▼] . You can either 'Open layer properties' or 'Open attribute table' with the double click.

- The following *Legend item styles* are possible:

    - ☑ *Capitalise layer names*

    - ☑ *Bold layer names*

    - ☑ *Bold group names*

    - ☑ *Display classification attribute names*

    - ☑ *Create raster icons (may be slow)*

9.3.7 Map tools Menu

This menu offers some options regarding the behaviour of the *Identify tool*.

- *Search radius for identifying and displaying map tips* is a tolerance factor expressed as a percentage of the map width. This means the identify tool will depict results as long as you click within this tolerance.

- *Highlight color* allows you to choose with which color should features being identified are to be highlighted.

- *Buffer* expressed as a percentage of the map width, determines a buffer distance to be rendered from the outline of the identify highlight.

- *Minimum width* expressed as a percentage of the map width, determines how thick should the outline of a highlighted object be.

Measure tool

- Define *Rubberband color* for measure tools
- Define *Decimal places*
- ☑ *Keep base unit*
- *Preferred measurements units* ⦿ ('Meters', 'Feet', 'Nautical Miles' or 'Degrees')'
- *Preferred angle units* ⦿ ('Degrees', 'Radians' or 'Gon')

Panning and zooming

- Define *Mouse wheel action* ▾ ('Zoom', 'Zoom and recenter', 'Zoom to mouse cursor', 'Nothing')
- Define *Zoom factor* for wheel mouse

Predefined scales

Here, you find a list of predefined scales. With the [+] and [-] buttons you can add or remove your individual scales.

9.3.8 Composer Menu

Composition defaults

You can define the *Default font* here.

Grid appearance

- Define the *Grid style* ▾ ('Solid', 'Dots', 'Crosses')
- Define the *Grid color*

Grid and guide defaults

- Define the *Grid spacing* 1,00 ↕
- Define the *Grid offset* 1,00 ↕ for x and y
- Define the *Snap tolerance* 1,00 ↕

9.3.9 Digitizing Menu

Feature creation

- ☑ *Suppress attributes pop-up windows after each created feature*
- ☑ *Reuse last entered attribute values*

- *Validate geometries*. Editing complex lines and polygons with many nodes can result in very slow rendering. This is because the default validation procedures in QGIS can take a lot of time. To speed up rendering, it is possible to select GEOS geometry validation (starting from GEOS 3.3) or to switch it off. GEOS geometry validation is much faster, but the disadvantage is that only the first geometry problem will be reported.

Rubberband

- Define Rubberband *Line width* and *Line color*

Snapping

- ☑ *Open snapping options in a dock window (QGIS restart required)*

- Define *Default snap mode* ⬚▼ ('To vertex', 'To segment', 'To vertex and segment', 'Off')

- Define *Default snapping tolerance* in map units or pixels

- Define the *Search radius for vertex edits* in map units or pixels

Vertex markers

- ☑ *Show markers only for selected features*

- Define vertex *Marker style* ⬚▼ ('Cross' (default), 'Semi transparent circle' or 'None')

- Define vertex *Marker size*

Curve offset tool

The next 3 options refer to the ⬭ Offset Curve tool in *Advanced digitizing*. Through the various settings, it is possible to influence the shape of the line offset. These options are possible starting from GEOS 3.3.

- *Join style*
- *Quadrant segments*
- *Miter limit*

9.3.10 GDAL Menu

GDAL is a data exchange library for raster files. In this tab, you can *Edit create options* and *Edit Pyramids Options* of the raster formats. Define which GDAL driver is to be used for a raster format, as in some cases more than one GDAL driver is available.

9.3.11 CRS Menu

Default CRS for new projects

- ⬚ *Don't enable 'on the fly' reprojection*

- ⦿ *Automatically enable 'on the fly' reprojection if layers have different CRS*

- ⬚ *Enable 'on the fly' reprojection by default*

- Select a CRS and *Always start new projects with this CRS*

CRS for new layers

This area allows you to define the action to take when a new layer is created, or when a layer without a CRS is loaded.

- ⦿ *Prompt for CRS*

- ⬚ *Use project CRS*

- ⬚ *Use default CRS*

Default datum transformations

- ☑ *Ask for datum transformation when no default is defined*

- If you have worked with the 'on-the-fly' CRS transformation you can see the result of the transformation in the window below. You can find information about 'Source CRS' and 'Destination CRS' as well as 'Source datum transform' and 'Destination datum transform'.

9.3.12 Locale Menu

- ☑ *Overwrite system locale* and *Locale to use instead*

- Information about active system locale

9.3.13 Network Menu

General

- Define *WMS search address*, default is `http://geopole.org/wms/search?search=\%1\&type=rss`

- Define *Timeout for network requests (ms)* - default is 60000

- Define *Default expiration period for WMSC/WMTS tiles (hours)* - default is 24

- Define *Max retry in case of tile request errors*

- Define *User-Agent*

Cache settings

Define the *Directory* and a *Size* for the cache.

- ☑ *Use proxy for web access* and define 'Host', 'Port', 'User', and 'Password'.

- Set the *Proxy type* ⬚▼ according to your needs.

  - *Default Proxy*: Proxy is determined based on the application proxy set using

  - *Socks5Proxy*: Generic proxy for any kind of connection. Supports TCP, UDP, binding to a port (incoming connections) and authentication.

  - *HttpProxy*: Implemented using the "CONNECT" command, supports only outgoing TCP connections; supports authentication.

  - *HttpCachingProxy*: Implemented using normal HTTP commands, it is useful only in the context of HTTP requests.

  - *FtpCachingProxy*: Implemented using an FTP proxy, it is useful only in the context of FTP requests.

Excluding some URLs can be added to the text box below the proxy settings (see Figure_Network_Tab).

If you need more detailed information about the different proxy settings, please refer to the manual of the underlying QT library documentation at http://doc.trolltech.com/4.5/qnetworkproxy.html#ProxyType-enum.

Tip: Using Proxies

Using proxies can sometimes be tricky. It is useful to proceed by 'trial and error' with the above proxy types, to check to see if they succeed in your case.

You can modify the options according to your needs. Some of the changes may require a restart of QGIS before they will be effective.

- 🐧 Settings are saved in a text file: `$HOME/.config/QGIS/QGIS2.conf`

- ❌ You can find your settings in: `$HOME/Library/Preferences/org.qgis.qgis.plist`

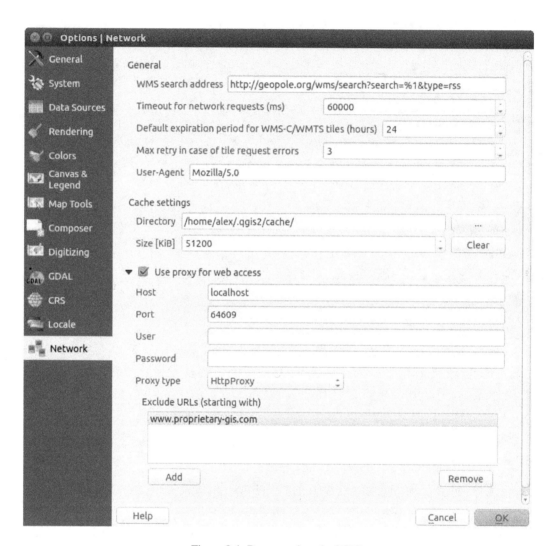

Figure 9.4: Proxy-settings in QGIS

- ![icon] Settings are stored in the registry under: `HKEY\CURRENT_USER\Software\QGIS\qgis`

9.4 Customization

The customization tool lets you (de)activate almost every element in the QGIS user interface. This can be very useful if you have a lot of plugins installed that you never use and that are filling your screen.

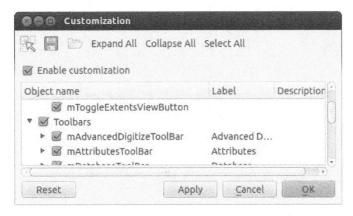

Figure 9.5: The Customization dialog ᐃ

QGIS Customization is divided into five groups. In ![icon] *Menus*, you can hide entries in the Menu bar. In ![icon] *Panels*, you find the panel windows. Panel windows are applications that can be started and used as a floating, top-level window or embedded to the QGIS main window as a docked widget (see also *Panels and Toolbars*). In the ![icon] *Status Bar*, features like the coordinate information can be deactivated. In ![icon] *Toolbars*, you can (de)activate the toolbar icons of QGIS, and in ![icon] *Widgets*, you can (de)activate dialogs as well as their buttons.

With ![icon] Switch to catching widgets in main application, you can click on elements in QGIS that you want to be hidden and find the corresponding entry in Customization (see figure_customization). You can also save your various setups for different use cases as well. Before your changes are applied, you need to restart QGIS.

.

## CHAPTER 10

Working with Projections

QGIS allows users to define a global and project-wide CRS (coordinate reference system) for layers without a pre-defined CRS. It also allows the user to define custom coordinate reference systems and supports on-the-fly (OTF) projection of vector and raster layers. All of these features allow the user to display layers with different CRSs and have them overlay properly.

10.1 Overview of Projection Support

QGIS has support for approximately 2,700 known CRSs. Definitions for each CRS are stored in a SQLite database that is installed with QGIS. Normally, you do not need to manipulate the database directly. In fact, doing so may cause projection support to fail. Custom CRSs are stored in a user database. See section *Custom Coordinate Reference System* for information on managing your custom coordinate reference systems.

The CRSs available in QGIS are based on those defined by the European Petroleum Search Group (EPSG) and the Institut Geographique National de France (IGNF) and are largely abstracted from the spatial reference tables used in GDAL. EPSG identifiers are present in the database and can be used to specify a CRS in QGIS.

In order to use OTF projection, either your data must contain information about its coordinate reference system or you will need to define a global, layer or project-wide CRS. For PostGIS layers, QGIS uses the spatial reference identifier that was specified when the layer was created. For data supported by OGR, QGIS relies on the presence of a recognized means of specifying the CRS. In the case of shapefiles, this means a file containing the well-known text (WKT) specification of the CRS. This projection file has the same base name as the shapefile and a `.prj` extension. For example, a shapefile named `alaska.shp` would have a corresponding projection file named `alaska.prj`.

Whenever you select a new CRS, the layer units will automatically be changed in the *General* tab of the ⚒ *Project Properties* dialog under the *Project* (Gnome, OS X) or *Settings* (KDE, Windows) menu.

10.2 Global Projection Specification

QGIS starts each new project using the global default projection. The global default CRS is EPSG:4326 - WGS 84 (`proj=longlat +ellps=WGS84 +datum=WGS84 +no_defs`), and it comes predefined in QGIS. This default can be changed via the **[Select...]** button in the first section, which is used to define the default coordinate reference system for new projects, as shown in figure_projection_1. This choice will be saved for use in subsequent QGIS sessions.

When you use layers that do not have a CRS, you need to define how QGIS responds to these layers. This can be done globally or project-wide in the *CRS* tab under *Settings* → ⚒ *Options*.

The options shown in figure_projection_1 are:

- ⦿ *Prompt for CRS*
- ◯ *Use project CRS*

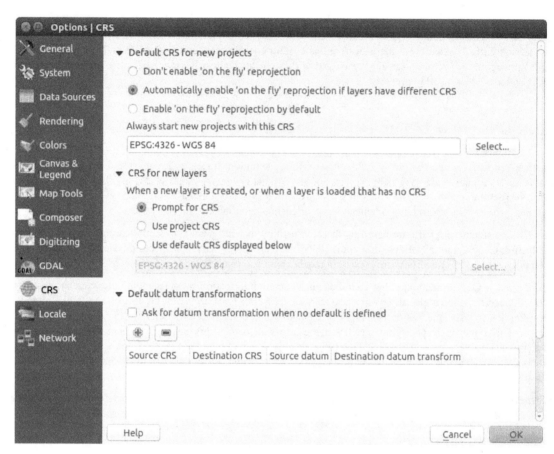

Figure 10.1: CRS tab in the QGIS Options Dialog

• ◯ *Use default CRS displayed below*

If you want to define the coordinate reference system for a certain layer without CRS information, you can also do that in the *General* tab of the raster and vector properties dialog (see *General Menu* for rasters and *General Menu* for vectors). If your layer already has a CRS defined, it will be displayed as shown in *Vector Layer Properties Dialog* .

Tip: CRS in the Map Legend

Right-clicking on a layer in the Map Legend (section *Map Legend*) provides two CRS shortcuts. *Set layer CRS* takes you directly to the Coordinate Reference System Selector dialog (see figure_projection_2). *Set project CRS from Layer* redefines the project CRS using the layer's CRS.

10.3 Define On The Fly (OTF) Reprojection

QGIS supports OTF reprojection for both raster and vector data. However, OTF is not activated by default. To use OTF projection, you must activate the ☑ *Enable on the fly CRS transformation* checkbox in the *CRS* tab of the ▱ *Project Properties* dialog.

There are three ways to do this:

1. Select ⚒ *Project Properties* from the *Project* (Gnome, OSX) or *Settings* (KDE, Windows) menu.

2. Click on the   CRS status icon in the lower right-hand corner of the status bar.

3. Turn OTF on by default in the *CRS* tab of the *Options* dialog by selecting ☑ *Enable 'on the fly' reprojection by default* or *Automatically enable 'on the fly' reprojection if layers have different CRS*.

If you have already loaded a layer and you want to enable OTF projection, the best practice is to open the *CRS* tab of the *Project Properties* dialog, select a CRS, and activate the ☑ *Enable 'on the fly' CRS transformation* checkbox. The   CRS status icon will no longer be greyed out, and all layers will be OTF projected to the CRS shown next to the icon.

The *CRS* tab of the *Project Properties* dialog contains five important components, as shown in Figure_projection_2 and described below:

1. **Enable 'on the fly' CRS transformation** — This checkbox is used to enable or disable OTF projection. When off, each layer is drawn using the coordinates as read from the data source, and the components described below are inactive. When on, the coordinates in each layer are projected to the coordinate reference system defined for the map canvas.

2. **Filter** — If you know the EPSG code, the identifier, or the name for a coordinate reference system, you can use the search feature to find it. Enter the EPSG code, the identifier or the name.

3. **Recently used coordinate reference systems** — If you have certain CRSs that you frequently use in your everyday GIS work, these will be displayed in this list. Click on one of these items to select the associated CRS.

4. **Coordinate reference systems of the world** — This is a list of all CRSs supported by QGIS, including Geographic, Projected and Custom coordinate reference systems. To define a CRS, select it from the list by expanding the appropriate node and selecting the CRS. The active CRS is preselected.

5. **PROJ.4 text** — This is the CRS string used by the PROJ.4 projection engine. This text is read-only and provided for informational purposes.

Tip: Project Properties Dialog

If you open the *Project Properties* dialog from the *Project* menu, you must click on the *CRS* tab to view the CRS settings.

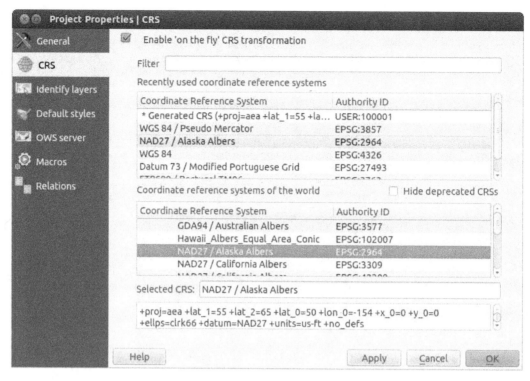

Figure 10.2: Project Properties Dialog Δ

Opening the dialog from the ᶜᴿˢ ˢᵗᵃᵗᵘˢ icon will automatically bring the *CRS* tab to the front.

10.4 Custom Coordinate Reference System

If QGIS does not provide the coordinate reference system you need, you can define a custom CRS. To define a CRS, select *Custom CRS...* from the *Settings* menu. Custom CRSs are stored in your QGIS user database. In addition to your custom CRSs, this database also contains your spatial bookmarks and other custom data.

Defining a custom CRS in QGIS requires a good understanding of the PROJ.4 projection library. To begin, refer to "Cartographic Projection Procedures for the UNIX Environment - A User's Manual" by Gerald I. Evenden, U.S. Geological Survey Open-File Report 90-284, 1990 (available at ftp://ftp.remotesensing.org/proj/OF90-284.pdf).

This manual describes the use of the `proj.4` and related command line utilities. The cartographic parameters used with `proj.4` are described in the user manual and are the same as those used by QGIS.

The *Custom Coordinate Reference System Definition* dialog requires only two parameters to define a user CRS:

1. A descriptive name

2. The cartographic parameters in PROJ.4 format

To create a new CRS, click the ☆ Add new CRS button and enter a descriptive name and the CRS parameters.

Note that the *Parameters* must begin with a `+proj=` block, to represent the new coordinate reference system.

You can test your CRS parameters to see if they give sane results. To do this, enter known WGS 84 latitude and longitude values in *North* and *East* fields, respectively. Click on [**Calculate**], and compare the results with the known values in your coordinate reference system.

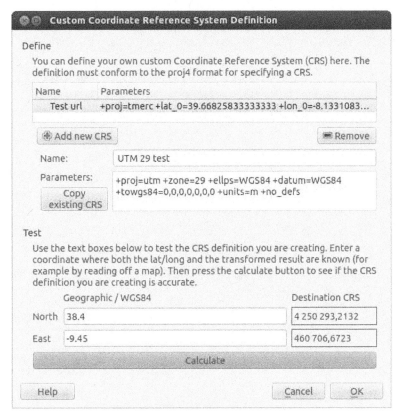

Figure 10.3: Custom CRS Dialog

10.5 Default datum transformations

OTF depends on being able to transform data into a 'default CRS', and QGIS uses WGS84. For some CRS there are a number of transforms available. QGIS allows you to define the transformation used otherwise QGIS uses a default transformation.

In the *CRS* tab under *Settings → ⚙ Options* you can:

- set QGIS to ask you when it needs define a transformation using ⦿ *Ask for datum transformation when no default is defined*

- edit a list of user defaults for transformations.

QGIS asks which transformation to use by opening a dialogue box displaying PROJ.4 text describing the source and destination transforms. Further information may be found by hovering over a transform. User defaults can be saved by selecting ⦿ *Remember selection.*

.

## CHAPTER 11

QGIS Browser

The QGIS Browser is a panel in QGIS that lets you easily navigate in your filesystem and manage geodata. You can have access to common vector files (e.g., ESRI shapefiles or MapInfo files), databases (e.g., PostGIS, Oracle, SpatiaLite or MS SQL Spatial) and WMS/WFS connections. You can also view your GRASS data (to get the data into QGIS, see *GRASS GIS Integration*).

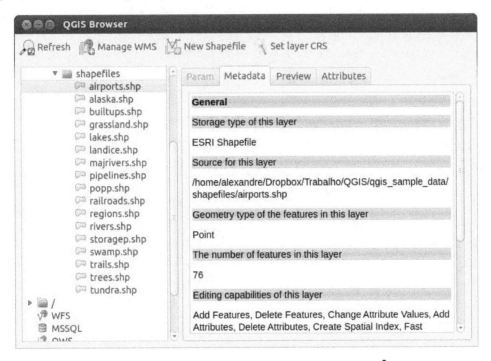

Figure 11.1: QGIS browser as a stand alone application 🐧

Use the QGIS Browser to preview your data. The drag-and-drop function makes it easy to get your data into the map view and the map legend.

1. Activate the QGIS Browser: Right-click on the toolbar and check ☑️*Browser* or select it from *Settings →
   Panels*.

2. Drag the panel into the legend window and release it.

3. Click on the *Browser* tab.

4. Browse in your filesystem and choose the `shapefile` folder from `qgis_sample_data` directory.

5. Press the `Shift` key and select the `airports.shp` and `alaska.shp` files.

6. Press the left mouse button, then drag and drop the files into the map canvas.

7. Right-click on a layer and choose *Set project CRS from layer*. For more information see *Working with Projections*.

8. Click on ⚲ Zoom Full to make the layers visible.

There is a second browser available under *Settings → Panels*. This is handy when you need to move files or layers between locations.

1. Activate a second QGIS Browser: Right-click on the toolbar and check ☑*Browser (2)*, or select it from *Settings → Panels*.

2. Drag the panel into the legend window.

3. Navigate to the *Browser (2)* tab and browse for a shapefile in your file system.

4. Select a file with the left mouse button. Now you can use the ⊕Add Selected Layers icon to add it into the current project.

QGIS automatically looks for the coordinate reference system (CRS) and zooms to the layer extent if you work in a blank QGIS project. If there are already files in your project, the file will just be added, and in the case that it has the same extent and CRS, it will be visualized. If the file has another CRS and layer extent, you must first right-click on the layer and choose *Set Project CRS from Layer*. Then choose *Zoom to Layer Extent*.

The ▮Filter files function works on a directory level. Browse to the folder where you want to filter files and enter a search word or wildcard. The Browser will show only matching filenames – other data won't be displayed.

It's also possible to run the QGIS Browser as a stand-alone application.

Start the QGIS browser

- 🐧 Type in "qbrowser" at a command prompt.

- 🪟 Start the QGIS Browser using the Start menu or desktop shortcut.

- X The QGIS Browser is available from your Applications folder.

In figure_browser_standalone_metadata, you can see the enhanced functionality of the stand-alone QGIS Browser. The *Param* tab provides the details of your connection-based datasets, like PostGIS or MSSQL Spatial. The *Metadata* tab contains general information about the file (see *Metadata Menu*). With the *Preview* tab, you can have a look at your files without importing them into your QGIS project. It's also possible to preview the attributes of your files in the *Attributes* tab.

## CHAPTER 12

Working with Vector Data

12.1 Supported Data Formats

QGIS uses the OGR library to read and write vector data formats, including ESRI shapefiles, MapInfo and Micro-Station file formats, AutoCAD DXF, PostGIS, SpatiaLite, Oracle Spatial and MSSQL Spatial databases, and many more. GRASS vector and PostgreSQL support is supplied by native QGIS data provider plugins. Vector data can also be loaded in read mode from zip and gzip archives into QGIS. As of the date of this document, 69 vector formats are supported by the OGR library (see OGR-SOFTWARE-SUITE in *Literature and Web References*). The complete list is available at http://www.gdal.org/ogr/ogr_formats.html.

Note: Not all of the listed formats may work in QGIS for various reasons. For example, some require external commercial libraries, or the GDAL/OGR installation of your OS may not have been built to support the format you want to use. Only those formats that have been well tested will appear in the list of file types when loading a vector into QGIS. Other untested formats can be loaded by selecting *∗.∗*.

Working with GRASS vector data is described in Section *GRASS GIS Integration*.

This section describes how to work with several common formats: ESRI shapefiles, PostGIS layers, SpatiaLite layers, OpenStreetMap vectors, and Comma Separated data (CSV). Many of the features available in QGIS work the same, regardless of the vector data source. This is by design, and it includes the identify, select, labeling and attributes functions.

12.1.1 ESRI Shapefiles

The standard vector file format used in QGIS is the ESRI shapefile. Support is provided by the OGR Simple Feature Library (http://www.gdal.org/ogr/).

A shapefile actually consists of several files. The following three are required:

1. .shp file containing the feature geometries

2. .dbf file containing the attributes in dBase format

3. .shx index file

Shapefiles also can include a file with a .prj suffix, which contains the projection information. While it is very useful to have a projection file, it is not mandatory. A shapefile dataset can contain additional files. For further details, see the ESRI technical specification at http://www.esri.com/library/whitepapers/pdfs/shapefile.pdf.

Loading a Shapefile

To load a shapefile, start QGIS and click on the $\checkmark$ Add Vector Layer toolbar button, or simply press Ctrl+Shift+V. This will bring up a new window (see figure_vector_1).

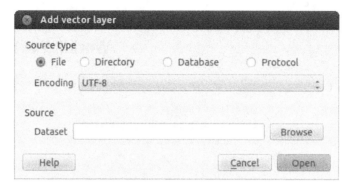

Figure 12.1: Add Vector Layer Dialog 🐧

From the available options check ● *File*. Click on **[Browse]**. That will bring up a standard open file dialog (see figure_vector_2), which allows you to navigate the file system and load a shapefile or other supported data source. The selection box *Filter* ⋯▼ allows you to preselect some OGR-supported file formats.

You can also select the encoding for the shapefile if desired.

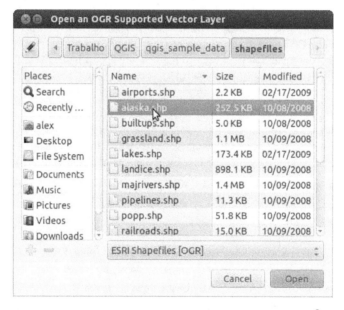

Figure 12.2: Open an OGR Supported Vector Layer Dialog 🐧

Selecting a shapefile from the list and clicking **[Open]** loads it into QGIS. Figure_vector_3 shows QGIS after loading the alaska.shp file.

Tip: Layer Colors

When you add a layer to the map, it is assigned a random color. When adding more than one layer at a time, different colors are assigned to each layer.

Once a shapefile is loaded, you can zoom around it using the map navigation tools. To change the style of a layer, open the *Layer Properties* dialog by double clicking on the layer name or by right-clicking on the name in the

---

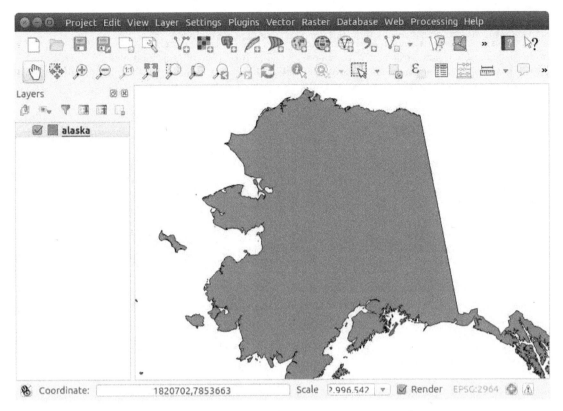

Figure 12.3: QGIS with Shapefile of Alaska loaded 🐧

legend and choosing *Properties* from the context menu. See section *Style Menu* for more information on setting symbology of vector layers.

Tip: Load layer and project from mounted external drives on OS X

On OS X, portable drives that are mounted beside the primary hard drive do not show up as expected under *File → Open Project*. We are working on a more OSX-native open/save dialog to fix this. As a workaround, you can type /Volumes in the *File name* box and press Enter. Then you can navigate to external drives and network mounts.

Improving Performance for Shapefiles

To improve the performance of drawing a shapefile, you can create a spatial index. A spatial index will improve the speed of both zooming and panning. Spatial indexes used by QGIS have a .qix extension.

Use these steps to create the index:

- Load a shapefile by clicking on the ⋁ Add Vector Layer toolbar button or pressing Ctrl+Shift+V.

- Open the *Layer Properties* dialog by double-clicking on the shapefile name in the legend or by right-clicking and choosing *Properties* from the context menu.

- In the *General* tab, click the [**Create Spatial Index**] button.

Problem loading a shape .prj file

If you load a shapefile with a .prj file and QGIS is not able to read the coordinate reference system from that file, you will need to define the proper projection manually within the *General* tab of the *Layer Properties* dialog

---

of the layer by clicking the **[Specify...]** button. This is due to the fact that `.prj` files often do not provide the complete projection parameters as used in QGIS and listed in the *CRS* dialog.

For the same reason, if you create a new shapefile with QGIS, two different projection files are created: a `.prj` file with limited projection parameters, compatible with ESRI software, and a `.qpj` file, providing the complete parameters of the used CRS. Whenever QGIS finds a `.qpj` file, it will be used instead of the `.prj`.

12.1.2 Loading a MapInfo Layer

To load a MapInfo layer, click on the Add Vector Layer toolbar button; or type `Ctrl+Shift+V`, change the file type filter *Files of type* : to 'Mapinfo File [OGR] (*.mif *.tab *.MIF *.TAB)' and select the MapInfo layer you want to load.

12.1.3 Loading an ArcInfo Binary Coverage

To load an ArcInfo Binary Coverage, click on the Add Vector Layer toolbar button or press `Ctrl+Shift+V` to open the *Add Vector Layer* dialog. Select Directory as *Source type*. Change the file type filter *Files of type* to 'Arc/Info Binary Coverage'. Navigate to the directory that contains the coverage file, and select it.

Similarly, you can load directory-based vector files in the UK National Transfer Format, as well as the raw TIGER Format of the US Census Bureau.

12.1.4 Delimited Text Files

Tabular data is a very common and widely used format because of its simplicity and readability – data can be viewed and edited even in a plain text editor. A delimited text file is an attribute table with each column separated by a defined character and each row separated by a line break. The first row usually contains the column names. A common type of delimited text file is a CSV (Comma Separated Values), with each column separated by a comma.

Such data files can also contain positional information in two main forms:

- As point coordinates in separate columns
- As well-known text (WKT) representation of geometry

QGIS allows you to load a delimited text file as a layer or ordinal table. But first check that the file meets the following requirements:

1. The file must have a delimited header row of field names. This must be the first line in the text file.

2. The header row must contain field(s) with geometry definition. These field(s) can have any name.

3. The X and Y coordinates (if geometry is defined by coordinates) must be specified as numbers. The coordinate system is not important.

As an example of a valid text file, we import the elevation point data file `elevp.csv` that comes with the QGIS sample dataset (see section *Sample Data*):

```
X;Y;ELEV
-300120;7689960;13
-654360;7562040;52
1640;7512840;3
[...]
```

Some items to note about the text file:

1. The example text file uses `;` (semicolon) as delimiter. Any character can be used to delimit the fields.

2. The first row is the header row. It contains the fields X, Y and ELEV.

3. No quotes (`"`) are used to delimit text fields.

4. The X coordinates are contained in the X field.

5. The Y coordinates are contained in the Y field.

Loading a delimited text file

Click the toolbar icon   Add Delimited Text Layer in the *Manage layers* toolbar to open the *Create a Layer from a Delimited Text File* dialog, as shown in figure_delimited_text_1.

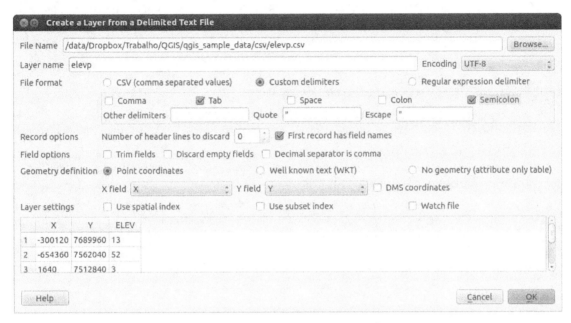

Figure 12.4: Delimited Text Dialog

First, select the file to import (e.g., `qgis_sample_data/csv/elevp.csv`) by clicking on the **[Browse]** button. Once the file is selected, QGIS attempts to parse the file with the most recently used delimiter. To enable QGIS to properly parse the file, it is important to select the correct delimiter. You can specify a delimiter by activating ⦿ *Custom delimiters*, or by activating ⦿ *Regular expression delimiter* and entering text into the *Expression* field. For example, to change the delimiter to tab, use `\t` (this is a regular expression for the tab character).

Once the file is parsed, set *Geometry definition* to ⦿ *Point coordinates* and choose the X and Y fields from the dropdown lists. If the coordinates are defined as degrees/minutes/seconds, activate the ☑ *DMS coordinates* checkbox.

Finally, enter a layer name (e.g., `elevp`), as shown in figure_delimited_text_1. To add the layer to the map, click **[OK]**. The delimited text file now behaves as any other map layer in QGIS.

There is also a helper option that allows you to trim leading and trailing spaces from fields — ☑ *Trim fields*. Also, it is possible to ☑ *Discard empty fields*. If necessary, you can force a comma to be the decimal separator by activating ☑ *Decimal separator is comma*.

If spatial information is represented by WKT, activate the ⦿ *Well Known Text* option and select the field with the WKT definition for point, line or polygon objects. If the file contains non-spatial data, activate ⦿ *No geometry (attribute only table)* and it will be loaded as an ordinal table.

Additionaly, you can enable:

- ☑ *Use spatial index* to improve the performance of displaying and spatially selecting features.

- ☑ *Use subset index.*

- ☑ *Watch file* to watch for changes to the file by other applications while QGIS is running.

12.1.5 OpenStreetMap data

In recent years, the OpenStreetMap project has gained popularity because in many countries no free geodata such as digital road maps are available. The objective of the OSM project is to create a free editable map of the world from GPS data, aerial photography or local knowledge. To support this objective, QGIS provides suppport for OSM data.

Loading OpenStreetMap Vectors

QGIS integrates OpenStreetMap import as a core functionality.

- To connect to the OSM server and download data, open the menu *Vector → Openstreetmap → Load data*. You can skip this step if you already obtained an `.osm` XML file using JOSM, Overpass API or any other source.

- The menu *Vector → Openstreetmap → Import topology from an XML file* will convert your `.osm` file into a SpatiaLite database and create a corresponding database connection.

- The menu *Vector → Openstreetmap → Export topology to SpatiaLite* then allows you to open the database connection, select the type of data you want (points, lines, or polygons) and choose tags to import. This creates a SpatiaLite geometry layer that you can add to your project by clicking on the ⚏ Add SpatiaLite Layer toolbar button or by selecting the ⚏ *Add SpatiaLite Layer...* option from the *Layer* menu (see section *SpatiaLite Layers*).

12.1.6 PostGIS Layers

PostGIS layers are stored in a PostgreSQL database. The advantages of PostGIS are the spatial indexing, filtering and query capabilities it provides. Using PostGIS, vector functions such as select and identify work more accurately than they do with OGR layers in QGIS.

Creating a stored Connection

⚏ The first time you use a PostGIS data source, you must create a connection to the PostgreSQL database that contains the data. Begin by clicking on the ⚏ Add PostGIS Layer toolbar button, selecting the ⚏ *Add PostGIS Layer...* option from the *Layer* menu, or typing `Ctrl+Shift+D`. You can also open the *Add Vector Layer* dialog and select ⦿ *Database*. The *Add PostGIS Table(s)* dialog will be displayed. To access the connection manager, click on the [**New**] button to display the *Create a New PostGIS Connection* dialog. The parameters required for a connection are:

- **Name**: A name for this connection. It can be the same as *Database*.

- **Service**: Service parameter to be used alternatively to hostname/port (and potentially database). This can be defined in `pg_service.conf`.

- **Host**: Name of the database host. This must be a resolvable host name such as would be used to open a telnet connection or ping the host. If the database is on the same computer as QGIS, simply enter *'localhost'* here.

- **Port**: Port number the PostgreSQL database server listens on. The default port is 5432.

- **Database**: Name of the database.

- **SSL mode**: How the SSL connection will be negotiated with the server. Note that massive speedups in PostGIS layer rendering can be achieved by disabling SSL in the connection editor. The following options are available:

  - Disable: Only try an unencrypted SSL connection.

  - Allow: Try a non-SSL connection. If that fails, try an SSL connection.

  - Prefer (the default): Try an SSL connection. If that fails, try a non-SSL connection.

  - Require: Only try an SSL connection.

- **Username**: User name used to log in to the database.

- **Password**: Password used with *Username* to connect to the database.

Optionally, you can activate the following checkboxes:

- ☑ *Save Username*

- ☑ *Save Password*

- ☑ *Only look in the geometry_columns table*

- ☑ *Don't resolve type of unrestricted columns (GEOMETRY)*

- ☑ *Only look in the 'public' schema*

- ☑ *Also list tables with no geometry*

- ☑ *Use estimated table metadata*

Once all parameters and options are set, you can test the connection by clicking on the **[Test Connect]** button.

Loading a PostGIS Layer

Once you have one or more connections defined, you can load layers from the PostgreSQL database. Of course, this requires having data in PostgreSQL. See section *Importing Data into PostgreSQL* for a discussion on importing data into the database.

To load a layer from PostGIS, perform the following steps:

- If the *Add PostGIS layers* dialog is not already open, selecting the *Add PostGIS Layer...* option from the *Layer* menu or typing `Ctrl+Shift+D` opens the dialog.

- Choose the connection from the drop-down list and click **[Connect]**.

- Select or unselect ☑ *Also list tables with no geometry*.

- Optionally, use some ☑ *Search Options* to define which features to load from the layer, or use the **[Build query]** button to start the *Query builder* dialog.

- Find the layer(s) you wish to add in the list of available layers.

- Select it by clicking on it. You can select multiple layers by holding down the `Shift` key while clicking. See section *Query Builder* for information on using the PostgreSQL Query Builder to further define the layer.

- Click on the **[Add]** button to add the layer to the map.

Tip: PostGIS Layers

Normally, a PostGIS layer is defined by an entry in the geometry_columns table. From version 0.9.0 on, QGIS can load layers that do not have an entry in the geometry_columns table. This includes both tables and views. Defining a spatial view provides a powerful means to visualize your data. Refer to your PostgreSQL manual for information on creating views.

Some details about PostgreSQL layers

This section contains some details on how QGIS accesses PostgreSQL layers. Most of the time, QGIS should simply provide you with a list of database tables that can be loaded, and it will load them on request. However, if you have trouble loading a PostgreSQL table into QGIS, the information below may help you understand any QGIS messages and give you direction on changing the PostgreSQL table or view definition to allow QGIS to load it.

QGIS requires that PostgreSQL layers contain a column that can be used as a unique key for the layer. For tables, this usually means that the table needs a primary key, or a column with a unique constraint on it. In QGIS, this column needs to be of type int4 (an integer of size 4 bytes). Alternatively, the ctid column can be used as primary key. If a table lacks these items, the oid column will be used instead. Performance will be improved if the column is indexed (note that primary keys are automatically indexed in PostgreSQL).

If the PostgreSQL layer is a view, the same requirement exists, but views do not have primary keys or columns with unique constraints on them. You have to define a primary key field (has to be integer) in the QGIS dialog before you can load the view. If a suitable column does not exist in the view, QGIS will not load the layer. If this occurs, the solution is to alter the view so that it does include a suitable column (a type of integer and either a primary key or with a unique constraint, preferably indexed).

QGIS offers a checkbox **Select at id** that is activated by default. This option gets the ids without the attributes which is faster in most cases. It can make sense to disable this option when you use expensive views.

Tip: Backup of PostGIS database with layers saved by QGIS

If you want to make a backup of your PostGIS database using the `pg_dump` and `pg_restore` commands the default layer styles as saved by QGIS are failing to restore afterwards. You need to set the XML option to `DOCUMENT` and the restore will work.

12.1.7 Importing Data into PostgreSQL

Data can be imported into PostgreSQL/PostGIS using several tools, including the SPIT plugin and the command line tools shp2pgsql and ogr2ogr.

DB Manager

QGIS comes with a core plugin named ![] DB Manager. It can be used to load shapefiles and other data formats, and it includes support for schemas. See section *DB Manager Plugin* for more information.

shp2pgsql

PostGIS includes an utility called **shp2pgsql** that can be used to import shapefiles into a PostGIS-enabled database. For example, to import a shapefile named `lakes.shp` into a PostgreSQL database named `gis_data`, use the following command:

```
shp2pgsql -s 2964 lakes.shp lakes_new | psql gis_data
```

This creates a new layer named `lakes_new` in the `gis_data` database. The new layer will have a spatial reference identifier (SRID) of 2964. See section *Working with Projections* for more information on spatial reference systems and projections.

Tip: Exporting datasets from PostGIS

Like the import tool **shp2pgsql**, there is also a tool to export PostGIS datasets as shapefiles: **pgsql2shp**. This is shipped within your PostGIS distribution.

ogr2ogr

Besides **shp2pgsql** and **DB Manager**, there is another tool for feeding geodata in PostGIS: **ogr2ogr**. This is part of your GDAL installation.

To import a shapefile into PostGIS, do the following:

```
ogr2ogr -f "PostgreSQL" PG:"dbname=postgis host=myhost.de user=postgres
password=topsecret" alaska.shp
```

This will import the shapefile `alaska.shp` into the PostGIS database *postgis* using the user *postgres* with the password *topsecret* on host server *myhost.de*.

Note that OGR must be built with PostgreSQL to support PostGIS. You can verify this by typing (in 🐧)

```
ogrinfo --formats | grep -i post
```

If you prefer to use PostgreSQL's **COPY** command instead of the default **INSERT INTO** method, you can export the following environment variable (at least available on 🐧 and **X**):

```
export PG_USE_COPY=YES
```

ogr2ogr does not create spatial indexes like **shp2pgsl** does. You need to create them manually, using the normal SQL command **CREATE INDEX** afterwards as an extra step (as described in the next section *Improving Performance*).

Improving Performance

Retrieving features from a PostgreSQL database can be time-consuming, especially over a network. You can improve the drawing performance of PostgreSQL layers by ensuring that a PostGIS spatial index exists on each layer in the database. PostGIS supports creation of a GiST (Generalized Search Tree) index to speed up spatial searches of the data (GiST index information is taken from the PostGIS documentation available at http://postgis.refractions.net).

The syntax for creating a GiST index is:

```
CREATE INDEX [indexname] ON [tablename]
  USING GIST ( [geometryfield] GIST_GEOMETRY_OPS );
```

Note that for large tables, creating the index can take a long time. Once the index is created, you should perform a VACUUM ANALYZE. See the PostGIS documentation (POSTGIS-PROJECT *Literature and Web References*) for more information.

The following is an example of creating a GiST index:

```
gsherman@madison:~/current$ psql gis_data
Welcome to psql 8.3.0, the PostgreSQL interactive terminal.

Type:  \copyright for distribution terms
       \h for help with SQL commands
       \? for help with psql commands
       \g or terminate with semicolon to execute query
       \q to quit

gis_data=# CREATE INDEX sidx_alaska_lakes ON alaska_lakes
gis_data-# USING GIST (the_geom GIST_GEOMETRY_OPS);
CREATE INDEX
gis_data=# VACUUM ANALYZE alaska_lakes;
VACUUM
gis_data=# \q
gsherman@madison:~/current$
```

12.1.8 Vector layers crossing 180° longitude

Many GIS packages don't wrap vector maps with a geographic reference system (lat/lon) crossing the 180 degrees longitude line (http://postgis.refractions.net/documentation/manual-2.0/ST_Shift_Longitude.html). As result, if we open such a map in QGIS, we will see two far, distinct locations, that should appear near each other. In Figure_vector_4, the tiny point on the far left of the map canvas (Chatham Islands) should be within the grid, to the right of the New Zealand main islands.

Figure 12.5: Map in lat/lon crossing the 180° longitude line 🐧

A work-around is to transform the longitude values using PostGIS and the **ST_Shift_Longitude** function. This function reads every point/vertex in every component of every feature in a geometry, and if the longitude coordinate is < 0°, it adds 360° to it. The result is a 0° - 360° version of the data to be plotted in a 180°-centric map.

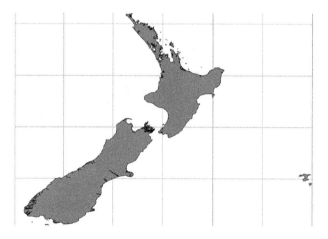

Figure 12.6: Crossing 180° longitude applying the **ST_Shift_Longitude** function

Usage

- Import data into PostGIS (*Importing Data into PostgreSQL*) using, for example, the DB Manager plugin.

- Use the PostGIS command line interface to issue the following command (in this example, "TABLE" is the actual name of your PostGIS table): `gis_data=# update TABLE set the_geom=ST_Shift_Longitude(the_geom);`

- If everything went well, you should receive a confirmation about the number of features that were updated. Then you'll be able to load the map and see the difference (Figure_vector_5).

12.1.9 SpatiaLite Layers

The first time you load data from a SpatiaLite database, begin by clicking on the Add SpatiaLite Layer toolbar button, or by selecting the *Add SpatiaLite Layer...* option from the *Layer* menu, or by typing Ctrl+Shift+L. This will bring up a window that will allow you either to connect to a SpatiaLite database already known to QGIS, which you can choose from the drop-down menu, or to define a new connection to a new database. To define a new connection, click on [**New**] and use the file browser to point to your SpatiaLite database, which is a file with a .sqlite extension.

If you want to save a vector layer to SpatiaLite format, you can do this by right clicking the layer in the legend. Then, click on *Save as..*, define the name of the output file, and select 'SpatiaLite' as format and the CRS. Also, you can select 'SQLite' as format and then add SPATIALITE=YES in the OGR data source creation option field. This tells OGR to create a SpatiaLite database. See also http://www.gdal.org/ogr/drv_sqlite.html.

QGIS also supports editable views in SpatiaLite.

Creating a new SpatiaLite layer

If you want to create a new SpatiaLite layer, please refer to section *Creating a new SpatiaLite layer*.

Tip: SpatiaLite data management Plugins

For SpatiaLite data management, you can also use several Python plugins: QSpatiaLite, SpatiaLite Manager or DB Manager (core plugin, recommended). If necessary, they can be downloaded and installed with the Plugin Installer.

12.1.10 MSSQL Spatial Layers

QGIS also provides native MS SQL 2008 support. The first time you load MSSQL Spatial data, begin by clicking on the Add MSSQL Spatial Layer toolbar button or by selecting the *Add MSSQL Spatial Layer...* option from the *Layer* menu, or by typing Ctrl+Shift+M.

12.1.11 Oracle Spatial Layers

The spatial features in Oracle Spatial aid users in managing geographic and location data in a native type within an Oracle database. QGIS now has support for such layers.

Creating a stored Connection

The first time you use an Oracle Spatial data source, you must create a connection to the database that contains the data. Begin by clicking on the Add Orcale Spatial Layer toolbar button, selecting the *Add Orcale Spatial Layer...* option from the *Layer* menu, or typing Ctrl+Shift+O. To access the connection manager, click on the [**New**] button to display the *Create a New Oracle Spatial Connection* dialog. The parameters required for a connection are:

- **Name**: A name for this connection. It can be the same as *Database*
- **Database**: SID or SERVICE_NAME of the Oracle instance.
- **Host**: Name of the database host. This must be a resolvable host name such as would be used to open a telnet connection or ping the host. If the database is on the same computer as QGIS, simply enter *'localhost'* here.
- **Port**: Port number the Oracle database server listens on. The default port is 1521.

- **Username**: Username used to login to the database.
- **Password**: Password used with *Username* to connect to the database.

Optionally, you can activate following checkboxes:

- ☑ *Save Username* Indicates whether to save the database username in the connection configuration.
- ☑ *Save Password* Indicates whether to save the database password in the connection settings.
- ☑ *Only look in meta data table* Restricts the displayed tables to those that are in the all_sdo_geom_metadata view. This can speed up the initial display of spatial tables.
- ☑ *Only look for user's tables* When searching for spatial tables, restrict the search to tables that are owned by the user.
- ☑ *Also list tables with no geometry* Indicates that tables without geometry should also be listed by default.
- ☑ *Use estimated table statistics for the layer metadata* When the layer is set up, various metadata are required for the Oracle table. This includes information such as the table row count, geometry type and spatial extents of the data in the geometry column. If the table contains a large number of rows, determining this metadata can be time-consuming. By activating this option, the following fast table metadata operations are done: Row count is determined from all_tables.num_rows. Table extents are always determined with the SDO_TUNE.EXTENTS_OF function, even if a layer filter is applied. Table geometry is determined from the first 100 non-null geometry rows in the table.
- ☑ *Only existing geometry types* Only list the existing geometry types and don't offer to add others.

Once all parameters and options are set, you can test the connection by clicking on the **[Test Connect]** button.

Tip: QGIS User Settings and Security

Depending on your computing environment, storing passwords in your QGIS settings may be a security risk. Passwords are saved in clear text in the system configuration and in the project files! Your customized settings for QGIS are stored based on the operating system:

- △ The settings are stored in your home directory in ~/.qgis2.
- The settings are stored in the registry.

Loading an Oracle Spatial Layer

Once you have one or more connections defined, you can load layers from the Oracle database. Of course, this requires having data in Oracle.

To load a layer from Oracle Spatial, perform the following steps:

- If the *Add Oracle Spatial layers* dialog is not already open, click on the Add Oracle Spatial Layer toolbar button.
- Choose the connection from the drop-down list and click **[Connect]**.
- Select or unselect ☑ *Also list tables with no geometry*.
- Optionally, use some ☑ *Search Options* to define which features to load from the layer or use the **[Build query]** button to start the *Query builder* dialog.
- Find the layer(s) you wish to add in the list of available layers.
- Select it by clicking on it. You can select multiple layers by holding down the Shift key while clicking. See section *Query Builder* for information on using the Oracle Query Builder to further define the layer.
- Click on the **[Add]** button to add the layer to the map.

Tip: Oracle Spatial Layers

Normally, an Oracle Spatial layer is defined by an entry in the **USER_SDO_METADATA** table.

.

12.2 The Symbol Library

12.2.1 Presentation

The Symbol Library is the place where users can create generic symbols to be used in several QGIS projects. It allows users to export and import symbols, groups symbols and add, edit and remove symbols. You can open it with the *Settings* → *Style Library* or from the **Style** tab in the vector layer's *Properties*.

Share and import symbols

Users can export and import symbols in two main formats: qml (QGIS format) and SLD (OGC standard). Note that SLD format is not fully supported by QGIS.

 share item displays a drop down list to let the user import or export symbols.

Groups and smart groups

Groups are categories of Symbols and smart groups are dynamic groups.

To create a group, right-click on an existing group or on the main **Groups** directory in the left of the library. You can also select a group and click on the 🞣 add item button.

To add a symbol into a group, you can either right click on a symbol then choose *Apply group* and then the group name added before. There is a second way to add several symbols into group: just select a group and click 🔤 and choose **Group Symbols**. All symbols display a checkbox that allow you to add the symbol into the selected groups. When finished, you can click on the same button, and choose **Finish Grouping**.

Create **Smart Symbols** is similar to creating group, but instead select **Smart Groups**. The dialog box allow user to choose the expression to select symbols in order to appear in the smart group (contains some tags, member of a group, have a string in its name, etc.)

Add, edit, remove symbol

With the *Style manager* from the **[Symbol]** 🔽 menu you can manage your symbols. You can 🞣 add item, ✏ edit item, 🔲 remove item and 👤 share item. 'Marker' symbols, 'Line' symbols, 'Fill' patterns and 'colour ramps' can be used to create the symbols. The symbols are then assigned to 'All Symbols', 'Groups' or 'Smart groups'.

For each kind of symbols, you will find always the same dialog structure:

- at the top left side a symbol representation
- under the symbol representation the symbol tree show the symbol layers
- at the right you can setup some parameter (unit,transparency, color, size and rotation)
- under these parameters you find some symbol from the symbols library

The symbol tree allow adding, removing or protect new simple symbol. You can move up or down the symbol layer.

More detailed settings can be made when clicking on the second level in the *Symbol layers* dialog. You can define *Symbol layers* that are combined afterwards. A symbol can consist of several *Symbol layers*. Settings will be shown later in this chapter.

Tip: Note that once you have set the size in the lower levels of the *Symbol layers* dialog, the size of the whole symbol can be changed with the *Size* menu in the first level again. The size of the lower levels changes accordingly, while the size ratio is maintained.

12.2.2 Marker Symbols

Marker symbols have several symbol layer types:

- Ellipse marker
- Font marker
- Simple marker (default)
- SVG marker
- Vector Field marker

The following settings are possible:

- *Symbol layer type*: You have the option to use Ellipse markers, Font markers, Simple markers, SVG markers and Vector Field markers.
- *colors*
- *Size*
- *Outline style*
- *Outline width*
- *Angle*
- *Offset X,Y*: You can shift the symbol in the x- or y-direction.
- *Anchor point*
- *Data defined properties ...*

12.2.3 Line Symbols

Line marker symbols have only two symbol layer types:

- Marker line
- Simple line (default)

The default symbol layer type draws a simple line whereas the other display a marker point regularly on the line. You can choose different location vertex, interval or central point. Marker line can have offset along the line or offset line. Finally, *rotation* allows you to change the orientation of the symbol.

The following settings are possible:

- *colour*
- *Pen width*
- *Offset*
- *Pen style*

- *Join style*
- *Cap style*
- ☑ *Use custom dash pattern*
- *Dash pattern unit*
- *Data defined properties ...*

12.2.4 Polygon Symbols

Polygon marker symbols have also several symbol layer types:

- Centroid fill
- Gradient fill
- Line pattern fill
- Point pattern fill
- Raster image fill
- SVG fill
- Shapeburst fill
- Simple fill (default)
- Outline: Marker line (same as line marker)
- Outline: simple line (same as line marker)

The following settings are possible:

- *Colors* for the border and the fill.
- *Fill style*
- *Border style*
- *Border width*
- *Offset X,Y*
- *Data defined properties ...*

Using the color combo box, you can drag and drop color for one color button to another button, copy-paste color, pick color from somewhere, choose a color from the palette or from recent or standard color. The combo box allow you to fill in the feature with transparency. You can also just click on the button to open the palettte dialog. Note that you can import color from some external software like GIMP.

With the 'Raster image fill' you can fill polygons with a tiled raster image. Options include (data defined) file name, opacity, image size (in pixels, mm or map units), coordinate mode (feature or view) and rotation.

'Gradient Fill' *Symbol layer type* allows you to select between a ⦿ *Two color* and ◯ *Color ramp* setting. You can use the ☑ *Feature centroid* as *Referencepoint*. All fills 'Gradient Fill' *Symbol layer type* is also available through the *Symbol* menu of the Categorized and Graduated Renderer and through the *Rule properties* menu of the Rule-based renderer. Other possibility is to choose a 'shapeburst fill' which is a buffered gradient fill, where a gradient is drawn from the boundary of a polygon towards the polygon's centre. Configurable parameters include distance from the boundary to shade, use of color ramps or simple two color gradients, optional blurring of the fill and offsets.

It is possible to only draw polygon borders inside the polygon. Using 'Outline: Simple line' select ☑ *Draw line only inside polygon*.

12.2.5 Color ramp

You can create a custom color ramp choosing *New color ramp...* from the *color ramp* drop-down menu. A dialog will prompt for the ramp type: Gradient, Random, colorBrewer, or cpt-city. The first three have options for number of steps and/or multiple stops in the color ramp. You can use the ✔ *Invert* option while classifying the data with a color ramp. See figure_symbology_3 for an example of custom color ramp and figure_symbology_3a for the cpt-city dialog.

Figure 12.7: Example of custom gradient color ramp with multiple stops 🐧

The cpt-city option opens a new dialog with hundreds of themes included 'out of the box'.

12.3 The Vector Properties Dialog

The *Layer Properties* dialog for a vector layer provides information about the layer, symbology settings and labeling options. If your vector layer has been loaded from a PostgreSQL/PostGIS datastore, you can also alter the underlying SQL for the layer by invoking the *Query Builder* dialog on the *General* tab. To access the *Layer Properties* dialog, double-click on a layer in the legend or right-click on the layer and select *Properties* from the pop-up menu.

12.3.1 Style Menu

The Style menu provides you with a comprehensive tool for rendering and symbolizing your vector data. You can use *Layer rendering* → tools that are common to all vector data, as well as special symbolizing tools that were designed for the different kinds of vector data.

Renderers

The renderer is responsible for drawing a feature together with the correct symbol. There are four types of renderers: single symbol, categorized, graduated and rule-based. There is no continuous color renderer, because it is in fact only a special case of the graduated renderer. The categorized and graduated renderers can be created by specifying a symbol and a color ramp - they will set the colors for symbols appropriately. For point layers, there is a point displacement renderer available. For each data type (points, lines and polygons), vector symbol layer

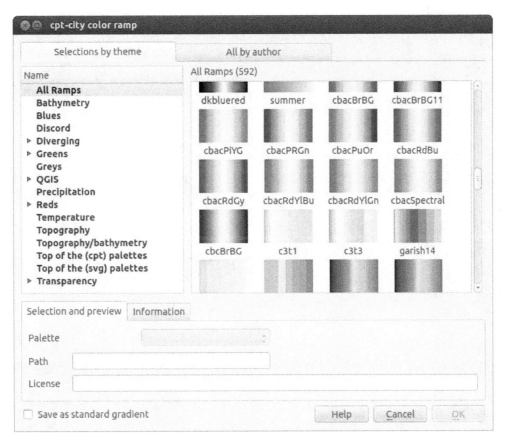

Figure 12.8: cpt-city dialog with hundreds of color ramps 🐧

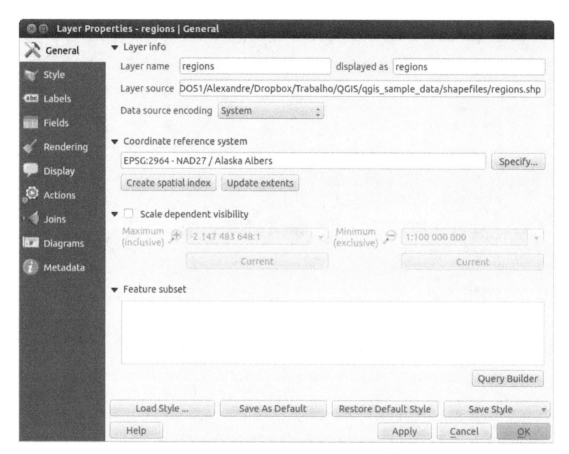

Figure 12.9: Vector Layer Properties Dialog △

types are available. Depending on the chosen renderer, the *Style* menu provides different additional sections. On the bottom right of the symbology dialog, there is a **[Symbol]** button, which gives access to the Style Manager (see *Presentation*). The Style Manager allows you to edit and remove existing symbols and add new ones.

After having made any needed changes, the symbol can be added to the list of current style symbols (using **[Symbol]** ⬚▾ *Save in symbol library*), and then it can easily be used in the future. Furthermore, you can use the **[Save Style]** ⬚▾ button to save the symbol as a QGIS layer style file (.qml) or SLD file (.sld). SLDs can be exported from any type of renderer – single symbol, categorized, graduated or rule-based – but when importing an SLD, either a single symbol or rule-based renderer is created. That means that categorized or graduated styles are converted to rule-based. If you want to preserve those renderers, you have to stick to the QML format. On the other hand, it can be very handy sometimes to have this easy way of converting styles to rule-based.

If you change the renderer type when setting the style of a vector layer the settings you made for the symbol will be maintained. Be aware that this procedure only works for one change. If you repeat changing the renderer type the settings for the symbol will get lost.

If the datasource of the layer is a database (PostGIS or Spatialite for example), you can save your layer style inside a table of the database. Just click on *Save Style* comboxbox and choose **Save in database** item then fill in the dialog to define a style name, add a description, an ui file and if the style is a default style. When loading a layer from the database, if a style already exists for this layer, QGIS will load the layer and its style. You can add several style in the database. Only one will be the default style anyway.

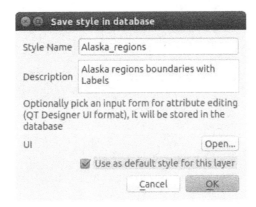

Figure 12.10: Save Style in database Dialog 🐧

Tip: Select and change multiple symbols

The Symbology allows you to select multiple symbols and right click to change color, transparency, size, or width of selected entries.

Single Symbol Renderer

The Single Symbol Renderer is used to render all features of the layer using a single user-defined symbol. The properties, which can be adjusted in the *Style* menu, depend partially on the type of layer, but all types share the following dialog structure. In the top-left part of the menu, there is a preview of the current symbol to be rendered. On the right part of the menu, there is a list of symbols already defined for the current style, prepared to be used by selecting them from the list. The current symbol can be modified using the menu on the right side. If you click on the first level in the *Symbol layers* dialog on the left side, it's possible to define basic parameters like *Size*, *Transparency*, *color* and *Rotation*. Here, the layers are joined together.

In any spinbox in this dialog you can enter expressions. E.g. you can calculate simple math like multiplying the existing size of a point by 3 without resorting to a calculator.

If you click on the second level in the *Symbol layers* dialog a 'Data-defined override' for nearly all settings is possible. When using a data-defined color one may want to link the color to a field 'budged'. Here a comment functionality is inserted.

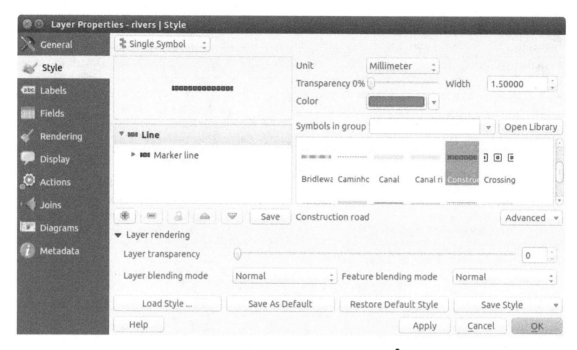

Figure 12.11: Single symbol line properties

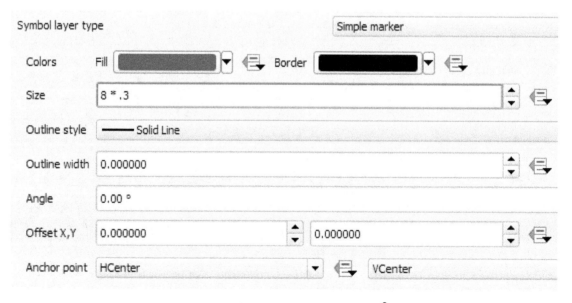

Figure 12.12: Expression in Size spinbox

```
/* This expression will return a color code depending on the field value.
 * Negative value: red
 * 0 value: yellow
 * Positive value: green
 */
CASE
  WHEN value < 0 THEN '#DC143C'  -- Negative value: red
  WHEN value = 0 THEN '#CCCC00'  -- Value 0: yellow
  ELSE '#228B22'                 -- Positive value: green
END
```

static/user_manual/working_with_vector/symbol_data_defined_e

Figure 12.13: Data-defined symbol with Edit... menu

Categorized Renderer

The Categorized Renderer is used to render all features from a layer, using a single user-defined symbol whose color reflects the value of a selected feature's attribute. The *Style* menu allows you to select:

- The attribute (using the Column listbox or the ε ... *Set column expression* function, see *Expressions*)

- The symbol (using the Symbol dialog)

- The colors (using the color Ramp listbox)

Then click on **Classify** button to create classes from the distinct value of the attribute column. Each classes can be disabled unchecking the checkbox at the left of the class name.

You can change symbol, value and/or label of the class, just double click on the item you want to change.

Right-click shows a contextual menu to **Copy/Paste**, **Change color**, **Change transparency**, **Change output unit**, **Change symbol width**.

The **[Advanced]** button in the lower-right corner of the dialog allows you to set the fields containing rotation and size scale information. For convenience, the center of the menu lists the values of all currently selected attributes together, including the symbols that will be rendered.

The example in figure_symbology_6 shows the category rendering dialog used for the rivers layer of the QGIS sample dataset.

Graduated Renderer

The Graduated Renderer is used to render all the features from a layer, using a single user-defined symbol whose color reflects the assignment of a selected feature's attribute to a class.

Like the Categorized Renderer, the Graduated Renderer allows you to define rotation and size scale from specified columns.

Also, analogous to the Categorized Renderer, the *Style* tab allows you to select:

- The attribute (using the Column listbox or the ε ... *Set column expression* function, see *Expressions* chapter)

- The symbol (using the Symbol Properties button)

- The colors (using the color Ramp list)

Additionally, you can specify the number of classes and also the mode for classifying features within the classes (using the Mode list). The available modes are:

- Equal Interval: each class has the same size (e.g. values from 0 to 16 and 4 classes, each class has a size of 4);

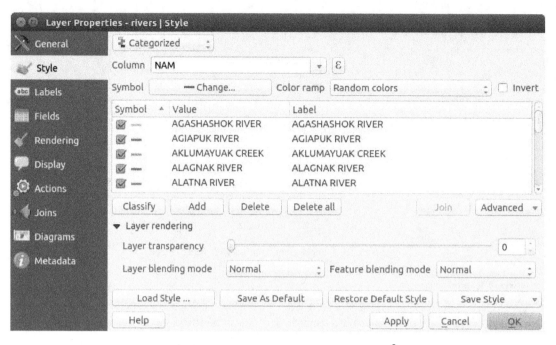

Figure 12.14: Categorized Symbolizing options

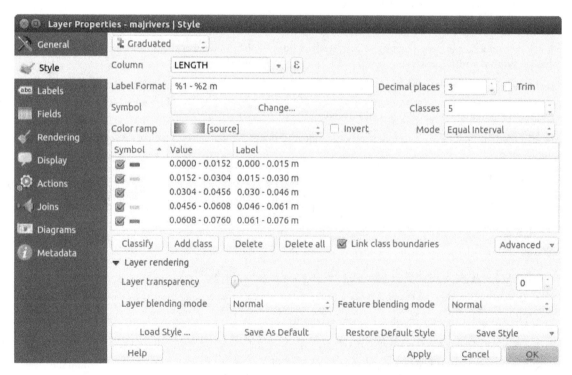

Figure 12.15: Graduated Symbolizing options

- Quantile: each class will have the same number of element inside (the idea of a boxplot);

- Natural Breaks (Jenks): the variance within each class is minimal while the variance between classes is maximal;

- Standard Deviation: classes are built depending on the standard deviation of the values;

- Pretty Breaks: the same of natural breaks but the extremes number of each class are integers.

The listbox in the center part of the *Style* menu lists the classes together with their ranges, labels and symbols that will be rendered.

Click on **Classify** button to create classes using the choosen mode. Each classes can be disabled unchecking the checkbox at the left of the class name.

You can change symbol, value and/or label of the clic, just double clicking on the item you want to change.

Right-click shows a contextual menu to **Copy/Paste**, **Change color**, **Change transparency**, **Change output unit**, **Change symbol width**.

The example in figure_symbology_7 shows the graduated rendering dialog for the rivers layer of the QGIS sample dataset.

Tip: Thematic maps using an expression

Categorized and graduated thematic maps can now be created using the result of an expression. In the properties dialog for vector layers, the attribute chooser has been augmented with a ε... *Set column expression* function. So now you no longer need to write the classification attribute to a new column in your attribute table if you want the classification attribute to be a composite of multiple fields, or a formula of some sort.

Rule-based rendering

The Rule-based Renderer is used to render all the features from a layer, using rule based symbols whose color reflects the assignment of a selected feature's attribute to a class. The rules are based on SQL statements. The dialog allows rule grouping by filter or scale, and you can decide if you want to enable symbol levels or use only the first-matched rule.

The example in figure_symbology_8 shows the rule-based rendering dialog for the rivers layer of the QGIS sample dataset.

To create a rule, activate an existing row by double-clicking on it, or click on '+' and click on the new rule. In the *Rule properties* dialog, you can define a label for the rule. Press the [....] button to open the expression string builder. In the **Function List**, click on *Fields and Values* to view all attributes of the attribute table to be searched. To add an attribute to the field calculator **Expression** field, double click its name in the *Fields and Values* list. Generally, you can use the various fields, values and functions to construct the calculation expression, or you can just type it into the box (see *Expressions*). You can create a new rule by copying and pasting an existing rule with the right mouse button. You can also use the 'ELSE' rule that will be run if none of the other rules on that level match. Since QGIS 2.8 the rules appear in a tree hierarchy in the map legend. Just double-klick the rules in the map legend and the Style menu of the layer properties appears showing the rule that is the background for the symbol in the tree.

Point displacement

The Point Displacement Renderer works to visualize all features of a point layer, even if they have the same location. To do this, the symbols of the points are placed on a displacement circle around a center symbol.

Tip: Export vector symbology

You have the option to export vector symbology from QGIS into Google *.kml, *.dxf and MapInfo *.tab files. Just open the right mouse menu of the layer and click on *Save selection as* → to specify the name of the output file and its format. In the dialog, use the *Symbology export* menu to save the symbology either as *Feature symbology* → or as *Symbol layer symbology* →. If you have used symbol layers, it is recommended to use the second setting.

Inverted Polygon

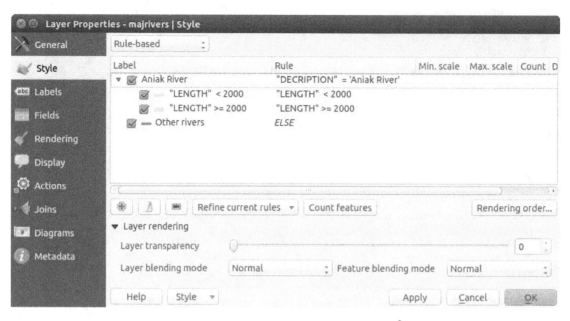

Figure 12.16: Rule-based Symbolizing options

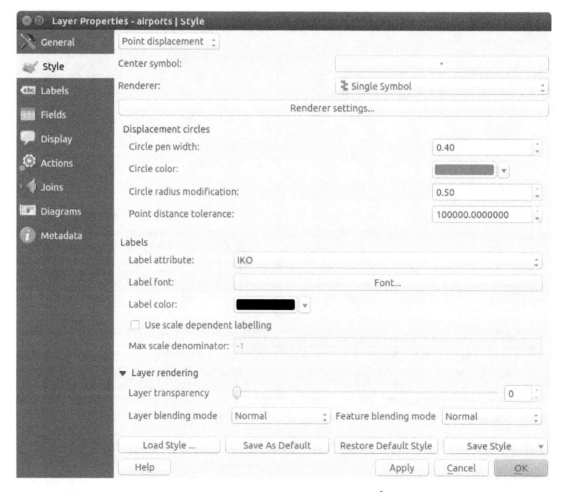

Figure 12.17: Point displacement dialog

Inverted polygon renderer allows user to define a symbol to fill in outside of the layer's polygons. As before you can select subrenderers. These subrenderers are the same as for the main renderers.

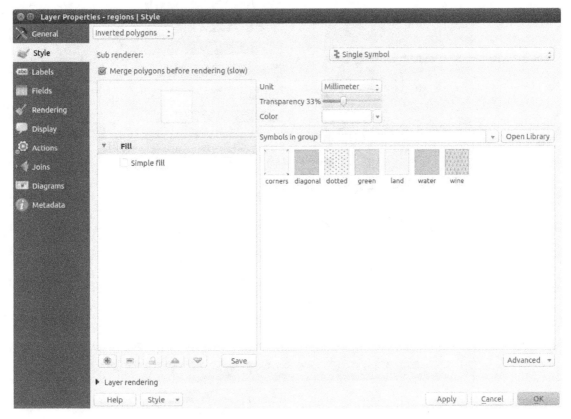

Figure 12.18: Inverted Polygon dialog △

Tip: Switch quickly between styles

Once you created one of the above mentioned styles you can right-klick on the layer and choose *Styles → Add* to save your style. Now you can easily switch between styles you created using the *Styles →* menu again.

Heatmap

With the Heatmap renderer you can create live dynamic heatmaps for (multi)point layers. You can specify the heatmap radius in pixels, mm or map units, choose a color ramp for the heatmap style and use a slider for selecting a tradeoff between render speed and quality. When adding or removing a feature the heatmap renderer updates the heatmap style automatically.

Color Picker

Regardless the type of style to be used, the *select color* dialog will show when you click to choose a color - either border or fill color. This dialog has four different tabs which allow you to select colors by ▦ color ramp, ◉ color wheel, ⊞ color swatches or ✐ color picker.

Whatever method you use, the selected color is always described through color sliders for HSV (Hue, Saturation, Value) and RGB (Red, Green, Blue) values. There is also an *opacity* slider to set transparency level. On the lower left part of the dialog you can see a comparison between the *current* and the *new* color you are presently selecting and on the lower right part you have the option to add the color you just tweaked into a color slot button.

With ▦ color ramp or with ◉ color wheel, you can browse to all possible color combinations. There are other

---

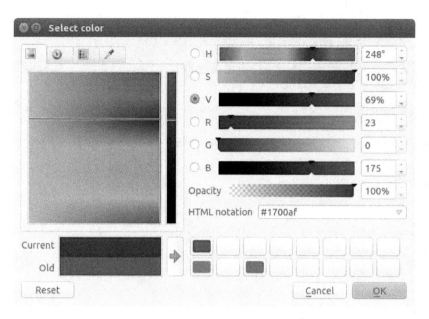

Figure 12.19: Color picker ramp tab 🐧

possibilities though. By using *color swatches* ▦ you can choose from a preselected list. This selected list is populated with one of three methods: *Recent colors*, *Standard colors* or *Project colors*

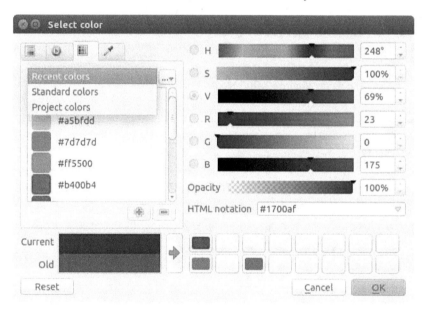

Figure 12.20: Color picker swatcher tab 🐧

Another option is to use the 🖊 color picker which allows you to sample a color from under your mouse pointer at any part of QGIS or even from another application by pressing the space bar. Please note that the color picker is OS dependent and is currently not supported by OSX.

Tip: quick color picker + copy/paste colors

You can quickly choose from *Recent colors*, from *Standard colors* or simply *copy* or *paste* a color by clicking the drop-down arrow that follows a current color box.

Figure 12.21: Quick color picker menu 🐧

Layer rendering

- *Layer transparency* [slider]: You can make the underlying layer in the map canvas visible with this tool. Use the slider to adapt the visibility of your vector layer to your needs. You can also make a precise definition of the percentage of visibility in the the menu beside the slider.

- *Layer blending mode* and *Feature blending mode*: You can achieve special rendering effects with these tools that you may previously only know from graphics programs. The pixels of your overlaying and underlaying layers are mixed through the settings described below.

  - Normal: This is the standard blend mode, which uses the alpha channel of the top pixel to blend with the pixel beneath it. The colors aren't mixed.

  - Lighten: This selects the maximum of each component from the foreground and background pixels. Be aware that the results tend to be jagged and harsh.

  - Screen: Light pixels from the source are painted over the destination, while dark pixels are not. This mode is most useful for mixing the texture of one layer with another layer (e.g., you can use a hillshade to texture another layer).

  - Dodge: Dodge will brighten and saturate underlying pixels based on the lightness of the top pixel. So, brighter top pixels cause the saturation and brightness of the underlying pixels to increase. This works best if the top pixels aren't too bright; otherwise the effect is too extreme.

  - Addition: This blend mode simply adds pixel values of one layer with the other. In case of values above one (in the case of RGB), white is displayed. This mode is suitable for highlighting features.

  - Darken: This creates a resultant pixel that retains the smallest components of the foreground and background pixels. Like lighten, the results tend to be jagged and harsh.

  - Multiply: Here, the numbers for each pixel of the top layer are multiplied with the corresponding pixels for the bottom layer. The results are darker pictures.

  - Burn: Darker colors in the top layer cause the underlying layers to darken. Burn can be used to tweak and colorise underlying layers.

  - Overlay: This mode combines the multiply and screen blending modes. In the resulting picture, light parts become lighter and dark parts become darker.

  - Soft light: This is very similar to overlay, but instead of using multiply/screen it uses color burn/dodge. This is supposed to emulate shining a soft light onto an image.

  - Hard light: Hard light is also very similar to the overlay mode. It's supposed to emulate projecting a very intense light onto an image.

  - Difference: Difference subtracts the top pixel from the bottom pixel, or the other way around, to always get a positive value. Blending with black produces no change, as the difference with all colors is zero.

– Subtract: This blend mode simply subtracts pixel values of one layer from the other. In case of negative values, black is displayed.

12.3.2 Labels Menu

The ^{abc} Labels core application provides smart labeling for vector point, line and polygon layers, and it only requires a few parameters. This new application also supports on-the-fly transformed layers. The core functions of the application have been redesigned. In QGIS, there are a number of other features that improve the labeling. The following menus have been created for labeling the vector layers:

- Text
- Formatting
- Buffer
- Background
- Shadow
- Placement
- Rendering

Let us see how the new menus can be used for various vector layers. **Labeling point layers**

Start QGIS and load a vector point layer. Activate the layer in the legend and click on the ^{abc} Layer Labeling Options icon in the QGIS toolbar menu.

The first step is to activate the ✔ *Label this layer with* checkbox and select an attribute column to use for labeling. Click ε… if you want to define labels based on expressions - See labeling_with_expressions.

The following steps describe a simple labeling without using the *Data defined override* functions, which are situated next to the drop-down menus.

You can define the text style in the *Text* menu (see Figure_labels_1). Use the *Type case* option to influence the text rendering. You have the possibility to render the text 'All uppercase', 'All lowercase' or 'Capitalize first letter'. Use the blend modes to create effects known from graphics programs (see blend_modes).

In the *Formatting* menu, you can define a character for a line break in the labels with the 'Wrap on character' function. Use the ✔ *Formatted numbers* option to format the numbers in an attribute table. Here, decimal places may be inserted. If you enable this option, three decimal places are initially set by default.

To create a buffer, just activate the ✔ *Draw text buffer* checkbox in the *Buffer* menu. The buffer color is variable. Here, you can also use blend modes (see blend_modes).

If the ✔ *color buffer's fill* checkbox is activated, it will interact with partially transparent text and give mixed color transparency results. Turning off the buffer fill fixes that issue (except where the interior aspect of the buffer's stroke intersects with the text's fill) and also allows you to make outlined text.

In the *Background* menu, you can define with *Size X* and *Size Y* the shape of your background. Use *Size type* to insert an additional 'Buffer' into your background. The buffer size is set by default here. The background then consists of the buffer plus the background in *Size X* and *Size Y*. You can set a *Rotation* where you can choose between 'Sync with label', 'Offset of label' and 'Fixed'. Using 'Offset of label' and 'Fixed', you can rotate the background. Define an *Offset X,Y* with X and Y values, and the background will be shifted. When applying *Radius X,Y*, the background gets rounded corners. Again, it is possible to mix the background with the underlying layers in the map canvas using the *Blend mode* (see blend_modes).

Use the *Shadow* menu for a user-defined *Drop shadow*. The drawing of the background is very variable. Choose between 'Lowest label component', 'Text', 'Buffer' and 'Background'. The *Offset* angle depends on the orientation of the label. If you choose the ✔ *Use global shadow* checkbox, then the zero point of the angle is always oriented to the north and doesn't depend on the orientation of the label. You can influence the appearance of the shadow with the *Blur radius*. The higher the number, the softer the shadows. The appearance of the drop shadow can also be altered by choosing a blend mode (see blend_modes).

Choose the *Placement* menu for the label placement and the labeling priority. Using the ● *Offset from point* setting, you now have the option to use *Quadrants* to place your label. Additionally, you can alter the angle of the label placement with the *Rotation* setting. Thus, a placement in a certain quadrant with a certain rotation is possible. In the *priority* section you can define with which priority the labels are rendered. It interacts with labels of the other vector layers in the map canvas. If there are labels from different layers in the same location then the label with the higher priority will be displayed and the other will be left out.

In the *Rendering* menu, you can define label and feature options. Under *Label options*, you find the scale-based visibility setting now. You can prevent QGIS from rendering only selected labels with the ☑ *Show all labels for this layer (including colliding labels)* checkbox. Under *Feature options*, you can define whether every part of a multipart feature is to be labeled. It's possible to define whether the number of features to be labeled is limited and to ☑ *Discourage labels from covering features*.

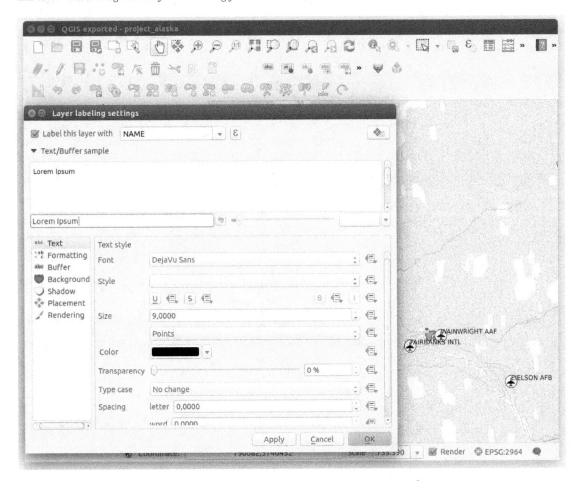

Figure 12.22: Smart labeling of vector point layers 🐧

Labeling line layers

The first step is to activate the ☑ *Label this layer* checkbox in the *Label settings* tab and select an attribute column to use for labeling. Click ε… if you want to define labels based on expressions - See labeling_with_expressions.

After that, you can define the text style in the *Text* menu. Here, you can use the same settings as for point layers.

Also, in the *Formatting* menu, the same settings as for point layers are possible.

The *Buffer* menu has the same functions as described in section labeling_point_layers.

The *Background* menu has the same entries as described in section labeling_point_layers.

Also, the *Shadow* menu has the same entries as described in section labeling_point_layers.

In the *Placement* menu, you find special settings for line layers. The label can be placed ⦿ *Parallel*, ◯ *Curved* or ◯ *Horizontal*. With the ⦿ *Parallel* and ◯ *Curved* option, you can define the position ☑ *Above line*, ☑ *On line* and ☑ *Below line*. It's possible to select several options at once. In that case, QGIS will look for the optimal position of the label. Remember that here you can also use the line orientation for the position of the label. Additionally, you can define a *Maximum angle between curved characters* when selecting the ◯ *Curved* option (see Figure_labels_2).

You can set up a minimum distance for repeating labels. Distance can be in mm or in map units.

Some Placement setup will display more options, for example, *Curved* and *Parallel* Placements will allow the user to set up the position of the label (above, below or on the line), *distance* from the line and for *Curved*, the user can also setup inside/outside max angle between curved label. As for point vector layers you have the possibility to define a *Priority* for the labels.

The *Rendering* menu has nearly the same entries as for point layers. In the *Feature options*, you can now *Suppress labeling of features smaller than*.

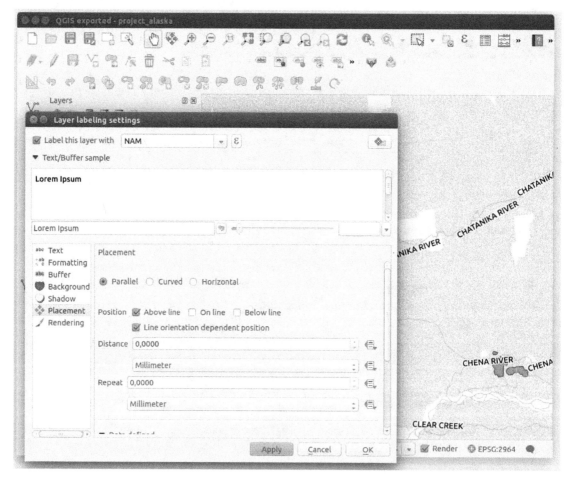

Figure 12.23: Smart labeling of vector line layers 🐧

Labeling polygon layers

The first step is to activate the ☑ *Label this layer* checkbox and select an attribute column to use for labeling. Click ε… if you want to define labels based on expressions - See labeling_with_expressions.

In the *Text* menu, define the text style. The entries are the same as for point and line layers.

The *Formatting* menu allows you to format multiple lines, also similar to the cases of point and line layers.

As with point and line layers, you can create a text buffer in the *Buffer* menu.

Use the *Background* menu to create a complex user-defined background for the polygon layer. You can use the menu also as with the point and line layers.

The entries in the *Shadow* menu are the same as for point and line layers.

In the *Placement* menu, you find special settings for polygon layers (see Figure_labels_3). ⦿ *Offset from centroid,* ⦾ *Horizontal (slow),* ⦾ *Around centroid,* ⦾ *Free* and ⦾ *Using perimeter* are possible.

In the ⦿ *Offset from centroid* settings, you can specify if the centroid is of the ⦿ *visible polygon* or ⦾ *whole polygon.* That means that either the centroid is used for the polygon you can see on the map or the centroid is determined for the whole polygon, no matter if you can see the whole feature on the map. You can place your label with the quadrants here, and define offset and rotation. The ⦾ *Around centroid* setting makes it possible to place the label around the centroid with a certain distance. Again, you can define ⦿ *visible polygon* or ⦾ *whole polygon* for the centroid. With the ⦾ *Using perimeter* settings, you can define a position and a distance for the label. For the position, ☑ *Above line,* ☑ *On line,* ☑ *Below line* and ☑ *Line orientation dependent position* are possible.

Related to the choice of Label Placement, several options will appear. As for Point Placement you can choose the distance for the polygon outline, repeat the label around the polygon perimeter.

As for point and line vector layers you have the possibility to define a *Priority* for the polygon vector layer.

The entries in the *Rendering* menu are the same as for line layers. You can also use *Suppress labeling of features smaller than* in the *Feature options.*   **Define labels based on expressions**

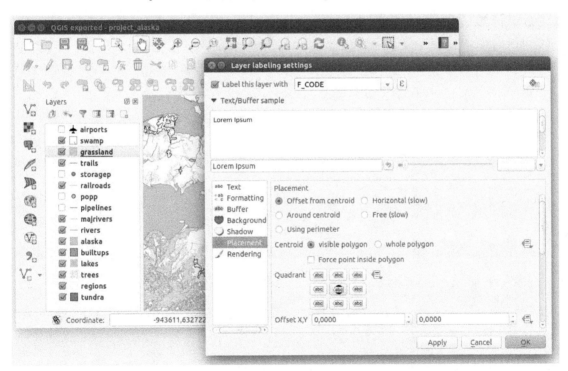

Figure 12.24: Smart labeling of vector polygon layers 🐧

QGIS allows to use expressions to label features. Just click the ε··· icon in the abc Labels menu of the properties dialog. In figure_labels_4 you see a sample expression to label the alaska regions with name and area size, based

---

on the field 'NAME_2', some descriptive text and the function '$area()' in combination with 'format_number()' to make it look nicer.

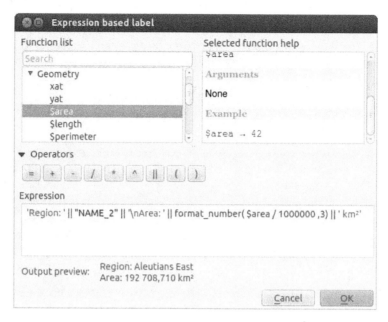

Figure 12.25: Using expressions for labeling

Expression based labeling is easy to work with. All you have to take care of is, that you need to combine all elements (strings, fields and functions) with a string concatenation sign '||' and that fields a written in "double quotes" and strings in 'single quotes'. Let's have a look at some examples:

```
# label based on two fields 'name' and 'place' with a comma as separater
"name" || ', ' || "place"

-> John Smith, Paris

# label based on two fields 'name' and 'place' separated by comma
'My name is ' || "name" || 'and I live in ' || "place"

-> My name is John Smith and I live in Paris

# label based on two fields 'name' and 'place' with a descriptive text
# and a line break (\n)
'My name is ' || "name" || '\nI live in ' || "place"

-> My name is John Smith
   I live in Paris

# create a multi-line label based on a field and the $area function
# to show the place name and its area size based on unit meter.
'The area of ' || "place" || 'has a size of ' || $area || 'm²'

-> The area of Paris has a size of 105000000 m²

# create a CASE ELSE condition. If the population value in field
# population is <= 50000 it is a town, otherwise a city.
'This place is a ' || CASE WHEN "population <= 50000" THEN 'town' ELSE 'city' END

-> This place is a town
```

As you can see in the expression builder, you have hundreds of functions available to create simple and very complex expressions to label your data in QGIS. See *Expressions* chapter for more information and examples on expressions.

Using data-defined override for labeling

With the data-defined override functions, the settings for the labeling are overridden by entries in the attribute table. You can activate and deactivate the function with the right-mouse button. Hover over the symbol and you see the information about the data-defined override, including the current definition field. We now describe an example using the data-defined override function for the 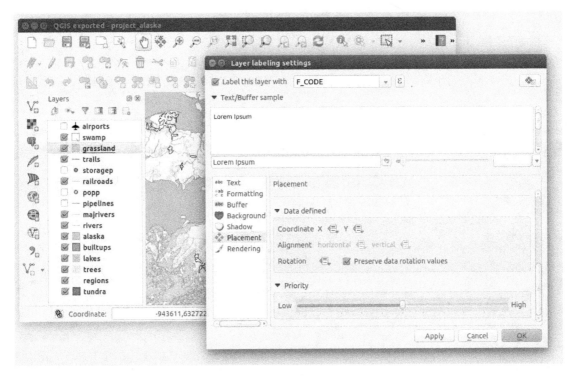Move label function (see figure_labels_5).

1. Import `lakes.shp` from the QGIS sample dataset.

2. Double-click the layer to open the Layer Properties. Click on *Labels* and *Placement*. Select 🔘 *Offset from centroid*.

3. Look for the *Data defined* entries. Click the 🗐 icon to define the field type for the *Coordinate*. Choose 'xlabel' for X and 'ylabel' for Y. The icons are now highlighted in yellow.

4. Zoom into a lake.

5. Go to the Label toolbar and click the 🔖 icon. Now you can shift the label manually to another position (see figure_labels_6). The new position of the label is saved in the 'xlabel' and 'ylabel' columns of the attribute table.

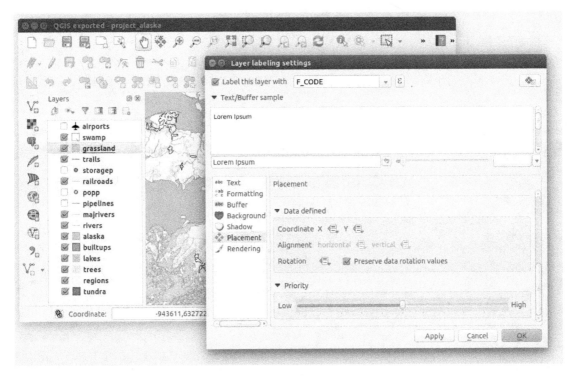

Figure 12.26: Labeling of vector polygon layers with data-defined override 🐧

12.3.3 Fields Menu

🗒 Within the *Fields* menu, the field attributes of the selected dataset can be manipulated. The buttons 🗐 New Column and 🗑 Delete Column can be used when the dataset is in 🖉 Editing mode.

Edit Widget

Within the *Fields* menu, you also find an **edit widget** column. This column can be used to define values or a range of values that are allowed to be added to the specific attribute table column. If you click on the [**edit widget**]

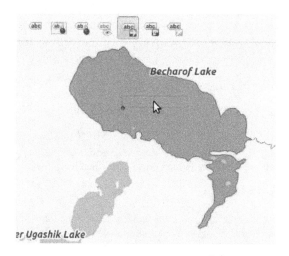

Figure 12.27: Move labels

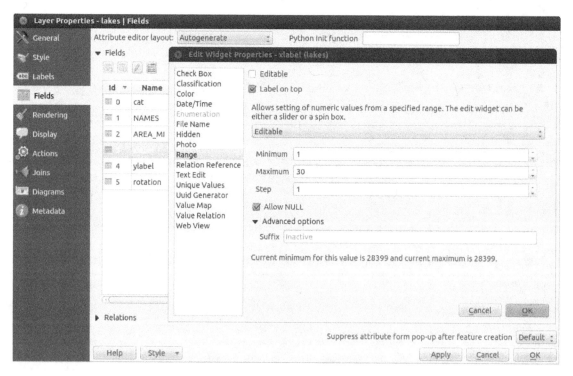

Figure 12.28: Dialog to select an edit widget for an attribute column

button, a dialog opens, where you can define different widgets. These widgets are:

- **Checkbox**: Displays a checkbox, and you can define what attribute is added to the column when the checkbox is activated or not.

- **Classification**: Displays a combo box with the values used for classification, if you have chosen 'unique value' as legend type in the *Style* menu of the properties dialog.

- **Color**: Displays a color button allowing user to choose a color from the color dialog window.

- **Date/Time**: Displays a line field which can open a calendar widget to enter a date, a time or both. Column type must be text. You can select a custom format, pop-up a calendar, etc.

- **Enumeration**: Opens a combo box with values that can be used within the columns type. This is currently only supported by the PostgreSQL provider.

- **File name**: Simplifies the selection by adding a file chooser dialog.

- **Hidden**: A hidden attribute column is invisible. The user is not able to see its contents.

- **Photo**: Field contains a filename for a picture. The width and height of the field can be defined.

- **Range**: Allows you to set numeric values from a specific range. The edit widget can be either a slider or a spin box.

- **Relation Reference**: This widged lets you embed the feature form of the referenced layer on the feature form of the actual layer. See *Creating one to many relations*.

- **Text edit** (default): This opens a text edit field that allows simple text or multiple lines to be used. If you choose multiple lines you can also choose html content.

- **Unique values**: You can select one of the values already used in the attribute table. If 'Editable' is activated, a line edit is shown with autocompletion support, otherwise a combo box is used.

- **UUID Generator**: Generates a read-only UUID (Universally Unique Identifiers) field, if empty.

- **Value map**: A combo box with predefined items. The value is stored in the attribute, the description is shown in the combo box. You can define values manually or load them from a layer or a CSV file.

- **Value Relation**: Offers values from a related table in a combobox. You can select layer, key column and value column.

- **Webview**: Field contains a URL. The width and height of the field is variable.

Note: QGIS has an advanced 'hidden' option to define your own field widget using python and add it to this impressive list of widgets. It is tricky but it is very well explained in following excellent blog that explains how to create a real time validation widget that can be used like described widgets. See http://blog.vitu.ch/10142013-1847/write-your-own-qgis-form-elements

---

With the **Attribute editor layout**, you can now define built-in forms (see figure_fields_2). This is usefull for data entry jobs or to identify objects using the option auto open form when you have objects with many attributes. You can create an editor with several tabs and named groups to present the attribute fields.

Choose 'Drag and drop designer' and an attribute column. Use the ⊕ icon to create a category to insert a tab or a named group (see figure_fields_3). When creating a new category, QGIS will insert a new tab or named group for the category in the built-in form. The next step will be to assign the relevant fields to a selected category with the ▷ icon. You can create more categories and use the same fields again.

Other options in the dialog are 'Autogenerate' and 'Provide ui-file'.

- 'Autogenerate' just creates editors for all fields and tabulates them.

- The 'Provide ui-file' option allows you to use complex dialogs made with the Qt-Designer. Using a UI-file allows a great deal of freedom in creating a dialog. For detailed information, see http://nathanw.net/2011/09/05/qgis-tips-custom-feature-forms-with-python-logic/.

QGIS dialogs can have a Python function that is called when the dialog is opened. Use this function to add extra logic to your dialogs. An example is (in module MyForms.py):

```
def open(dialog,layer,feature):
geom = feature.geometry()
control = dialog.findChild(QWidged,"My line edit")
```

Reference in Python Init Function like so: MyForms.open

MyForms.py must live on PYTHONPATH, in .qgis2/python, or inside the project folder.

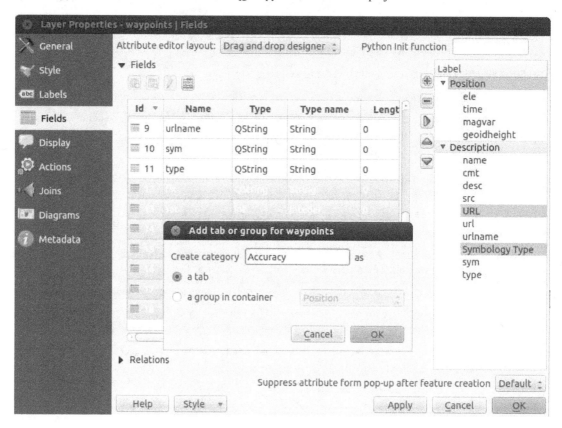

Figure 12.29: Dialog to create categories with the **Attribute editor layout**

12.3.4 General Menu

Use this menu to make general settings for the vector layer. There are several options available:

Layer Info

- Change the display name of the layer in *displayed as*
- Define the *Layer source* of the vector layer
- Define the *Data source encoding* to define provider-specific options and to be able to read the file

Coordinate Reference System

- *Specify* the coordinate reference system. Here, you can view or change the projection of the specific vector layer.
- Create a *Spatial Index* (only for OGR-supported formats)
- *Update Extents* information for a layer

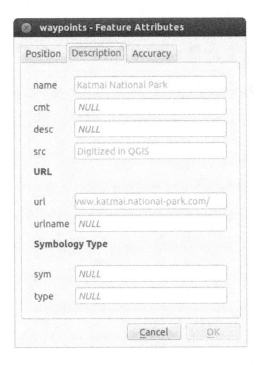

Figure 12.30: Resulting built-in form with tabs and named groups

• View or change the projection of the specific vector layer, clicking on *Specify ...*

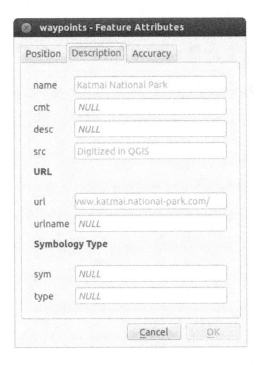 *Scale dependent visibility*

• You can set the *Maximum (inclusive)* and *Minimum (exclusive)* scale. The scale can also be set by the **[Current]** buttons.

Feature subset

• With the **[Query Builder]** button, you can create a subset of the features in the layer that will be visualized (also refer to section *Query Builder*).

12.3.5 Rendering Menu

QGIS 2.2 introduces support for on-the-fly feature generalisation. This can improve rendering times when drawing many complex features at small scales. This feature can be enabled or disabled in the layer settings using the *Simplify geometry* option. There is also a new global setting that enables generalisation by default for newly added layers (see section *Options*). **Note**: Feature generalisation may introduce artefacts into your rendered output in some cases. These may include slivers between polygons and inaccurate rendering when using offset-based symbol layers.

12.3.6 Display Menu

This menu is specifically created for Map Tips. It includes a new feature: Map Tip display text in HTML. While you can still choose a *Field* to be displayed when hovering over a feature on the map, it is now possible to insert HTML code that creates a complex display when hovering over a feature. To activate Map Tips, select the menu option *View → MapTips*. Figure Display 1 shows an example of HTML code.

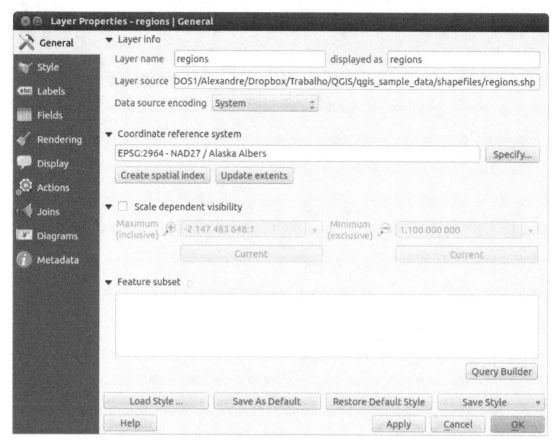

Figure 12.31: General menu in vector layers properties dialog △

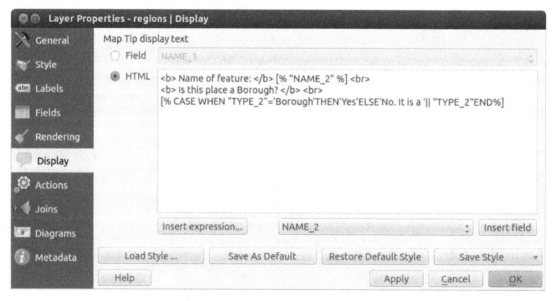

Figure 12.32: HTML code for map tip △

Figure 12.33: Map tip made with HTML code 🐧

12.3.7 Actions Menu

QGIS provides the ability to perform an action based on the attributes of a feature. This can be used to perform any number of actions, for example, running a program with arguments built from the attributes of a feature or passing parameters to a web reporting tool.

Actions are useful when you frequently want to run an external application or view a web page based on one or more values in your vector layer. They are divided into six types and can be used like this:

- Generic, Mac, Windows and Unix actions start an external process.

- Python actions execute a Python expression.

- Generic and Python actions are visible everywhere.

- Mac, Windows and Unix actions are visible only on the respective platform (i.e., you can define three 'Edit' actions to open an editor and the users can only see and execute the one 'Edit' action for their platform to run the editor).

There are several examples included in the dialog. You can load them by clicking on [**Add default actions**]. One example is performing a search based on an attribute value. This concept is used in the following discussion.

Defining Actions

Attribute actions are defined from the vector *Layer Properties* dialog. To define an action, open the vector *Layer Properties* dialog and click on the *Actions* menu. Go to the *Action properties*. Select 'Generic' as type and provide a descriptive name for the action. The action itself must contain the name of the application that will be executed when the action is invoked. You can add one or more attribute field values as arguments to the application. When the action is invoked, any set of characters that start with a % followed by the name of a field will be replaced by the value of that field. The special characters %% will be replaced by the value of the field that was selected from the identify results or attribute table (see using_actions below). Double quote marks can be used to group text into a single argument to the program, script or command. Double quotes will be ignored if preceded by a backslash.

If you have field names that are substrings of other field names (e.g., col1 and col10), you should indicate that by surrounding the field name (and the % character) with square brackets (e.g., [%col10]). This will prevent the %col10 field name from being mistaken for the %col1 field name with a 0 on the end. The brackets will be removed by QGIS when it substitutes in the value of the field. If you want the substituted field to be surrounded by square brackets, use a second set like this: [[%col10]].

Using the *Identify Features* tool, you can open the *Identify Results* dialog. It includes a *(Derived)* item that contains information relevant to the layer type. The values in this item can be accessed in a similar way to the other fields by preceding the derived field name with (Derived).. For example, a point layer has an X and Y field, and

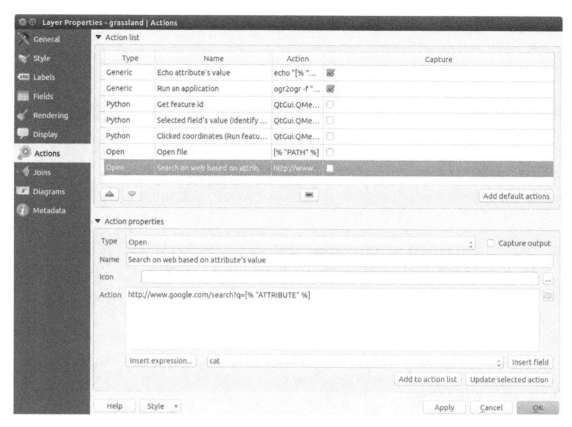

Figure 12.34: Overview action dialog with some sample actions 🐧

the values of these fields can be used in the action with `%(Derived).X` and `%(Derived).Y`. The derived attributes are only available from the *Identify Results* dialog box, not the *Attribute Table* dialog box.

Two example actions are shown below:

- `konqueror http://www.google.com/search?q=%nam`

- `konqueror http://www.google.com/search?q=%%`

In the first example, the web browser konqueror is invoked and passed a URL to open. The URL performs a Google search on the value of the `nam` field from our vector layer. Note that the application or script called by the action must be in the path, or you must provide the full path. To be certain, we could rewrite the first example as: `/opt/kde3/bin/konqueror http://www.google.com/search?q=%nam`. This will ensure that the konqueror application will be executed when the action is invoked.

The second example uses the %% notation, which does not rely on a particular field for its value. When the action is invoked, the %% will be replaced by the value of the selected field in the identify results or attribute table.

Using Actions

Actions can be invoked from either the *Identify Results* dialog, an *Attribute Table* dialog or from *Run Feature Action* (recall that these dialogs can be opened by clicking   Identify Features or ▦ Open Attribute Table or Run Feature Action). To invoke an action, right click on the record and choose the action from the pop-up menu. Actions are listed in the popup menu by the name you assigned when defining the action. Click on the action you wish to invoke.

If you are invoking an action that uses the `%%` notation, right-click on the field value in the *Identify Results* dialog or the *Attribute Table* dialog that you wish to pass to the application or script.

Here is another example that pulls data out of a vector layer and inserts it into a file using bash and the `echo` command (so it will only work on 🐧 or perhaps ✗). The layer in question has fields for a species name `taxon_name`, latitude `lat` and longitude `long`. We would like to be able to make a spatial selection of localities and export these field values to a text file for the selected record (shown in yellow in the QGIS map area). Here is the action to achieve this:

```
bash -c "echo \"%taxon_name %lat %long\" >> /tmp/species_localities.txt"
```

After selecting a few localities and running the action on each one, opening the output file will show something like this:

```
Acacia mearnsii -34.0800000000 150.0800000000
Acacia mearnsii -34.9000000000 150.1200000000
Acacia mearnsii -35.2200000000 149.9300000000
Acacia mearnsii -32.2700000000 150.4100000000
```

As an exercise, we can create an action that does a Google search on the `lakes` layer. First, we need to determine the URL required to perform a search on a keyword. This is easily done by just going to Google and doing a simple search, then grabbing the URL from the address bar in your browser. From this little effort, we see that the format is http://google.com/search?q=qgis, where `QGIS` is the search term. Armed with this information, we can proceed:

1. Make sure the `lakes` layer is loaded.

2. Open the *Layer Properties* dialog by double-clicking on the layer in the legend, or right-click and choose *Properties* from the pop-up menu.

3. Click on the *Actions* menu.

4. Enter a name for the action, for example `Google Search`.

5. For the action, we need to provide the name of the external program to run. In this case, we can use Firefox. If the program is not in your path, you need to provide the full path.

6. Following the name of the external application, add the URL used for doing a Google search, up to but not including the search term: `http://google.com/search?q=`

7. The text in the *Action* field should now look like this: `firefox http://google.com/search?q=`

8. Click on the drop-down box containing the field names for the `lakes` layer. It's located just to the left of the **[Insert Field]** button.

9. From the drop-down box, select 'NAMES' and click **[Insert Field]**.

10. Your action text now looks like this:

    `firefox http://google.com/search?q=%NAMES`

11. To finalize the action, click the **[Add to action list]** button.

This completes the action, and it is ready to use. The final text of the action should look like this:

```
firefox http://google.com/search?q=%NAMES
```

We can now use the action. Close the *Layer Properties* dialog and zoom in to an area of interest. Make sure the `lakes` layer is active and identify a lake. In the result box you'll now see that our action is visible:

When we click on the action, it brings up Firefox and navigates to the URL http://www.google.com/search?q=Tustumena. It is also possible to add further attribute fields to the action. Therefore, you can add a + to the end of the action text, select another field and click on **[Insert Field]**. In this example, there is just no other field available that would make sense to search for.

You can define multiple actions for a layer, and each will show up in the *Identify Results* dialog.

There are all kinds of uses for actions. For example, if you have a point layer containing locations of images or photos along with a file name, you could create an action to launch a viewer to display the image. You could also use actions to launch web-based reports for an attribute field or combination of fields, specifying them in the same way we did in our Google search example.

We can also make more complex examples, for instance, using **Python** actions.

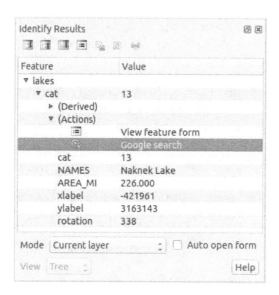

Figure 12.35: Select feature and choose action ⏻

Usually, when we create an action to open a file with an external application, we can use absolute paths, or eventually relative paths. In the second case, the path is relative to the location of the external program executable file. But what about if we need to use relative paths, relative to the selected layer (a file-based one, like a shapefile or SpatiaLite)? The following code will do the trick:

```
command = "firefox";
imagerelpath = "images_test/test_image.jpg";
layer = qgis.utils.iface.activeLayer();
import os.path;
layerpath = layer.source() if layer.providerType() == 'ogr'
  else (qgis.core.QgsDataSourceURI(layer.source()).database()
  if layer.providerType() == 'spatialite' else None);
path = os.path.dirname(str(layerpath));
image = os.path.join(path,imagerelpath);
import subprocess;
subprocess.Popen( [command, image ] );
```

We just have to remember that the action is one of type *Python* and the *command* and *imagerelpath* variables must be changed to fit our needs.

But what about if the relative path needs to be relative to the (saved) project file? The code of the Python action would be:

```
command="firefox";
imagerelpath="images/test_image.jpg";
projectpath=qgis.core.QgsProject.instance().fileName();
import os.path; path=os.path.dirname(str(projectpath)) if projectpath != '' else None;
image=os.path.join(path, imagerelpath);
import subprocess;
subprocess.Popen( [command, image ] );
```

Another Python action example is the one that allows us to add new layers to the project. For instance, the following examples will add to the project respectively a vector and a raster. The names of the files to be added to the project and the names to be given to the layers are data driven (*filename* and *layername* are column names of the table of attributes of the vector where the action was created):

```
qgis.utils.iface.addVectorLayer('/yourpath/[% "filename" %].shp','[% "layername" %]',
  'ogr')
```

To add a raster (a TIF image in this example), it becomes:

```
qgis.utils.iface.addRasterLayer('/yourpath/[% "filename" %].tif','[% "layername" %]
')
```

12.3.8 Joins Menu

The *Joins* menu allows you to join a loaded attribute table to a loaded vector layer. After clicking ⊕, the *Add vector join* dialog appears. As key columns, you have to define a join layer you want to connect with the target vector layer. Then, you have to specify the join field that is common to both the join layer and the target layer. Now you can also specify a subset of fields from the joined layer based on the checkbox ☑ *Choose which fields are joined*. As a result of the join, all information from the join layer and the target layer are displayed in the attribute table of the target layer as joined information. If you specified a subset of fields only these fields are displayed in the attribute table of the target layer.

QGIS currently has support for joining non-spatial table formats supported by OGR (e.g., CSV, DBF and Excel), delimited text and the PostgreSQL provider (see figure_joins_1).

Figure 12.36: Join an attribute table to an existing vector layer △

Additionally, the add vector join dialog allows you to:

- ☑ *Cache join layer in virtual memory*

- ☑ *Create attribute index on the join field*

- ☑ *Choose which fields are joined*

- Create a ☑ *Custom field name prefix*

12.3.9 Diagrams Menu

The *Diagrams* menu allows you to add a graphic overlay to a vector layer (see figure_diagrams_1).

The current core implementation of diagrams provides support for pie charts, text diagrams and histograms.

The menu is divided into four tabs: *Appearance*, *Size*, *Postion* and *Options*.

In the cases of the text diagram and pie chart, text values of different data columns are displayed one below the other with a circle or a box and dividers. In the *Size* tab, diagram size is based on a fixed size or on linear scaling according to a classification attribute. The placement of the diagrams, which is done in the *Position* tab, interacts with the new labeling, so position conflicts between diagrams and labels are detected and solved. In addition, chart positions can be fixed manually.

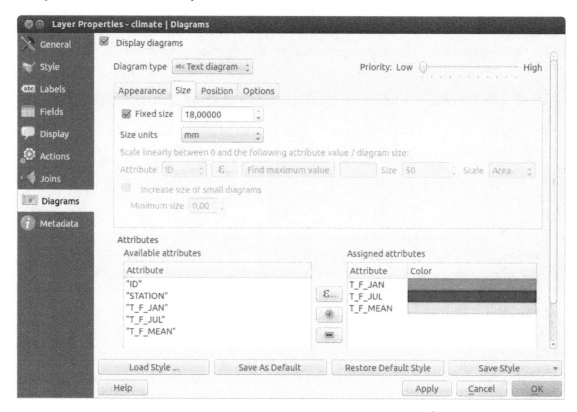

Figure 12.37: Vector properties dialog with diagram menu

We will demonstrate an example and overlay on the Alaska boundary layer a text diagram showing temperature data from a climate vector layer. Both vector layers are part of the QGIS sample dataset (see section *Sample Data*).

1. First, click on the `Load Vector` icon, browse to the QGIS sample dataset folder, and load the two vector shape layers `alaska.shp` and `climate.shp`.

2. Double click the `climate` layer in the map legend to open the *Layer Properties* dialog.

3. Click on the *Diagrams* menu, activate ☑ *Display diagrams*, and from the *Diagram type* combo box, select 'Text diagram'.

4. In the *Appearance* tab, we choose a light blue as background color, and in the *Size* tab, we set a fixed size to 18 mm.

5. In the *Position* tab, placement could be set to 'Around Point'.

6. In the diagram, we want to display the values of the three columns T_F_JAN, T_F_JUL and T_F_MEAN. First select T_F_JAN as *Attributes* and click the ✚ button, then T_F_JUL, and finally T_F_MEAN.

7. Now click [**Apply**] to display the diagram in the QGIS main window.

8. You can adapt the chart size in the *Size* tab. Deactivate the ☑ *Fixed size* and set the size of the diagrams on the basis of an attribute with the [**Find maximum value**] button and the *Size* menu. If the diagrams appear too small on the screen, you can activate the ☑ *Increase size of small diagrams* checkbox and define the minimum size of the diagrams.

9. Change the attribute colors by double clicking on the color values in the *Assigned attributes* field. Figure_diagrams_2 gives an idea of the result.

10. Finally, click [**Ok**].

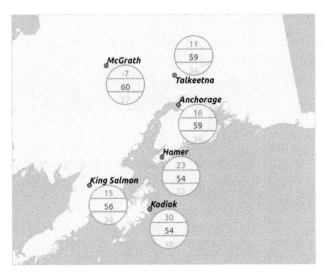

Figure 12.38: Diagram from temperature data overlayed on a map 🐧

Remember that in the *Position* tab, a ☑ *Data defined position* of the diagrams is possible. Here, you can use attributes to define the position of the diagram. You can also set a scale-dependent visibility in the *Appearance* tab.

The size and the attributes can also be an expression. Use the ε... button to add an expression. See *Expressions* chapter for more information and example.

12.3.10 Metadata Menu

ⓘ The *Metadata* menu consists of *Description*, *Attribution*, *MetadataURL* and *Properties* sections.

In the *Properties* section, you get general information about the layer, including specifics about the type and location, number of features, feature type, and editing capabilities. The *Extents* table provides you with layer extent information and the *Layer Spatial Reference System*, which is information about the CRS of the layer. This is a quick way to get information about the layer.

Additionally, you can add or edit a title and abstract for the layer in the *Description* section. It's also possible to define a *Keyword list* here. These keyword lists can be used in a metadata catalogue. If you want to use a title from an XML metadata file, you have to fill in a link in the *DataUrl* field. Use *Attribution* to get attribute data from an XML metadata catalogue. In *MetadataUrl*, you can define the general path to the XML metadata catalogue. This information will be saved in the QGIS project file for subsequent sessions and will be used for QGIS server.

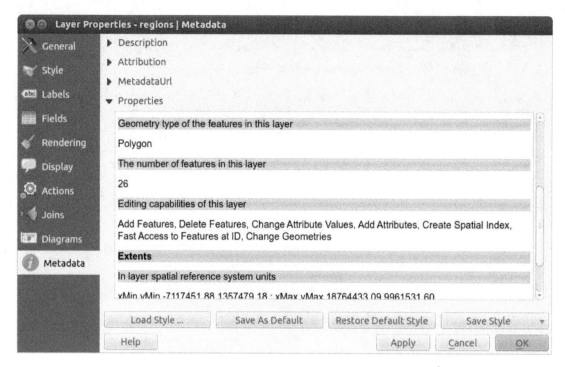

Figure 12.39: Metadata menu in vector layers properties dialog

12.4 Expressions

The **Expressions** feature are available through the field calculator or the add a new column button in the attribut table or the Field tab in the Layer properties ; through the graduaded, categorized and rule-based rendering in the Style tab of the Layer properties ; through the expression-based labeling in the Labeling core application ; through the feature selection and through the diagram tab of the Layer properties as well as the *Main properties* of the label item and the *Atlas generation* tab in the Print Composer.

They are a powerful way to manipulate attribute value in order to dynamically change the final value in order to change the geometry style, the content of the label, the value for diagram, select some feature or create virtual column.

12.4.1 Functions List

The **Function List** contains functions as well as fields and values. View the help function in the **Selected Function Help**. In **Expression** you see the calculation expressions you create with the **Function List**. For the most commonly used operators, see **Operators**.

In the **Function List**, click on *Fields and Values* to view all attributes of the attribute table to be searched. To add an attribute to the Field calculator **Expression** field, double click its name in the *Fields and Values* list. Generally, you can use the various fields, values and functions to construct the calculation expression, or you can just type it into the box. To display the values of a field, you just right click on the appropriate field. You can choose between *Load top 10 unique values* and *Load all unique values*. On the right side, the **Field Values** list opens with the unique values. To add a value to the Field calculator **Expression** box, double click its name in the **Field Values** list.

The *Operators*, *Math*, *Conversions*, *String*, *Geometry* and *Record* groups provide several functions. In *Operators*, you find mathematical operators. Look in *Math* for mathematical functions. The *Conversions* group contains functions that convert one data type to another. The *String* group provides functions for data strings. In the *Geometry* group, you find functions for geometry objects. With *Record* group functions, you can add a numeration to your data set. To add a function to the Field calculator **Expression** box, click on the > and then double click the function.

Operators

This group contains operators (e.g., +, -, *).

```
a + b       a plus b
a - b       a minus b
a * b       a multiplied by b
a / b       a divided by b
a % b       a modulo b (for example, 7 % 2 = 1, or 2 fits into 7 three
            times with remainder 1)
a ^ b       a power b (for example, 2^2=4 or 2^3=8)
a = b       a and b are equal
a > b       a is larger than b
a < b       a is smaller than b
a <> b      a and b are not equal
a != b      a and b are not equal
a <= b      a is less than or equal to b
a >= b      a is larger than or equal to b
a ~ b       a matches the regular expression b
+ a         positive sign
- a         negative value of a
||          joins two values together into a string 'Hello' || ' world'
LIKE        returns 1 if the string matches the supplied pattern
ILIKE       returns 1 if the string matches case-insensitive the supplied
            pattern (ILIKE can be used instead of LIKE to make the match
            case-insensitive)
IS          returns 1 if a is the same as b
OR          returns 1 when condition a or b is true
AND         returns 1 when condition a and b are true
NOT         returns 1 if a is not the same as b
column name "column name"       value of the field column name, take
                                care to not be confused with simple
                                quote, see below
'string'                        a string value, take care to not be
                                confused with double quote, see above
NULL                            null value
a IS NULL                       a has no value
a IS NOT NULL                   a has a value
a IN (value[,value])            a is below the values listed
a NOT IN (value[,value])        a is not below the values listed
```

Some examples:

- Joins a string and a value from a column name:

```
'My feature's id is: ' || "gid"
```

- Test if the "description" attribute field starts with the 'Hello' string in the value (note the position of the % character):

```
"description" LIKE 'Hello%'
```

Conditionals

This group contains functions to handle conditional checks in expressions.

```
CASE                        evaluates multiple expressions and returns a
                            result
CASE ELSE                   evaluates multiple expressions and returns a
                            result
```

| coalesce | returns the first non-NULL value from the expression list |
| regexp_match | returns true if any part of a string matches the supplied regular expression |

Some example:

- Send back a value if the first condition is true, else another value:

```
CASE WHEN "software" LIKE '%QGIS%' THEN 'QGIS' ELSE 'Other'
```

Mathematical Functions

This group contains math functions (e.g., square root, sin and cos).

sqrt(a)	square root of a
abs	returns the absolute value of a number
sin(a)	sine of a
cos(a)	cosine of a
tan(a)	tangent of a
asin(a)	arcsin of a
acos(a)	arccos of a
atan(a)	arctan of a
atan2(y,x)	arctan of y/x using the signs of the two arguments to determine the quadrant of the result
exp	exponential of a value
ln	value of the natural logarithm of the passed expression
log10	value of the base 10 logarithm of the passed expression
log	value of the logarithm of the passed value and base
round	round to number of decimal places
rand	random integer within the range specified by the minimum and maximum argument (inclusive)
randf	random float within the range specified by the minimum and maximum argument (inclusive)
max	largest value in a set of values
min	smallest value in a set of values
clamp	restricts an input value to a specified range
scale_linear	transforms a given value from an input domain to an output range using linear interpolation
scale_exp	transforms a given value from an input domain to an output range using an exponential curve
floor	rounds a number downwards
ceil	rounds a number upwards
$pi	pi as value for calculations

Conversions

This group contains functions to convert one data type to another (e.g., string to integer, integer to string).

toint	converts a string to integer number
toreal	converts a string to real number
tostring	converts number to string

```
todatetime              converts a string into Qt data time type
todate                  converts a string into Qt data type
totime                  converts a string into Qt time type
tointerval              converts a string to an interval type (can be
                        used to take days, hours, months, etc. off a
                        date)
```

Date and Time Functions

This group contains functions for handling date and time data.

```
$now        current date and time
age         difference between two dates
year        extract the year part from a date, or the number of years from
            an interval
month       extract the month part from a date, or the number of months
            from an interval
week        extract the week number from a date, or the number of weeks
            from an interval
day         extract the day from a date, or the number of days from an
            interval
hour        extract the hour from a datetime or time, or the number
            of hours from an interval
minute      extract the minute from a datetime or time, or the number
            of minutes from an interval
second      extract the second from a datetime or time, or the number
            of minutes from an interval
```

Some example:

- Get the month and the year of today in the format "10/2014"

```
month($now)  ||  '/'  ||  year($now)
```

String Functions

This group contains functions that operate on strings (e.g., that replace, convert to upper case).

```
lower                       convert string a to lower case
upper                       convert string a to upper case
title                       converts all words of a string to title
                            case (all words lower case with leading
                            capital letter)
trim                        removes all leading and trailing white
                            space (spaces, tabs, etc.) from a string
wordwrap                    returns a string wrapped to a maximum/
                            minimum number of characters
length                      length of string a
replace                     returns a string with the supplied string
                            replaced
regexp_replace(a,this,that) returns a string with the supplied regular
                            expression replaced
regexp_substr               returns the portion of a string which matches
                            a supplied regular expression
substr(*a*,from,len)        returns a part of a string
concat                      concatenates several strings to one
strpos                      returns the index of a regular expression
                            in a string
left                        returns a substring that contains the n
                            leftmost characters of the string
right                       returns a substring that contains the n
```

	rightmost characters of the string
rpad	returns a string with supplied width padded using the fill character
lpad	returns a string with supplied width padded using the fill character
format	formats a string using supplied arguments
format_number	returns a number formatted with the locale separator for thousands (also truncates the number to the number of supplied places)
format_date	formats a date type or string into a custom string format

Color Functions

This group contains functions for manipulating colors.

color_rgb	returns a string representation of a color based on its red, green, and blue components
color_rgba	returns a string representation of a color based on its red, green, blue, and alpha (transparency) components
ramp_color	returns a string representing a color from a color ramp
color_hsl	returns a string representation of a color based on its hue, saturation, and lightness attributes
color_hsla	returns a string representation of a color based on its hue, saturation, lightness and alpha (transparency) attributes
color_hsv	returns a string representation of a color based on its hue, saturation, and value attributes
color_hsva	returns a string representation of a color based on its hue, saturation, value and alpha (transparency) attributes
color_cmyk	returns a string representation of a color based on its cyan, magenta, yellow and black components
color_cmyka	returns a string representation of a color based on its cyan, magenta, yellow, black and alpha (transparency) components

Geometry Functions

This group contains functions that operate on geometry objects (e.g., length, area).

$geometry	returns the geometry of the current feature (can be used for processing with other functions)
$area	returns the area size of the current feature
$length	returns the length size of the current feature
$perimeter	returns the perimeter length of the current feature
$x	returns the x coordinate of the current feature
$y	returns the y coordinate of the current feature
xat	retrieves the nth x coordinate of the current feature. n given as a parameter of the function
yat	retrieves the nth y coordinate of the current feature. n given as a parameter of the function
xmin	returns the minimum x coordinate of a geometry. Calculations are in the Spatial Reference System of this Geometry
xmax	returns the maximum x coordinate of a geometry. Calculations are in the Spatial Reference System of this Geometry
ymin	returns the minimum y coordinate of a geometry. Calculations are in the Spatial Reference System of this Geometry

ymax	returns the maximum y coordinate of a geometry. Calculations are in the Spatial Reference System of this Geometry
geomFromWKT	returns a geometry created from a well-known text (WKT) representation
geomFromGML bbox	returns a geometry from a GML representation of geometry
disjoint	returns 1 if the geometries do not share any space together
intersects	returns 1 if the geometries spatially intersect (share any portion of space) and 0 if they don't
touches	returns 1 if the geometries have at least one point in common, but their interiors do not intersect
crosses	returns 1 if the supplied geometries have some, but not all, interior points in common
contains	returns true if and only if no points of b lie in the exterior of a, and at least one point of the interior of b lies in the interior of a
overlaps	returns 1 if the geometries share space, are of the same dimension, but are not completely contained by each other
within	returns 1 if geometry a is completely inside geometry b
buffer	returns a geometry that represents all points whose distance from this geometry is less than or equal to distance
centroid	returns the geometric center of a geometry
bounds	returns a geometry which represents the bounding box of an input geometry. Calculations are in the Spatial Reference System of this Geometry.
bounds_width	returns the width of the bounding box of a geometry. Calculations are in the Spatial Reference System of this Geometry.
bounds_height	returns the height of the bounding box of a geometry. Calculations are in the Spatial Reference System of this Geometry.
convexHull	returns the convex hull of a geometry (this represents the minimum convex geometry that encloses all geometries within the set)
difference	returns a geometry that represents that part of geometry a that does not intersect with geometry b
distance	returns the minimum distance (based on spatial ref) between two geometries in projected units
intersection	returns a geometry that represents the shared portion of geometry a and geometry b
symDifference	returns a geometry that represents the portions of a and b that do not intersect
combine	returns the combination of geometry a and geometry b
union	returns a geometry that represents the point set union of the geometries
geomToWKT	returns the well-known text (WKT) representation of the geometry without SRID metadata
geometry	returns the feature's geometry
transform	returns the geometry transformed from the source CRS to the dest CRS

Record Functions

This group contains functions that operate on record identifiers.

$rownum	returns the number of the current row
$id	returns the feature id of the current row
$currentfeature	returns the current feature being evaluated.

	This can be used with the 'attribute' function to evaluate attribute values from the current feature.
$scale	returns the current scale of the map canvas
$uuid	generates a Universally Unique Identifier (UUID) for each row. Each UUID is 38 characters long.
getFeature	returns the first feature of a layer matching a given attribute value.
attribute	returns the value of a specified attribute from a feature.
$map	returns the id of the current map item if the map is being drawn in a composition, or "canvas" if the map is being drawn within the main QGIS window.

Fields and Values

Contains a list of fields from the layer. Sample values can also be accessed via right-click.

Select the field name from the list, then right-click to access a context menu with options to load sample values from the selected field.

Fields name should be double-quoted. Values or string should be simple-quoted.

.

12.5 Editing

QGIS supports various capabilities for editing OGR, SpatiaLite, PostGIS, MSSQL Spatial and Oracle Spatial vector layers and tables.

Note: The procedure for editing GRASS layers is different - see section *Digitizing and editing a GRASS vector layer* for details.

Tip: Concurrent Edits

This version of QGIS does not track if somebody else is editing a feature at the same time as you are. The last person to save their edits wins.

12.5.1 Setting the Snapping Tolerance and Search Radius

Before we can edit vertices, we must set the snapping tolerance and search radius to a value that allows us an optimal editing of the vector layer geometries.

Snapping tolerance

Snapping tolerance is the distance QGIS uses to `search` for the closest vertex and/or segment you are trying to connect to when you set a new vertex or move an existing vertex. If you aren't within the snapping tolerance, QGIS will leave the vertex where you release the mouse button, instead of snapping it to an existing vertex and/or segment. The snapping tolerance setting affects all tools that work with tolerance.

1. A general, project-wide snapping tolerance can be defined by choosing *Settings* → ✎ *Options*. On Mac, go to *QGIS* → ✎ *Preferences....* On Linux: *Edit* → ✎ *Options*. In the *Digitizing* tab, you can select between 'to vertex', 'to segment' or 'to vertex and segment' as default snap mode. You can also define a default snapping tolerance and a search radius for vertex edits. The tolerance can be set either in map units or in pixels. The advantage of choosing pixels is that the snapping tolerance doesn't have to be changed after

zoom operations. In our small digitizing project (working with the Alaska dataset), we define the snapping units in feet. Your results may vary, but something on the order of 300 ft at a scale of 1:10000 should be a reasonable setting.

2. A layer-based snapping tolerance can be defined by choosing *Settings →* (or *File →*) *Snapping options...* to enable and adjust snapping mode and tolerance on a layer basis (see figure_edit_1).

Note that this layer-based snapping overrides the global snapping option set in the Digitizing tab. So, if you need to edit one layer and snap its vertices to another layer, then enable snapping only on the `snap to` layer, then decrease the global snapping tolerance to a smaller value. Furthermore, snapping will never occur to a layer that is not checked in the snapping options dialog, regardless of the global snapping tolerance. So be sure to mark the checkbox for those layers that you need to snap to.

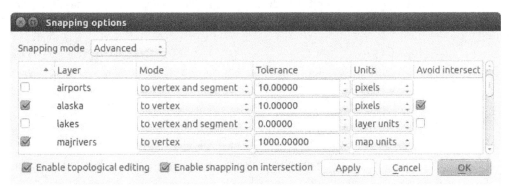

Figure 12.40: Edit snapping options on a layer basis (Advanced mode)

The *Snapping options* enables you to make a quick and simple general setting for all layers in the project so that the pointer snaps to all existing vertices and/or segments when using the 'All layers' snapping mode. In most cases it is sufficient to use this snapping mode.

It is important to consider that the per-layer tolerance in 'map units' was actually in layer units. So if working with a layer in WGS84 reprojected to UTM, setting tolerance to 1 map unit (i.e. 1 meter) wouldn't work correctly because the units would be actually degrees. So now the 'map units' has been relabeled to 'layer units' and the new entry 'map units' operates with units of the map view. While working with 'on-the-fly' CRS transformation it is now possible to use a snapping tolerance that refers to either the units of the reprojected layer (setting 'layer units') or the units of the map view (setting 'map units').

Search radius

Search radius is the distance QGIS uses to `search` for the closest vertex you are trying to move when you click on the map. If you aren't within the search radius, QGIS won't find and select any vertex for editing, and it will pop up an annoying warning to that effect. Snap tolerance and search radius are set in map units or pixels, so you may find you need to experiment to get them set right. If you specify too big of a tolerance, QGIS may snap to the wrong vertex, especially if you are dealing with a large number of vertices in close proximity. Set search radius too small, and it won't find anything to move.

The search radius for vertex edits in layer units can be defined in the *Digitizing* tab under *Settings →* ⚙ *Options*. This is the same place where you define the general, project- wide snapping tolerance.

12.5.2 Zooming and Panning

Before editing a layer, you should zoom in to your area of interest. This avoids waiting while all the vertex markers are rendered across the entire layer.

Apart from using the 🖑 pan and 🔍 zoom-in / 🔍 zoom-out icons on the toolbar with the mouse, navigating can also be done with the mouse wheel, spacebar and the arrow keys.

Zooming and panning with the mouse wheel

While digitizing, you can press the mouse wheel to pan inside of the main window, and you can roll the mouse wheel to zoom in and out on the map. For zooming, place the mouse cursor inside the map area and roll it forward (away from you) to zoom in and backwards (towards you) to zoom out. The mouse cursor position will be the center of the zoomed area of interest. You can customize the behavior of the mouse wheel zoom using the *Map tools* tab under the *Settings → * 🔧 *Options* menu.

Panning with the arrow keys

Panning the map during digitizing is possible with the arrow keys. Place the mouse cursor inside the map area, and click on the right arrow key to pan east, left arrow key to pan west, up arrow key to pan north, and down arrow key to pan south.

You can also use the space bar to temporarily cause mouse movements to pan the map. The PgUp and PgDown keys on your keyboard will cause the map display to zoom in or out without interrupting your digitizing session.

12.5.3 Topological editing

Besides layer-based snapping options, you can also define topological functionalities in the *Snapping options...* dialog in the *Settings* (or *File*) menu. Here, you can define ☑ *Enable topological editing*, and/or for polygon layers, you can activate the column ☑ *Avoid Int.*, which avoids intersection of new polygons.

Enable topological editing

The option ☑ *Enable topological editing* is for editing and maintaining common boundaries in polygon mosaics. QGIS 'detects' a shared boundary in a polygon mosaic, so you only have to move the vertex once, and QGIS will take care of updating the other boundary.

Avoid intersections of new polygons

The second topological option in the ☑ *Avoid Int.* column, called *Avoid intersections of new polygons*, avoids overlaps in polygon mosaics. It is for quicker digitizing of adjacent polygons. If you already have one polygon, it is possible with this option to digitize the second one such that both intersect, and QGIS then cuts the second polygon to the common boundary. The advantage is that you don't have to digitize all vertices of the common boundary.

Enable snapping on intersections

Another option is to use ☑ *Enable snapping on intersection*. It allows you to snap on an intersection of background layers, even if there's no vertex on the intersection.

12.5.4 Digitizing an existing layer

By default, QGIS loads layers read-only. This is a safeguard to avoid accidentally editing a layer if there is a slip of the mouse. However, you can choose to edit any layer as long as the data provider supports it, and the underlying data source is writable (i.e., its files are not read-only).

In general, tools for editing vector layers are divided into a digitizing and an advanced digitizing toolbar, described in section *Advanced digitizing*. You can select and unselect both under *View*

→ *Toolbars* →. Using the basic digitizing tools, you can perform the following functions:

Icon	Purpose	Icon	Purpose
	Current edits		Toggle editing
	Adding Features: Capture Point		Adding Features: Capture Line
	Adding Features: Capture Polygon		Move Feature
	Node Tool		Delete Selected
	Cut Features		Copy Features
	Paste Features		Save layer edits

Table Editing: Vector layer basic editing toolbar

All editing sessions start by choosing the Toggle editing option. This can be found in the context menu after right clicking on the legend entry for a given layer.

Alternatively, you can use the Toggle Editing Toggle editing button from the digitizing toolbar to start or stop the editing mode. Once the layer is in edit mode, markers will appear at the vertices, and additional tool buttons on the editing toolbar will become available.

Tip: Save Regularly

Remember to Save Layer Edits regularly. This will also check that your data source can accept all the changes.

Adding Features

You can use the Add Feature, Add Feature or Add Feature icons on the toolbar to put the QGIS cursor into digitizing mode.

For each feature, you first digitize the geometry, then enter its attributes. To digitize the geometry, left-click on the map area to create the first point of your new feature.

For lines and polygons, keep on left-clicking for each additional point you wish to capture. When you have finished adding points, right-click anywhere on the map area to confirm you have finished entering the geometry of that feature.

The attribute window will appear, allowing you to enter the information for the new feature. Figure_edit_2 shows setting attributes for a fictitious new river in Alaska. In the *Digitizing* menu under the *Settings* → *Options* menu, you can also activate *Suppress attributes pop-up windows after each created feature* and *Reuse last entered attribute values*.

Figure 12.41: Enter Attribute Values Dialog after digitizing a new vector feature

With the Move Feature(s) icon on the toolbar, you can move existing features.

Tip: Attribute Value Types

For editing, the attribute types are validated during entry. Because of this, it is not possible to enter a number into a text column in the dialog *Enter Attribute Values* or vice versa. If you need to do so, you should edit the attributes in a second step within the *Attribute table* dialog.

Current Edits

This feature allows the digitization of multiple layers. Choose 🖫 *Save for Selected Layers* to save all changes you made in multiple layers. You also have the opportunity to 🔄 *Rollback for Selected Layers*, so that the digitization may be withdrawn for all selected layers. If you want to stop editing the selected layers, ⊘ *Cancel for Selected Layer(s)* is an easy way.

The same functions are available for editing all layers of the project.

Node Tool

For shapefile-based layers as well as SpatialLite, PostgreSQL/PostGIS, MSSQL Spatial, and Oracle Spatial tables, the 🖊 Node Tool provides manipulation capabilities of feature vertices similar to CAD programs. It is possible to simply select multiple vertices at once and to move, add or delete them altogether. The node tool also works with 'on the fly' projection turned on, and it supports the topological editing feature. This tool is, unlike other tools in QGIS, persistent, so when some operation is done, selection stays active for this feature and tool. If the node tool is unable to find any features, a warning will be displayed.

It is important to set the property *Settings → ⚒ Options → Digitizing → Search Radius:* 1,00 ◇ to a number greater than zero (i.e., 10). Otherwise, QGIS will not be able to tell which vertex is being edited.

Tip: Vertex Markers

The current version of QGIS supports three kinds of vertex markers: 'Semi-transparent circle', 'Cross' and 'None'. To change the marker style, choose ⚒ *Options* from the *Settings* menu, click on the *Digitizing* tab and select the appropriate entry.

Basic operations

Start by activating the 🖊 Node Tool and selecting a feature by clicking on it. Red boxes will appear at each vertex of this feature.

- **Selecting vertices**: You can select vertices by clicking on them one at a time, by clicking on an edge to select the vertices at both ends, or by clicking and dragging a rectangle around some vertices. When a vertex is selected, its color changes to blue. To add more vertices to the current selection, hold down the Ctrl key while clicking. Hold down Ctrl or Shift when clicking to toggle the selection state of vertices (vertices that are currently unselected will be selected as usual, but also vertices that are already selected will become unselected).

- **Adding vertices**: To add a vertex, simply double click near an edge and a new vertex will appear on the edge near to the cursor. Note that the vertex will appear on the edge, not at the cursor position; therefore, it should be moved if necessary.

- **Deleting vertices**: After selecting vertices for deletion, click the Delete key. Note that you cannot use the 🖊 Node Tool to delete a complete feature; QGIS will ensure it retains the minimum number of vertices for the feature type you are working on. To delete a complete feature use the 🗑 Delete Selected tool.

- **Moving vertices**: Select all the vertices you want to move. Click on a selected vertex or edge and drag in the direction you wish to move. All the selected vertices will move together. If snapping is enabled, the whole selection can jump to the nearest vertex or line.

Each change made with the node tool is stored as a separate entry in the Undo dialog. Remember that all operations support topological editing when this is turned on. On-the-fly projection is also supported, and the node tool provides tooltips to identify a vertex by hovering the pointer over it.

Cutting, Copying and Pasting Features

Selected features can be cut, copied and pasted between layers in the same QGIS project, as long as destination layers are set to ⟋ Toggle editing beforehand.

Features can also be pasted to external applications as text. That is, the features are represented in CSV format, with the geometry data appearing in the OGC Well-Known Text (WKT) format.

However, in this version of QGIS, text features from outside QGIS cannot be pasted to a layer within QGIS. When would the copy and paste function come in handy? Well, it turns out that you can edit more than one layer at a time and copy/paste features between layers. Why would we want to do this? Say we need to do some work on a new layer but only need one or two lakes, not the 5,000 on our `big_lakes` layer. We can create a new layer and use copy/paste to plop the needed lakes into it.

As an example, we will copy some lakes to a new layer:

1. Load the layer you want to copy from (source layer)
2. Load or create the layer you want to copy to (target layer)
3. Start editing for target layer
4. Make the source layer active by clicking on it in the legend
5. Use the ⬚⬚ Select Single Feature tool to select the feature(s) on the source layer
6. Click on the ▤ Copy Features tool
7. Make the destination layer active by clicking on it in the legend
8. Click on the ▦ Paste Features tool
9. Stop editing and save the changes

What happens if the source and target layers have different schemas (field names and types are not the same)? QGIS populates what matches and ignores the rest. If you don't care about the attributes being copied to the target layer, it doesn't matter how you design the fields and data types. If you want to make sure everything - the feature and its attributes - gets copied, make sure the schemas match.

Tip: Congruency of Pasted Features

If your source and destination layers use the same projection, then the pasted features will have geometry identical to the source layer. However, if the destination layer is a different projection, then QGIS cannot guarantee the geometry is identical. This is simply because there are small rounding-off errors involved when converting between projections.

Tip: Copy string attribute into another

If you have created a new column in your attribute table with type 'string' and want to paste values from another attribute column that has a greater length the length of the column size will be extended to the same amount. This is because the GDAL Shapefile driver starting with GDAL/OGR 1.10 knows to auto-extend string and integer fields to dynamically accomodate for the length of the data to be inserted.

Deleting Selected Features

If we want to delete an entire polygon, we can do that by first selecting the polygon using the regular
Select Single Feature tool. You can select multiple features for deletion. Once you have the selection set, use the
Delete Selected tool to delete the features.

The Cut Features tool on the digitizing toolbar can also be used to delete features. This effectively deletes the
feature but also places it on a "spatial clipboard". So, we cut the feature to delete. We could then use the
Paste Features tool to put it back, giving us a one-level undo capability. Cut, copy, and paste work on the currently
selected features, meaning we can operate on more than one at a time.

Saving Edited Layers

When a layer is in editing mode, any changes remain in the memory of QGIS. Therefore, they are not commit-
ted/saved immediately to the data source or disk. If you want to save edits to the current layer but want to continue
editing without leaving the editing mode, you can click the Save Layer Edits button. When you turn editing mode
off with Toggle editing (or quit QGIS for that matter), you are also asked if you want to save your changes or
discard them.

If the changes cannot be saved (e.g., disk full, or the attributes have values that are out of range), the QGIS
in-memory state is preserved. This allows you to adjust your edits and try again.

Tip: Data Integrity

It is always a good idea to back up your data source before you start editing. While the authors of QGIS have
made every effort to preserve the integrity of your data, we offer no warranty in this regard.

12.5.5 Advanced digitizing

Icon	Purpose	Icon	Purpose
	Undo		Redo
	Rotate Feature(s)		Simplify Feature
	Add Ring		Add Part
	Fill Ring		Delete Ring
	Delete Part		Reshape Features
	Offset Curve		Split Features
	Split Parts		Merge Selected Features
	Merge Attributes of Selected Features		Rotate Point Symbols

Table Advanced Editing: Vector layer advanced editing toolbar

Undo and Redo

The Undo and Redo tools allows you to undo or redo vector editing operations. There is also a dockable
widget, which shows all operations in the undo/redo history (see Figure_edit_3). This widget is not displayed by
default; it can be displayed by right clicking on the toolbar and activating the Undo/Redo checkbox. Undo/Redo
is however active, even if the widget is not displayed.

Figure 12.42: Redo and Undo digitizing steps ⌂

When Undo is hit, the state of all features and attributes are reverted to the state before the reverted operation happened. Changes other than normal vector editing operations (for example, changes done by a plugin), may or may not be reverted, depending on how the changes were performed.

To use the undo/redo history widget, simply click to select an operation in the history list. All features will be reverted to the state they were in after the selected operation.

Rotate Feature(s)

Use ⬚Rotate Feature(s) to rotate one or multiple features in the map canvas. Press the ⬚Rotate Feature(s) icon and then click on the feature to rotate. Either click on the map to place the rotated feature or enter an angle in the user input widget. If you want to rotate several features, they shall be selected first.

If you enable the map tool with feature(s) selected, its (their) centroid appears and will be the rotation anchor point. If you want to move the anchor point, hold the Ctrl button and click on the map to place it.

If you hold Shift before clicking on the map, the rotation will be done in 45 degree steps, which can be modified afterwards in the user input widget.

Simplify Feature

The ⬡ Simplify Feature tool allows you to reduce the number of vertices of a feature, as long as the geometry doesn't change. With the tool you can also simplify multi-part features. First, drag a rectangle over the feature. The vertices will be highlighted in red while the color of the feature will change and a dialog where you can define a tolerance in map units or pixels will appear. QGIS calculates the amount of vertices that can be deleted while maintaining the geometry using the given tolerance. The higher the tolerance is the more vertices can be deleted. After gaining the statistics about the simplification just klick the *OK* button. The tolerance you used will be saved when leaving a project or when leaving an edit session. So you can go back to the same tolerance the next time when simplifying a feature.

Add Ring

You can create ring polygons using the ⬚ Add Ring icon in the toolbar. This means that inside an existing area, it is possible to digitize further polygons that will occur as a 'hole', so only the area between the boundaries of the outer and inner polygons remains as a ring polygon.

Add Part

You can ⬚ add part polygons to a selected multipolygon. The new part polygon must be digitized outside the selected multi-polygon.

Fill Ring

You can use the [icon] Fill Ring function to add a ring to a polygon and add a new feature to the layer at the same time. Thus you need not first use the [icon] Add Ring icon and then the [icon] Add feature function anymore.

Delete Ring

The [icon] Delete Ring tool allows you to delete ring polygons inside an existing area. This tool only works with polygon layers. It doesn't change anything when it is used on the outer ring of the polygon. This tool can be used on polygon and multi-polygon features. Before you select the vertices of a ring, adjust the vertex edit tolerance.

Delete Part

The [icon] Delete Part tool allows you to delete parts from multifeatures (e.g., to delete polygons from a multi-polygon feature). It won't delete the last part of the feature; this last part will stay untouched. This tool works with all multi-part geometries: point, line and polygon. Before you select the vertices of a part, adjust the vertex edit tolerance.

Reshape Features

You can reshape line and polygon features using the [icon] Reshape Features icon on the toolbar. It replaces the line or polygon part from the first to the last intersection with the original line. With polygons, this can sometimes lead to unintended results. It is mainly useful to replace smaller parts of a polygon, not for major overhauls, and the reshape line is not allowed to cross several polygon rings, as this would generate an invalid polygon.

For example, you can edit the boundary of a polygon with this tool. First, click in the inner area of the polygon next to the point where you want to add a new vertex. Then, cross the boundary and add the vertices outside the polygon. To finish, right-click in the inner area of the polygon. The tool will automatically add a node where the new line crosses the border. It is also possible to remove part of the area from the polygon, starting the new line outside the polygon, adding vertices inside, and ending the line outside the polygon with a right click.

Note: The reshape tool may alter the starting position of a polygon ring or a closed line. So, the point that is represented 'twice' will not be the same any more. This may not be a problem for most applications, but it is something to consider.

Offset Curves

The [icon] Offset Curve tool creates parallel shifts of line layers. The tool can be applied to the edited layer (the geometries are modified) or also to background layers (in which case it creates copies of the lines / rings and adds them to the the edited layer). It is thus ideally suited for the creation of distance line layers. The displacement is shown at the bottom left of the taskbar.

To create a shift of a line layer, you must first go into editing mode and activate the [icon] Offset Curve tool. Then click on a feature to shift it. Move the mouse and click where wanted or enter the desired distance in the user input widget. Your changes may then be saved with the |mActionSaveEdits|:sup:*Save Layer Edits* tool.

QGIS options dialog (Digitizing tab then **Curve offset tools** section) allows you to configure some parameters like **Join style**, **Quadrant segments**, **Miter limit**.

Split Features

You can split features using the ^Split Features^ icon on the toolbar. Just draw a line across the feature you want to split.

Split parts

In QGIS 2.0 it is now possible to split the parts of a multi part feature so that the number of parts is increased. Just draw a line across the part you want to split using the ^Split Parts^ icon.

Merge selected features

The ^Merge Selected Features^ tool allows you to merge features. A new dialog will allow you to choose which value to choose between each selected features or select a function (Minimum, Maximum, Median, Sum, Skip Attribute) to use for each column. If features don't have a common boundaries, a multipolygon will be created.

Merge attributes of selected features

The ^Merge Attributes of Selected Features^ tool allows you to merge attributes of features with common boundaries and attributes without merging their boundaries. First, select several features at once. Then press the ^Merge Attributes of Selected Features^ button. Now QGIS asks you which attributes are to be applied to all selected objects. As a result, all selected objects have the same attribute entries.

Rotate Point Symbols

^Rotate Point Symbols^ allows you to change the rotation of point symbols in the map canvas. You must first define a rotation column from the attribute table of the point layer in the *Advanced* menu of the *Style* menu of the *Layer Properties*. Also, you will need to go into the 'SVG marker' and choose *Data defined properties ....* Activate *Angle* and choose 'rotation' as field. Without these settings, the tool is inactive.

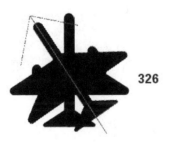

Figure 12.43: Rotate Point Symbols

To change the rotation, select a point feature in the map canvas and rotate it, holding the left mouse button pressed. A red arrow with the rotation value will be visualized (see Figure_edit_4). When you release the left mouse button again, the value will be updated in the attribute table.

Note: If you hold the `Ctrl` key pressed, the rotation will be done in 15 degree steps.

12.5.6 The Advanced Digitizing panel

When capturing new geometries or geometry parts you also have the possibility to use the Advanced Digitizing panel. You can digitize lines exactly parallel or at a specific angle or lock lines to specific angles. Furthermore you can enter coordinates directly so that you can make a precise definition for your new geomtry.

_figure_advanced_edit 1:

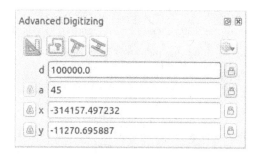

Figure 12.44: The Advanced Digitizing panel

The tools are not enabled if the map view is in geographic coordinates.

12.5.7 Creating new Vector layers

QGIS allows you to create new shapefile layers, new SpatiaLite layers, new GPX layers and New Temporary Scratch Layers. Creation of a new GRASS layer is supported within the GRASS plugin. Please refer to section *Creating a new GRASS vector layer* for more information on creating GRASS vector layers.

Creating a new Shapefile layer

To create a new shape layer for editing, choose *New →* New Shapefile Layer... from the *Layer* menu. The *New Vector Layer* dialog will be displayed as shown in Figure_edit_5. Choose the type of layer (point, line or polygon) and the CRS (coordinate reference system).

Note that QGIS does not yet support creation of 2.5D features (i.e., features with X,Y,Z coordinates).

To complete the creation of the new shapefile layer, add the desired attributes by clicking on the **[Add to attributes list]** button and specifying a name and type for the attribute. A first 'id' column is added as default but can be removed, if not wanted. Only *Type: real* , *Type: integer* , *Type: string* and *Type:date* attributes are supported. Additionally and according to the attribute type, you can also define the width and precision of the new attribute column. Once you are happy with the attributes, click **[OK]** and provide a name for the shapefile. QGIS will automatically add a .shp extension to the name you specify. Once the layer has been created, it will be added to the map, and you can edit it in the same way as described in section *Digitizing an existing layer* above.

Creating a new SpatiaLite layer

To create a new SpatiaLite layer for editing, choose *New →* New SpatiaLite Layer... from the *Layer* menu. The *New SpatiaLite Layer* dialog will be displayed as shown in Figure_edit_6.

The first step is to select an existing SpatiaLite database or to create a new SpatiaLite database. This can be done with the browse button to the right of the database field. Then, add a name for the new layer, define the layer type, and specify the coordinate reference system with **[Specify CRS]**. If desired, you can select *Create an autoincrementing primary key.*

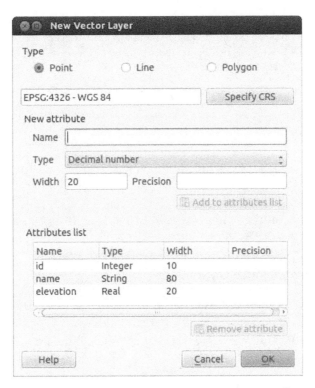

Figure 12.45: Creating a new Shapefile layer Dialog

Figure 12.46: Creating a New SpatiaLite layer Dialog

To define an attribute table for the new SpatiaLite layer, add the names of the attribute columns you want to create with the corresponding column type, and click on the [**Add to attribute list**] button. Once you are happy with the attributes, click [**OK**]. QGIS will automatically add the new layer to the legend, and you can edit it in the same way as described in section *Digitizing an existing layer* above.

Further management of SpatiaLite layers can be done with the DB Manager. See *DB Manager Plugin*.

Creating a new GPX layer

To create a new GPX file, you need to load the GPS plugin first. *Plugins →* ![icon] *Plugin Manager...* opens the Plugin Manager Dialog. Activate the ![icon] *GPS Tools* checkbox.

When this plugin is loaded, choose *New →* ![icon] *Create new GPX Layer...* from the *Layer* menu. In the *Save new GPX file as* dialog, you can choose where to save the new GPX layer.

Creating a new Temporary Scratch Layer

Empty, editable memory layers can be defined using *Layer → Create Layer → New Temporary Scratch Layer*. Here you can even create ![icon] *Multipoint*, ![icon] *Multiline* and ![icon] *Multipolygon* Layers beneath ![icon] *Point*, ![icon] *Line* and ![icon] *Polygon* Layers. Temporary Scratch Layers are not saved and will be discarded when QGIS is closed. See also paste_into_layer .

12.5.8 Working with the Attribute Table

The attribute table displays features of a selected layer. Each row in the table represents one map feature, and each column contains a particular piece of information about the feature. Features in the table can be searched, selected, moved or even edited.

To open the attribute table for a vector layer, make the layer active by clicking on it in the map legend area. Then, from the main *Layer* menu, choose ![icon] *Open Attribute Table*. It is also possible to right click on the layer and choose ![icon] *Open Attribute Table* from the drop-down menu, and to click on the ![icon] *Open Attribute Table* button in the Attributes toolbar.

This will open a new window that displays the feature attributes for the layer (figure_attributes_1). The number of features and the number of selected features are shown in the attribute table title.

Figure 12.47: Attribute Table for regions layer △

Selecting features in an attribute table

Each selected row in the attribute table displays the attributes of a selected feature in the layer. If the set of features selected in the main window is changed, the selection is also updated in the attribute table. Likewise, if the set of rows selected in the attribute table is changed, the set of features selected in the main window will be updated.

Rows can be selected by clicking on the row number on the left side of the row. **Multiple rows** can be marked by holding the Ctrl key. A **continuous selection** can be made by holding the Shift key and clicking on several row headers on the left side of the rows. All rows between the current cursor position and the clicked row are selected. Moving the cursor position in the attribute table, by clicking a cell in the table, does not change the row selection. Changing the selection in the main canvas does not move the cursor position in the attribute table.

The table can be sorted by any column, by clicking on the column header. A small arrow indicates the sort order (downward pointing means descending values from the top row down, upward pointing means ascending values from the top row down).

For a **simple search by attributes** on only one column, choose the *Column filter* → from the menu in the bottom left corner. Select the field (column) on which the search should be performed from the drop-down menu, and hit the **[Apply]** button. Then, only the matching features are shown in the attribute table.

To make a selection, you have to use the $\mathcal{E}$ Select features using an Expression icon on top of the attribute table. $\mathcal{E}$ Select features using an Expression allows you to define a subset of a table using a *Function List* like in the 🔢 Field Calculator (see *Field Calculator*). The query result can then be saved as a new vector layer. For example, if you want to find regions that are boroughs from regions.shp of the QGIS sample data, you have to open the *Fields and Values* menu and choose the field that you want to query. Double-click the field 'TYPE_2' and also **[Load all unique values]** . From the list, choose and double-click 'Borough'. In the *Expression* field, the following query appears:

```
"TYPE_2" = 'Borough'
```

Here you can also use the *Function list* → *Recent (Selection)* to make a selection that you used before. The expression builder remembers the last 20 used expressions.

The matching rows will be selected, and the total number of matching rows will appear in the title bar of the attribute table, as well as in the status bar of the main window. For searches that display only selected features on the map, use the Query Builder described in section *Query Builder*.

To show selected records only, use *Show Selected Features* from the menu at the bottom left.

The field calculator bar allows you to make calculations on the selected rows only. For example, you can alter the number of the ID field of the file:*regions.shp* with the expression

```
ID+5
```

as shown in figure_attributes_1 .

The other buttons at the top of the attribute table window provide the following functionality:

- 🖉 Toggle editing mode to edit single values and to enable functionalities described below (also with Ctrl+E)

- 💾 Save Edits (also with Ctrl+S)

- 🔲 Unselect all (also with Ctrl+U)

- 🔼 Move selected to top (also with Ctrl+T)

- 🔄 Invert selection (also with Ctrl+R)

- 📄 Copy selected rows to clipboard (also with Ctrl+C)

- 🔍 Zoom map to the selected rows (also with Ctrl+J)

- ⬡ Pan map to the selected rows (also with Ctrl+P)

- ⊠ Delete selected features (also with Ctrl+D)

- ▦ New Column for PostGIS layers and for OGR layers with GDAL version >= 1.6 (also with Ctrl+W)

- ▦ Delete Column for PostGIS layers and for OGR layers with GDAL version >= 1.9 (also with Ctrl+L)

- ▦ Open field calculator (also with Ctrl+I)

Below these buttons is the Field Calculator bar, which allows calculations to be quickly applied attributes visible in the table. This bar uses the same expressions as the ▦ Field Calculator (see *Field Calculator*).

Tip: Skip WKT geometry

If you want to use attribute data in external programs (such as Excel), use the ▤ Copy selected rows to clipboard button. You can copy the information without vector geometries if you deactivate *Settings → Options →* Data sources menu ☑ *Copy geometry in WKT representation from attribute table*.

Save selected features as new layer

The selected features can be saved as any OGR-supported vector format and also transformed into another coordinate reference system (CRS). Just open the right mouse menu of the layer and click on *Save as* to define the name of the output file, its format and CRS (see section *Map Legend*). To save the selection ensure that the ☑ *Save only selected features* is selected. It is also possible to specify OGR creation options within the dialog.

Paste into new layer

Features that are on the clipboard may be pasted into a new layer. To do this, first make a layer editable. Select some features, copy them to the clipboard, and then paste them into a new layer using *Edit → Paste Features as* and choosing *New vector layer* or *New memory layer*.

This applies to features selected and copied within QGIS and also to features from another source defined using well-known text (WKT).

Working with non spatial attribute tables

QGIS allows you also to load non-spatial tables. This currently includes tables supported by OGR and delimited text, as well as the PostgreSQL, MSSQL and Oracle provider. The tables can be used for field lookups or just generally browsed and edited using the table view. When you load the table, you will see it in the legend field. It can be opened with the ▦ Open Attribute Table tool and is then editable like any other layer attribute table.

As an example, you can use columns of the non-spatial table to define attribute values, or a range of values that are allowed, to be added to a specific vector layer during digitizing. Have a closer look at the edit widget in section *Fields Menu* to find out more.

12.5.9 Creating one to many relations

Relations are a technique often used in databases. The concept is, that features (rows) of different layers (tables) can belong to each other.

As an example you have a layer with all regions of alaska (polygon) which provides some attributes about its name and region type and a unique id (which acts as primary key).

Foreign keys

Then you get another point layer or table with information about airports that are located in the regions and you also want to keep track of these. If you want to add them to the region layer, you need to create a one to many relation using foreign keys, because there are several airports in most regions.

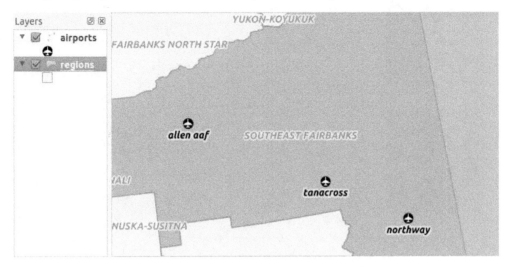

Figure 12.48: Alaska region with airports

In addition to the already existing attributes in the airports attribute table another field fk_region which acts as a foreign key (if you have a database, you will probably want to define a constraint on it).

This field fk_region will always contain an id of a region. It can be seen like a pointer to the region it belongs to. And you can design a custom edit form for the editing and QGIS takes care about the setup. It works with different providers (so you can also use it with shape and csv files) and all you have to do is to tell QGIS the relations between your tables.

Layers

QGIS makes no difference between a table and a vector layer. Basically, a vector layer is a table with a geometry. So can add your table as a vector layer. To demostrate you can load the 'region' shapefile (with geometries) and the 'airport' csv table (without geometries) and a foreign key (fk_region) to the layer region. This means, that each airport belongs to exactly one region while each region can have any number of airports (a typical one to many relation).

Definition (Relation Manager)

The first thing we are going to do is to let QGIS know about the relations between the layer. This is done in *Settings* → *Project Properties*. Open the *Relations* menu and click on *Add*.

- **name** is going to be used as a title. It should be a human readable string, describing, what the relation is used for. We will just call say "Airports" in this case.

- **referencing layer** is the one with the foreign key field on it. In our case this is the airports layer

- **referencing field** will say, which field points to the other layer so this is fk_region in this case

- **referenced layer** is the one with the primary key, pointed to, so here it is the regions layer

- **referenced field** is the primary key of the referenced layer so it is ID

- **id** will be used for internal purposes and has to be unique. You may need it to build custom forms once this is supported. If you leave it empty, one will be generated for you but you can assign one yourself to get one that is easier to handle.

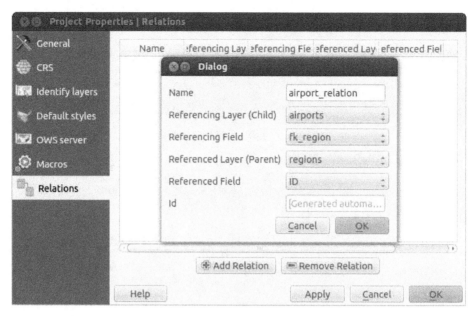

Figure 12.49: Relation Manager

Forms

Now that QGIS knows about the relation, it will be used to improve the forms it generates. As we did not change the default form method (autogenerated) it will just add a new widget in our form. So let's select the layer region in the legend and use the identify tool. Depending on your settings, the form might open directly or you will have to choose to open it in the identification dialog under actions.

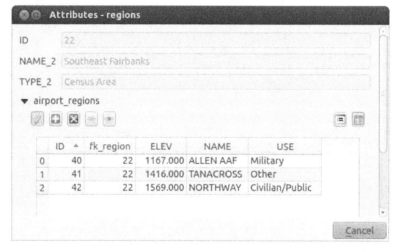

Figure 12.50: Identification dialog regions with relation to airports

As you can see, the airports assigned to this particular region are all shown in a table. And there are also some buttons available. Let's review them shortly

- The ⟋ button is for toggling the edit mode. Be aware that it toggles the edit mode of the airport layer, although we are in the feature form of a feature from the region layer. But the table is representing features of the airport layer.

- The ⊕ button will add a new feature to the airport layer. And it will assign the new airport to the current region by default.

- The 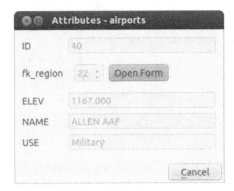 button will delete the selected airport permanently.

- The symbol will open a new dialog where you can select any existing airport which will then be assigned to the current region. This may be handy if you created the airport on the wrong region by accident.

- The symbol will unlink the selected airport from the current region, leaving them unassigned (the foreign key is set to NULL) effectively.

- The two buttons to the right switch between table view and form view where the later let's you view all the airports in their respective form.

If you work on the airport table, a new widget type is available which lets you embed the feature form of the referenced region on the feature form of the airports. It can be used when you open the layer properties of the airports table, switch to the *Fields* menu and change the widget type of the foreign key field 'fk_region' to Relation Reference.

If you look at the feature dialog now, you will see, that the form of the region is embedded inside the airports form and will even have a combobox, which allows you to assign the current airport to another region.

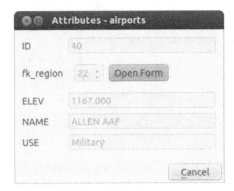

Figure 12.51: Identification dialog airport with relation to regions

12.6 Query Builder

The Query Builder allows you to define a subset of a table using a SQL-like WHERE clause and to display the result in the main window. The query result can then be saved as a new vector layer.

12.6.1 Query

Open the **Query Builder** by opening the Layer Properties and going to the *General* menu. Under *Feature subset*, click on the **[Query Builder]** button to open the *Query builder*. For example, if you have a regions layer with a TYPE_2 field, you could select only regions that are borough in the *Provider specific filter expression* box of the Query Builder. Figure_attributes_2 shows an example of the Query Builder populated with the regions.shp layer from the QGIS sample data. The Fields, Values and Operators sections help you to construct the SQL-like query.

The **Fields list** contains all attribute columns of the attribute table to be searched. To add an attribute column to the SQL WHERE clause field, double click its name in the Fields list. Generally, you can use the various fields, values and operators to construct the query, or you can just type it into the SQL box.

The **Values list** lists the values of an attribute table. To list all possible values of an attribute, select the attribute in the Fields list and click the **[all]** button. To list the first 25 unique values of an attribute column, select the attribute column in the Fields list and click the **[Sample]** button. To add a value to the SQL WHERE clause field, double click its name in the Values list.

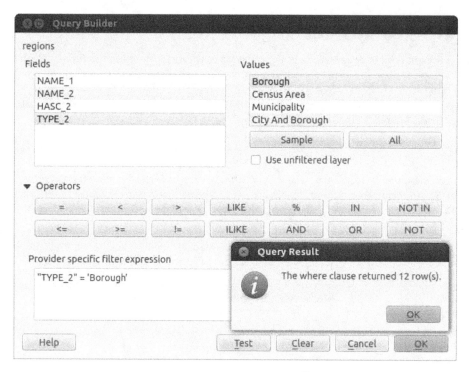

Figure 12.52: Query Builder

The **Operators section** contains all usable operators. To add an operator to the SQL WHERE clause field, click the appropriate button. Relational operators (= , > , ...), string comparison operator (LIKE), and logical operators (AND, OR, ...) are available.

The **[Test]** button shows a message box with the number of features satisfying the current query, which is useful in the process of query construction. The **[Clear]** button clears the text in the SQL WHERE clause text field. The **[OK]** button closes the window and selects the features satisfying the query. The **[Cancel]** button closes the window without changing the current selection.

QGIS treats the resulting subset acts as if it where the entire layer. For example if you applied the filter above for 'Borough', you can not display, query, save or edit Anchorage, because that is a 'Municipality' and therefore not part of the subset.

The only exception is that unless your layer is part of a database, using a subset will prevent you from editing the layer.

.

12.7 Field Calculator

The ⌗ Field Calculator button in the attribute table allows you to perform calculations on the basis of existing attribute values or defined functions, for instance, to calculate length or area of geometry features. The results can be written to a new attribute field, a virtual field, or they can be used to update values in an existing field.

Tip: Virtual Fields

- Virtual fields are not permanent and are not saved.
- To make a field virtual it must be done when the field is made.

The field calculator is now available on any layer that supports edit. When you click on the field calculator icon the dialog opens (see figure_attributes_3). If the layer is not in edit mode, a warning is displayed and using the field calculator will cause the layer to be put in edit mode before the calculation is made.

The quick field calculation bar on top of the attribute table is only visible if the layer is editable.

In quick field calculation bar, you first select the existing field name then open the expression dialog to create your expression or write it directly in the field then click on **Update All** button.

12.7.1 Expression tab

In the field calculator dialog, you first must select whether you want to only update selected features, create a new attribute field where the results of the calculation will be added or update an existing field.

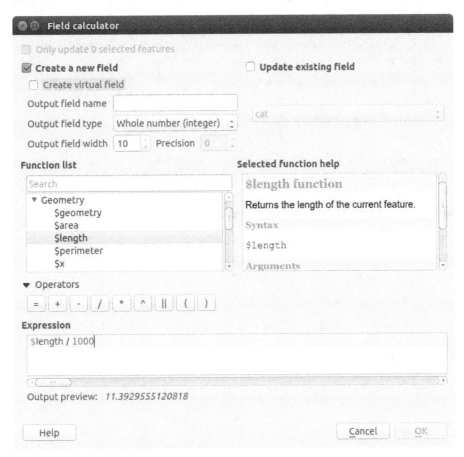

Figure 12.53: Field Calculator

If you choose to add a new field, you need to enter a field name, a field type (integer, real or string), the total field width, and the field precision (see figure_attributes_3). For example, if you choose a field width of 10 and a field precision of 3, it means you have 6 digits before the dot, then the dot and another 3 digits for the precision.

A short example illustrates how field calculator works when using the *Expression* tab. We want to calculate the length in km of the `railroads` layer from the QGIS sample dataset:

1. Load the shapefile `railroads.shp` in QGIS and press ⊞ Open Attribute Table.

2. Click on ✏ Toggle editing mode and open the ⊞ Field Calculator dialog.

3. Select the ☑ *Create a new field* checkbox to save the calculations into a new field.

4. Add `length` as Output field name and `real` as Output field type, and define Output field width to be 10 and Precision, 3.

5. Now double click on function $length in the *Geometry* group to add it into the Field calculator expression box.

6. Complete the expression by typing ''/ 1000" in the Field calculator expression box and click [**Ok**].

7. You can now find a new field length in the attribute table.

The available functions are listed in *Expressions* chapter.

12.7.2 Function Editor tab

With the Function Editor you are able to define your own Python custom functions in a comfortable way. The function editor will create new Python files in qgis2pythonexpressions and will auto load all functions defined when starting QGIS. Be aware that new functions are only saved in the expressions folder and not in the project file. If you have a project that uses one of your custom functions you will need to also share the .py file in the expressions folder.

Here's a short example on how to create your own functions:

```
@qgsfunction(args="auto", group='Custom')
def myfunc(value1, value2 feature, parent):
    pass
```

The short example creates a function 'myfunc' that will give you a function with two values. When using the args='auto' function argument the number of function arguments required will be calculated by the number of arguments the function has been defined with in Python (minus 2 - feature, and parent).

This function then can be used with the following expression:

```
myfunc('test1', 'test2')
```

Your function will be implemented in the 'Custom' *Functions* of the *Expression* tab after using the *Run Script* button.

Further information about creating Python code can be found on http://www.qgis.org/html/en/docs/pyqgis_developer_cookbook/inc

The function editor is not only limited to working with the field calculator, it can be found whenever you work with expressions. See also *Expressions*.

.

## CHAPTER 13

Working with Raster Data

13.1 Working with Raster Data

This section describes how to visualize and set raster layer properties. QGIS uses the GDAL library to read and write raster data formats, including ArcInfo Binary Grid, ArcInfo ASCII Grid, GeoTIFF, ERDAS IMAGINE, and many more. GRASS raster support is supplied by a native QGIS data provider plugin. The raster data can also be loaded in read mode from zip and gzip archives into QGIS.

As of the date of this document, more than 100 raster formats are supported by the GDAL library (see GDAL-SOFTWARE-SUITE in *Literature and Web References*). A complete list is available at http://www.gdal.org/formats_list.html.

Note: Not all of the listed formats may work in QGIS for various reasons. For example, some require external commercial libraries, or the GDAL installation of your OS may not have been built to support the format you want to use. Only those formats that have been well tested will appear in the list of file types when loading a raster into QGIS. Other untested formats can be loaded by selecting the [GDAL] All files (*) filter.

Working with GRASS raster data is described in section *GRASS GIS Integration*.

13.1.1 What is raster data?

Raster data in GIS are matrices of discrete cells that represent features on, above or below the earth's surface. Each cell in the raster grid is the same size, and cells are usually rectangular (in QGIS they will always be rectangular). Typical raster datasets include remote sensing data, such as aerial photography, or satellite imagery and modelled data, such as an elevation matrix.

Unlike vector data, raster data typically do not have an associated database record for each cell. They are geocoded by pixel resolution and the x/y coordinate of a corner pixel of the raster layer. This allows QGIS to position the data correctly in the map canvas.

QGIS makes use of georeference information inside the raster layer (e.g., GeoTiff) or in an appropriate world file to properly display the data.

13.1.2 Loading raster data in QGIS

Raster layers are loaded either by clicking on the ▨ Add Raster Layer icon or by selecting the *Layer* → ▨ *Add Raster Layer* menu option. More than one layer can be loaded at the same time by holding down the Ctrl or Shift key and clicking on multiple items in the *Open a GDAL Supported Raster Data Source* dialog.

Once a raster layer is loaded in the map legend, you can click on the layer name with the right mouse button to select and activate layer-specific features or to open a dialog to set raster properties for the layer.

Right mouse button menu for raster layers

- *Zoom to Layer Extent*
- *Zoom to Best Scale (100%)*
- *Stretch Using Current Extend*
- *Show in Overview*
- *Remove*
- *Duplicate*
- *Set Layer CRS*
- *Set Project CRS from Layer*
- *Save as ...*
- *Properties*
- *Rename*
- *Copy Style*
- *Add New Group*
- *Expand all*
- *Collapse all*
- *Update Drawing Order*

13.2 Raster Properties Dialog

To view and set the properties for a raster layer, double click on the layer name in the map legend, or right click on the layer name and choose *Properties* from the context menu. This will open the *Raster Layer Properties* dialog (see figure_raster_1).

There are several menus in the dialog:

- *General*
- *Style*
- *Transparency*
- *Pyramids*
- *Histogram*
- *Metadata*

13.2.1 General Menu

Layer Info

The *General* menu displays basic information about the selected raster, including the layer source path, the display name in the legend (which can be modified), and the number of columns, rows and no-data values of the raster.

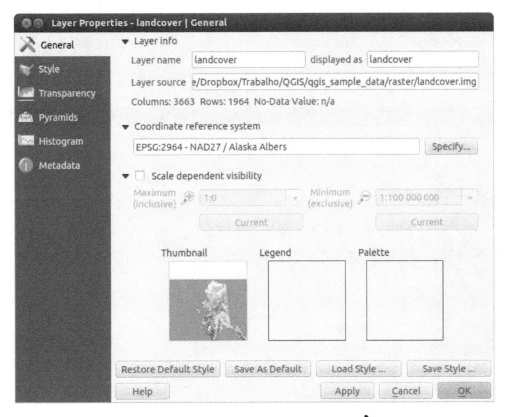

Figure 13.1: Raster Layers Properties Dialog

Coordinate reference system

Here, you find the coordinate reference system (CRS) information printed as a PROJ.4 string. If this setting is not correct, it can be modified by clicking the **[Specify]** button.

Scale Dependent visibility

Additionally scale-dependent visibility can be set in this tab. You will need to check the checkbox and set an appropriate scale where your data will be displayed in the map canvas.

At the bottom, you can see a thumbnail of the layer, its legend symbol, and the palette.

13.2.2 Style Menu

Band rendering

QGIS offers four different *Render types*. The renderer chosen is dependent on the data type.

1. Multiband color - if the file comes as a multiband with several bands (e.g., used with a satellite image with several bands)

2. Paletted - if a single band file comes with an indexed palette (e.g., used with a digital topographic map)

3. Singleband gray - (one band of) the image will be rendered as gray; QGIS will choose this renderer if the file has neither multibands nor an indexed palette nor a continous palette (e.g., used with a shaded relief map)

4. Singleband pseudocolor - this renderer is possible for files with a continuous palette, or color map (e.g., used with an elevation map)

Multiband color

With the multiband color renderer, three selected bands from the image will be rendered, each band representing the red, green or blue component that will be used to create a color image. You can choose several *Contrast enhancement* methods: 'No enhancement', 'Stretch to MinMax', 'Stretch and clip to MinMax' and 'Clip to min max'.

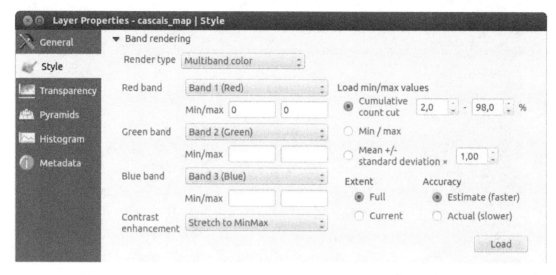

Figure 13.2: Raster Renderer - Multiband color 🐧

This selection offers you a wide range of options to modify the appearance of your raster layer. First of all, you have to get the data range from your image. This can be done by choosing the *Extent* and pressing **[Load]**. QGIS can ⦿ *Estimate (faster)* the *Min* and *Max* values of the bands or use the ○ *Actual (slower) Accuracy*.

Now you can scale the colors with the help of the *Load min/max values* section. A lot of images have a few very low and high data. These outliers can be eliminated using the ⦿ *Cumulative count cut* setting. The standard data range is set from 2% to 98% of the data values and can be adapted manually. With this setting, the gray character of the image can disappear. With the scaling option ○ *Min/max*, QGIS creates a color table with all of the data included in the original image (e.g., QGIS creates a color table with 256 values, given the fact that you have 8 bit bands). You can also calculate your color table using the ○ *Mean +/- standard deviation x* 1,00 ⌄. Then, only the values within the standard deviation or within multiple standard deviations are considered for the color table. This is useful when you have one or two cells with abnormally high values in a raster grid that are having a negative impact on the rendering of the raster.

All calculations can also be made for the ○ *Current* extent.

Tip: Viewing a Single Band of a Multiband Raster

If you want to view a single band of a multiband image (for example, Red), you might think you would set the Green and Blue bands to "Not Set". But this is not the correct way. To display the Red band, set the image type to 'Singleband gray', then select Red as the band to use for Gray.

Paletted

This is the standard render option for singleband files that already include a color table, where each pixel value is assigned to a certain color. In that case, the palette is rendered automatically. If you want to change colors assigned to certain values, just double-click on the color and the *Select color* dialog appears. Also, in QGIS 2.2. it's now possible to assign a label to the color values. The label appears in the legend of the raster layer then.

Contrast enhancement

Note: When adding GRASS rasters, the option *Contrast enhancement* will always be set automatically to *stretch to min max*, regardless of if this is set to another value in the QGIS general options.

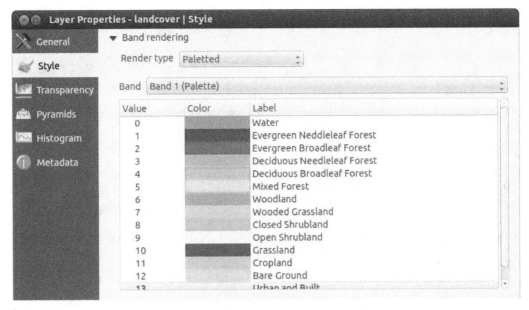

Figure 13.3: Raster Renderer - Paletted △

Singleband gray

This renderer allows you to render a single band layer with a *Color gradient*: 'Black to white' or 'White to black'. You can define a *Min* and a *Max* value by choosing the *Extent* first and then pressing [**Load**]. QGIS can ◉ *Estimate (faster)* the *Min* and *Max* values of the bands or use the ◯ *Actual (slower) Accuracy*.

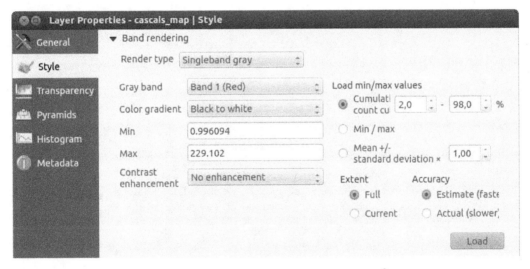

Figure 13.4: Raster Renderer - Singleband gray △

With the *Load min/max values* section, scaling of the color table is possible. Outliers can be eliminated using the ◉ *Cumulative count cut* setting. The standard data range is set from 2% to 98% of the data values and can be adapted manually. With this setting, the gray character of the image can disappear. Further settings can be made with ◯ *Min/max* and ◯ *Mean +/- standard deviation x* 1,00 ◇ . While the first one creates a color table with all of the data included in the original image, the second creates a color table that only considers values within the standard deviation or within multiple standard deviations. This is useful when you have one or two cells with abnormally high values in a raster grid that are having a negative impact on the rendering of the raster.

Singleband pseudocolor

This is a render option for single-band files, including a continous palette. You can also create individual color maps for the single bands here.   Three types of color interpolation are available:

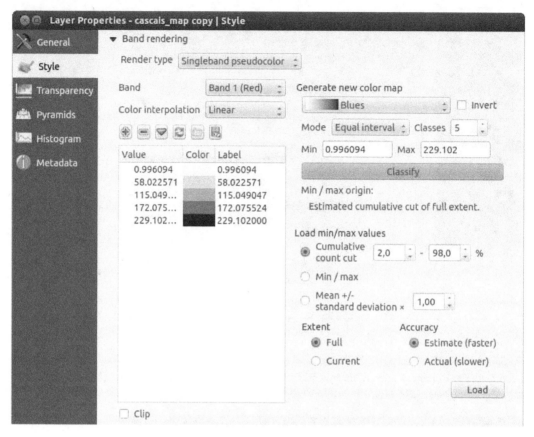

Figure 13.5: Raster Renderer - Singleband pseudocolor

1. Discrete

2. Linear

3. Exact

In the left block, the button Add values manually adds a value to the individual color table. The button Remove selected row deletes a value from the individual color table, and the Sort colormap items button sorts the color table according to the pixel values in the value column. Double clicking on the value column lets you insert a specific value. Double clicking on the color column opens the dialog *Change color*, where you can select a color to apply on that value. Further, you can also add labels for each color, but this value won't be displayed when you use the identify feature tool. You can also click on the button   Load color map from band, which tries to load the table from the band (if it has any). And you can use the buttons   Load color map from file or   Export color map to file to load an existing color table or to save the defined color table for other sessions.

In the right block, *Generate new color map* allows you to create newly categorized color maps. For the *Classification mode*   'Equal interval', you only need to select the *number of classes* 1,00 and press the button *Classify*. You can invert the colors of the color map by clicking the   *Invert* checkbox. In the case of the *Mode*   'Continous', QGIS creates classes automatically depending on the *Min* and *Max*. Defining *Min/Max* values can be done with the help of the *Load min/max values* section. A lot of images have a few very low and high data. These outliers can be eliminated using the   *Cumulative count cut* setting. The standard data range is set from 2% to 98% of the data values and can be adapted manually. With this setting, the gray character of the image can disappear. With the scaling option   *Min/max*, QGIS creates a color table with all of the data included in the original image (e.g., QGIS creates a color table with 256 values, given the fact that you have 8 bit bands). You can also calculate your color table using the ◯ *Mean +/- standard deviation x* `1,00 ◇`. Then, only the values within the standard deviation or within multiple standard deviations are considered for the color table.

Color rendering

For every *Band rendering*, a *Color rendering* is possible.

You can also achieve special rendering effects for your raster file(s) using one of the blending modes (see *The Vector Properties Dialog*).

Further settings can be made in modifiying the *Brightness*, the *Saturation* and the *Contrast*. You can also use a *Grayscale* option, where you can choose between 'By lightness', 'By luminosity' and 'By average'. For one hue in the color table, you can modify the 'Strength'.

Resampling

The *Resampling* option makes its appearance when you zoom in and out of an image. Resampling modes can optimize the appearance of the map. They calculate a new gray value matrix through a geometric transformation.

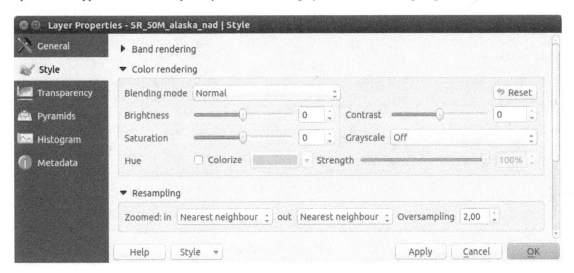

Figure 13.6: Raster Rendering - Resampling ◬

When applying the 'Nearest neighbour' method, the map can have a pixelated structure when zooming in. This appearance can be improved by using the 'Bilinear' or 'Cubic' method, which cause sharp features to be blurred. The effect is a smoother image. This method can be applied, for instance, to digital topographic raster maps.

13.2.3 Transparency Menu

QGIS has the ability to display each raster layer at a different transparency level. Use the transparency slider ▭ to indicate to what extent the underlying layers (if any) should be visible though the current raster layer. This is very useful if you like to overlay more than one raster layer (e.g., a shaded relief map overlayed by a classified raster map). This will make the look of the map more three dimensional.

Additionally, you can enter a raster value that should be treated as *NODATA* in the *Additional no data value* menu.

An even more flexible way to customize the transparency can be done in the *Custom transparency options* section. The transparency of every pixel can be set here.

As an example, we want to set the water of our example raster file `landcover.tif` to a transparency of 20%. The following steps are neccessary:

1. Load the raster file `landcover.tif`.

2. Open the *Properties* dialog by double-clicking on the raster name in the legend, or by right-clicking and choosing *Properties* from the pop-up menu.

3. Select the *Transparency* menu.

4. From the *Transparency band* menu, choose 'None'.

5. Click the ⊕ Add values manually button. A new row will appear in the pixel list.

6. Enter the raster value in the 'From' and 'To' column (we use 0 here), and adjust the transparency to 20%.

7. Press the **[Apply]** button and have a look at the map.

You can repeat steps 5 and 6 to adjust more values with custom transparency.

As you can see, it is quite easy to set custom transparency, but it can be quite a lot of work. Therefore, you can use the button 🖫 Export to file to save your transparency list to a file. The button 🗁 Import from file loads your transparency settings and applies them to the current raster layer.

13.2.4 Pyramids Menu

Large resolution raster layers can slow navigation in QGIS. By creating lower resolution copies of the data (pyramids), performance can be considerably improved, as QGIS selects the most suitable resolution to use depending on the level of zoom.

You must have write access in the directory where the original data is stored to build pyramids.

Several resampling methods can be used to calculate the pyramids:

- Nearest Neighbour
- Average
- Gauss
- Cubic
- Mode
- None

If you choose 'Internal (if possible)' from the *Overview format* menu, QGIS tries to build pyramids internally. You can also choose 'External' and 'External (Erdas Imagine)'.

Please note that building pyramids may alter the original data file, and once created they cannot be removed. If you wish to preserve a 'non-pyramided' version of your raster, make a backup copy prior to building pyramids.

13.2.5 Histogram Menu

The *Histogram* menu allows you to view the distribution of the bands or colors in your raster. The histogram is generated automatically when you open the *Histogram* menu. All existing bands will be displayed together. You can save the histogram as an image with the 🖫 button. With the *Visibility* option in the *Prefs/Actions* menu, you can display histograms of the individual bands. You will need to select the option ◔ *Show selected band*. The *Min/max options* allow you to 'Always show min/max markers', to 'Zoom to min/max' and to 'Update style to min/max'. With the *Actions* option, you can 'Reset' and 'Recompute histogram' after you have chosen the *Min/max options*.

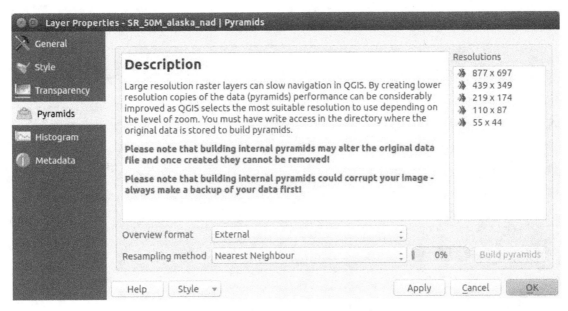

Figure 13.7: The Pyramids Menu

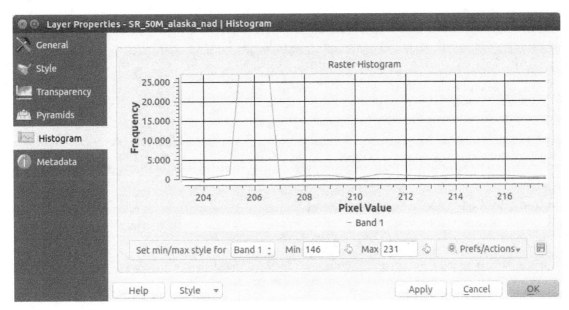

Figure 13.8: Raster Histogram

13.2.6 Metadata Menu

The *Metadata* menu displays a wealth of information about the raster layer, including statistics about each band in the current raster layer. From this menu, entries may be made for the *Description*, *Attribution*, *MetadataUrl* and *Properties*. In *Properties*, statistics are gathered on a 'need to know' basis, so it may well be that a given layer's statistics have not yet been collected.

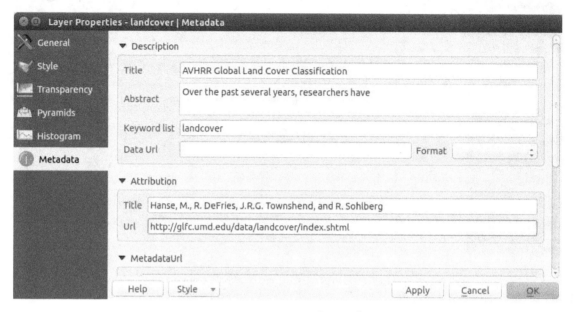

Figure 13.9: Raster Metadata ⬤

13.3 Raster Calculator

The *Raster Calculator* in the *Raster* menu allows you to perform calculations on the basis of existing raster pixel values (see figure_raster_10). The results are written to a new raster layer with a GDAL-supported format.

The **Raster bands** list contains all loaded raster layers that can be used. To add a raster to the raster calculator expression field, double click its name in the Fields list. You can then use the operators to construct calculation expressions, or you can just type them into the box.

In the **Result layer** section, you will need to define an output layer. You can then define the extent of the calculation area based on an input raster layer, or based on X,Y coordinates and on columns and rows, to set the resolution of the output layer. If the input layer has a different resolution, the values will be resampled with the nearest neighbor algorithm.

The **Operators** section contains all available operators. To add an operator to the raster calculator expression box, click the appropriate button. Mathematical calculations (+, −, *, ...) and trigonometric functions (sin, cos, tan, ...) are available. Stay tuned for more operators to come!

With the ✅ *Add result to project* checkbox, the result layer will automatically be added to the legend area and can be visualized.

13.3.1 Examples

Convert elevation values from meters to feet

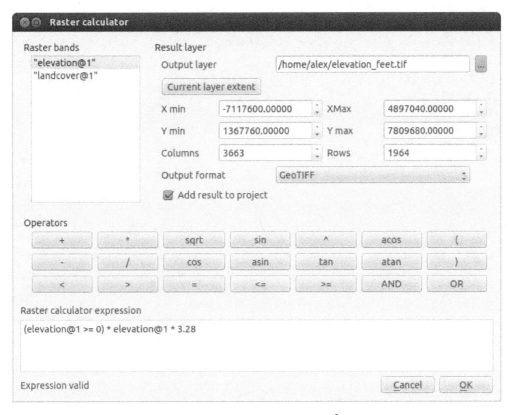

Figure 13.10: Raster Calculator △

Creating an elevation raster in feet from a raster in meters, you need to use the conversion factor for meters to feet: 3.28. The expression is:

```
"elevation@1" * 3.28
```

Using a mask

If you want to mask out parts of a raster – say, for instance, because you are only interested in elevations above 0 meters – you can use the following expression to create a mask and apply the result to a raster in one step.

```
("elevation@1" >= 0) * "elevation@1"
```

In other words, for every cell greater than or equal to 0, set its value to 1. Otherwise set it to 0. This creates the mask on the fly.

If you want to classify a raster – say, for instance into two elevation classes, you can use the following expression to create a raster with two values 1 and 2 in one step.

```
("elevation@1" < 50) * 1 + ("elevation@1" >= 50) * 2
```

In other words, for every cell less than 50 set its value to 1. For every cell greater than or equal 50 set its value to 2.

## CHAPTER 14

Working with OGC Data

14.1 QGIS as OGC Data Client

The Open Geospatial Consortium (OGC) is an international organization with membership of more than 300 commercial, governmental, nonprofit and research organizations worldwide. Its members develop and implement standards for geospatial content and services, GIS data processing and exchange.

Describing a basic data model for geographic features, an increasing number of specifications are developed by OGC to serve specific needs for interoperable location and geospatial technology, including GIS. Further information can be found at http://www.opengeospatial.org/.

Important OGC specifications supported by QGIS are:

- **WMS** — Web Map Service (*WMS/WMTS Client*)

- **WMTS** — Web Map Tile Service (*WMS/WMTS Client*)

- **WFS** — Web Feature Service (*WFS and WFS-T Client*)

- **WFS-T** — Web Feature Service - Transactional (*WFS and WFS-T Client*)

- **WCS** — Web Coverage Service (*WCS Client*)

- **SFS** — Simple Features for SQL (*PostGIS Layers*)

- **GML** — Geography Markup Language

OGC services are increasingly being used to exchange geospatial data between different GIS implementations and data stores. QGIS can deal with the above specifications as a client, being **SFS** (through support of the PostgreSQL / PostGIS data provider, see section *PostGIS Layers*).

14.1.1 WMS/WMTS Client

Overview of WMS Support

QGIS currently can act as a WMS client that understands WMS 1.1, 1.1.1 and 1.3 servers. In particular, it has been tested against publicly accessible servers such as DEMIS.

A WMS server acts upon requests by the client (e.g., QGIS) for a raster map with a given extent, set of layers, symbolization style, and transparency. The WMS server then consults its local data sources, rasterizes the map, and sends it back to the client in a raster format. For QGIS, this format would typically be JPEG or PNG.

WMS is generically a REST (Representational State Transfer) service rather than a full-blown Web service. As such, you can actually take the URLs generated by QGIS and use them in a web browser to retrieve the same images that QGIS uses internally. This can be useful for troubleshooting, as there are several brands of WMS server on the market and they all have their own interpretation of the WMS standard.

WMS layers can be added quite simply, as long as you know the URL to access the WMS server, you have a serviceable connection to that server, and the server understands HTTP as the data transport mechanism.

Overview of WMTS Support

QGIS can also act as a WMTS client. WMTS is an OGC standard for distributing tile sets of geospatial data. This is a faster and more efficient way of distributing data than WMS because with WMTS, the tile sets are pre-generated, and the client only requests the transmission of the tiles, not their production. A WMS request typically involves both the generation and transmission of the data. A well-known example of a non-OGC standard for viewing tiled geospatial data is Google Maps.

In order to display the data at a variety of scales close to what the user might want, the WMTS tile sets are produced at several different scale levels and are made available for the GIS client to request them.

This diagram illustrates the concept of tile sets:

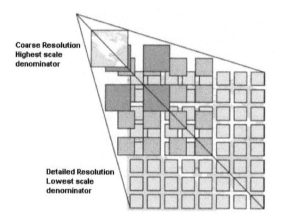

Figure 14.1: Concept of WMTS tile sets

The two types of WMTS interfaces that QGIS supports are via Key-Value-Pairs (KVP) and RESTful. These two interfaces are different, and you need to specify them to QGIS differently.

1) In order to access a **WMTS KVP** service, a QGIS user must open the WMS/WMTS interface and add the following string to the URL of the WMTS tile service:

```
"?SERVICE=WMTS&REQUEST=GetCapabilities"
```

An example of this type of address is

```
http://opencache.statkart.no/gatekeeper/gk/gk.open_wmts?\
  service=WMTS&request=GetCapabilities
```

For testing the topo2 layer in this WMTS works nicely. Adding this string indicates that a WMTS web service is to be used instead of a WMS service.

2. The **RESTful WMTS** service takes a different form, a straightforward URL. The format recommended by the OGC is:

```
{WMTSBaseURL}/1.0.0/WMTSCapabilities.xml
```

This format helps you to recognize that it is a RESTful address. A RESTful WMTS is accessed in QGIS by simply adding its address in the WMS setup in the URL field of the form. An example of this type of address for the case of an Austrian basemap is http://maps.wien.gv.at/basemap/1.0.0/WMTSCapabilities.xml.

Note: You can still find some old services called WMS-C. These services are quite similar to WMTS (i.e., same purpose but working a little bit differently). You can manage them the same as you do WMTS services. Just add ?tiled=true at the end of the url. See http://wiki.osgeo.org/wiki/Tile_Map_Service_Specification for more information about this specification.

When you read WMTS, you can often think WMS-C also.

Selecting WMS/WMTS Servers

The first time you use the WMS feature in QGIS, there are no servers defined.

Begin by clicking the ^Add WMS layer^ button on the toolbar, or selecting *Layer → Add WMS Layer....*

The dialog *Add Layer(s) from a Server* for adding layers from the WMS server appears. You can add some servers to play with by clicking the **[Add default servers]** button. This will add two WMS demo servers for you to use: the WMS servers of the DM Solutions Group and Lizardtech. To define a new WMS server in the *Layers* tab, select the **[New]** button. Then enter the parameters to connect to your desired WMS server, as listed in table_OGC_1:

Name	A name for this connection. This name will be used in the Server Connections drop-down box so that you can distinguish it from other WMS servers.
URL	URL of the server providing the data. This must be a resolvable host name – the same format as you would use to open a telnet connection or ping a host.
Username	Username to access a secured WMS server. This parameter is optional.
Password	Password for a basic authenticated WMS server. This parameter is optional.
Ignore GetMap URI	☑ *Ignore GetMap URI reported in capabilities.* Use given URI from URL field above.
Ignore GetFeatureInfo URI	☑ *Ignore GetFeatureInfo URI reported in capabilities.* Use given URI from URL field above.

Table OGC 1: WMS Connection Parameters

If you need to set up a proxy server to be able to receive WMS services from the internet, you can add your proxy server in the options. Choose *Settings → Options* and click on the *Network & Proxy* tab. There, you can add your proxy settings and enable them by setting ☑ *Use proxy for web access.* Make sure that you select the correct proxy type from the *Proxy type* [⋯▼] drop-down menu.

Once the new WMS server connection has been created, it will be preserved for future QGIS sessions.

Tip: On WMS Server URLs

Be sure, when entering the WMS server URL, that you have the base URL only. For example, you shouldn't have fragments such as `request=GetCapabilities` or `version=1.0.0` in your URL.

Loading WMS/WMTS Layers

Once you have successfully filled in your parameters, you can use the **[Connect]** button to retrieve the capabilities of the selected server. This includes the image encoding, layers, layer styles and projections. Since this is a network operation, the speed of the response depends on the quality of your network connection to the WMS server. While downloading data from the WMS server, the download progress is visualized in the lower left of the WMS dialog.

Your screen should now look a bit like figure_OGR_1, which shows the response provided by the European Soil Portal WMS server.

Image Encoding

The *Image encoding* section lists the formats that are supported by both the client and server. Choose one depending on your image accuracy requirements.

Tip: Image Encoding

You will typically find that a WMS server offers you the choice of JPEG or PNG image encoding. JPEG is a lossy compression format, whereas PNG faithfully reproduces the raw raster data.

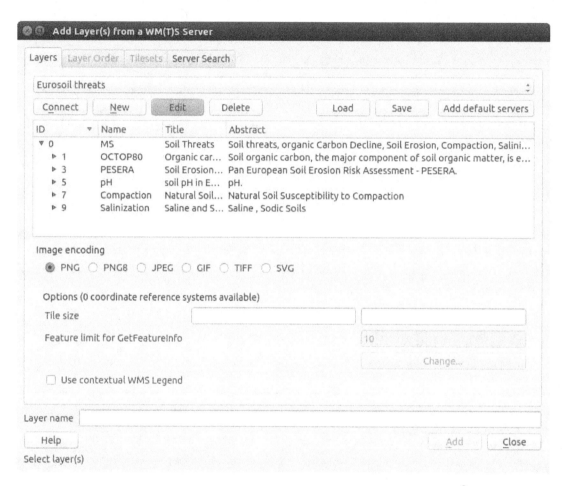

Figure 14.2: Dialog for adding a WMS server, showing its available layers △

Use JPEG if you expect the WMS data to be photographic in nature and/or you don't mind some loss in picture quality. This trade-off typically reduces by five times the data transfer requirement compared with PNG.

Use PNG if you want precise representations of the original data and you don't mind the increased data transfer requirements.

Options

The Options area of the dialog provides a text field where you can add a *Layer name* for the WMS layer. This name will appear in the legend after loading the layer.

Below the layer name, you can define *Tile size* if you want to set tile sizes (e.g., 256x256) to split up the WMS request into multiple requests.

The *Feature limit for GetFeatureInfo* defines what features from the server to query.

If you select a WMS from the list, a field with the default projection provided by the mapserver appears. If the [**Change...**] button is active, you can click on it and change the default projection of the WMS to another CRS provided by the WMS server.

Finally you can activate ☑ *Use contextual WMS-Legend* if the WMS Server supports this feature. Then only the relevant legend for your current map view extent will be shown and thus will not include legend items for things you can't see in the current map.

Layer Order

The *Layer Order* tab lists the selected layers available from the current connected WMS server. You may notice that some layers are expandable; this means that the layer can be displayed in a choice of image styles.

You can select several layers at once, but only one image style per layer. When several layers are selected, they will be combined at the WMS server and transmitted to QGIS in one go.

Tip: WMS Layer Ordering

WMS layers rendered by a server are overlaid in the order listed in the Layers section, from top to bottom of the list. If you want to change the overlay order, you can use the *Layer Order* tab.

Transparency

In this version of QGIS, the *Global transparency* setting from the *Layer Properties* is hard coded to be always on, where available.

Tip: WMS Layer Transparency

The availability of WMS image transparency depends on the image encoding used: PNG and GIF support transparency, whilst JPEG leaves it unsupported.

Coordinate Reference System

A coordinate reference system (CRS) is the OGC terminology for a QGIS projection.

Each WMS layer can be presented in multiple CRSs, depending on the capability of the WMS server.

To choose a CRS, select [**Change...**] and a dialog similar to Figure Projection 3 in *Working with Projections* will appear. The main difference with the WMS version of the dialog is that only those CRSs supported by the WMS server will be shown.

Server search

Within QGIS, you can search for WMS servers. Figure_OGC_2 shows the *Server Search* tab with the *Add Layer(s) from a Server* dialog.

As you can see, it is possible to enter a search string in the text field and hit the [**Search**] button. After a short while, the search result will be populated into the list below the text field. Browse the result list and inspect your

---

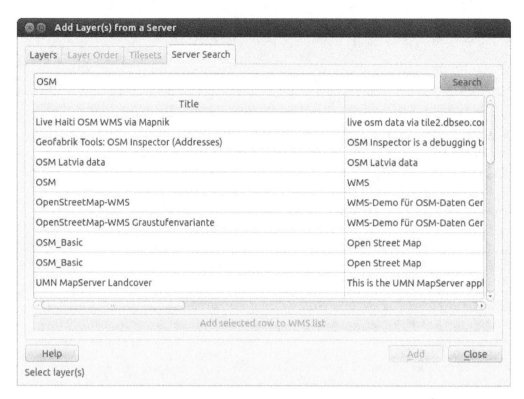

Figure 14.3: Dialog for searching WMS servers after some keywords △

search results within the table. To visualize the results, select a table entry, press the [**Add selected row to WMS list**] button and change back to the *Layers* tab. QGIS has automatically updated your server list, and the selected search result is already enabled in the list of saved WMS servers in the *Layers* tab. You only need to request the list of layers by clicking the [**Connect**] button. This option is quite handy when you want to search maps by specific keywords.

Basically, this option is a front end to the API of http://geopole.org.

Tilesets

When using WMTS (Cached WMS) services like

```
http://opencache.statkart.no/gatekeeper/gk/gk.open_wmts?\
    service=WMTS&request=GetCapabilities
```

you are able to browse through the *Tilesets* tab given by the server. Additional information like tile size, formats and supported CRS are listed in this table. In combination with this feature, you can use the tile scale slider by selecting *Settings* → *Panels* (KDE and Windows) or *View* → *Panels* (Gnome and MacOSX), then choosing *Tile scale*. This gives you the available scales from the tile server with a nice slider docked in.

Using the Identify Tool

Once you have added a WMS server, and if any layer from a WMS server is queryable, you can then use the ^{Identify} tool to select a pixel on the map canvas. A query is made to the WMS server for each selection made. The results of the query are returned in plain text. The formatting of this text is dependent on the particular WMS server used. **Format selection**

If multiple output formats are supported by the server, a combo box with supported formats is automatically added to the identify results dialog and the selected format may be stored in the project for the layer. **GML format support**

The ^{Identify} tool supports WMS server response (GetFeatureInfo) in GML format (it is called Feature in the QGIS GUI in this context). If "Feature" format is supported by the server and selected, results of the Identify tool are vector features, as from a regular vector layer. When a single feature is selected in the tree, it is highlighted in the map and it can be copied to the clipboard and pasted to another vector layer. See the example setup of the UMN Mapserver below to support GetFeatureInfo in GML format.

```
# in layer METADATA add which fields should be included and define geometry (example):

"gml_include_items"    "all"
"ows_geometries"       "mygeom"
"ows_mygeom_type"      "polygon"

# Then there are two possibilities/formats available, see a) and b):

# a) basic (output is generated by Mapserver and does not contain XSD)
# in WEB METADATA define formats (example):
"wms_getfeatureinfo_formatlist" "application/vnd.ogc.gml,text/html"

# b) using OGR (output is generated by OGR, it is send as multipart and contains XSD)
# in MAP define OUTPUTFORMAT (example):
OUTPUTFORMAT
    NAME "OGRGML"
    MIMETYPE "ogr/gml"
    DRIVER "OGR/GML"
    FORMATOPTION "FORM=multipart"
END

# in WEB METADATA define formats (example):
"wms_getfeatureinfo_formatlist" "OGRGML,text/html"
```

Viewing Properties

Once you have added a WMS server, you can view its properties by right-clicking on it in the legend and selecting *Properties*. **Metadata Tab**

The tab *Metadata* displays a wealth of information about the WMS server, generally collected from the capabilities statement returned from that server. Many definitions can be gleaned by reading the WMS standards (see OPEN-GEOSPATIAL-CONSORTIUM in *Literature and Web References*), but here are a few handy definitions:

- **Server Properties**

    - **WMS Version** — The WMS version supported by the server.

    - **Image Formats** — The list of MIME-types the server can respond with when drawing the map. QGIS supports whatever formats the underlying Qt libraries were built with, which is typically at least `image/png` and `image/jpeg`.

    - **Identity Formats** — The list of MIME-types the server can respond with when you use the Identify tool. Currently, QGIS supports the `text-plain` type.

- **Layer Properties**

    - **Selected** — Whether or not this layer was selected when its server was added to this project.

    - **Visible** — Whether or not this layer is selected as visible in the legend (not yet used in this version of QGIS).

    - **Can Identify** — Whether or not this layer will return any results when the Identify tool is used on it.

    - **Can be Transparent** — Whether or not this layer can be rendered with transparency. This version of QGIS will always use transparency if this is `Yes` and the image encoding supports transparency.

    - **Can Zoom In** — Whether or not this layer can be zoomed in by the server. This version of QGIS assumes all WMS layers have this set to `Yes`. Deficient layers may be rendered strangely.

- **Cascade Count** — WMS servers can act as a proxy to other WMS servers to get the raster data for a layer. This entry shows how many times the request for this layer is forwarded to peer WMS servers for a result.

- **Fixed Width, Fixed Height** — Whether or not this layer has fixed source pixel dimensions. This version of QGIS assumes all WMS layers have this set to nothing. Deficient layers may be rendered strangely.

- **WGS 84 Bounding Box** — The bounding box of the layer, in WGS 84 coordinates. Some WMS servers do not set this correctly (e.g., UTM coordinates are used instead). If this is the case, then the initial view of this layer may be rendered with a very 'zoomed-out' appearance by QGIS. The WMS webmaster should be informed of this error, which they may know as the WMS XML elements `LatLonBoundingBox`, `EX_GeographicBoundingBox` or the CRS:84 `BoundingBox`.

- **Available in CRS** — The projections that this layer can be rendered in by the WMS server. These are listed in the WMS-native format.

- **Available in style** — The image styles that this layer can be rendered in by the WMS server.

Show WMS legend graphic in table of contents and composer

The QGIS WMS data provider is able to display a legend graphic in the table of contents' layer list and in the map composer. The WMS legend will be shown only if the WMS server has GetLegendGraphic capability and the layer has getCapability url specified, so you additionally have to select a styling for the layer.

If a legendGraphic is available, it is shown below the layer. It is little and you have to click on it to open it in real dimension (due to QgsLegendInterface architectural limitation). Clicking on the layer's legend will open a frame with the legend at full resolution.

In the print composer, the legend will be integrated at it's original (dowloaded) dimension. Resolution of the legend graphic can be set in the item properties under Legend -> WMS LegendGraphic to match your printing requirements

The legend will display contextual information based on your current scale. The WMS legend will be shown only if the WMS server has GetLegendGraphic capability and the layer has getCapability url specified, so you have to select a styling.

WMS Client Limitations

Not all possible WMS client functionality had been included in this version of QGIS. Some of the more noteworthy exceptions follow.

Editing WMS Layer Settings

Once you've completed the ^{Add WMS layer} procedure, there is no way to change the settings. A work-around is to delete the layer completely and start again.

WMS Servers Requiring Authentication

Currently, publicly accessible and secured WMS services are supported. The secured WMS servers can be accessed by public authentication. You can add the (optional) credentials when you add a WMS server. See section *Selecting WMS/WMTS Servers* for details.

Tip: Accessing secured OGC-layers

If you need to access secured layers with secured methods other than basic authentication, you can use InteProxy as a transparent proxy, which does support several authentication methods. More information can be found in the InteProxy manual at http://inteproxy.wald.intevation.org.

Tip: QGIS WMS Mapserver

Since Version 1.7.0, QGIS has its own implementation of a WMS 1.3.0 Mapserver. Read more about this in chapter *QGIS as OGC Data Server*.

14.1.2 WCS Client

A Web Coverage Service (WCS) provides access to raster data in forms that are useful for client-side rendering, as input into scientific models, and for other clients. The WCS may be compared to the WFS and the WMS. As WMS and WFS service instances, a WCS allows clients to choose portions of a server's information holdings based on spatial constraints and other query criteria.

QGIS has a native WCS provider and supports both version 1.0 and 1.1 (which are significantly different), but currently it prefers 1.0, because 1.1 has many issues (i.e., each server implements it in a different way with various particularities).

The native WCS provider handles all network requests and uses all standard QGIS network settings (especially proxy). It is also possible to select cache mode ('always cache', 'prefer cache', 'prefer network', 'always network'), and the provider also supports selection of time position, if temporal domain is offered by the server.

14.1.3 WFS and WFS-T Client

In QGIS, a WFS layer behaves pretty much like any other vector layer. You can identify and select features, and view the attribute table. Since QGIS 1.6, editing WFS-T is also supported.

In general, adding a WFS layer is very similar to the procedure used with WMS. The difference is that there are no default servers defined, so we have to add our own.

Loading a WFS Layer

As an example, we use the DM Solutions WFS server and display a layer. The URL is: http://www2.dmsolutions.ca/cgi-bin/mswfs_gmap

1. Click on the ᴬᵈᵈ ᵂᶠˢ ᴸᵃʸᵉʳ tool on the Layers toolbar. The *Add WFS Layer from a Server* dialog appears.
2. Click on [**New**].
3. Enter 'DM Solutions' as name.
4. Enter the URL (see above).
5. Click [**OK**].
6. Choose 'DM Solutions' from the *Server Connections* drop-down list.
7. Click [**Connect**].
8. Wait for the list of layers to be populated.
9. Select the *Parks* layer in the list.
10. Click [**Apply**] to add the layer to the map.

Note that any proxy settings you may have set in your preferences are also recognized.

You'll notice the download progress is visualized in the lower left of the QGIS main window. Once the layer is loaded, you can identify and select a province or two and view the attribute table.

Only WFS 1.0.0 is supported. At this time, there have not been many tests against WFS versions implemented in other WFS servers. If you encounter problems with any other WFS server, please do not hesitate to contact the development team. Please refer to section *Help and Support* for further information about the mailing lists.

Tip: Finding WFS Servers

You can find additional WFS servers by using Google or your favorite search engine. There are a number of lists with public URLs, some of them maintained and some not.

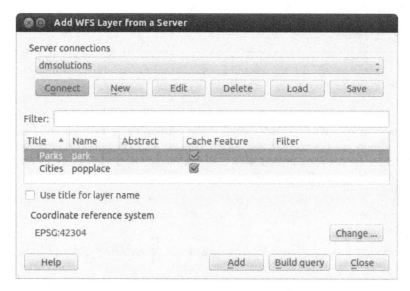

Figure 14.4: Adding a WFS layer

14.2 QGIS as OGC Data Server

QGIS Server is an open source WMS 1.3, WFS 1.0.0 and WCS 1 1.1.1 implementation that, in addition, implements advanced cartographic features for thematic mapping. The QGIS Server is a FastCGI/CGI (Common Gateway Interface) application written in C++ that works together with a web server (e.g., Apache, Lighttpd). It has Python plugin support allowing for fast and efficient development and deployment of new features. It is funded by the EU projects Orchestra, Sany and the city of Uster in Switzerland.

QGIS Server uses QGIS as back end for the GIS logic and for map rendering. Furthermore, the Qt library is used for graphics and for platform-independent C++ programming. In contrast to other WMS software, the QGIS Server uses cartographic rules as a configuration language, both for the server configuration and for the user-defined cartographic rules.

As QGIS desktop and QGIS Server use the same visualization libraries, the maps that are published on the web look the same as in desktop GIS.

In one of the following manuals, we will provide a sample configuration to set up a QGIS Server. For now, we recommend to read one of the following URLs to get more information:

- http://karlinapp.ethz.ch/qgis_wms/

- http://hub.qgis.org/projects/quantum-gis/wiki/QGIS_Server_Tutorial

- http://linfiniti.com/2010/08/qgis-mapserver-a-wms-server-for-the-masses/

14.2.1 Sample installation on Debian Squeeze

At this point, we will give a short and simple sample installation how-to for a minimal working configuration using Apache2 on Debian Squeeze. Many other OSs provide packages for QGIS Server, too. If you have to build it all from source, please refer to the URLs above.

Firstly, add the following debian GIS repository by adding the following repository:

```
$ cat /etc/apt/sources.list.d/debian-gis.list
deb http://qgis.org/debian trusty main
deb-src http://qgis.org/debian trusty main

$ # Add keys
$ sudo gpg --recv-key DD45F6C3
$ sudo gpg --export --armor DD45F6C3 | sudo apt-key add -

$ # Update package list
$ sudo apt-get update && sudo apt-get upgrade
```

Now, install QGIS-Server:

```
$ sudo apt-get install qgis-server python-qgis
```

Installation of a HelloWorld example plugin for testing the servers. You create a directory to hold server plugins. This will be specified in the virtual host configuration and passed on to the server through an environment variable:

```
$ sudo mkdir -p /opt/qgis-server/plugins
$ cd /opt/qgis-server/plugins
$ sudo wget https://github.com/elpaso/qgis-helloserver/archive/master.zip
$ # In case unzip was not installed before:
$ sudo apt-get install unzip
$ sudo unzip master.zip
$ sudo mv qgis-helloserver-master HelloServer
```

Install the Apache server in a separate virtual host listening on port 80. Enable the rewrite module to pass HTTP BASIC auth headers:

```
$ sudo a2enmod rewrite
$ cat /etc/apache2/conf-available/qgis-server-port.conf
Listen 80
$ sudo a2enconf qgis-server-port
```

This is the virtual host configuration, stored in /etc/apache2/sites-available/001-qgis-server.conf :

```
<VirtualHost *:80>
  ServerAdmin webmaster@localhost
  DocumentRoot /var/www/html

  ErrorLog ${APACHE_LOG_DIR}/qgis-server-error.log
  CustomLog ${APACHE_LOG_DIR}/qgis-server-access.log combined

  # Longer timeout for WPS... default = 40
  FcgidIOTimeout 120
  FcgidInitialEnv LC_ALL "en_US.UTF-8"
  FcgidInitialEnv PYTHONIOENCODING UTF-8
  FcgidInitialEnv LANG "en_US.UTF-8"
  FcgidInitialEnv QGIS_DEBUG 1
  FcgidInitialEnv QGIS_SERVER_LOG_FILE /tmp/qgis-000.log
  FcgidInitialEnv QGIS_SERVER_LOG_LEVEL 0
  FcgidInitialEnv QGIS_PLUGINPATH "/opt/qgis-server/plugins"

  # ABP: needed for QGIS HelloServer plugin HTTP BASIC auth
  <IfModule mod_fcgid.c>
      RewriteEngine on
      RewriteCond %{HTTP:Authorization} .
      RewriteRule .* - [E=HTTP_AUTHORIZATION:%{HTTP:Authorization}]
  </IfModule>

  ScriptAlias /cgi-bin/ /usr/lib/cgi-bin/
  <Directory "/usr/lib/cgi-bin">
      AllowOverride All
```

```
      Options +ExecCGI -MultiViews +FollowSymLinks
      # for apache2 > 2.4
      Require all granted
      #Allow from all
   </Directory>
 </VirtualHost>
```

Now enable the virtual host and restart Apache:

```
$ sudo a2ensite 001-qgis-server
$ sudo service apache2 restart
```

Test the server with the HelloWorld plugin:

```
$ wget -q -O - "http://localhost/cgi-bin/qgis_mapserv.fcgi?SERVICE=HELLO"
HelloServer!
```

You can have a look at the default GetCpabilities of the QGIS server at: `http://localhost/cgi-bin/qgis_mapserv.fcgi?SERVICE=WMS&VERSION=1.3.0&REQUEST=GetCapabil`

Tip: If you work with a feature that has many nodes then modyfying and adding a new feature will fail. In this case it is possible to insert the following code into the `001-qgis-server.conf` file:

```
<IfModule mod_fcgid.c>
FcgidMaxRequestLen 26214400
FcgidConnectTimeout 60
</IfModule>
```

14.2.2 Creating a WMS/WFS/WCS from a QGIS project

To provide a new QGIS Server WMS, WFS or WCS, we have to create a QGIS project file with some data. Here, we use the 'Alaska' shapefile from the QGIS sample dataset. Define the colors and styles of the layers in QGIS and the project CRS, if not already defined.

Then, go to the *OWS Server* menu of the *Project → Project Properties* dialog and provide some information about the OWS in the fields under *Service Capabilities*. This will appear in the GetCapabilities response of the WMS, WFS or WCS. If you don't check ☑ *Service capabilities*, QGIS Server will use the information given in the `wms_metadata.xml` file located in the `cgi-bin` folder.

WMS capabilities

In the *WMS capabilities* section, you can define the extent advertised in the WMS GetCapabilities response by entering the minimum and maximum X and Y values in the fields under *Advertised extent*. Clicking *Use Current Canvas Extent* sets these values to the extent currently displayed in the QGIS map canvas. By checking ☑ *CRS restrictions*, you can restrict in which coordinate reference systems (CRS) QGIS Server will offer to render maps.

Use the ⊕ button below to select those CRS from the Coordinate Reference System Selector, or click *Used* to add the CRS used in the QGIS project to the list.

If you have print composers defined in your project, they will be listed in the GetCapabilities response, and they can be used by the GetPrint request to create prints, using one of the print composer layouts as a template. This is a QGIS-specific extension to the WMS 1.3.0 specification. If you want to exclude any print composer from being published by the WMS, check ☑ *Exclude composers* and click the ⊕ button below. Then, select a print composer from the *Select print composer* dialog in order to add it to the excluded composers list.

If you want to exclude any layer or layer group from being published by the WMS, check ☑ *Exclude Layers* and click the ⊕ button below. This opens the *Select restricted layers and groups* dialog, which allows you to choose the layers and groups that you don't want to be published. Use the `Shift` or `Ctrl` key if you want to select multiple entries at once.

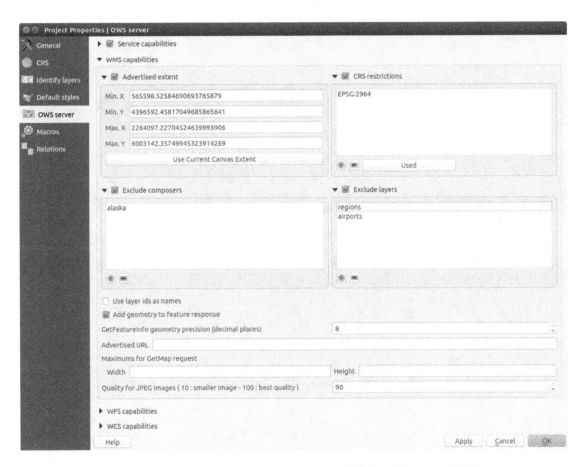

Figure 14.5: Definitions for a QGIS Server WMS/WFS/WCS project (KDE)

You can receive requested GetFeatureInfo as plain text, XML and GML. Default is XML, text or GML format depends the output format choosen for the GetFeatureInfo request.

If you wish, you can check ☑ *Add geometry to feature response*. This will include in the GetFeatureInfo response the geometries of the features in a text format. If you want QGIS Server to advertise specific request URLs in the WMS GetCapabilities response, enter the corresponding URL in the *Advertised URL* field. Furthermore, you can restrict the maximum size of the maps returned by the GetMap request by entering the maximum width and height into the respective fields under *Maximums for GetMap request*.

If one of your layers uses the Map Tip display (i.e. to show text using expressions) this will be listed inside the GetFeatureInfo output. If the layer uses a Value Map for one of his attributes, also this information will be shown in the GetFeatureInfo output.

QGIS support the following request for WMS service:

- GetCapabilities
- GetMap
- GetFeatureInfo
- GetLegendGraphic (SLD profile)
- DescribeLayer (SLD profile)
- GetStyles (custom QGIS profile)

WFS capabilities

In the *WFS capabilities* area, you can select the layers that you want to publish as WFS, and specify if they will allow the update, insert and delete operations. If you enter a URL in the *Advertised URL* field of the *WFS capabilities* section, QGIS Server will advertise this specific URL in the WFS GetCapabilities response.

QGIS support the following request for WFS service:

- GetCapabilities
- DescribeFeatureType
- GetFeature
- Transaction

WCS capabilities

In the *WCS capabilities* area, you can select the layers that you want to publish as WCS. If you enter a URL in the *Advertised URL* field of the *WCS capabilities* section, QGIS Server will advertise this specific URL in the WCS GetCapabilities response.

Now, save the session in a project file `alaska.qgs`. To provide the project as a WMS/WFS, we create a new folder `/usr/lib/cgi-bin/project` with admin privileges and add the project file `alaska.qgs` and a copy of the `qgis_mapserv.fcgi` file - that's all.

Now we test our project WMS, WFS and WCS. Add the WMS, WFS and WCS as described in *Loading WMS/WMTS Layers*, *WFS and WFS-T Client* and *WCS Client* to QGIS and load the data. The URL is:

`http://localhost/cgi-bin/project/qgis_mapserv.fcgi`

QGIS support the following request for WCS service:

- GetCapabilities
- DescribeCoverage
- GetCoverage

Fine tuning your OWS

For vector layers, the *Fields* menu of the *Layer → Properties* dialog allows you to define for each attribute if it will be published or not. By default, all the attributes are published by your WMS and WFS. If you want a specific attribute not to be published, uncheck the corresponding checkbox in the *WMS* or *WFS* column.

You can overlay watermarks over the maps produced by your WMS by adding text annotations or SVG annotations to the project file. See section Annotation Tools in *General Tools* for instructions on creating annotations. For annotations to be displayed as watermarks on the WMS output, the *Fixed map position* check box in the *Annotation text* dialog must be unchecked. This can be accessed by double clicking the annotation while one of the annotation tools is active. For SVG annotations, you will need either to set the project to save absolute paths (in the *General* menu of the *Project → Project Properties* dialog) or to manually modify the path to the SVG image in a way that it represents a valid relative path.

Extra parameters supported by the WMS GetMap request

In the WMS GetMap request, QGIS Server accepts a couple of extra parameters in addition to the standard parameters according to the OCG WMS 1.3.0 specification:

- **MAP** parameter: Similar to MapServer, the `MAP` parameter can be used to specify the path to the QGIS project file. You can specify an absolute path or a path relative to the location of the server executable (`qgis_mapserv.fcgi`). If not specified, QGIS Server searches for .qgs files in the directory where the server executable is located.

  Example:

  ```
  http://localhost/cgi-bin/qgis_mapserv.fcgi?\
      REQUEST=GetMap&MAP=/home/qgis/mymap.qgs&...
  ```

- **DPI** parameter: The `DPI` parameter can be used to specify the requested output resolution.

  Example:

  ```
  http://localhost/cgi-bin/qgis_mapserv.fcgi?REQUEST=GetMap&DPI=300&...
  ```

- **OPACITIES** parameter: Opacity can be set on layer or group level. Allowed values range from 0 (fully transparent) to 255 (fully opaque).

  Example:

  ```
  http://localhost/cgi-bin/qgis_mapserv.fcgi?\
      REQUEST=GetMap&LAYERS=mylayer1,mylayer2&OPACITIES=125,200&...
  ```

QGIS Server logging

To log requests send to server, set the following environment variables:

- **QGIS_SERVER_LOG_FILE**: Specify path and filename. Make sure that server has proper permissions for writing to file. File should be created automatically, just send some requests to server. If it's not there, check permissions.

- **QGIS_SERVER_LOG_LEVEL**: Specify desired log level. Available values are:

  - 0 INFO (log all requests),
  - 1 WARNING,
  - 2 CRITICAL (log just critical errors, suitable for production purposes).

  Example:

  ```
  SetEnv QGIS_SERVER_LOG_FILE /var/tmp/qgislog.txt
  SetEnv QGIS_SERVER_LOG_LEVEL 0
  ```

Note

- When using Fcgid module use FcgidInitialEnv instead of SetEnv!
- Server logging is enabled also if executable is compiled in release mode.

Environment variables

- **QGIS_OPTIONS_PATH**: The variable specifies path to directory with settings. It works the same ways as QGIS application –optionspath option. It is looking for settings file in <QGIS_OPTIONS_PATH>/QGIS/QGIS2.ini. For exaple, to set QGIS server on Apache to use /path/to/config/QGIS/QGIS2.ini settings file, add to Apache config:

```
SetEnv QGIS_OPTIONS_PATH "/path/to/config/"
```

.

## CHAPTER 15

Working with GPS Data

15.1 GPS Plugin

15.1.1 What is GPS?

GPS, the Global Positioning System, is a satellite-based system that allows anyone with a GPS receiver to find their exact position anywhere in the world. GPS is used as an aid in navigation, for example in airplanes, in boats and by hikers. The GPS receiver uses the signals from the satellites to calculate its latitude, longitude and (sometimes) elevation. Most receivers also have the capability to store locations (known as **waypoints**), sequences of locations that make up a planned **route** and a tracklog or **track** of the receiver's movement over time. Waypoints, routes and tracks are the three basic feature types in GPS data. QGIS displays waypoints in point layers, while routes and tracks are displayed in linestring layers.

15.1.2 Loading GPS data from a file

There are dozens of different file formats for storing GPS data. The format that QGIS uses is called GPX (GPS eXchange format), which is a standard interchange format that can contain any number of waypoints, routes and tracks in the same file.

To load a GPX file, you first need to load the plugin. *Plugins → 🕸 Plugin Manager...* opens the Plugin Manager Dialog. Activate the ☑ *GPS Tools* checkbox. When this plugin is loaded, a button with a small handheld GPS device will show up in the toolbar and in *Layer → Create Layer →* :

- ⊟ GPS Tools

- ▣ *Create new GPX Layer*

For working with GPS data, we provide an example GPX file available in the QGIS sample dataset: `qgis_sample_data/gps/national_monuments.gpx`. See section *Sample Data* for more information about the sample data.

1. Select *Vector → GPS → GPS Tools* or click the ⊟ GPS Tools icon in the toolbar and open the *Load GPX file* tab (see figure_GPS_1).

2. Browse to the folder `qgis_sample_data/gps/`, select the GPX file `national_monuments.gpx` and click **[Open]**.

Use the **[Browse...]** button to select the GPX file, then use the checkboxes to select the feature types you want to load from that GPX file. Each feature type will be loaded in a separate layer when you click **[OK]**. The file `national_monuments.gpx` only includes waypoints.

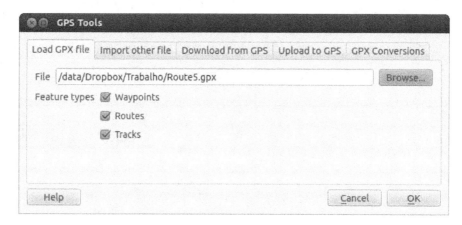

Figure 15.1: The *GPS Tools* dialog window 🐧

Note: GPS units allow you to store data in different coordinate systems. When downloading a GPX file (from your GPS unit or a web site) and then loading it in QGIS, be sure that the data stored in the GPX file uses WGS 84 (latitude/longitude). QGIS expects this, and it is the official GPX specification. See http://www.topografix.com/GPX/1/1/.

15.1.3 GPSBabel

Since QGIS uses GPX files, you need a way to convert other GPS file formats to GPX. This can be done for many formats using the free program GPSBabel, which is available at http://www.gpsbabel.org. This program can also transfer GPS data between your computer and a GPS device. QGIS uses GPSBabel to do these things, so it is recommended that you install it. However, if you just want to load GPS data from GPX files you will not need it. Version 1.2.3 of GPSBabel is known to work with QGIS, but you should be able to use later versions without any problems.

15.1.4 Importing GPS data

To import GPS data from a file that is not a GPX file, you use the tool *Import other file* in the GPS Tools dialog. Here, you select the file that you want to import (and the file type), which feature type you want to import from it, where you want to store the converted GPX file and what the name of the new layer should be. Note that not all GPS data formats will support all three feature types, so for many formats you will only be able to choose between one or two types.

15.1.5 Downloading GPS data from a device

QGIS can use GPSBabel to download data from a GPS device directly as new vector layers. For this we use the *Download from GPS* tab of the GPS Tools dialog (see Figure_GPS_2). Here, we select the type of GPS device, the port that it is connected to (or USB if your GPS supports this), the feature type that you want to download, the GPX file where the data should be stored, and the name of the new layer.

The device type you select in the GPS device menu determines how GPSBabel tries to communicate with your GPS device. If none of the available types work with your GPS device, you can create a new type (see section *Defining new device types*).

The port may be a file name or some other name that your operating system uses as a reference to the physical port in your computer that the GPS device is connected to. It may also be simply USB, for USB-enabled GPS units.

- 🐧 On Linux, this is something like `/dev/ttyS0` or `/dev/ttyS1`.

- 🪟 On Windows, it is `COM1` or `COM2`.

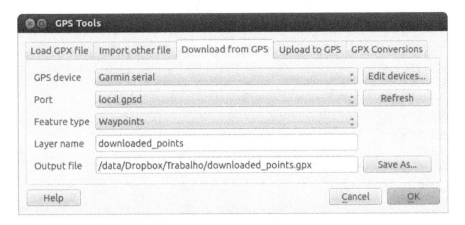

Figure 15.2: The download tool

When you click [**OK**], the data will be downloaded from the device and appear as a layer in QGIS.

15.1.6 Uploading GPS data to a device

You can also upload data directly from a vector layer in QGIS to a GPS device using the *Upload to GPS* tab of the GPS Tools dialog. To do this, you simply select the layer that you want to upload (which must be a GPX layer), your GPS device type, and the port (or USB) that it is connected to. Just as with the download tool, you can specify new device types if your device isn't in the list.

This tool is very useful in combination with the vector-editing capabilities of QGIS. It allows you to load a map, create waypoints and routes, and then upload them and use them on your GPS device.

15.1.7 Defining new device types

There are lots of different types of GPS devices. The QGIS developers can't test all of them, so if you have one that does not work with any of the device types listed in the *Download from GPS* and *Upload to GPS* tools, you can define your own device type for it. You do this by using the GPS device editor, which you start by clicking the [**Edit devices**] button in the download or the upload tab.

To define a new device, you simply click the [**New device**] button, enter a name, enter download and upload commands for your device, and click the [**Update device**] button. The name will be listed in the device menus in the upload and download windows – it can be any string. The download command is the command that is used to download data from the device to a GPX file. This will probably be a GPSBabel command, but you can use any other command line program that can create a GPX file. QGIS will replace the keywords %type, %in, and %out when it runs the command.

%type will be replaced by -w if you are downloading waypoints, -r if you are downloading routes and -t if you are downloading tracks. These are command-line options that tell GPSBabel which feature type to download.

%in will be replaced by the port name that you choose in the download window and %out will be replaced by the name you choose for the GPX file that the downloaded data should be stored in. So, if you create a device type with the download command gpsbabel %type -i garmin -o gpx %in %out (this is actually the download command for the predefined device type 'Garmin serial') and then use it to download waypoints from port /dev/ttyS0 to the file output.gpx, QGIS will replace the keywords and run the command gpsbabel -w -i garmin -o gpx /dev/ttyS0 output.gpx.

The upload command is the command that is used to upload data to the device. The same keywords are used, but %in is now replaced by the name of the GPX file for the layer that is being uploaded, and %out is replaced by the port name.

You can learn more about GPSBabel and its available command line options at http://www.gpsbabel.org.

Once you have created a new device type, it will appear in the device lists for the download and upload tools.

15.1.8 Download of points/tracks from GPS units

As described in previous sections QGIS uses GPSBabel to download points/tracks directly in the project. QGIS comes out of the box with a pre-defined profile to download from Garmin devices. Unfortunately there is a bug #6318 that does not allow create other profiles, so downloading directly in QGIS using the GPS Tools is at the moment limited to Garmin USB units.

Garmin GPSMAP 60cs

MS Windows

Install the Garmin USB drivers from http://www8.garmin.com/support/download_details.jsp?id=591

Connect the unit. Open GPS Tools and use `type=garmin serial` and `port=usb`: Fill the fields *Layer name* and *Output file*. Sometimes it seems to have problems saving in a certain folder, using something like `c:\temp` usually works.

Ubuntu/Mint GNU/Linux

It is first needed an issue about the permissions of the device, as described at https://wiki.openstreetmap.org/wiki/USB_Garmin_on_GNU/Linux. You can try to create a file `/etc/udev/rules.d/51-garmin.rules` containing this rule

```
ATTRS{idVendor}=="091e", ATTRS{idProduct}=="0003", MODE="666"
```

After that is necessary to be sure that the `garmin_gps` kernel module is not loaded

```
rmmod garmin_gps
```

and then you can use the GPS Tools. Unfortunately there seems to be a bug #7182 and usually QGIS freezes several times before the operation work fine.

BTGP-38KM datalogger (only Bluetooth)

MS Windows

The already referred bug does not allow to download the data from within QGIS, so it is needed to use GPSBabel from the command line or using its interface. The working command is

```
gpsbabel -t -i skytraq,baud=9600,initbaud=9600 -f COM9 -o gpx -F C:/GPX/aaa.gpx
```

Ubuntu/Mint GNU/Linux

Use same command (or settings if you use GPSBabel GUI) as in Windows. On Linux it maybe somehow common to get a message like

```
skytraq: Too many read errors on serial port
```

it is just a matter to turn off and on the datalogger and try again.

BlueMax GPS-4044 datalogger (both BT and USB)

MS Windows

Note: It needs to install its drivers before using it on Windows 7. See in the manufacturer site for the proper download.

Downloading with GPSBabel, both with USB and BT returns always an error like

```
gpsbabel -t -i mtk -f COM12 -o gpx -F C:/temp/test.gpx
mtk_logger: Can't create temporary file data.bin
Error running gpsbabel: Process exited unsuccessfully with code 1
```

Ubuntu/Mint GNU/Linux

With USB

After having connected the cable use the `dmesg` command to understand what port is being used, for example `/dev/ttyACM3`. Then as usual use GPSBabel from the CLI or GUI

```
gpsbabel -t -i mtk -f /dev/ttyACM3 -o gpx -F /home/user/bluemax.gpx
```

With Bluetooth

Use Blueman Device Manager to pair the device and make it available through a system port, then run GPSBabel

```
gpsbabel -t -i mtk -f /dev/rfcomm0 -o gpx -F /home/user/bluemax_bt.gpx
```

15.2 Live GPS tracking

To activate live GPS tracking in QGIS, you need to select *Settings → Panels* ☑ *GPS information*. You will get a new docked window on the left side of the canvas.

There are four possible screens in this GPS tracking window:

- ✏ GPS position coordinates and an interface for manually entering vertices and features

- ▮▮▮ GPS signal strength of satellite connections

- ✳ GPS polar screen showing number and polar position of satellites

- ✎ GPS options screen (see figure_gps_options)

With a plugged-in GPS receiver (has to be supported by your operating system), a simple click on **[Connect]** connects the GPS to QGIS. A second click (now on **[Disconnect]**) disconnects the GPS receiver from your computer. For GNU/Linux, gpsd support is integrated to support connection to most GPS receivers. Therefore, you first have to configure gpsd properly to connect QGIS to it.

> **Warning:** If you want to record your position to the canvas, you have to create a new vector layer first and switch it to editable status to be able to record your track.

15.2.1 Position and additional attributes

✏ If the GPS is receiving signals from satellites, you will see your position in latitude, longitude and altitude together with additional attributes.

15.2.2 GPS signal strength

▮▮▮ Here, you can see the signal strength of the satellites you are receiving signals from.

15.2.3 GPS polar window

✳ If you want to know where in the sky all the connected satellites are, you have to switch to the polar screen. You can also see the ID numbers of the satellites you are receiving signals from.

Figure 15.3: GPS tracking position and additional attributes

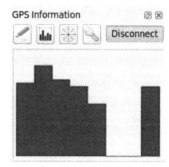

Figure 15.4: GPS tracking signal strength

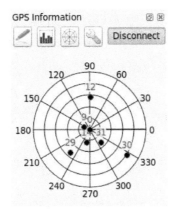

Figure 15.5: GPS tracking polar window

15.2.4 GPS options

In case of connection problems, you can switch between:

- Autodetect
- Internal
- Serial device
- gpsd (selecting the Host, Port and Device your GPS is connected to)

A click on **[Connect]** again initiates the connection to the GPS receiver.

You can activate *Automatically save added features* when you are in editing mode. Or you can activate *Automatically add points* to the map canvas with a certain width and color.

Activating *Cursor*, you can use a slider to shrink and grow the position cursor on the canvas.

Activating *Map centering* allows you to decide in which way the canvas will be updated. This includes 'always', 'when leaving', if your recorded coordinates start to move out of the canvas, or 'never', to keep map extent.

Finally, you can activate *Log file* and define a path and a file where log messages about the GPS tracking are logged.

If you want to set a feature manually, you have to go back to Position and click on **[Add Point]** or **[Add track point]**.

15.2.5 Connect to a Bluetooth GPS for live tracking

With QGIS you can connect a Bluetooth GPS for field data collection. To perform this task you need a GPS Bluetooth device and a Bluetooth receiver on your computer.

At first you must let your GPS device be recognized and paired to the computer. Turn on the GPS, go to the Bluetooth icon on your notification area and search for a New Device.

On the right side of the Device selection mask make sure that all devices are selected so your GPS unit will probably appear among those available. In the next step a serial connection service should be available, select it and click on **[Configure]** button.

Remember the number of the COM port assigned to the GPS connection as resulting by the Bluetooth properties.

After the GPS has been recognized, make the pairing for the connection. Usually the autorization code is 0000.

Figure 15.6: GPS tracking options window △

Now open *GPS information* panel and switch to ✎ GPS options screen. Select the COM port assigned to the GPS connection and click the **[Connect]**. After a while a cursor indicating your position should appear.

If QGIS can't receive GPS data, then you should restart your GPS device, wait 5-10 seconds then try to connect again. Usually this solution work. If you receive again a connection error make sure you don't have another Bluetooth receiver near you, paired with the same GPS unit.

15.2.6 Using GPSMAP 60cs

MS Windows

Easiest way to make it work is to use a middleware (freeware, not open) called GPSGate.

Launch the program, make it scan for GPS devices (works for both USB and BT ones) and then in QGIS just click **[Connect]** in the Live tracking panel using the ⊙ *Autodetect* mode.

Ubuntu/Mint GNU/Linux

As for Windows the easiest way is to use a server in the middle, in this case GPSD, so

```
sudo apt-get install gpsd
```

Then load the `garmin_gps` kernel module

```
sudo modprobe garmin_gps
```

And then connect the unit. Then check with `dmesg` the actual device being used bu the unit, for example `/dev/ttyUSB0`. Now you can launch gpsd

```
gpsd /dev/ttyUSB0
```

And finally connect with the QGIS live tracking tool.

15.2.7 Using BTGP-38KM datalogger (only Bluetooth)

Using GPSD (under Linux) or GPSGate (under Windows) is effortless.

15.2.8 Using BlueMax GPS-4044 datalogger (both BT and USB)

MS Windows

The live tracking works for both USB and BT modes, by using GPSGate or even without it, just use the ⊙ *Autodetect* mode, or point the tool the right port.

Ubuntu/Mint GNU/Linux

For USB

The live tracking works both with GPSD

```
gpsd /dev/ttyACM3
```

or without it, by connecting the QGIS live tracking tool directly to the device (for example `/dev/ttyACM3`).

For Bluetooth

The live tracking works both with GPSD

```
gpsd /dev/rfcomm0
```

or without it, by connecting the QGIS live tracking tool directly to the device (for example /dev/rfcomm0).

.

## CHAPTER 16

GRASS GIS Integration

The GRASS plugin provides access to GRASS GIS databases and functionalities (see GRASS-PROJECT in *Literature and Web References*). This includes visualizing GRASS raster and vector layers, digitizing vector layers, editing vector attributes, creating new vector layers and analysing GRASS 2-D and 3-D data with more than 400 GRASS modules.

In this section, we'll introduce the plugin functionalities and give some examples of managing and working with GRASS data. The following main features are provided with the toolbar menu when you start the GRASS plugin, as described in section sec_starting_grass:

- Open mapset
- New mapset
- Close mapset
- Add GRASS vector layer
- Add GRASS raster layer
- Create new GRASS vector
- Edit GRASS vector layer
- Open GRASS tools
- Display current GRASS region
- Edit current GRASS region

16.1 Starting the GRASS plugin

To use GRASS functionalities and/or visualize GRASS vector and raster layers in QGIS, you must select and load the GRASS plugin with the Plugin Manager. Therefore, go to the menu *Plugins* → *Manage Plugins*, select *GRASS* and click [**OK**].

You can now start loading raster and vector layers from an existing GRASS LOCATION (see section sec_load_grassdata). Or, you can create a new GRASS LOCATION with QGIS (see section *Creating a new GRASS LOCATION*) and import some raster and vector data (see section *Importing data into a GRASS LOCATION*) for further analysis with the GRASS Toolbox (see section *The GRASS Toolbox*).

16.2 Loading GRASS raster and vector layers

With the GRASS plugin, you can load vector or raster layers using the appropriate button on the toolbar menu. As an example, we will use the QGIS Alaska dataset (see section *Sample Data*). It includes a small sample GRASS LOCATION with three vector layers and one raster elevation map.

1. Create a new folder called `grassdata`, download the QGIS 'Alaska' dataset `qgis_sample_data.zip` from http://download.osgeo.org/qgis/data/ and unzip the file into `grassdata`.

2. Start QGIS.

3. If not already done in a previous QGIS session, load the GRASS plugin clicking on *Plugins* → ⚙ *Manage Plugins* and activate ☑ *GRASS*. The GRASS toolbar appears in the QGIS main window.

4. In the GRASS toolbar, click the ▣ Open mapset icon to bring up the *MAPSET* wizard.

5. For `Gisdbase`, browse and select or enter the path to the newly created folder `grassdata`.

6. You should now be able to select the *LOCATION* ⤵ `alaska` and the *MAPSET* ⤵ `demo`.

7. Click [**OK**]. Notice that some previously disabled tools in the GRASS toolbar are now enabled.

8. Click on ▣ Add GRASS raster layer, choose the map name `gtopo30` and click [**OK**]. The elevation layer will be visualized.

9. Click on ▣ Add GRASS vector layer, choose the map name `alaska` and click [**OK**]. The Alaska boundary vector layer will be overlayed on top of the `gtopo30` map. You can now adapt the layer properties as described in chapter *The Vector Properties Dialog* (e.g., change opacity, fill and outline color).

10. Also load the other two vector layers, `rivers` and `airports`, and adapt their properties.

As you see, it is very simple to load GRASS raster and vector layers in QGIS. See the following sections for editing GRASS data and creating a new LOCATION. More sample GRASS LOCATIONs are available at the GRASS website at http://grass.osgeo.org/download/sample-data/.

Tip: GRASS Data Loading

If you have problems loading data or QGIS terminates abnormally, check to make sure you have loaded the GRASS plugin properly as described in section *Starting the GRASS plugin*.

16.3 GRASS LOCATION and MAPSET

GRASS data are stored in a directory referred to as GISDBASE. This directory, often called `grassdata`, must be created before you start working with the GRASS plugin in QGIS. Within this directory, the GRASS GIS data are organized by projects stored in subdirectories called LOCATIONs. Each LOCATION is defined by its coordinate system, map projection and geographical boundaries. Each LOCATION can have several MAPSETs (subdirectories of the LOCATION) that are used to subdivide the project into different topics or subregions, or as workspaces for individual team members (see Neteler & Mitasova 2008 in *Literature and Web References*). In order to analyze vector and raster layers with GRASS modules, you must import them into a GRASS LOCATION. (This is not strictly true – with the GRASS modules `r.external` and `v.external` you can create read-only links to external GDAL/OGR-supported datasets without importing them. But because this is not the usual way for beginners to work with GRASS, this functionality will not be described here.)

16.3.1 Creating a new GRASS LOCATION

As an example, here is how the sample GRASS LOCATION `alaska`, which is projected in Albers Equal Area projection with unit feet was created for the QGIS sample dataset. This sample GRASS LOCATION `alaska`

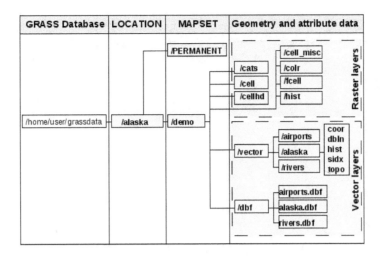

Figure 16.1: GRASS data in the alaska LOCATION

will be used for all examples and exercises in the following GRASS-related sections. It is useful to download and install the dataset on your computer (see *Sample Data*).

1. Start QGIS and make sure the GRASS plugin is loaded.

2. Visualize the `alaska.shp` shapefile (see section *Loading a Shapefile*) from the QGIS Alaska dataset (see *Sample Data*).

3. In the GRASS toolbar, click on the ▨ New mapset icon to bring up the *MAPSET* wizard.

4. Select an existing GRASS database (GISDBASE) folder `grassdata`, or create one for the new `LOCATION` using a file manager on your computer. Then click [**Next**].

5. We can use this wizard to create a new `MAPSET` within an existing `LOCATION` (see section *Adding a new MAPSET*) or to create a new `LOCATION` altogether. Select ⦿ *Create new location* (see figure_grass_location_2).

6. Enter a name for the `LOCATION` – we used 'alaska' – and click [**Next**].

7. Define the projection by clicking on the radio button ⦿ *Projection* to enable the projection list.

8. We are using Albers Equal Area Alaska (feet) projection. Since we happen to know that it is represented by the EPSG ID 2964, we enter it in the search box. (Note: If you want to repeat this process for another `LOCATION` and projection and haven't memorized the EPSG ID, click on the ⊕ CRS Status icon in the lower right-hand corner of the status bar (see section *Working with Projections*)).

9. In *Filter*, insert 2964 to select the projection.

10. Click [**Next**].

11. To define the default region, we have to enter the `LOCATION` bounds in the north, south, east, and west directions. Here, we simply click on the button [**Set current |qg| extent**], to apply the extent of the loaded layer `alaska.shp` as the GRASS default region extent.

12. Click [**Next**].

13. We also need to define a `MAPSET` within our new `LOCATION` (this is necessary when creating a new `LOCATION`). You can name it whatever you like - we used 'demo'. GRASS automatically creates a special `MAPSET` called `PERMANENT`, designed to store the core data for the project, its default spatial extent and coordinate system definitions (see Neteler & Mitasova 2008 in *Literature and Web References*).

14. Check out the summary to make sure it's correct and click [**Finish**].

15. The new `LOCATION`, 'alaska', and two `MAPSET`s, 'demo' and 'PERMANENT', are created. The currently opened working set is 'demo', as you defined.

16. Notice that some of the tools in the GRASS toolbar that were disabled are now enabled.

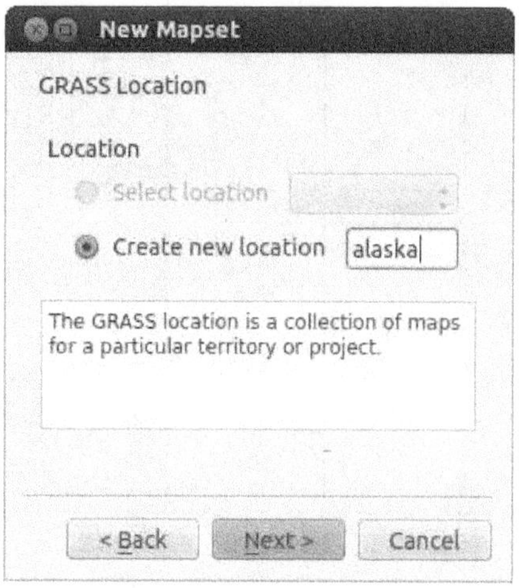

Figure 16.2: Creating a new GRASS LOCATION or a new MAPSET in QGIS

If that seemed like a lot of steps, it's really not all that bad and a very quick way to create a LOCATION. The LOCATION 'alaska' is now ready for data import (see section *Importing data into a GRASS LOCATION*). You can also use the already-existing vector and raster data in the sample GRASS LOCATION 'alaska', included in the QGIS 'Alaska' dataset *Sample Data*, and move on to section *The GRASS vector data model*.

16.3.2 Adding a new MAPSET

A user has write access only to a GRASS MAPSET he or she created. This means that besides access to your own MAPSET, you can read maps in other users' MAPSETs (and they can read yours), but you can modify or remove only the maps in your own MAPSET.

All MAPSETs include a WIND file that stores the current boundary coordinate values and the currently selected raster resolution (see Neteler & Mitasova 2008 in *Literature and Web References*, and section *The GRASS region tool*).

1. Start QGIS and make sure the GRASS plugin is loaded.

2. In the GRASS toolbar, click on the [⊞] New mapset icon to bring up the *MAPSET* wizard.

3. Select the GRASS database (GISDBASE) folder grassdata with the LOCATION 'alaska', where we want to add a further MAPSET called 'test'.

4. Click [**Next**].

5. We can use this wizard to create a new MAPSET within an existing LOCATION or to create a new LOCATION altogether. Click on the radio button [●] *Select location* (see figure_grass_location_2) and click [**Next**].

6. Enter the name text for the new MAPSET. Below in the wizard, you see a list of existing MAPSETs and corresponding owners.

7. Click [**Next**], check out the summary to make sure it's all correct and click [**Finish**].

16.4 Importing data into a GRASS LOCATION

This section gives an example of how to import raster and vector data into the 'alaska' GRASS LOCATION provided by the QGIS 'Alaska' dataset. Therefore, we use the landcover raster map landcover.img and the vector GML file lakes.gml from the QGIS 'Alaska' dataset (see *Sample Data*).

1. Start QGIS and make sure the GRASS plugin is loaded.

2. In the GRASS toolbar, click the ▦ Open MAPSET icon to bring up the *MAPSET* wizard.

3. Select as GRASS database the folder `grassdata` in the QGIS Alaska dataset, as LOCATION 'alaska', as MAPSET 'demo' and click [**OK**].

4. Now click the ▦ Open GRASS tools icon. The GRASS Toolbox (see section *The GRASS Toolbox*) dialog appears.

5. To import the raster map `landcover.img`, click the module `r.in.gdal` in the *Modules Tree* tab. This GRASS module allows you to import GDAL-supported raster files into a GRASS LOCATION. The module dialog for `r.in.gdal` appears.

6. Browse to the folder `raster` in the QGIS 'Alaska' dataset and select the file `landcover.img`.

7. As raster output name, define `landcover_grass` and click [**Run**]. In the *Output* tab, you see the currently running GRASS command `r.in.gdal -o input=/path/to/landcover.img output=landcover_grass`.

8. When it says **Succesfully finished**, click [**View output**]. The `landcover_grass` raster layer is now imported into GRASS and will be visualized in the QGIS canvas.

9. To import the vector GML file `lakes.gml`, click the module `v.in.ogr` in the *Modules Tree* tab. This GRASS module allows you to import OGR-supported vector files into a GRASS LOCATION. The module dialog for `v.in.ogr` appears.

10. Browse to the folder `gml` in the QGIS 'Alaska' dataset and select the file `lakes.gml` as OGR file.

11. As vector output name, define `lakes_grass` and click [**Run**]. You don't have to care about the other options in this example. In the *Output* tab you see the currently running GRASS command `v.in.ogr -o dsn=/path/to/lakes.gml output=lakes\_grass`.

12. When it says **Succesfully finished**, click [**View output**]. The `lakes_grass` vector layer is now imported into GRASS and will be visualized in the QGIS canvas.

16.5 The GRASS vector data model

It is important to understand the GRASS vector data model prior to digitizing.

In general, GRASS uses a topological vector model.

This means that areas are not represented as closed polygons, but by one or more boundaries. A boundary between two adjacent areas is digitized only once, and it is shared by both areas. Boundaries must be connected and closed without gaps. An area is identified (and labeled) by the **centroid** of the area.

Besides boundaries and centroids, a vector map can also contain points and lines. All these geometry elements can be mixed in one vector and will be represented in different so-called 'layers' inside one GRASS vector map. So in GRASS, a layer is not a vector or raster map but a level inside a vector layer. This is important to distinguish carefully. (Although it is possible to mix geometry elements, it is unusual and, even in GRASS, only used in special cases such as vector network analysis. Normally, you should prefer to store different geometry elements in different layers.)

It is possible to store several 'layers' in one vector dataset. For example, fields, forests and lakes can be stored in one vector. An adjacent forest and lake can share the same boundary, but they have separate attribute tables. It is also possible to attach attributes to boundaries. An example might be the case where the boundary between a lake and a forest is a road, so it can have a different attribute table.

The 'layer' of the feature is defined by the 'layer' inside GRASS. 'Layer' is the number which defines if there is more than one layer inside the dataset (e.g., if the geometry is forest or lake). For now, it can be only a number. In the future, GRASS will also support names as fields in the user interface.

Attributes can be stored inside the GRASS LOCATION as dBase or SQLite3 or in external database tables, for example, PostgreSQL, MySQL, Oracle, etc.

Attributes in database tables are linked to geometry elements using a 'category' value.

'Category' (key, ID) is an integer attached to geometry primitives, and it is used as the link to one key column in the database table.

Tip: Learning the GRASS Vector Model

The best way to learn the GRASS vector model and its capabilities is to download one of the many GRASS tutorials where the vector model is described more deeply. See http://grass.osgeo.org/documentation/manuals/ for more information, books and tutorials in several languages.

16.6 Creating a new GRASS vector layer

To create a new GRASS vector layer with the GRASS plugin, click the toolbar icon. Enter a name in the text box, and you can start digitizing point, line or polygon geometries following the procedure described in section *Digitizing and editing a GRASS vector layer*.

In GRASS, it is possible to organize all sorts of geometry types (point, line and area) in one layer, because GRASS uses a topological vector model, so you don't need to select the geometry type when creating a new GRASS vector. This is different from shapefile creation with QGIS, because shapefiles use the Simple Feature vector model (see section *Creating new Vector layers*).

Tip: Creating an attribute table for a new GRASS vector layer

If you want to assign attributes to your digitized geometry features, make sure to create an attribute table with columns before you start digitizing (see figure_grass_digitizing_5).

16.7 Digitizing and editing a GRASS vector layer

The digitizing tools for GRASS vector layers are accessed using the icon on the toolbar. Make sure you have loaded a GRASS vector and it is the selected layer in the legend before clicking on the edit tool. Figure figure_grass_digitizing_2 shows the GRASS edit dialog that is displayed when you click on the edit tool. The tools and settings are discussed in the following sections.

Tip: Digitizing polygons in GRASS

If you want to create a polygon in GRASS, you first digitize the boundary of the polygon, setting the mode to 'No category'. Then you add a centroid (label point) into the closed boundary, setting the mode to 'Next not used'. The reason for this is that a topological vector model links the attribute information of a polygon always to the centroid and not to the boundary.

Toolbar

In figure_grass_digitizing_1, you see the GRASS digitizing toolbar icons provided by the GRASS plugin. Table table_grass_digitizing_1 explains the available functionalities.

Figure 16.3: GRASS Digitizing Toolbar

Icon	Tool	Purpose
° °⊡	New Point	Digitize new point
⌐⊡	New Line	Digitize new line
⌐⊡	New Boundary	Digitize new boundary (finish by selecting new tool)
⌐⊡	New Centroid	Digitize new centroid (label existing area)
⌐⊡	Move vertex	Move one vertex of existing line or boundary and identify new position
⌐⊡	Add vertex	Add a new vertex to existing line
⌐⊠	Delete vertex	Delete vertex from existing line (confirm selected vertex by another click)
⌐⊡	Move element	Move selected boundary, line, point or centroid and click on new position
⌐	Split line	Split an existing line into two parts
⌐⊠	Delete element	Delete existing boundary, line, point or centroid (confirm selected element by another click)
📄	Edit attributes	Edit attributes of selected element (note that one element can represent more features, see above)
⏻	Close	Close session and save current status (rebuilds topology afterwards)

Table GRASS Digitizing 1: GRASS Digitizing Tools

Category Tab

The *Category* tab allows you to define the way in which the category values will be assigned to a new geometry element.

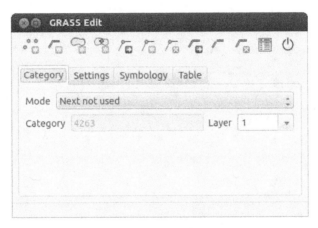

Figure 16.4: GRASS Digitizing Category Tab

- **Mode**: The category value that will be applied to new geometry elements.
  - Next not used - Apply next not yet used category value to geometry element.
  - Manual entry - Manually define the category value for the geometry element in the 'Category' entry field.
  - No category - Do not apply a category value to the geometry element. This is used, for instance, for area boundaries, because the category values are connected via the centroid.
- **Category** - The number (ID) that is attached to each digitized geometry element. It is used to connect each geometry element with its attributes.

16.7. Digitizing and editing a GRASS vector layer

- **Field (layer)** - Each geometry element can be connected with several attribute tables using different GRASS geometry layers. The default layer number is 1.

Tip: Creating an additional GRASS 'layer' with |qg|

If you would like to add more layers to your dataset, just add a new number in the 'Field (layer)' entry box and press return. In the Table tab, you can create your new table connected to your new layer.

Settings Tab

The *Settings* tab allows you to set the snapping in screen pixels. The threshold defines at what distance new points or line ends are snapped to existing nodes. This helps to prevent gaps or dangles between boundaries. The default is set to 10 pixels.

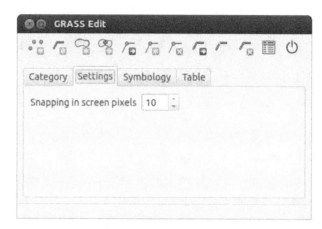

Figure 16.5: GRASS Digitizing Settings Tab

Symbology Tab

The *Symbology* tab allows you to view and set symbology and color settings for various geometry types and their topological status (e.g., closed / opened boundary).

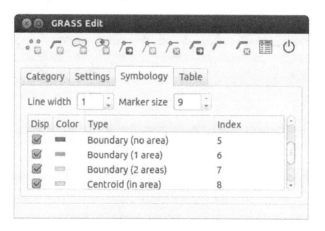

Figure 16.6: GRASS Digitizing Symbology Tab

Table Tab

The *Table* tab provides information about the database table for a given 'layer'. Here, you can add new columns to an existing attribute table, or create a new database table for a new GRASS vector layer (see section *Creating a new GRASS vector layer*).

Tip: GRASS Edit Permissions

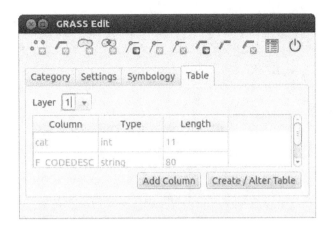

Figure 16.7: GRASS Digitizing Table Tab

You must be the owner of the GRASS MAPSET you want to edit. It is impossible to edit data layers in a MAPSET that is not yours, even if you have write permission.

16.8 The GRASS region tool

The region definition (setting a spatial working window) in GRASS is important for working with raster layers. Vector analysis is by default not limited to any defined region definitions. But all newly created rasters will have the spatial extension and resolution of the currently defined GRASS region, regardless of their original extension and resolution. The current GRASS region is stored in the $LOCATION/$MAPSET/WIND file, and it defines north, south, east and west bounds, number of columns and rows, horizontal and vertical spatial resolution.

It is possible to switch on and off the visualization of the GRASS region in the QGIS canvas using the Display current GRASS region button.

With the Edit current GRASS region icon, you can open a dialog to change the current region and the symbology of the GRASS region rectangle in the QGIS canvas. Type in the new region bounds and resolution, and click [**OK**]. The dialog also allows you to select a new region interactively with your mouse on the QGIS canvas. Therefore, click with the left mouse button in the QGIS canvas, open a rectangle, close it using the left mouse button again and click [**OK**].

The GRASS module g.region provides a lot more parameters to define an appropriate region extent and resolution for your raster analysis. You can use these parameters with the GRASS Toolbox, described in section *The GRASS Toolbox*.

16.9 The GRASS Toolbox

The Open GRASS Tools box provides GRASS module functionalities to work with data inside a selected GRASS LOCATION and MAPSET. To use the GRASS Toolbox you need to open a LOCATION and MAPSET that you have write permission for (usually granted, if you created the MAPSET). This is necessary, because new raster or vector layers created during analysis need to be written to the currently selected LOCATION and MAPSET.

16.9.1 Working with GRASS modules

The GRASS shell inside the GRASS Toolbox provides access to almost all (more than 300) GRASS modules in a command line interface. To offer a more user-friendly working environment, about 200 of the available GRASS modules and functionalities are also provided by graphical dialogs within the GRASS plugin Toolbox.

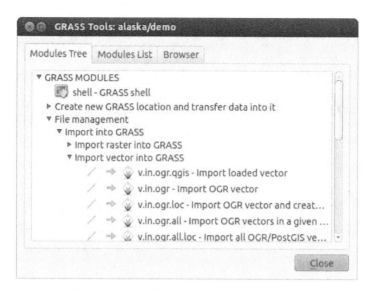

Figure 16.8: GRASS Toolbox and Module Tree 🐧

A complete list of GRASS modules available in the graphical Toolbox in QGIS version 2.8 is available in the GRASS wiki at http://grass.osgeo.org/wiki/GRASS-QGIS_relevant_module_list.

It is also possible to customize the GRASS Toolbox content. This procedure is described in section *Customizing the GRASS Toolbox*.

As shown in figure_grass_toolbox_1, you can look for the appropriate GRASS module using the thematically grouped *Modules Tree* or the searchable *Modules List* tab.

By clicking on a graphical module icon, a new tab will be added to the Toolbox dialog, providing three new sub-tabs: *Options*, *Output* and *Manual*.

Options

The *Options* tab provides a simplified module dialog where you can usually select a raster or vector layer visualized in the QGIS canvas and enter further module-specific parameters to run the module.

The provided module parameters are often not complete to keep the dialog clear. If you want to use further module parameters and flags, you need to start the GRASS shell and run the module in the command line.

A new feature since QGIS 1.8 is the support for a *Show Advanced Options* button below the simplified module dialog in the *Options* tab. At the moment, it is only added to the module v.in.ascii as an example of use, but it will probably be part of more or all modules in the GRASS Toolbox in future versions of QGIS. This allows you to use the complete GRASS module options without the need to switch to the GRASS shell.

Output

The *Output* tab provides information about the output status of the module. When you click the **[Run]** button, the module switches to the *Output* tab and you see information about the analysis process. If all works well, you will finally see a Successfully finished message.

Manual

The *Manual* tab shows the HTML help page of the GRASS module. You can use it to check further module parameters and flags or to get a deeper knowledge about the purpose of the module. At the end of each module manual page, you see further links to the Main Help index, the Thematic index and the Full index. These links provide the same information as the module g.manual.

Tip: Display results immediately

If you want to display your calculation results immediately in your map canvas, you can use the 'View Output' button at the bottom of the module tab.

Figure 16.9: GRASS Toolbox Module Options 🐧

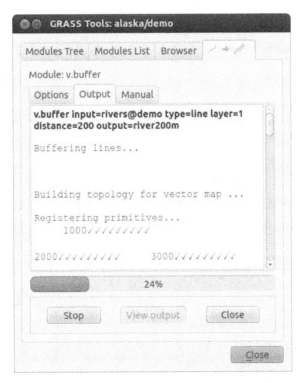

Figure 16.10: GRASS Toolbox Module Output 🐧

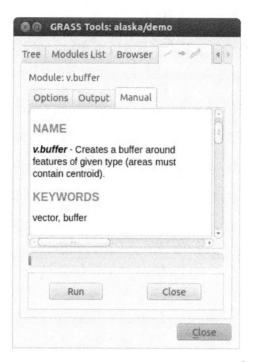

Figure 16.11: GRASS Toolbox Module Manual △

16.9.2 GRASS module examples

The following examples will demonstrate the power of some of the GRASS modules.

Creating contour lines

The first example creates a vector contour map from an elevation raster (DEM). Here, it is assumed that you have the Alaska LOCATION set up as explained in section *Importing data into a GRASS LOCATION*.

- First, open the location by clicking the 📚 Open mapset button and choosing the Alaska location.

- Now load the gtopo30 elevation raster by clicking 📇 Add GRASS raster layer and selecting the gtopo30 raster from the demo location.

- Now open the Toolbox with the 🔧 Open GRASS tools button.

- In the list of tool categories, double-click *Raster → Surface Management → Generate vector contour lines*.

- Now a single click on the tool **r.contour** will open the tool dialog as explained above (see *Working with GRASS modules*). The gtopo30 raster should appear as the *Name of input raster*.

- Type into the *Increment between Contour levels* 1,00 ◇ the value 100. (This will create contour lines at intervals of 100 meters.)

- Type into the *Name for output vector map* the name ctour_100.

- Click **[Run]** to start the process. Wait for several moments until the message Successfully finished appears in the output window. Then click **[View Output]** and **[Close]**.

Since this is a large region, it will take a while to display. After it finishes rendering, you can open the layer properties window to change the line color so that the contours appear clearly over the elevation raster, as in *The Vector Properties Dialog*.

Next, zoom in to a small, mountainous area in the center of Alaska. Zooming in close, you will notice that the contours have sharp corners. GRASS offers the **v.generalize** tool to slightly alter vector maps while keeping their overall shape. The tool uses several different algorithms with different purposes. Some of the algorithms (i.e., Douglas Peuker and Vertex Reduction) simplify the line by removing some of the vertices. The resulting vector will load faster. This process is useful when you have a highly detailed vector, but you are creating a very small-scale map, so the detail is unnecessary.

Tip: The simplify tool

Note that the QGIS fTools plugin has a *Simplify geometries* → tool that works just like the GRASS **v.generalize** Douglas-Peuker algorithm.

However, the purpose of this example is different. The contour lines created by `r.contour` have sharp angles that should be smoothed. Among the **v.generalize** algorithms, there is Chaiken's, which does just that (also Hermite splines). Be aware that these algorithms can **add** additional vertices to the vector, causing it to load even more slowly.

- Open the GRASS Toolbox and double-click the categories *Vector* → *Develop map* → *Generalization*, then click on the **v.generalize** module to open its options window.

- Check that the 'ctour_100' vector appears as the *Name of input vector*.

- From the list of algorithms, choose Chaiken's. Leave all other options at their default, and scroll down to the last row to enter in the field *Name for output vector map* 'ctour_100_smooth', and click **[Run]**.

- The process takes several moments. Once `Successfully finished` appears in the output windows, click **[View output]** and then **[Close]**.

- You may change the color of the vector to display it clearly on the raster background and to contrast with the original contour lines. You will notice that the new contour lines have smoother corners than the original while staying faithful to the original overall shape.

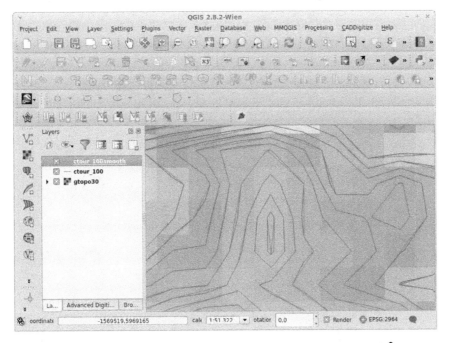

Figure 16.12: GRASS module v.generalize to smooth a vector map

---

Tip: Other uses for r.contour

The procedure described above can be used in other equivalent situations. If you have a raster map of precipitation data, for example, then the same method will be used to create a vector map of isohyetal (constant rainfall) lines.

Creating a Hillshade 3-D effect

Several methods are used to display elevation layers and give a 3-D effect to maps. The use of contour lines, as shown above, is one popular method often chosen to produce topographic maps. Another way to display a 3-D effect is by hillshading. The hillshade effect is created from a DEM (elevation) raster by first calculating the slope and aspect of each cell, then simulating the sun's position in the sky and giving a reflectance value to each cell. Thus, you get sun-facing slopes lighted; the slopes facing away from the sun (in shadow) are darkened.

- Begin this example by loading the gtopo30 elevation raster. Start the GRASS Toolbox, and under the Raster category, double-click to open *Spatial analysis → Terrain analysis*.

- Then click **r.shaded.relief** to open the module.

- Change the *azimuth angle* 1.00 ◇ 270 to 315.

- Enter gtopo30_shade for the new hillshade raster, and click **[Run]**.

- When the process completes, add the hillshade raster to the map. You should see it displayed in grayscale.

- To view both the hillshading and the colors of the gtopo30 together, move the hillshade map below the gtopo30 map in the table of contents, then open the *Properties* window of gtopo30, switch to the *Transparency* tab and set its transparency level to about 25%.

You should now have the gtopo30 elevation with its colormap and transparency setting displayed **above** the grayscale hillshade map. In order to see the visual effects of the hillshading, turn off the gtopo30_shade map, then turn it back on.

Using the GRASS shell

The GRASS plugin in QGIS is designed for users who are new to GRASS and not familiar with all the modules and options. As such, some modules in the Toolbox do not show all the options available, and some modules do not appear at all. The GRASS shell (or console) gives the user access to those additional GRASS modules that do not appear in the Toolbox tree, and also to some additional options to the modules that are in the Toolbox with the simplest default parameters. This example demonstrates the use of an additional option in the **r.shaded.relief** module that was shown above.

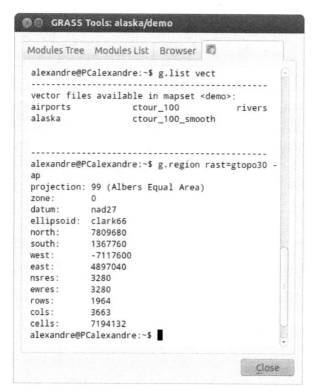

Figure 16.13: The GRASS shell, r.shaded.relief module △

The module **r.shaded.relief** can take a parameter `zmult`, which multiplies the elevation values relative to the X-Y coordinate units so that the hillshade effect is even more pronounced.

- Load the `gtopo30` elevation raster as above, then start the GRASS Toolbox and click on the GRASS shell. In the shell window, type the command `r.shaded.relief map=gtopo30 shade=gtopo30_shade2 azimuth=315 zmult=3` and press [**Enter**].

- After the process finishes, shift to the *Browse* tab and double-click on the new `gtopo30_shade2` raster to display it in QGIS.

- As explained above, move the shaded relief raster below the `gtopo30` raster in the table of contents, then check the transparency of the colored `gtopo30` layer. You should see that the 3-D effect stands out more strongly compared with the first shaded relief map.

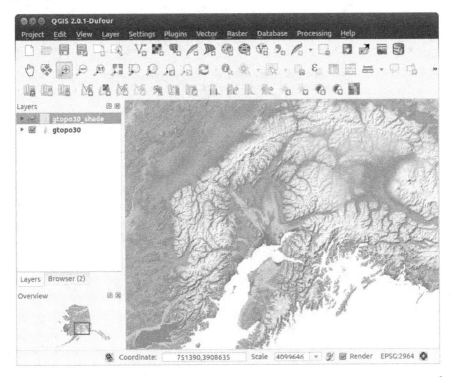

Figure 16.14: Displaying shaded relief created with the GRASS module r.shaded.relief 🐧

Raster statistics in a vector map

The next example shows how a GRASS module can aggregate raster data and add columns of statistics for each polygon in a vector map.

- Again using the Alaska data, refer to *Importing data into a GRASS LOCATION* to import the trees shapefile from the `shapefiles` directory into GRASS.

- Now an intermediate step is required: centroids must be added to the imported trees map to make it a complete GRASS area vector (including both boundaries and centroids).

- From the Toolbox, choose *Vector → Manage features*, and open the module **v.centroids**.

- Enter as the *output vector map* 'forest_areas' and run the module.

- Now load the `forest_areas` vector and display the types of forests - deciduous, evergreen, mixed - in different colors: In the layer *Properties* window, *Symbology* tab, choose from *Legend type* [...▼] 'Unique value' and set the *Classification field* to 'VEGDESC'. (Refer to the explanation of the symbology tab in *Style Menu* of the vector section.)

- Next, reopen the GRASS Toolbox and open *Vector → Vector update* by other maps.

- Click on the **v.rast.stats** module. Enter `gtopo30` and `forest_areas`.

- Only one additional parameter is needed: Enter *column prefix* `elev`, and click **[Run]**. This is a computationally heavy operation, which will run for a long time (probably up to two hours).

- Finally, open the `forest_areas` attribute table, and verify that several new columns have been added, including `elev_min`, `elev_max`, `elev_mean`, etc., for each forest polygon.

16.9.3 Working with the GRASS LOCATION browser

Another useful feature inside the GRASS Toolbox is the GRASS `LOCATION` browser. In figure_grass_module_7, you can see the current working `LOCATION` with its `MAPSET`s.

In the left browser windows, you can browse through all `MAPSET`s inside the current `LOCATION`. The right browser window shows some meta-information for selected raster or vector layers (e.g., resolution, bounding box, data source, connected attribute table for vector data, and a command history).

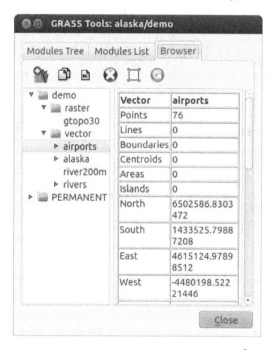

Figure 16.15: GRASS LOCATION browser ⬠

The toolbar inside the *Browser* tab offers the following tools to manage the selected `LOCATION`:

- *Add selected map to canvas*

- *Copy selected map*

- *Rename selected map*

- *Delete selected map*

- *Set current region to selected map*

- *Refresh browser window*

The *Rename selected map* and *Delete selected map* only work with maps inside your currently selected `MAPSET`. All other tools also work with raster and vector layers in another `MAPSET`.

16.9.4 Customizing the GRASS Toolbox

Nearly all GRASS modules can be added to the GRASS Toolbox. An XML interface is provided to parse the pretty simple XML files that configure the modules' appearance and parameters inside the Toolbox.

A sample XML file for generating the module v.buffer (v.buffer.qgm) looks like this:

```
<?xml version="1.0" encoding="UTF-8"?>
<!DOCTYPE qgisgrassmodule SYSTEM "http://mrcc.com/qgisgrassmodule.dtd">

<qgisgrassmodule label="Vector buffer" module="v.buffer">
        <option key="input" typeoption="type" layeroption="layer" />
        <option key="buffer"/>
        <option key="output" />
</qgisgrassmodule>
```

The parser reads this definition and creates a new tab inside the Toolbox when you select the module. A more detailed description for adding new modules, changing a module's group, etc., can be found on the QGIS wiki at http://hub.qgis.org/projects/quantum-gis/wiki/Adding_New_Tools_to_the_GRASS_Toolbox.

QGIS processing framework

17.1 Introduction

This chapter introduces the QGIS processing framework, a geoprocessing environment that can be used to call native and third-party algorithms from QGIS, making your spatial analysis tasks more productive and easy to accomplish.

In the following sections, we will review how to use the graphical elements of this framework and make the most out of each one of them.

There are four basic elements in the framework GUI, which are used to run algorithms for different purposes. Choosing one tool or another will depend on the kind of analysis that is to be performed and the particular characteristics of each user and project. All of them (except for the batch processing interface, which is called from the toolbox, as we will see) can be accessed from the *Processing* menu item. (You will see more than four entries. The remaining ones are not used to execute algorithms and will be explained later in this chapter.)

- The toolbox. The main element of the GUI, it is used to execute a single algorithm or run a batch process based on that algorithm.

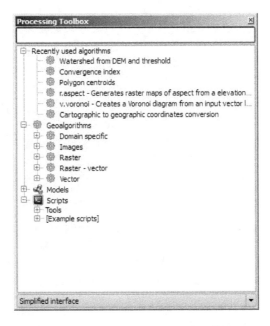

Figure 17.1: Processing Toolbox

- The graphical modeler. Several algorithms can be combined graphically using the modeler to define a workflow, creating a single process that involves several subprocesses.

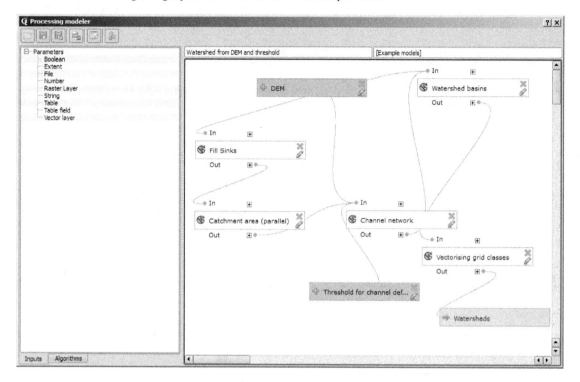

Figure 17.2: Processing Modeler

- The history manager. All actions performed using any of the aforementioned elements are stored in a history file and can be later easily reproduced using the history manager.

- The batch processing interface. This interface allows you to execute batch processes and automate the execution of a single algorithm on multiple datasets.

In the following sections, we will review each one of these elements in detail.

.

17.2 The toolbox

The *Toolbox* is the main element of the processing GUI, and the one that you are more likely to use in your daily work. It shows the list of all available algorithms grouped in different blocks, and it is the access point to run them, whether as a single process or as a batch process involving several executions of the same algorithm on different sets of inputs.

The toolbox contains all the available algorithms, divided into predefined groups. All these groups are found under a single tree entry named *Geoalgorithms*.

Additionally, two more entries are found, namely *Models* and *Scripts*. These include user-created algorithms, and they allow you to define your own workflows and processing tasks. We will devote a full section to them a bit later.

In the upper part of the toolbox, you will find a text box. To reduce the number of algorithms shown in the toolbox and make it easier to find the one you need, you can enter any word or phrase on the text box. Notice that, as you type, the number of algorithms in the toolbox is reduced to just those that contain the text you have entered in their names.

In the lower part, you will find a box that allows you to switch between the simplified algorithm list (the one explained above) and the advanced list. If you change to the advanced mode, the toolbox will look like this:

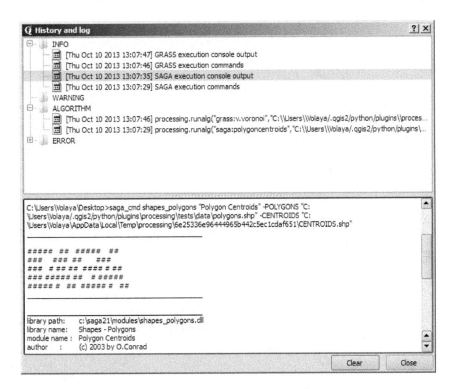

Figure 17.3: Processing History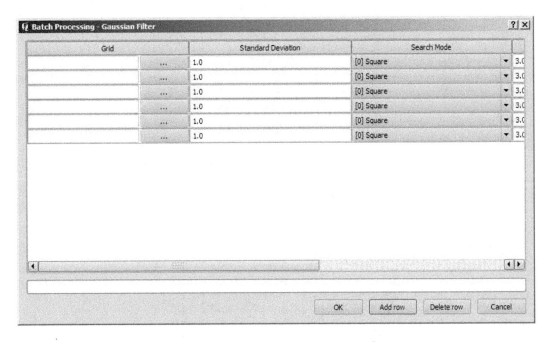

Figure 17.4: Batch Processing interface

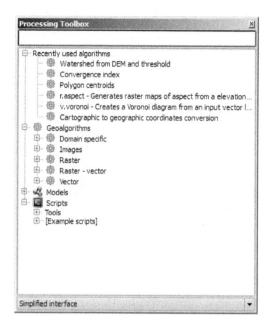

Figure 17.5: Processing Toolbox

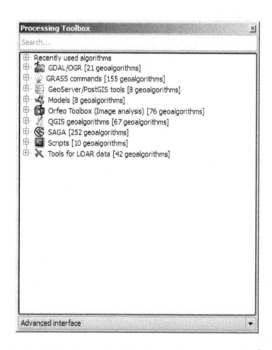

Figure 17.6: Processing Toolbox (advanced mode)

In the advanced view, each group represents a so-called 'algorithm provider', which is a set of algorithms coming from the same source, for instance, from a third-party application with geoprocessing capabilities. Some of these groups represent algorithms from third-party applications like SAGA, GRASS or R, while others contain algorithms directly coded as part of the processing plugin, not relying on any additional software.

This view is recommended to those users who have a certain knowledge of the applications that are backing the algorithms, since they will be shown with their original names and groups.

Also, some additional algorithms are available only in the advanced view, such as LiDAR tools and scripts based on the R statistical computing software, among others. Independent QGIS plugins that add new algorithms to the toolbox will only be shown in the advanced view.

In particular, the simplified view contains algorithms from the following providers:

- GRASS
- SAGA
- OTB
- Native QGIS algorithms

In the case of running QGIS under Windows, these algorithms are fully-functional in a fresh installation of QGIS, and they can be run without requiring any additional installation. Also, running them requires no prior knowledge of the external applications they use, making them more accesible for first-time users.

If you want to use an algorithm not provided by any of the above providers, switch to the advanced mode by selecting the corresponding option at the bottom of the toolbox.

To execute an algorithm, just double-click on its name in the toolbox.

17.2.1 The algorithm dialog

Once you double-click on the name of the algorithm that you want to execute, a dialog similar to that in the figure below is shown (in this case, the dialog corresponds to the SAGA 'Convergence index' algorithm).

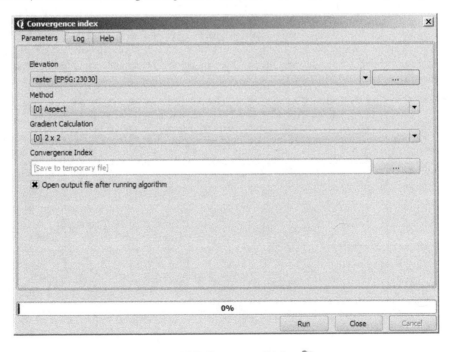

Figure 17.7: Parameters Dialog

This dialog is used to set the input values that the algorithm needs to be executed. It shows a table where input values and configuration parameters are to be set. It of course has a different content, depending on the requirements of the algorithm to be executed, and is created automatically based on those requirements. On the left side, the name of the parameter is shown. On the right side, the value of the parameter can be set.

Although the number and type of parameters depend on the characteristics of the algorithm, the structure is similar for all of them. The parameters found in the table can be of one of the following types.

- A raster layer, to select from a list of all such layers available (currently opened) in QGIS. The selector contains as well a button on its right-hand side, to let you select filenames that represent layers currently not loaded in QGIS.

- A vector layer, to select from a list of all vector layers available in QGIS. Layers not loaded in QGIS can be selected as well, as in the case of raster layers, but only if the algorithm does not require a table field selected from the attributes table of the layer. In that case, only opened layers can be selected, since they need to be open so as to retrieve the list of field names available.

You will see a button by each vector layer selector, as shown in the figure below.

Figure 17.8: Vector iterator button

If the algorithm contains several of them, you will be able to toggle just one of them. If the button corresponding to a vector input is toggled, the algorithm will be executed iteratively on each one of its features, instead of just once for the whole layer, producing as many outputs as times the algorithm is executed. This allows for automating the process when all features in a layer have to be processed separately.

- A table, to select from a list of all available in QGIS. Non-spatial tables are loaded into QGIS like vector layers, and in fact they are treated as such by the program. Currently, the list of available tables that you will see when executing an algorithm that needs one of them is restricted to tables coming from files in dBase (.dbf) or Comma-Separated Values (.csv) formats.

- An option, to choose from a selection list of possible options.

- A numerical value, to be introduced in a text box. You will find a button by its side. Clicking on it, you will see a dialog that allows you to enter a mathematical expression, so you can use it as a handy calculator. Some useful variables related to data loaded into QGIS can be added to your expression, so you can select a value derived from any of these variables, such as the cell size of a layer or the northernmost coordinate of another one.

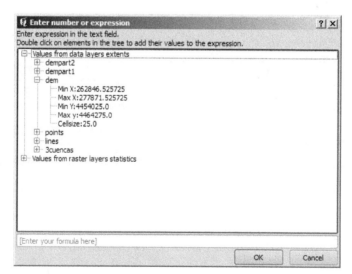

Figure 17.9: Number Selector

- A range, with min and max values to be introduced in two text boxes.

- A text string, to be introduced in a text box.

- A field, to choose from the attributes table of a vector layer or a single table selected in another parameter.

- A coordinate reference system. You can type the EPSG code directly in the text box, or select it from the CRS selection dialog that appears when you click on the button on the right-hand side.

- An extent, to be entered by four numbers representing its xmin, xmax, ymin, ymax limits. Clicking on the button on the right-hand side of the value selector, a pop-up menu will appear, giving you two options: to select the value from a layer or the current canvas extent, or to define it by dragging directly onto the map canvas.

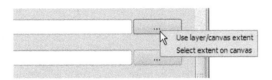

Figure 17.10: Extent selector

If you select the first option, you will see a window like the next one.

Figure 17.11: Extent List

If you select the second one, the parameters window will hide itself, so you can click and drag onto the canvas. Once you have defined the selected rectangle, the dialog will reappear, containing the values in the extent text box.

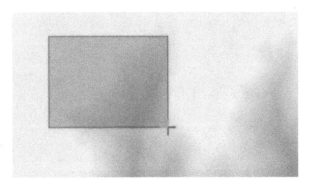

Figure 17.12: Extent Drag

- A list of elements (whether raster layers, vector layers or tables), to select from the list of such layers available in QGIS. To make the selection, click on the small button on the left side of the corresponding row to see a dialog like the following one.

- A small table to be edited by the user. These are used to define parameters like lookup tables or convolution kernels, among others.

  Click on the button on the right side to see the table and edit its values.

Figure 17.13: Multiple Selection

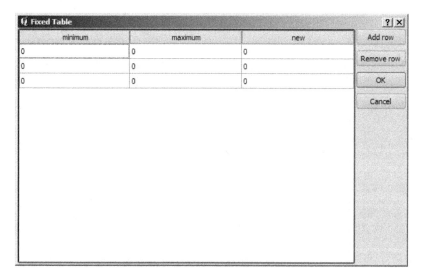

Figure 17.14: Fixed Table

Depending on the algorithm, the number of rows can be modified or not by using the buttons on the right side of the window.

You will find a **[Help]** tab in the the parameters dialog. If a help file is available, it will be shown, giving you more information about the algorithm and detailed descriptions of what each parameter does. Unfortunately, most algorithms lack good documentation, but if you feel like contributing to the project, this would be a good place to start.

A note on projections

Algorithms run from the processing framework — this is also true of most of the external applications whose algorithms are exposed through it. Do not perform any reprojection on input layers and assume that all of them are already in a common coordinate system and ready to be analized. Whenever you use more than one layer as input to an algorithm, whether vector or raster, it is up to you to make sure that they are all in the same coordinate system.

Note that, due to QGIS's on-the-fly reprojecting capabilities, although two layers might seem to overlap and match, that might not be true if their original coordinates are used without reprojecting them onto a common coordinate system. That reprojection should be done manually, and then the resulting files should be used as input to the algorithm. Also, note that the reprojection process can be performed with the algorithms that are available in the processing framework itself.

By default, the parameters dialog will show a description of the CRS of each layer along with its name, making it easy to select layers that share the same CRS to be used as input layers. If you do not want to see this additional information, you can disable this functionality in the processing configuration dialog, unchecking the *Show CRS* option.

If you try to execute an algorithm using as input two or more layers with unmatching CRSs, a warning dialog will be shown.

You still can execute the algorithm, but be aware that in most cases that will produce wrong results, such as empty layers due to input layers not overlapping.

17.2.2 Data objects generated by algorithms

Data objects generated by an algorithm can be of any of the following types:

- A raster layer
- A vector layer
- A table
- An HTML file (used for text and graphical outputs)

These are all saved to disk, and the parameters table will contain a text box corresponding to each one of these outputs, where you can type the output channel to use for saving it. An output channel contains the information needed to save the resulting object somewhere. In the most usual case, you will save it to a file, but the architecture allows for any other way of storing it. For instance, a vector layer can be stored in a database or even uploaded to a remote server using a WFS-T service. Although solutions like these are not yet implemented, the processing framework is prepared to handle them, and we expect to add new kinds of output channels in a near feature.

To select an output channel, just click on the button on the right side of the text box. That will open a save file dialog, where you can select the desired file path. Supported file extensions are shown in the file format selector of the dialog, depending on the kind of output and the algorithm.

The format of the output is defined by the filename extension. The supported formats depend on what is supported by the algorithm itself. To select a format, just select the corresponding file extension (or add it, if you are directly typing the file path instead). If the extension of the file path you entered does not match any of the supported formats, a default extension (usually `.dbf`' for tables, `.tif` for raster layers and `.shp` for vector layers) will be appended to the file path, and the file format corresponding to that extension will be used to save the layer or table.

If you do not enter any filename, the result will be saved as a temporary file in the corresponding default file format, and it will be deleted once you exit QGIS (take care with that, in case you save your project and it contains temporary layers).

You can set a default folder for output data objects. Go to the configuration dialog (you can open it from the *Processing* menu), and in the *General* group, you will find a parameter named *Output folder*. This output folder is used as the default path in case you type just a filename with no path (i.e., `myfile.shp`) when executing an algorithm.

When running an algorithm that uses a vector layer in iterative mode, the entered file path is used as the base path for all generated files, which are named using the base name and appending a number representing the index of the iteration. The file extension (and format) is used for all such generated files.

Apart from raster layers and tables, algorithms also generate graphics and text as HTML files. These results are shown at the end of the algorithm execution in a new dialog. This dialog will keep the results produced by any algorithm during the current session, and can be shown at any time by selecting *Processing → Results viewer* from the QGIS main menu.

Some external applications might have files (with no particular extension restrictions) as output, but they do not belong to any of the categories above. Those output files will not be processed by QGIS (opened or included into the current QGIS project), since most of the time they correspond to file formats or elements not supported by QGIS. This is, for instance, the case with LAS files used for LiDAR data. The files get created, but you won't see anything new in your QGIS working session.

For all the other types of output, you will find a checkbox that you can use to tell the algorithm whether to load the file once it is generated by the algorithm or not. By default, all files are opened.

Optional outputs are not supported. That is, all outputs are created. However, you can uncheck the corresponding checkbox if you are not interested in a given output, which essentially makes it behave like an optional output (in other words, the layer is created anyway, but if you leave the text box empty, it will be saved to a temporary file and deleted once you exit QGIS).

17.2.3 Configuring the processing framework

As has been mentioned, the configuration menu gives access to a new dialog where you can configure how algorithms work. Configuration parameters are structured in separate blocks that you can select on the left-hand side of the dialog.

Along with the aforementioned *Output folder* entry, the *General* block contains parameters for setting the default rendering style for output layers (that is, layers generated by using algorithms from any of the framework GUI components). Just create the style you want using QGIS, save it to a file, and then enter the path to that file in the settings so the algorithms can use it. Whenever a layer is loaded by SEXTANTE and added to the QGIS canvas, it will be rendered with that style.

Rendering styles can be configured individually for each algorithm and each one of its outputs. Just right-click on the name of the algorithm in the toolbox and select *Edit rendering styles*. You will see a dialog like the one shown next.

Select the style file (`.qml`) that you want for each output and press **[OK]**.

Other configuration parameters in the *General* group are listed below:

- *Use filename as layer name*. The name of each resulting layer created by an algorithm is defined by the algorithm itself. In some cases, a fixed name might be used, meaning that the same output name will be used, no matter which input layer is used. In other cases, the name might depend on the name of the input layer or some of the parameters used to run the algorithm. If this checkbox is checked, the name will be taken from the output filename instead. Notice that, if the output is saved to a temporary file, the filename of this temporary file is usually a long and meaningless one intended to avoid collision with other already existing filenames.

- *Use only selected features*. If this option is selected, whenever a vector layer is used as input for an algorithm, only its selected features will be used. If the layer has no selected features, all features will be used.

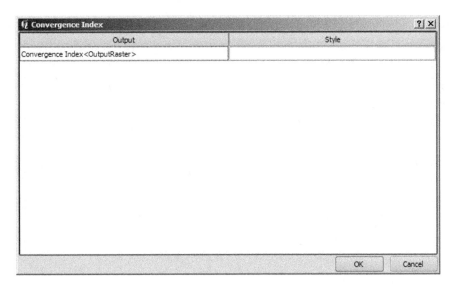

Figure 17.15: Rendering Styles

- *Pre-execution script file* and *Post-execution script file.* These parameters refer to scripts written using the processing scripting functionality, and are explained in the section covering scripting and the console.

Apart from the *General* block in the settings dialog, you will also find a block for algorithm providers. Each entry in this block contains an *Activate* item that you can use to make algorithms appear or not in the toolbox. Also, some algorithm providers have their own configuration items, which we will explain later when covering particular algorithm providers.

17.3 The graphical modeler

The *graphical modeler* allows you to create complex models using a simple and easy-to-use interface. When working with a GIS, most analysis operations are not isolated, but rather part of a chain of operations instead. Using the graphical modeler, that chain of processes can be wrapped into a single process, so it is as easy and convenient to execute as a single process later on a different set of inputs. No matter how many steps and different algorithms it involves, a model is executed as a single algorithm, thus saving time and effort, especially for larger models.

The modeler can be opened from the processing menu.

The modeler has a working canvas where the structure of the model and the workflow it represents are shown. On the left part of the window, a panel with two tabs can be used to add new elements to the model.

Creating a model involves two steps:

1. *Definition of necessary inputs.* These inputs will be added to the parameters window, so the user can set their values when executing the model. The model itself is an algorithm, so the parameters window is generated automatically as it happens with all the algorithms available in the processing framework.

2. *Definition of the workflow.* Using the input data of the model, the workflow is defined by adding algorithms and selecting how they use those inputs or the outputs generated by other algorithms already in the model.

17.3.1 Definition of inputs

The first step to create a model is to define the inputs it needs. The following elements are found in the *Inputs* tab on the left side of the modeler window:

- Raster layer

Figure 17.16: Modeler

- Vector layer

- String

- Table field

- Table

- Extent

- Number

- Boolean

- File

Double-clicking on any of these elements, a dialog is shown to define its characteristics. Depending on the parameter itself, the dialog may contain just one basic element (the description, which is what the user will see when executing the model) or more of them. For instance, when adding a numerical value, as can be seen in the next figure, apart from the description of the parameter, you have to set a default value and a range of valid values.

For each added input, a new element is added to the modeler canvas.

You can also add inputs by dragging the input type from the list and dropping it in the modeler canvas, in the position where you want to place it.

17.3.2 Definition of the workflow

Once the inputs have been defined, it is time to define the algorithms to apply on them. Algorithms can be found in the *Algorithms* tab, grouped much in the same way as they are in the toolbox.

The appearance of the toolbox has two modes here as well: simplified and advanced. However, there is no element to switch between views in the modeler, so you have to do it in the toolbox. The mode that is selected in the toolbox

Figure 17.17: Model Parameters

Figure 17.18: Model Parameters

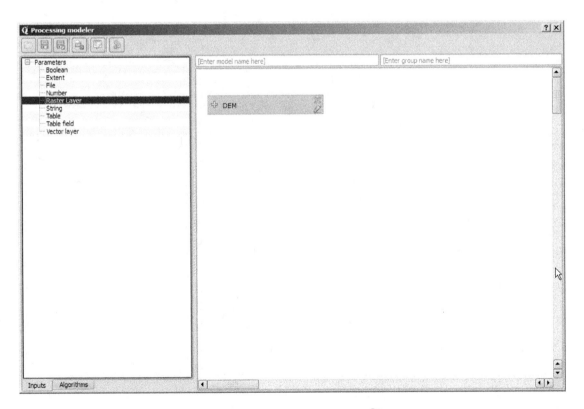

Figure 17.19: Model Parameters

is the one that will be used for the list of algorithms in the modeler.

To add an algorithm to a model, double-click on its name or drag and drop it, just like it was done when adding inputs. An execution dialog will appear, with a content similar to the one found in the execution panel that is shown when executing the algorithm from the toolbox. The one shown next corresponds to the SAGA 'Convergence index' algorithm, the same example we saw in the section dedicated to the toolbox.

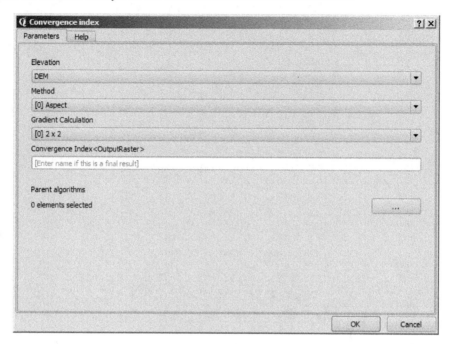

Figure 17.20: Model Parameters

As you can see, some differences exist. Instead of the file output box that was used to set the file path for output layers and tables, a simple text box is used here. If the layer generated by the algorithm is just a temporary result that will be used as the input of another algorithm and should not be kept as a final result, just do not edit that text box. Typing anything in it means that the result is final and the text that you supply will be the description for the output, which will be the output the user will see when executing the model.

Selecting the value of each parameter is also a bit different, since there are important differences between the context of the modeler and that of the toolbox. Let's see how to introduce the values for each type of parameter.

- Layers (raster and vector) and tables. These are selected from a list, but in this case, the possible values are not the layers or tables currently loaded in QGIS, but the list of model inputs of the corresponding type, or other layers or tables generated by algorithms already added to the model.

- Numerical values. Literal values can be introduced directly in the text box. But this text box is also a list that can be used to select any of the numerical value inputs of the model. In this case, the parameter will take the value introduced by the user when executing the model.

- String. As in the case of numerical values, literal strings can be typed, or an input string can be selected.

- Table field. The fields of the parent table or layer cannot be known at design time, since they depend on the selection of the user each time the model is executed. To set the value for this parameter, type the name of a field directly in the text box, or use the list to select a table field input already added to the model. The validity of the selected field will be checked at run time.

In all cases, you will find an additional parameter named *Parent algorithms* that is not available when calling the algorithm from the toolbox. This parameter allows you to define the order in which algorithms are executed by explicitly defining one algorithm as a parent of the current one, which will force the parent algorithm to be executed before the current one.

When you use the output of a previous algorithm as the input of your algorithm, that implicitly sets the previous algorithm as parent of the current one (and places the corresponding arrow in the modeler canvas). However, in some cases an algorithm might depend on another one even if it does not use any output object from it (for instance, an algorithm that executes an SQL sentence on a PostGIS database and another one that imports a layer into that same database). In that case, just select the previous algorithm in the *Parent algorithms* parameter and the two steps will be executed in the correct order.

Once all the parameters have been assigned valid values, click on **[OK]** and the algorithm will be added to the canvas. It will be linked to all the other elements in the canvas, whether algorithms or inputs, that provide objects that are used as inputs for that algorithm.

Elements can be dragged to a different position within the canvas, to change the way the module structure is displayed and make it more clear and intuitive. Links between elements are updated automatically. You can zoom in and out by using the mouse wheel.

You can run your algorithm anytime by clicking on the **[Run]** button. However, in order to use the algorithm from the toolbox, it has to be saved and the modeler dialog closed, to allow the toolbox to refresh its contents.

17.3.3 Saving and loading models

Use the **[Save]** button to save the current model and the **[Open]** button to open any model previously saved. Models are saved with the .model extension. If the model has been previously saved from the modeler window, you will not be prompted for a filename. Since there is already a file associated with that model, the same file will be used for any subsequent saves.

Before saving a model, you have to enter a name and a group for it, using the text boxes in the upper part of the window.

Models saved on the models folder (the default folder when you are prompted for a filename to save the model) will appear in the toolbox in the corresponding branch. When the toolbox is invoked, it searches the models folder for files with the .model extension and loads the models they contain. Since a model is itself an algorithm, it can be added to the toolbox just like any other algorithm.

The models folder can be set from the processing configuration dialog, under the *Modeler* group.

Models loaded from the models folder appear not only in the toolbox, but also in the algorithms tree in the *Algorithms* tab of the modeler window. That means that you can incorporate a model as a part of a bigger model, just as you add any other algorithm.

In some cases, a model might not be loaded because not all the algorithms included in its workflow are available. If you have used a given algorithm as part of your model, it should be available (that is, it should appear in the toolbox) in order to load that model. Deactivating an algorithm provider in the processing configuration window renders all the algorithms in that provider unusable by the modeler, which might cause problems when loading models. Keep that in mind when you have trouble loading or executing models.

17.3.4 Editing a model

You can edit the model you are currently creating, redefining the workflow and the relationships between the algorithms and inputs that define the model itself.

If you right-click on an algorithm in the canvas representing the model, you will see a context menu like the one shown next:

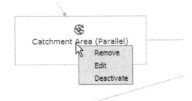

Figure 17.21: Modeler Right Click

Selecting the *Remove* option will cause the selected algorithm to be removed. An algorithm can be removed only if there are no other algorithms depending on it. That is, if no output from the algorithm is used in a different one as input. If you try to remove an algorithm that has others depending on it, a warning message like the one you can see below will be shown:

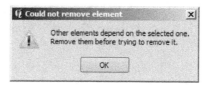

Figure 17.22: Cannot Delete Algorithm

Selecting the *Edit* option or simply double-clicking on the algorithm icon will show the parameters dialog of the algorithm, so you can change the inputs and parameter values. Not all input elements available in the model will appear in this case as available inputs. Layers or values generated at a more advanced step in the workflow defined by the model will not be available if they cause circular dependencies.

Select the new values and then click on the [**OK**] button as usual. The connections between the model elements will change accordingly in the modeler canvas.

17.3.5 Editing model help files and meta-information

You can document your models from the modeler itself. Just click on the [**Edit model help**] button and a dialog like the one shown next will appear.

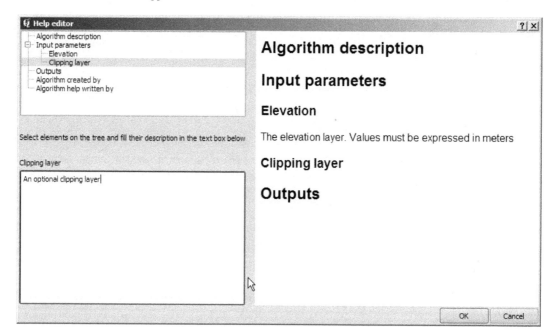

Figure 17.23: Help Edition

On the right-hand side, you will see a simple HTML page, created using the description of the input parameters and outputs of the algorithm, along with some additional items like a general description of the model or its author. The first time you open the help editor, all these descriptions are empty, but you can edit them using the elements on the left-hand side of the dialog. Select an element on the upper part and then write its description in the text box below.

Model help is saved in a file in the same folder as the model itself. You do not have to worry about saving it, since it is done automatically.

17.3.6 About available algorithms

You might notice that some algorithms that can be be executed from the toolbox do not appear in the list of available algorithms when you are designing a model. To be included in a model, an algorithm must have a correct semantic, so as to be properly linked to others in the workflow. If an algorithm does not have such a well-defined semantic (for instance, if the number of output layers cannot be known in advance), then it is not possible to use it within a model, and thus, it does not appear in the list of algorithms that you can find in the modeler dialog.

Additionally, you will see some algorithms in the modeler that are not found in the toolbox. These algorithms are meant to be used exclusively as part of a model, and they are of no interest in a different context. The 'Calculator' algorithm is an example of that. It is just a simple arithmetic calculator that you can use to modify numerical values (entered by the user or generated by some other algorithm). This tool is really useful within a model, but outside of that context, it doesn't make too much sense.

.

17.4 The batch processing interface

17.4.1 Introduction

All algorithms (including models) can be executed as a batch process. That is, they can be executed using not just a single set of inputs, but several of them, executing the algorithm as many times as needed. This is useful when processing large amounts of data, since it is not necessary to launch the algorithm many times from the toolbox.

To execute an algorithm as a batch process, right-click on its name in the toolbox and select the *Execute as batch process* option in the pop-up menu that will appear.

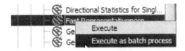

Figure 17.24: Batch Processing Right Click

17.4.2 The parameters table

Executing a batch process is similar to performing a single execution of an algorithm. Parameter values have to be defined, but in this case we need not just a single value for each parameter, but a set of them instead, one for each time the algorithm has to be executed. Values are introduced using a table like the one shown next.

Each line of this table represents a single execution of the algorithm, and each cell contains the value of one of the parameters. It is similar to the parameters dialog that you see when executing an algorithm from the toolbox, but with a different arrangement.

By default, the table contains just two rows. You can add or remove rows using the buttons on the lower part of the window.

Once the size of the table has been set, it has to be filled with the desired values.

17.4.3 Filling the parameters table

For most parameters, setting the value is trivial. Just type the value or select it from the list of available options, depending on the parameter type.

The main differences are found for parameters representing layers or tables, and for output file paths. Regarding input layers and tables, when an algorithm is executed as part of a batch process, those input data objects are taken directly from files, and not from the set of them already opened in QGIS. For this reason, any algorithm can be

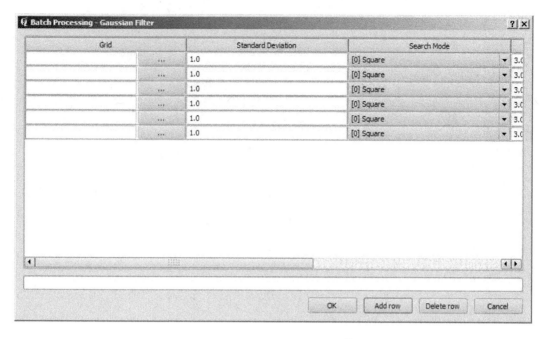

Figure 17.25: Batch Processing

executed as a batch process, even if no data objects at all are opened and the algorithm cannot be run from the toolbox.

Filenames for input data objects are introduced directly typing or, more conveniently, clicking on the ⌐.⌐ button on the right hand of the cell, which shows a typical file chooser dialog. Multiple files can be selected at once. If the input parameter represents a single data object and several files are selected, each one of them will be put in a separate row, adding new ones if needed. If the parameter represents a multiple input, all the selected files will be added to a single cell, separated by semicolons (;).

Output data objects are always saved to a file and, unlike when executing an algorithm from the toolbox, saving to a temporary file is not permitted. You can type the name directly or use the file chooser dialog that appears when clicking on the accompanying button.

Once you select the file, a new dialog is shown to allow for autocompletion of other cells in the same column (same parameter).

Figure 17.26: Batch Processing Save

If the default value ('Do not autocomplete') is selected, it will just put the selected filename in the selected cell from the parameters table. If any of the other options is selected, all the cells below the selected one will be automatically filled based on a defined criteria. This way, it is much easier to fill the table, and the batch process can be defined with less effort.

Automatic filling can be done by simply adding correlative numbers to the selected file path, or by appending the value of another field at the same row. This is particularly useful for naming output data objects according to input ones.

Figure 17.27: Batch Processing File Path

17.4.4 Executing the batch process

To execute the batch process once you have introduced all the necessary values, just click on **[OK]**. Progress of the global batch task will be shown in the progress bar in the lower part of the dialog.

17.5 Using processing algorithms from the console

The console allows advanced users to increase their productivity and perform complex operations that cannot be performed using any of the other GUI elements of the processing framework. Models involving several algorithms can be defined using the command-line interface, and additional operations such as loops and conditional sentences can be added to create more flexible and powerful workflows.

There is not a proccesing console in QGIS, but all processing commands are available instead from the QGIS built-in Python console. That means that you can incorporate those commands into your console work and connect processing algorithms to all the other features (including methods from the QGIS API) available from there.

The code that you can execute from the Python console, even if it does not call any specific processing method, can be converted into a new algorithm that you can later call from the toolbox, the graphical modeler or any other component, just like you do with any other algorithm. In fact, some algorithms that you can find in the toolbox are simple scripts.

In this section, we will see how to use processing algorithms from the QGIS Python console, and also how to write algorithms using Python.

17.5.1 Calling algorithms from the Python console

The first thing you have to do is to import the processing functions with the following line:

```
>>> import processing
```

Now, there is basically just one (interesting) thing you can do with that from the console: execute an algorithm. That is done using the `runalg()` method, which takes the name of the algorithm to execute as its first parameter, and then a variable number of additional parameters depending on the requirements of the algorithm. So the first thing you need to know is the name of the algorithm to execute. That is not the name you see in the toolbox, but rather a unique command–line name. To find the right name for your algorithm, you can use the `algslist()` method. Type the following line in your console:

```
>>> processing.alglist()
```

You will see something like this.

```
Accumulated Cost (Anisotropic)----------------->saga:accumulatedcost(anisotropic)
Accumulated Cost (Isotropic)------------------->saga:accumulatedcost(isotropic)
Add Coordinates to points---------------------->saga:addcoordinatestopoints
Add Grid Values to Points---------------------->saga:addgridvaluestopoints
Add Grid Values to Shapes---------------------->saga:addgridvaluestoshapes
Add Polygon Attributes to Points--------------->saga:addpolygonattributestopoints
```

```
Aggregate----------------------------------->saga:aggregate
Aggregate Point Observations----------------->saga:aggregatepointobservations
Aggregation Index---------------------------->saga:aggregationindex
Analytical Hierarchy Process----------------->saga:analyticalhierarchyprocess
Analytical Hillshading----------------------->saga:analyticalhillshading
Average With Mask 1-------------------------->saga:averagewithmask1
Average With Mask 2-------------------------->saga:averagewithmask2
Average With Thereshold 1-------------------->saga:averagewiththereshold1
Average With Thereshold 2-------------------->saga:averagewiththereshold2
Average With Thereshold 3-------------------->saga:averagewiththereshold3
B-Spline Approximation----------------------->saga:b-splineapproximation
...
```

That's a list of all the available algorithms, alphabetically ordered, along with their corresponding command-line names.

You can use a string as a parameter for this method. Instead of returning the full list of algorithms, it will only display those that include that string. If, for instance, you are looking for an algorithm to calculate slope from a DEM, type `alglist("slope")` to get the following result:

```
DTM Filter (slope-based)--------------------->saga:dtmfilter(slope-based)
Downslope Distance Gradient------------------>saga:downslopedistancegradient
Relative Heights and Slope Positions--------->saga:relativeheightsandslopepositions
Slope Length--------------------------------->saga:slopelength
Slope, Aspect, Curvature--------------------->saga:slopeaspectcurvature
Upslope Area--------------------------------->saga:upslopearea
Vegetation Index[slope based]---------------->saga:vegetationindex[slopebased]
```

This result might change depending on the algorithms you have available.

It is easier now to find the algorithm you are looking for and its command-line name, in this case `saga:slopeaspectcurvature`.

Once you know the command-line name of the algorithm, the next thing to do is to determine the right syntax to execute it. That means knowing which parameters are needed and the order in which they have to be passed when calling the `runalg()` method. There is a method to describe an algorithm in detail, which can be used to get a list of the parameters that an algorithm requires and the outputs that it will generate. To get this information, you can use the `alghelp(name_of_the_algorithm)` method. Use the command-line name of the algorithm, not the full descriptive name.

Calling the method with `saga:slopeaspectcurvature` as parameter, you get the following description:

```
>>> processing.alghelp("saga:slopeaspectcurvature")
ALGORITHM: Slope, Aspect, Curvature
    ELEVATION <ParameterRaster>
    METHOD <ParameterSelection>
    SLOPE <OutputRaster>
    ASPECT <OutputRaster>
    CURV <OutputRaster>
    HCURV <OutputRaster>
    VCURV <OutputRaster>
```

Now you have everything you need to run any algorithm. As we have already mentioned, there is only one single command to execute algorithms: `runalg()`. Its syntax is as follows:

```
>>> processing.runalg(name_of_the_algorithm, param1, param2, ..., paramN,
        Output1, Output2, ..., OutputN)
```

The list of parameters and outputs to add depends on the algorithm you want to run, and is exactly the list that the `alghelp()` method gives you, in the same order as shown.

Depending on the type of parameter, values are introduced differently. The next list gives a quick review of how to introduce values for each type of input parameter:

- Raster Layer, Vector Layer or Table. Simply use a string with the name that identifies the data object to use (the name it has in the QGIS Table of Contents) or a filename (if the corresponding layer is not opened, it will be opened but not added to the map canvas). If you have an instance of a QGIS object representing the layer, you can also pass it as parameter. If the input is optional and you do not want to use any data object, use None.

- Selection. If an algorithm has a selection parameter, the value of that parameter should be entered using an integer value. To know the available options, you can use the algoptions() command, as shown in the following example:

```
>>> processing.algoptions("saga:slopeaspectcurvature")
METHOD(Method)
	0 -  [0] Maximum Slope (Travis et al. 1975)
	1 -  [1] Maximum Triangle Slope (Tarboton 1997)
	2 -  [2] Least Squares Fitted Plane (Horn 1981, Costa-Cabral & Burgess 1996)
	3 -  [3] Fit 2.Degree Polynom (Bauer, Rohdenburg, Bork 1985)
	4 -  [4] Fit 2.Degree Polynom (Heerdegen & Beran 1982)
	5 -  [5] Fit 2.Degree Polynom (Zevenbergen & Thorne 1987)
	6 -  [6] Fit 3.Degree Polynom (Haralick 1983)
```

In this case, the algorithm has one such parameter, with seven options. Notice that ordering is zero-based.

- Multiple input. The value is a string with input descriptors separated by semicolons (;). As in the case of single layers or tables, each input descriptor can be the data object name, or its file path.

- Table Field from XXX. Use a string with the name of the field to use. This parameter is case-sensitive.

- Fixed Table. Type the list of all table values separated by commas (,) and enclosed between quotes ("). Values start on the upper row and go from left to right. You can also use a 2-D array of values representing the table.

- CRS. Enter the EPSG code number of the desired CRS.

- Extent. You must use a string with xmin, xmax, ymin and ymax values separated by commas (,).

Boolean, file, string and numerical parameters do not need any additional explanations.

Input parameters such as strings, booleans, or numerical values have default values. To use them, specify None in the corresponding parameter entry.

For output data objects, type the file path to be used to save it, just as it is done from the toolbox. If you want to save the result to a temporary file, use None. The extension of the file determines the file format. If you enter a file extension not supported by the algorithm, the default file format for that output type will be used, and its corresponding extension appended to the given file path.

Unlike when an algorithm is executed from the toolbox, outputs are not added to the map canvas if you execute that same algorithm from the Python console. If you want to add an output to the map canvas, you have to do it yourself after running the algorithm. To do so, you can use QGIS API commands, or, even easier, use one of the handy methods provided for such tasks.

The runalg method returns a dictionary with the output names (the ones shown in the algorithm description) as keys and the file paths of those outputs as values. You can load those layers by passing the corresponding file paths to the load() method.

17.5.2 Additional functions for handling data

Apart from the functions used to call algorithms, importing the processing package will also import some additional functions that make it easier to work with data, particularly vector data. They are just convenience functions that wrap some functionality from the QGIS API, usually with a less complex syntax. These functions should be used when developing new algorithms, as they make it easier to operate with input data.

Below is a list of some of these commands. More information can be found in the classes under the processing/tools package, and also in the example scripts provided with QGIS.

- `getObject(obj)`: Returns a QGIS object (a layer or table) from the passed object, which can be a filename or the name of the object in the QGIS Table of Contents.

- `values(layer, fields)`: Returns the values in the attributes table of a vector layer, for the passed fields. Fields can be passed as field names or as zero-based field indices. Returns a dict of lists, with the passed field identifiers as keys. It considers the existing selection.

- `features(layer)`: Returns an iterator over the features of a vector layer, considering the existing selection.

- `uniqueValues(layer, field)`: Returns a list of unique values for a given attribute. Attributes can be passed as a field name or a zero-based field index. It considers the existing selection.

17.5.3 Creating scripts and running them from the toolbox

You can create your own algorithms by writing the corresponding Python code and adding a few extra lines to supply additional information needed to define the semantics of the algorithm. You can find a *Create new script* menu under the *Tools* group in the *Script* algorithms block of the toolbox. Double-click on it to open the script editing dialog. That's where you should type your code. Saving the script from there in the `scripts` folder (the default folder when you open the save file dialog) with `.py` extension will automatically create the corresponding algorithm.

The name of the algorithm (the one you will see in the toolbox) is created from the filename, removing its extension and replacing low hyphens with blank spaces.

Let's have a look at the following code, which calculates the Topographic Wetness Index (TWI) directly from a DEM.

```
##dem=raster
##twi=output
ret_slope = processing.runalg("saga:slopeaspectcurvature", dem, 0, None,
                None, None, None, None)
ret_area = processing.runalg("saga:catchmentarea(mass-fluxmethod)", dem,
                0, False, False, False, False, None, None, None, None, None)
processing.runalg("saga:topographicwetnessindex(twi), ret_slope['SLOPE'],
                ret_area['AREA'], None, 1, 0, twi)
```

As you can see, the calculation involves three algorithms, all of them coming from SAGA. The last one calculates the TWI, but it needs a slope layer and a flow accumulation layer. We do not have these layers, but since we have the DEM, we can calculate them by calling the corresponding SAGA algorithms.

The part of the code where this processing takes place is not difficult to understand if you have read the previous sections in this chapter. The first lines, however, need some additional explanation. They provide the information that is needed to turn your code into an algorithm that can be run from any of the GUI components, like the toolbox or the graphical modeler.

These lines start with a double Python comment symbol (##) and have the following structure:

```
[parameter_name]=[parameter_type] [optional_values]
```

Here is a list of all the parameter types that are supported in processing scripts, their syntax and some examples.

- `raster`. A raster layer.

- `vector`. A vector layer.

- `table`. A table.

- `number`. A numerical value. A default value must be provided. For instance, `depth=number 2.4`.

- `string`. A text string. As in the case of numerical values, a default value must be added. For instance, `name=string Victor`.

- `boolean`. A boolean value. Add `True` or `False` after it to set the default value. For example, `verbose=boolean True`.

- `multiple raster`. A set of input raster layers.

- `multiple vector`. A set of input vector layers.

- `field`. A field in the attributes table of a vector layer. The name of the layer has to be added after the `field` tag. For instance, if you have declared a vector input with `mylayer=vector`, you could use `myfield=field mylayer` to add a field from that layer as parameter.

- `folder`. A folder.

- `file`. A filename.

The parameter name is the name that will be shown to the user when executing the algorithm, and also the variable name to use in the script code. The value entered by the user for that parameter will be assigned to a variable with that name.

When showing the name of the parameter to the user, the name will be edited to improve its appearance, replacing low hyphens with spaces. So, for instance, if you want the user to see a parameter named `A numerical value`, you can use the variable name `A_numerical_value`.

Layers and table values are strings containing the file path of the corresponding object. To turn them into a QGIS object, you can use the `processing.getObjectFromUri()` function. Multiple inputs also have a string value, which contains the file paths to all selected object, separated by semicolons (`;`).

Outputs are defined in a similar manner, using the following tags:

- `output raster`

- `output vector`

- `output table`

- `output html`

- `output file`

- `output number`

- `output string`

The value assigned to the output variables is always a string with a file path. It will correspond to a temporary file path in case the user has not entered any output filename.

When you declare an output, the algorithm will try to add it to QGIS once it is finished. That is why, although the `runalg()` method does not load the layers it produces, the final TWI layer will be loaded (using the case of our previous example), since it is saved to the file entered by the user, which is the value of the corresponding output.

Do not use the `load()` method in your script algorithms, just when working with the console line. If a layer is created as output of an algorithm, it should be declared as such. Otherwise, you will not be able to properly use the algorithm in the modeler, since its syntax (as defined by the tags explained above) will not match what the algorithm really creates.

Hidden outputs (numbers and strings) do not have a value. Instead, you have to assign a value to them. To do so, just set the value of a variable with the name you used to declare that output. For instance, if you have used this declaration,

```
##average=output number
```

the following line will set the value of the output to 5:

```
average = 5
```

In addition to the tags for parameters and outputs, you can also define the group under which the algorithm will be shown, using the `group` tag.

If your algorithm takes a long time to process, it is a good idea to inform the user. You have a global named `progress` available, with two possible methods: `setText(text)` and `setPercentage(percent)` to modify the progress text and the progress bar.

Several examples are provided. Please check them to see real examples of how to create algorithms using the processing framework classes. You can right-click on any script algorithm and select *Edit script* to edit its code or just to see it.

17.5.4 Documenting your scripts

As in the case of models, you can create additional documentation for your scripts, to explain what they do and how to use them. In the script editing dialog, you will find an **[Edit script help]** button. Click on it and it will take you to the help editing dialog. Check the section about the graphical modeler to know more about this dialog and how to use it.

Help files are saved in the same folder as the script itself, adding the `.help` extension to the filename. Notice that you can edit your script's help before saving the script for the first time. If you later close the script editing dialog without saving the script (i.e., you discard it), the help content you wrote will be lost. If your script was already saved and is associated to a filename, saving the help content is done automatically.

17.5.5 Pre- and post-execution script hooks

Scripts can also be used to set pre- and post-execution hooks that are run before and after an algorithm is run. This can be used to automate tasks that should be performed whenever an algorithm is executed.

The syntax is identical to the syntax explained above, but an additional global variable named `alg` is available, representing the algorithm that has just been (or is about to be) executed.

In the *General* group of the processing configuration dialog, you will find two entries named *Pre-execution script file* and *Post-execution script file* where the filename of the scripts to be run in each case can be entered.

.

17.6 The history manager

17.6.1 The processing history

Every time you execute an algorithm, information about the process is stored in the history manager. Along with the parameters used, the date and time of the execution are also saved.

This way, it is easy to track and control all the work that has been developed using the processing framework, and easily reproduce it.

The history manager is a set of registry entries grouped according to their date of execution, making it easier to find information about an algorithm executed at any particular moment.

Process information is kept as a command-line expression, even if the algorithm was launched from the toolbox. This makes it also useful for those learning how to use the command-line interface, since they can call an algorithm using the toolbox and then check the history manager to see how that same algorithm could be called from the command line.

Apart from browsing the entries in the registry, you can also re-execute processes by simply double-clicking on the corresponding entry.

Along with recording algorithm executions, the processing framework communicates with the user by means of the other groups of the registry, namely *Errors*, *Warnings* and *Information*. In case something is not working properly, having a look at the *Errors* might help you to see what is happening. If you get in contact with a developer to report a bug or error, the information in that group will be very useful for her or him to find out what is going wrong.

Third-party algorithms are usually executed by calling their command-line interfaces, which communicate with the user via the console. Although that console is not shown, a full dump of it is stored in the *Information* group each time you run one of those algorithms. If, for instance, you are having problems executing a SAGA algorithm,

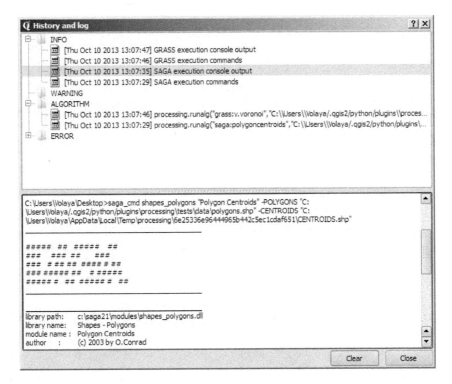

Figure 17.28: History

look for an entry named 'SAGA execution console output' to check all the messages generated by SAGA and try to find out where the problem is.

Some algorithms, even if they can produce a result with the given input data, might add comments or additional information to the *Warning* block if they detect potential problems with the data, in order to warn you. Make sure you check those messages if you are having unexpected results.

17.7 Writing new Processing algorithms as python scripts

You can create your own algorithms by writing the corresponding Python code and adding a few extra lines to supply additional information needed to define the semantics of the algorithm. You can find a *Create new script* menu under the *Tools* group in the *Script* algorithms block of the toolbox. Double-click on it to open the script edition dialog. That's where you should type your code. Saving the script from there in the scripts folder (the default one when you open the save file dialog), with .py extension, will automatically create the corresponding algorithm.

The name of the algorithm (the one you will see in the toolbox) is created from the filename, removing its extension and replacing low hyphens with blank spaces.

Let's have the following code, which calculates the Topographic Wetness Index (TWI) directly from a DEM

```
##dem=raster
##twi=output raster
ret_slope = processing.runalg("saga:slopeaspectcurvature", dem, 0, None,
            None, None, None, None)
ret_area = processing.runalg("saga:catchmentarea", dem,
            0, False, False, False, False, None, None, None, None, None)
processing.runalg("saga:topographicwetnessindextwi, ret_slope['SLOPE'],
            ret_area['AREA'], None, 1, 0, twi)
```

As you can see, it involves 3 algorithms, all of them coming from SAGA. The last one of them calculates the TWI, but it needs a slope layer and a flow accumulation layer. We do not have these ones, but since we have the DEM, we can calculate them calling the corresponding SAGA algorithms.

The part of the code where this processing takes place is not difficult to understand if you have read the previous chapter. The first lines, however, need some additional explanation. They provide the information that is needed to turn your code into an algorithm that can be run from any of the GUI components, like the toolbox or the graphical modeler.

These lines start with a double Python comment symbol (##) and have the following structure

```
[parameter_name]=[parameter_type] [optional_values]
```

Here is a list of all the parameter types that are supported in processign scripts, their syntax and some examples.

- `raster`. A raster layer
- `vector`. A vector layer
- `table`. A table
- `number`. A numerical value. A default value must be provided. For instance, `depth=number 2.4`
- `string`. A text string. As in the case of numerical values, a default value must be added. For instance, `name=string Victor`
- `longstring`. Same as string, but a larger text box will be shown, so it is better suited for long strings, such as for a script expecting a small code snippet.
- `boolean`. A boolean value. Add `True` or `False` after it to set the default value. For example, `verbose=boolean True`.
- `multiple raster`. A set of input raster layers.
- `multiple vector`. A set of input vector layers.
- `field`. A field in the attributes table of a vector layer. The name of the layer has to be added after the `field` tag. For instance, if you have declared a vector input with `mylayer=vector`, you could use `myfield=field mylayer` to add a field from that layer as parameter.
- `folder`. A folder
- `file`. A filename
- `crs`. A Coordinate Reference System

The parameter name is the name that will be shown to the user when executing the algorithm, and also the variable name to use in the script code. The value entered by the user for that parameter will be assigned to a variable with that name.

When showing the name of the parameter to the user, the name will be edited it to improve its appearance, replacing low hyphens with spaces. So, for instance, if you want the user to see a parameter named `A numerical value`, you can use the variable name `A_numerical_value`.

Layers and tables values are strings containing the filepath of the corresponding object. To turn them into a QGIS object, you can use the `processing.getObjectFromUri()` function. Multiple inputs also have a string value, which contains the filepaths to all selected objects, separated by semicolons (`;`).

Outputs are defined in a similar manner, using the following tags:

- `output raster`
- `output vector`
- `output table`
- `output html`
- `output file`
- `output number`
- `output string`

- `output extent`

The value assigned to the output variables is always a string with a filepath. It will correspond to a temporary filepath in case the user has not entered any output filename.

In addition to the tags for parameters and outputs, you can also define the group under which the algorithm will be shown, using the `group` tag.

The last tag that you can use in your script header is `##nomodeler`. Use that when you do not want your algorithm to be shown in the modeler window. This should be used for algorithms that do not have a clear syntax (for instance, if the number of layers to be created is not known in advance, at design time), which make them unsuitable for the graphical modeler

17.8 Handing data produced by the algorithm

When you declare an output representing a layer (raster, vector or table), the algorithm will try to add it to QGIS once it is finished. That is the reason why, although the `runalg()` method does not load the layers it produces, the final *TWI* layer will be loaded, since it is saved to the file entered by the user, which is the value of the corresponding output.

Do not use the `load()` method in your script algorithms, but just when working with the console line. If a layer is created as output of an algorithm, it should be declared as such. Otherwise, you will not be able to properly use the algorithm in the modeler, since its syntax (as defined by the tags explained above) will not match what the algorithm really creates.

Hidden outputs (numbers and strings) do not have a value. Instead, it is you who has to assign a value to them. To do so, just set the value of a variable with the name you used to declare that output. For instance, if you have used this declaration,

```
##average=output number
```

the following line will set the value of the output to 5:

```
average = 5
```

17.9 Communicating with the user

If your algorithm takes a long time to process, it is a good idea to inform the user. You have a global named `progress` available, with two available methods: `setText(text)` and `setPercentage(percent)` to modify the progress text and the progress bar.

If you have to provide some information to the user, not related to the progress of the algorithm, you can use the `setInfo(text)` method, also from the `progress` object.

If your script has some problem, the correct way of propagating it is to raise an exception of type `GeoAlgorithmExecutionException()`. You can pass a message as argument to the constructor of the exception. Processing will take care of handling it and communicating with the user, depending on where the algorithm is being executed from (toolbox, modeler, Python console...)

17.10 Documenting your scripts

As in the case of models, you can create additional documentation for your script, to explain what they do and how to use them. In the script editing dialog you will find a **[Edit script help]** button. Click on it and it will take you to the help editing dialog. Check the chapter about the graphical modeler to know more about this dialog and how to use it.

Help files are saved in the same folder as the script itself, adding the `.help` extension to the filename. Notice that you can edit your script's help before saving it for the first time. If you later close the script editing dialog without

---

saving the script (i.e. you discard it), the help content you wrote will be lost. If your script was already saved and is associated to a filename, saving is done automatically.

17.11 Example scripts

Several examples are available in the on-line collection of scripts, which you can access by selecting the *Get script from on-line script collection* tool under the *Scripts/tools* entry in the toolbox.

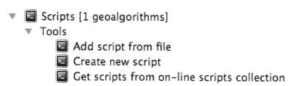

Please, check them to see real examples of how to create algorithms using the processing framework classes. You can right-click on any script algorithm and select *Edit script* to edit its code or just to see it.

17.12 Best practices for writing script algorithms

Here's a quick summary of ideas to consider when creating your script algorithms and, especially, if you want to share with other QGIS users. Following these simple rules will ensure consistency across the different Processing elements such as the toolbox, the modeler or the batch processing interface.

- Do not load resulting layers. Let Processing handle your results and load your layers if needed.

- Always declare the outputs your algorithm creates. Avoid things such as declaring one output and then using the destination filename set for that output to create a collection of them. That will break the correct semantics of the algorithm and make it impossible to use it safely in the modeler. If you have to write an algorithm like that, make sure you add the `##nomodeler` tag.

- Do not show message boxes or use any GUI element from the script. If you want to communicate with the user, use the `setInfo()` method or throw an `GeoAlgorithmExecutionException`

- As a rule of thumb, do not forget that your algorithm might be executed in a context other than the Processing toolbox.

17.13 Pre- and post-execution script hooks

Scripts can also be used to set pre- and post-execution hooks that are run before and after an algorithm is run. This can be used to automate tasks that should be performed whenever an algorithm is executed.

The syntax is identical to the syntax explained above, but an additional global variable named `alg` is available, representing the algorithm that has just been (or is about to be) executed.

In the *General* group of the processing config dialog you will find two entries named *Pre-execution script file* and *Post-execution script file* where the filename of the scripts to be run in each case can be entered.

.

17.14 Configuring external applications

The processing framework can be extended using additional applications. Currently, SAGA, GRASS, OTB (Orfeo Toolbox) and R are supported, along with some other command-line applications that provide spatial data analysis functionalities. Algorithms relying on an external application are managed by their own algorithm provider.

This section will show you how to configure the processing framework to include these additional applications, and it will explain some particular features of the algorithms based on them. Once you have correctly configured the system, you will be able to execute external algorithms from any component like the toolbox or the graphical modeler, just like you do with any other geoalgorithm.

By default, all algorithms that rely on an external appplication not shipped with QGIS are not enabled. You can enable them in the configuration dialog. Make sure that the corresponding application is already installed in your system. Enabling an algorithm provider without installing the application it needs will cause the algorithms to appear in the toolbox, but an error will be thrown when you try to execute them.

This is because the algorithm descriptions (needed to create the parameters dialog and provide the information needed about the algorithm) are not included with each application, but with QGIS instead. That is, they are part of QGIS, so you have them in your installation even if you have not installed any other software. Running the algorithm, however, needs the application binaries to be installed in your system.

17.14.1 A note for Windows users

If you are not an advanced user and you are running QGIS on Windows, you might not be interested in reading the rest of this chapter. Make sure you install QGIS in your system using the standalone installer. That will automatically install SAGA, GRASS and OTB in your system and configure them so they can be run from QGIS. All the algorithms in the simplified view of the toolbox will be ready to be run without needing any further configuration. If installing through OSGeo4W application, make sure you select for insttallation SAGA and OTB as well.

If you want to know more about how these providers work, or if you want to use some algorithms not included in the simplified toolbox (such as R scripts), keep on reading.

17.14.2 A note on file formats

When using an external software, opening a file in QGIS does not mean that it can be opened and processed as well in that other software. In most cases, other software can read what you have opened in QGIS, but in some cases, that might not be true. When using databases or uncommon file formats, whether for raster or vector layers, problems might arise. If that happens, try to use well-known file formats that you are sure are understood by both programs, and check the console output (in the history and log dialog) to know more about what is going wrong.

Using GRASS raster layers is, for instance, one case in which you might have trouble and not be able to complete your work if you call an external algorithm using such a layer as input. For this reason, these layers will not appear as available to algorithms.

You should, however, find no problems at all with vector layers, since QGIS automatically converts from the original file format to one accepted by the external application before passing the layer to it. This adds extra processing time, which might be significant if the layer has a large size, so do not be surprised if it takes more time to process a layer from a DB connection than it does to process one of a similar size stored in a shapefile.

Providers not using external applications can process any layer that you can open in QGIS, since they open it for analysis through QGIS.

Regarding output formats, all formats supported by QGIS as output can be used, both for raster and vector layers. Some providers do not support certain formats, but all can export to common raster layer formats that can later be transformed by QGIS automatically. As in the case of input layers, if this conversion is needed, that might increase the processing time.

If the extension of the filename specified when calling an algorithm does not match the extension of any of the formats supported by QGIS, then a suffix will be added to set a default format. In the case of raster layers, the `.tif` extension is used, while `.shp` is used for vector layers.

17.14.3 A note on vector layer selections

External applications may also be made aware of the selections that exist in vector layers within QGIS. However, that requires rewriting all input vector layers, just as if they were originally in a format not supported by the external application. Only when no selection exists, or the *Use only selected features* option is not enabled in the processing general configuration, can a layer be directly passed to an external application.

In other cases, exporting only selected features is needed, which causes execution times to be longer.

SAGA

SAGA algorithms can be run from QGIS if you have SAGA installed in your system and you configure the processing framework properly so it can find SAGA executables. In particular, the SAGA command-line executable is needed to run SAGA algorithms.

If you are running Windows, both the stand-alone installer and the OSGeo4W installer include SAGA along with QGIS, and the path is automatically configured, so there is no need to do anything else.

If you have installed SAGA yourself (remember, you need version 2.1), the path to the SAGA executable must be configured. To do this, open the configuration dialog. In the *SAGA* block, you will find a setting named *SAGA Folder*. Enter the path to the folder where SAGA is installed. Close the configuration dialog, and now you are ready to run SAGA algorithms from QGIS.

If you are running Linux, SAGA binaries are not included with SEXTANTE, so you have to download and install the software yourself. Please check the SAGA website for more information. SAGA 2.1 is needed.

In this case, there is no need to configure the path to the SAGA executable, and you will not see those folders. Instead, you must make sure that SAGA is properly installed and its folder is added to the PATH environment variable. Just open a console and type `saga_cmd` to check that the system can find where the SAGA binaries are located.

17.14.4 About SAGA grid system limitations

Most SAGA algorithms that require several input raster layers require them to have the same grid system. That is, they must cover the same geographic area and have the same cell size, so their corresponding grids match. When calling SAGA algorithms from QGIS, you can use any layer, regardless of its cell size and extent. When multiple raster layers are used as input for a SAGA algorithm, QGIS resamples them to a common grid system and then passes them to SAGA (unless the SAGA algorithm can operate with layers from different grid systems).

The definition of that common grid system is controlled by the user, and you will find several parameters in the SAGA group of the settings window to do so. There are two ways of setting the target grid system:

- Setting it manually. You define the extent by setting the values of the following parameters:

  - *Resampling min X*

  - *Resampling max X*

  - *Resampling min Y*

  - *Resampling max Y*

  - *Resampling cellsize*

  Notice that QGIS will resample input layers to that extent, even if they do not overlap with it.

- Setting it automatically from input layers. To select this option, just check the *Use min covering grid system for resampling* option. All the other settings will be ignored and the minimum extent that covers all the input layers will be used. The cell size of the target layer is the maximum of all cell sizes of the input layers.

For algorithms that do not use multiple raster layers, or for those that do not need a unique input grid system, no resampling is performed before calling SAGA, and those parameters are not used.

17.14.5 Limitations for multi-band layers

Unlike QGIS, SAGA has no support for multi-band layers. If you want to use a multiband layer (such as an RGB or multispectral image), you first have to split it into single-banded images. To do so, you can use the 'SAGA/Grid

- Tools/Split RGB image' algorithm (which creates three images from an RGB image) or the 'SAGA/Grid - Tools/Extract band' algorithm (to extract a single band).

17.14.6 Limitations in cell size

SAGA assumes that raster layers have the same cell size in the X and Y axis. If you are working with a layer with different values for horizontal and vertical cell size, you might get unexpected results. In this case, a warning will be added to the processing log, indicating that an input layer might not be suitable to be processed by SAGA.

17.14.7 Logging

When QGIS calls SAGA, it does so using its command-line interface, thus passing a set of commands to perform all the required operations. SAGA shows its progress by writing information to the console, which includes the percentage of processing already done, along with additional content. This output is filtered and used to update the progress bar while the algorithm is running.

Both the commands sent by QGIS and the additional information printed by SAGA can be logged along with other processing log messages, and you might find them useful to track in detail what is going on when QGIS runs a SAGA algorithm. You will find two settings, namely *Log console output* and *Log execution commands*, to activate that logging mechanism.

Most other providers that use an external application and call it through the command-line have similar options, so you will find them as well in other places in the processing settings list.

R. Creating R scripts

R integration in QGIS is different from that of SAGA in that there is not a predefined set of algorithms you can run (except for a few examples). Instead, you should write your scripts and call R commands, much like you would do from R, and in a very similar manner to what we saw in the section dedicated to processing scripts. This section shows you the syntax to use to call those R commands from QGIS and how to use QGIS objects (layers, tables) in them.

The first thing you have to do, as we saw in the case of SAGA, is to tell QGIS where your R binaries are located. You can do this using the *R folder* entry in the processing configuration dialog. Once you have set that parameter, you can start creating and executing your own R scripts.

Once again, this is different in Linux, and you just have to make sure that the R folder is included in the PATH environment variable. If you can start R just typing R in a console, then you are ready to go.

To add a new algorithm that calls an R function (or a more complex R script that you have developed and you would like to have available from QGIS), you have to create a script file that tells the processing framework how to perform that operation and the corresponding R commands to do so.

R script files have the extension .rsx, and creating them is pretty easy if you just have a basic knowledge of R syntax and R scripting. They should be stored in the R scripts folder. You can set this folder in the *R* settings group (available from the processing settings dialog), just like you do with the folder for regular processing scripts.

Let's have a look at a very simple script file, which calls the R method spsample to create a random grid within the boundary of the polygons in a given polygon layer. This method belongs to the maptools package. Since almost all the algorithms that you might like to incorporate into QGIS will use or generate spatial data, knowledge of spatial packages like maptools and, especially, sp, is mandatory.

```
##polyg=vector
##numpoints=number 10
##output=output vector
##sp=group
pts=spsample(polyg,numpoints,type="random")
output=SpatialPointsDataFrame(pts, as.data.frame(pts))
```

The first lines, which start with a double Python comment sign (##), tell QGIS the inputs of the algorithm described in the file and the outputs that it will generate. They work with exactly the same syntax as the SEXTANTE scripts that we have already seen, so they will not be described here again.

When you declare an input parameter, QGIS uses that information for two things: creating the user interface to ask the user for the value of that parameter and creating a corresponding R variable that can later be used as input for R commands.

In the above example, we are declaring an input of type `vector` named `polyg`. When executing the algorithm, QGIS will open in R the layer selected by the user and store it in a variable also named `polyg`. So, the name of a parameter is also the name of the variable that we can use in R for accesing the value of that parameter (thus, you should avoid using reserved R words as parameter names).

Spatial elements such as vector and raster layers are read using the `readOGR()` and `brick()` commands (you do not have to worry about adding those commands to your description file – QGIS will do it), and they are stored as `Spatial*DataFrame` objects. Table fields are stored as strings containing the name of the selected field.

Tables are opened using the `read.csv()` command. If a table entered by the user is not in CSV format, it will be converted prior to importing it into R.

Additionally, raster files can be read using the `readGDAL()` command instead of `brick()` by using the `##usereadgdal`.

If you are an advanced user and do not want QGIS to create the object representing the layer, you can use the `##passfilename` tag to indicate that you prefer a string with the filename instead. In this case, it is up to you to open the file before performing any operation on the data it contains.

With the above information, we can now understand the first line of our first example script (the first line not starting with a Python comment).

```
pts=spsample(polyg,numpoints,type="random")
```

The variable `polygon` already contains a `SpatialPolygonsDataFrame` object, so it can be used to call the `spsample` method, just like the `numpoints` one, which indicates the number of points to add to the created sample grid.

Since we have declared an output of type vector named `out`, we have to create a variable named `out` and store a `Spatial*DataFrame` object in it (in this case, a `SpatialPointsDataFrame`). You can use any name for your intermediate variables. Just make sure that the variable storing your final result has the same name that you used to declare it, and that it contains a suitable value.

In this case, the result obtained from the `spsample` method has to be converted explicitly into a `SpatialPointsDataFrame` object, since it is itself an object of class `ppp`, which is not a suitable class to be returned to QGIS.

If your algorithm generates raster layers, the way they are saved will depend on whether or not you have used the `#dontuserasterpackage` option. In you have used it, layers are saved using the `writeGDAL()` method. If not, the `writeRaster()` method from the `raster` package will be used.

If you have used the `#passfilename` option, outputs are generated using the `raster` package (with `writeRaster()`), even though it is not used for the inputs.

If your algorithm does not generate any layer, but rather a text result in the console instead, you have to indicate that you want the console to be shown once the execution is finished. To do so, just start the command lines that produce the results you want to print with the > ('greater') sign. The output of all other lines will not be shown. For instance, here is the description file of an algorithm that performs a normality test on a given field (column) of the attributes of a vector layer:

```
##layer=vector
##field=field layer
##nortest=group
library(nortest)
>lillie.test(layer[[field]])
```

The output of the last line is printed, but the output of the first is not (and neither are the outputs from other command lines added automatically by QGIS).

Chapter 17. QGIS processing framework

If your algorithm creates any kind of graphics (using the `plot()` method), add the following line:

```
##showplots
```

This will cause QGIS to redirect all R graphical outputs to a temporary file, which will be opened once R execution has finished.

Both graphics and console results will be shown in the processing results manager.

For more information, please check the script files provided with SEXTANTE. Most of them are rather simple and will greatly help you understand how to create your own scripts.

Note: `rgdal` and `maptools` libraries are loaded by default, so you do not have to add the corresponding `library()` commands (you just have to make sure that those two packages are installed in your R distribution). However, other additional libraries that you might need have to be explicitly loaded. Just add the necessary commands at the beginning of your script. You also have to make sure that the corresponding packages are installed in the R distribution used by QGIS. The processing framework will not take care of any package installation. If you run a script that requires a package that is not installed, the execution will fail, and Processing will try to detect which packages are missing. You must install those missing libraries manually before you can run the algorithm.

GRASS

Configuring GRASS is not much different from configuring SAGA. First, the path to the GRASS folder has to be defined, but only if you are running Windows. Additionaly, a shell interpreter (usually `msys.exe`, which can be found in most GRASS for Windows distributions) has to be defined and its path set up as well.

By default, the processing framework tries to configure its GRASS connector to use the GRASS distribution that ships along with QGIS. This should work without problems in most systems, but if you experience problems, you might have to configure the GRASS connector manually. Also, if you want to use a different GRASS installation, you can change that setting and point to the folder where the other version is installed. GRASS 6.4 is needed for algorithms to work correctly.

If you are running Linux, you just have to make sure that GRASS is correctly installed, and that it can be run without problem from a console.

GRASS algorithms use a region for calculations. This region can be defined manually using values similar to the ones found in the SAGA configuration, or automatically, taking the minimum extent that covers all the input layers used to execute the algorithm each time. If the latter approach is the behaviour you prefer, just check the *Use min covering region* option in the GRASS configuration parameters.

The last parameter that has to be configured is related to the mapset. A mapset is needed to run GRASS, and the processing framework creates a temporary one for each execution. You have to specify if the data you are working with uses geographical (lat/lon) coordinates or projected ones.

GDAL

No additional configuration is needed to run GDAL algorithms. Since they are already incorporated into QGIS, the algorithms can infer their configuration from it.

Orfeo Toolbox

Orfeo Toolbox (OTB) algorithms can be run from QGIS if you have OTB installed in your system and you have configured QGIS properly, so it can find all necessary files (command-line tools and libraries).

As in the case of SAGA, OTB binaries are included in the stand-alone installer for Windows, but they are not included if you are runing Linux, so you have to download and install the software yourself. Please check the OTB website for more information.

Once OTB is installed, start QGIS, open the processing configuration dialog and configure the OTB algorithm provider. In the *Orfeo Toolbox (image analysis)* block, you will find all settings related to OTB. First, ensure that algorithms are enabled.

Then, configure the path to the folder where OTB command-line tools and libraries are installed:

- Usually *OTB applications folder* points to `/usr/lib/otb/applications` and *OTB command line tools folder* is `/usr/bin`.

- If you use the OSGeo4W installer, then install `otb-bin` package and enter `C:\OSGeo4W\apps\orfeotoolbox\applications` as *OTB applications folder* and `C:\OSGeo4W\bin` as *OTB command line tools folder*. These values should be configured by default, but if you have a different OTB installation, configure them to the corresponding values in your system.

TauDEM

To use this provider, you need to install TauDEM command line tools.

17.14.8 Windows

Please visit the TauDEM homepage for installation instructions and precompiled binaries for 32-bit and 64-bit systems. **IMPORTANT**: You need TauDEM 5.0.6 executables. Version 5.2 is currently not supported.

17.14.9 Linux

There are no packages for most Linux distributions, so you should compile TauDEM by yourself. As TauDEM uses MPICH2, first install it using your favorite package manager. Alternatively, TauDEM works fine with Open MPI, so you can use it instead of MPICH2.

Download TauDEM 5.0.6 source code and extract the files in some folder.

Open the `linearpart.h` file, and after line

```
#include "mpi.h"
```

add a new line with

```
#include <stdint.h>
```

so you'll get

```
#include "mpi.h"
#include <stdint.h>
```

Save the changes and close the file. Now open `tiffIO.h`, find line `#include "stdint.h"` and replace quotes (`""`) with `<>`, so you'll get

```
#include <stdint.h>
```

Save the changes and close the file. Create a build directory and cd into it

```
mkdir build
cd build
```

Configure your build with the command

```
CXX=mpicxx cmake -DCMAKE_INSTALL_PREFIX=/usr/local ..
```

and then compile

```
make
```

Finally, to install TauDEM into `/usr/local/bin`, run

```
sudo make install
```

17.15 The QGIS Commander

Processing includes a practical tool that allows you to run algorithms without having to use the toolbox, but just by typing the name of the algorithm you want to run.

This tool is known as the *QGIS commander*, and it is just a simple text box with autocompletion where you type the command you want to run.

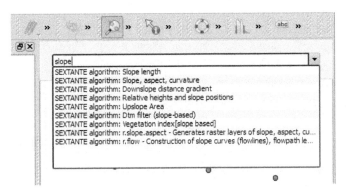

Figure 17.29: The QGIS Commander

The Commander is started from the *Analysis* menu or, more practically, by pressing `Shift + Ctrl + M` (you can change that default keyboard shortcut in the QGIS configuration if you prefer a different one). Apart from executing Processing algorithms, the Commander gives you access to most of the functionality in QGIS, which means that it gives you a practical and efficient way of running QGIS tasks and allows you to control QGIS with reduced usage of buttons and menus.

Moreover, the Commander is configurable, so you can add your custom commands and have them just a few keystrokes away, making it a powerful tool to help you become more productive in your daily work with QGIS.

17.15.1 Available commands

The commands available in the Commander fall in the following categories:

- Processing algorithms. These are shown as `Processing algorithm: <name of the algorithm>`.

- Menu items. These are shown as `Menu item: <menu entry text>`. All menus items available from the QGIS interface are available, even if they are included in a submenu.

- Python functions. You can create short Python functions that will be then included in the list of available commands. They are shown as `Function: <function name>`.

To run any of the above, just start typing and then select the corresponding element from the list of available commands that appears after filtering the whole list of commands with the text you have entered.

In the case of calling a Python function, you can select the entry in the list, which is pre-fixed by `Function:` (for instance, `Function: removeall`), or just directly type the function name (``removeall` in the previous example). There is no need to add brackets after the function name.

17.15.2 Creating custom functions

Custom functions are added by entering the corresponding Python code in the `commands.py` file that is found in the `.qgis/sextante/commander` `directory` in your user folder. It is just a simple Python file where you can add the functions that you need.

The file is created with a few example functions the first time you open the Commander. If you haven't launched the Commander yet, you can create the file yourself. To edit the commands file, use your favorite text editor. You can also use a built-in editor by calling the `edit` command from the Commander. It will open the editor with the commands file, and you can edit it directly and then save your changes.

For instance, you can add the following function, which removes all layers:

```
from qgis.gui import *

def removeall():
    mapreg = QgsMapLayerRegistry.instance()
    mapreg.removeAllMapLayers()
```

Once you have added the function, it will be available in the Commander, and you can invoke it by typing `removeall`. There is no need to do anything apart from writing the function itself.

Functions can receive parameters. Add `*args` to your function definition to receive arguments. When calling the function from the Commander, parameters have to be passed separated by spaces.

Here is an example of a function that loads a layer and takes a parameter with the filename of the layer to load.

```
import processing

def load(*args):
  processing.load(args[0])
```

If you want to load the layer in `/home/myuser/points.shp`, type `load /home/myuser/points.shp` in the Commander text box.

.

Chapter 17. QGIS processing framework

## CHAPTER 18

Print Composer

With the Print Composer you can create nice maps and atlasses that can be printed or saved as PDF-file, an image or an SVG-file. This is a powerfull way to share geographical information produced with QGIS that can be included in reports or published.

The Print Composer provides growing layout and printing capabilities. It allows you to add elements such as the QGIS map canvas, text labels, images, legends, scale bars, basic shapes, arrows, attribute tables and HTML frames. You can size, group, align, position and rotate each element and adjust the properties to create your layout. The layout can be printed or exported to image formats, PostScript, PDF or to SVG (export to SVG is not working properly with some recent Qt4 versions; you should try and check individually on your system). You can save the layout as a template and load it again in another session. Finally, generating several maps based on a template can be done through the atlas generator. See a list of tools in table_composer_1:

Icon	Purpose	Icon	Purpose
	Save Project		New Composer
	Duplicate Composer		Composer Manager
	Load from template		Save as template
	Print or export as PostScript		Export to an image format
	Export print composition to SVG		Export as PDF
	Revert last change		Restore last change
	Zoom to full extent		Zoom to 100%
	Zoom in		Zoom out
	Refresh View		
	Pan		Zoom to specific region
	Select/Move item in print composition		Move content within an item
	Add new map from QGIS map canvas		Add image to print composition
	Add label to print composition		Add new legend to print composition
	Add scale bar to print composition		Add basic shape to print composition
	Add arrow to print composition		Add attribute table to print composition
	Add an HTML frame		
	Group items of print composition		Ungroup items of print composition
	Lock Selected Items		Unlock All items
	Raise selected items		Lower selected items
	Move selected items to top		Move selected items to bottom
	Align selected items left		Align selected items right
	Align selected items center		Align selected items center vertical
	Align selected items top		Align selected items bottom
	Preview Atlas		First Feature
	Previous Feature		Next Feature
	Last feature		Print Atlas
	Export Atlas as Image		Atlas Settings

Table Composer 1: Print Composer Tools

All Print Composer tools are available in menus and as icons in a toolbar. The toolbar can be switched off and on using the right mouse button over the toolbar.

18.1 First steps

18.1.1 Open a new Print Composer Template

Before you start to work with the Print Composer, you need to load some raster and vector layers in the QGIS map canvas and adapt their properties to suit your own convenience. After everything is rendered and symbolized to your liking, click the ⌐ New Print Composer icon in the toolbar or choose *File → New Print Composer*. You will be prompted to choose a title for the new Composer.

18.1.2 Overview of the Print Composer

Opening the Print Composer provides you with a blank canvas that represents the paper surface when using the print option. Initially you find buttons on the left beside the canvas to add map composer items; the current QGIS map canvas, text labels, images, legends, scale bars, basic shapes, arrows, attribute tables and HTML frames. In this toolbar you also find toolbar buttons to navigate, zoom in on an area and pan the view on the composer and toolbar buttons to select a map composer item and to move the contents of the map item.

Figure_composer_overview shows the initial view of the Print Composer before any elements are added.

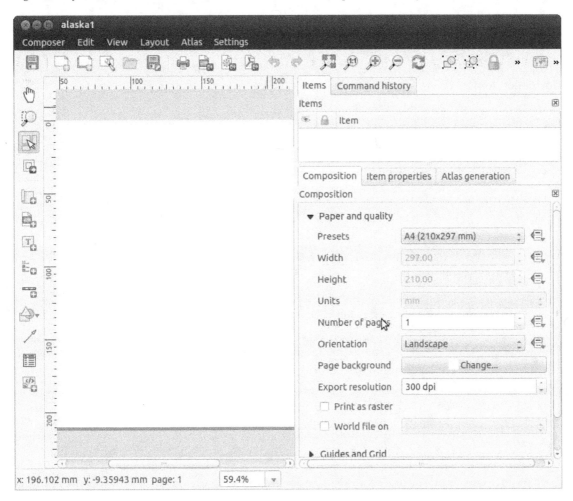

Figure 18.1: Print Composer

On the right beside the canvas you find two panels. The upper panel holds the tabs *Items* and *Command History* and the lower panel holds the tabs *Composition*, *Item properties* and *Atlas generation*.

- The *Items* tab provides a list of all map composer items added to the canvas.

- The *Command history* tab displays a history of all changes applied to the Print Composer layout. With a mouse click, it is possible to undo and redo layout steps back and forth to a certain status.

- The *Composition* tab allows you to set paper size, orientation, the page background, number of pages and print quality for the output file in dpi. Furthermore, you can also activate the ☑ *Print as raster* checkbox. This means all items will be converted to raster before printing or saving as PostScript or PDF. In this tab, you can also customize settings for grid and smart guides.

- The *Item Properties* tab displays the properties for the selected item. Click the ⬚ Select/Move item icon to select an item (e.g., legend, scale bar or label) on the canvas. Then click the *Item Properties* tab and customize the settings for the selected item.

- The *Atlas generation* tab allows you to enable the generation of an atlas for the current Composer and gives access to its parameters.

- Finally, you can save your print composition with the ⬚ Save Project button.

In the bottom part of the Print Composer window, you can find a status bar with mouse position, current page number and a combo box to set the zoom level.

You can add multiple elements to the Composer. It is also possible to have more than one map view or legend or scale bar in the Print Composer canvas, on one or several pages. Each element has its own properties and, in the case of the map, its own extent. If you want to remove any elements from the Composer canvas you can do that with the Delete or the Backspace key.

Navigation tools

To navigate in the canvas layout, the Print Composer provides some general tools:

- ⬚ Zoom in

- ⬚ Zoom out

- ⬚ Zoom full

- ⬚ Zoom to 100%

- Refresh view (if you find the view in an inconsistent state)

- ⬚ Pan composer

- ⬚ Zoom (zoom to a specific region of the Composer)

You can change the zoom level also using the mouse wheel or the combo box in the status bar. If you need to switch to pan mode while working in the Composer area, you can hold the Spacebar or the the mouse wheel. With Ctrl+Spacebar, you can temporarily switch to zoom mode, and with Ctrl+Shift+Spacebar, to zoom out mode.

18.1.3 Sample Session

To demonstrate how to create a map please follow the next instructions.

1. On the left site, select the ⬚ Add new map toolbar button and draw a rectangle on the canvas holding down the left mouse button. Inside the drawn rectangle the QGIS map view to the canvas.

2. Select the ⬚ Add new scalebar toolbar button and place the map item with the left mouse button on the Print Composer canvas. A scalebar will be added to the canvas.

3. Select the ⬚ Add new legend toolbar button and draw a rectangle on the canvas holding down the left mouse button. Inside the drawn rectangle the legend will be drawn.

4. Select the ⬚ Select/Move item icon to select the map on the canvas and move it a bit.

5. While the map item is still selected you can also change the size of the map item. Click while holding down the left mouse button, in a white little rectangle in one of the corners of the map item and drag it to a new location to change it's size.

6. Click the *Item Properties* tab on the left lower panel and find the setting for the orientation. Change the value of the setting *Map orientation* to '15.00° '. You should see the orientation of the map item change.

7. Finally, you can save your print composition with the 💾 Save Project button.

18.1.4 Print Composer Options

From *Settings → Composer Options* you can set some options that will be used as default during your work.

- *Compositions defaults* let you specify the default font to use.

- With *Grid appearance*, you can set the grid style and its color. There are three types of grid: **Dots**, **Solid** lines and **Crosses**.

- *Grid and guide defaults* defines spacing, offset and tolerance of the grid.

18.1.5 Composition tab — General composition setup

In the *Composition* tab, you can define the global settings of your composition.

- You can choose one of the *Presets* for your paper sheet, or enter your custom *width* and *height*.

- Composition can now be divided into several pages. For instance, a first page can show a map canvas, and a second page can show the attribute table associated with a layer, while a third one shows an HTML frame linking to your organization website. Set the *Number of pages* to the desired value. You can choose the page *Orientation* and its *Exported resolution*. When checked, ✅ *print as raster* means all elements will be rasterized before printing or saving as PostScript or PDF.

- *Grid and guides* lets you customize grid settings like *spacings*, *offsets* and *tolerance* to your need. The tolerance is the maximum distance below which an item is snapped to smart guides.

Snap to grid and/or to smart guides can be enabled from the *View* menu. In this menu, you can also hide or show the grid and smart guides.

18.1.6 Composer items common options

Composer items have a set of common properties you will find on the bottom of the *Item Properties* tab: Position and size, Rotation, Frame, Background, Item ID and Rendering (See figure_composer_common_1).

- The *Position and size* dialog lets you define size and position of the frame that contains the item. You can also choose which *Reference point* will be set at the **X** and **Y** coordinates previously defined.

- The *Rotation* sets the rotation of the element (in degrees).

- The ✅ *Frame* shows or hides the frame around the label. Use the *Frame color* and *Thickness* menus to adjust those properties.

- Use the *Background color* menu for setting a background color. With the dialog you can pick a color (see *Color Picker*).

- Use the *Item ID* to create a relationship to other Print Composer items. This is used with QGIS server and any potential web client. You can set an ID on an item (e.g., a map and a label), and then the web client can send data to set a property (e.g., label text) for that specific item. The GetProjectSettings command will list what items and which IDs are available in a layout.

- *Rendering* mode can be selected in the option field. See Rendering_Mode.

Note:

- If you checked ✅ *Use live-updating color chooser dialogs* in the QGIS general options, the color button will update as soon as you choose a new color from **Color Dialog** windows. If not, you need to close the **Color Dialog**.

Figure 18.2: Common Item properties Dialogs △

- The  Data defined override icon next to a field means that you can associate the field with data in the map item or use expressions. These are particularly helpful with atlas generation (See atlas_data_defined_overrides).

18.2 Rendering mode

QGIS now allows advanced rendering for Composer items just like vector and raster layers.

Figure 18.3: Rendering mode △

- *Transparency* ◯────── : You can make the underlying item in the Composer visible with this tool. Use the slider to adapt the visibility of your item to your needs. You can also make a precise definition of the percentage of visibility in the menu beside the slider.

- ☑ *Exclude item from exports*: You can decide to make an item not visible in all exports. After activating this checkbox, the item will not be included in PDF's, prints etc..

- *Blending mode*: You can achieve special rendering effects with these tools that you previously only may know from graphics programs. The pixels of your overlaying and underlaying items are mixed through the settings described below.

  - Normal: This is the standard blend mode, which uses the alpha channel of the top pixel to blend with the pixel beneath it; the colors aren't mixed.

  - Lighten: This selects the maximum of each component from the foreground and background pixels. Be aware that the results tend to be jagged and harsh.

– Screen: Light pixels from the source are painted over the destination, while dark pixels are not. This mode is most useful for mixing the texture of one layer with another layer (e.g., you can use a hillshade to texture another layer).

– Dodge: Dodge will brighten and saturate underlying pixels based on the lightness of the top pixel. So, brighter top pixels cause the saturation and brightness of the underlying pixels to increase. This works best if the top pixels aren't too bright; otherwise the effect is too extreme.

– Addition: This blend mode simply adds pixel values of one layer with pixel values of the other. In case of values above 1 (as in the case of RGB), white is displayed. This mode is suitable for highlighting features.

– Darken: This creates a resultant pixel that retains the smallest components of the foreground and background pixels. Like lighten, the results tend to be jagged and harsh.

– Multiply: Here, the numbers for each pixel of the top layer are multiplied with the numbers for the corresponding pixel of the bottom layer. The results are darker pictures.

– Burn: Darker colors in the top layer cause the underlying layers to darken. Burn can be used to tweak and colorise underlying layers.

– Overlay: This mode combines the multiply and screen blending modes. In the resulting picture, light parts become lighter and dark parts become darker.

– Soft light: This is very similar to overlay, but instead of using multiply/screen it uses color burn/dodge. This mode is supposed to emulate shining a soft light onto an image.

– Hard light: Hard light is very similar to the overlay mode. It's supposed to emulate projecting a very intense light onto an image.

– Difference: Difference subtracts the top pixel from the bottom pixel, or the other way around, to always get a positive value. Blending with black produces no change, as the difference with all colors is zero.

– Subtract: This blend mode simply subtracts pixel values of one layer with pixel values of the other. In case of negative values, black is displayed.

18.3 Composer Items

18.3.1 The Map item

Click on the ⬚ Add new map toolbar button in the Print Composer toolbar to add the QGIS map canvas. Now, drag a rectangle onto the Composer canvas with the left mouse button to add the map. To display the current map, you can choose between three different modes in the map *Item Properties* tab:

- **Rectangle** is the default setting. It only displays an empty box with a message 'Map will be printed here'.

- **Cache** renders the map in the current screen resolution. If you zoom the Composer window in or out, the map is not rendered again but the image will be scaled.

- **Render** means that if you zoom the Composer window in or out, the map will be rendered again, but for space reasons, only up to a maximum resolution.

Cache is the default preview mode for newly added Print Composer maps.

You can resize the map element by clicking on the ⬚ Select/Move item button, selecting the element, and dragging one of the blue handles in the corner of the map. With the map selected, you can now adapt more properties in the map *Item Properties* tab.

To move layers within the map element, select the map element, click the ⬚ Move item content icon and move the layers within the map item frame with the left mouse button. After you have found the right place for an item, you can lock the item position within the Print Composer canvas. Select the map item and use the toolbar 🔒

Lock Selected Items or the *Items* tab to Lock the item. A locked item can only be selected using the *Items* tab. Once selected you can use the *Items* tab to unlock individual items. The <img> Unlock All Items icon will unlock all locked composer items.

Main properties

The *Main properties* dialog of the map *Item Properties* tab provides the following functionalities (see figure_composer_map_1):

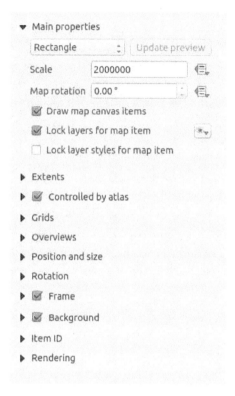

Figure 18.4: Map Item properties Tab △

- The **Preview** area allows you to define the preview modes 'Rectangle', 'Cache' and 'Render', as described above. If you change the view on the QGIS map canvas by changing vector or raster properties, you can update the Print Composer view by selecting the map element in the Print Composer and clicking the **[Update preview]** button.

- The field *Scale* 1.00 ◊ sets a manual scale.

- The field *Map rotation* 1.00 ◊ allows you to rotate the map element content clockwise in degrees. The rotation of the map view can be imitated here. Note that a correct coordinate frame can only be added with the default value 0 and that once you defined a *Map rotation* it currently cannot be changed.

- ☑ *Draw map canvas items* lets you show annotations that may be placed on the map canvas in the main QGIS window.

- You can choose to lock the layers shown on a map item. Check ☑ *Lock layers for map item*. After this is checked, any layer that would be displayed or hidden in the main QGIS window will not appear or be hidden in the map item of the Composer. But style and labels of a locked layer are still refreshed according to the main QGIS interface. You can prevent this by using *Lock layer styles for map item*.

- The 👁 button allows you to add quickly all the presets views you have prepared in QGIS. Clicking on the 👁 button you will see the list of all the preset views: just select the preset you want to display. The map canvas will automatically lock the preset layers by enabling the 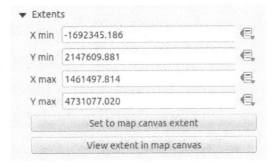 *Lock layers for map item*: if you want to unselect the preset, just uncheck the and press on the button. See *Map Legend* to find out how to create presets views.

Extents

The *Extents* dialog of the map item tab provides the following functionalities (see figure_composer_map_2):

Figure 18.5: Map Extents Dialog

- The **Map extents** area allows you to specify the map extent using X and Y min/max values and by clicking the **[Set to map canvas extent]** button. This button sets the map extent of the composer map item to the extent of the current map view in the main QGIS application. The button **[View extent in map canvas]** does exactly the opposite, it updates the extent of the map view in the QGIS application to the extent of the composer map item.

If you change the view on the QGIS map canvas by changing vector or raster properties, you can update the Print Composer view by selecting the map element in the Print Composer and clicking the **[Update preview]** button in the map *Item Properties* tab (see figure_composer_map_1).

Grids

The *Grids* dialog of the map *Item Properties* tab provides the possibility to add several grids to a map item.

- With the plus and minus button you can add or remove a selected grid.
- With the up and down button you can move a grid in the list and set the drawing priority.

When you double click on the added grid you can give it another name.

Figure 18.6: Map Grids Dialog

After you have added a grid, you can activate the checkbox 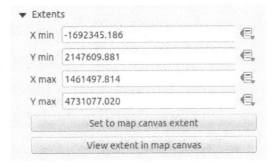 *Show grid* to overlay a grid onto the map element. Expand this option to provide a lot of configuration options, see Figure_composer_map_4.

As grid type, you can specify to use a 'Solid', 'Cross', 'Markers' or 'Frame and annotations only'. 'Frame and annotations only' is especially useful when working with rotated maps or reprojected grids. In the devisions

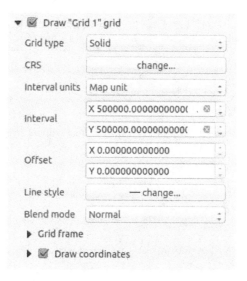

Figure 18.7: Draw Grid Dialog △

section of the Grid Frame Dialog mentioned below you then have a corresponding setting. Symbology of the grid can be chosen. See section Rendering_Mode. Furthermore, you can define an interval in the X and Y directions, an X and Y offset, and the width used for the cross or line grid type.

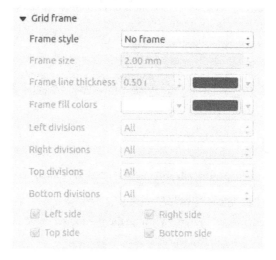

Figure 18.8: Grid Frame Dialog △

- There are different options to style the frame that holds the map. Following options are available: No Frame, Zebra, Interior ticks, Exterior ticks, Interior and Exterior ticks and Lineborder.

- With 'LatitudeY/ only' and 'Longitude/X only' setting in the devisions section you have the possibility to prevent a mix of latitude/y and longitude/x coordinates showing on a side when working with rotated maps or reprojected grids.

- Advanced rendering mode is also available for grids (see section Rendering_mode).

- The ☑ *Draw coordinates* checkbox allows you to add coordinates to the map frame. You can choose the annotation numeric format, the options range from decimal to degrees, minute and seconds, with or without suffix, and aligned or not. You can choose which annotation to show. The options are: show all, latitude only, longitude only, or disable(none). This is useful when the map is rotated. The annotation can be drawn inside or outside the map frame. The annotation direction can be defined as horizontal, vertical ascending or vertical descending. In case of map rotation you can Finally, you can define the annotation font, the annotation font color, the annotation distance from the map frame and the precision of the drawn coordinates.

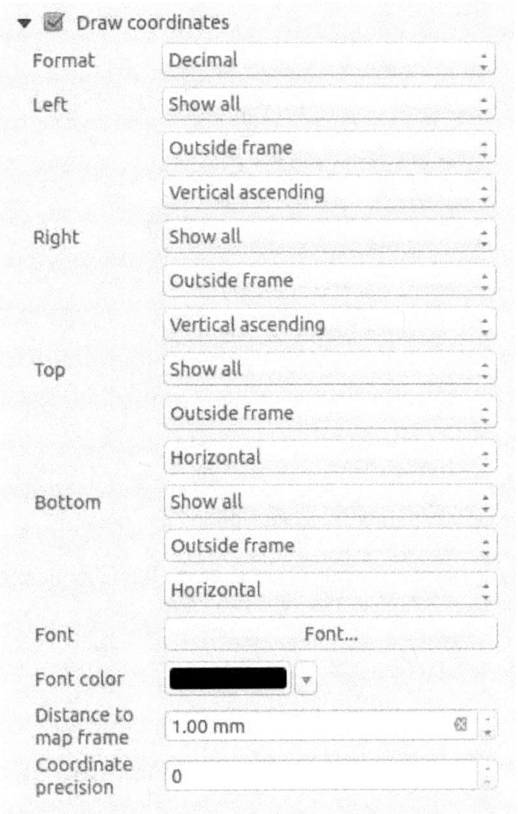

Figure 18.9: Grid Draw Coordinates dialog

Overviews

The *Overviews* dialog of the map *Item Properties* tab provides the following functionalities:

You can choose to create an overview map, which shows the extents of the other map(s) that are available in the composer. First you need to create the map(s) you want to include in the overview map. Next you create the map you want to use as the overview map, just like a normal map.

- With the plus and minus button you can add or remove an overview.

- With the up and down button you can move an overview in the list and set the drawing priority.

Open *Overviews* and press the green plus icon-button to add an overview. Initially this overview is named 'Overview 1' (see Figure_composer_map_7). You can change the name when you double-click on the overview item in the list named 'Overview 1' and change it to another name.

When you select the overview item in the list you can customize it.

- The ☑ *Draw "<name_overview>" overview* needs to be activated to draw the extent of selected map frame.

- The *Map frame* combo list can be used to select the map item whose extents will be drawn on the present map item.

- The *Frame Style* allows you to change the style of the overview frame.

- The *Blending mode* allows you to set different transparency blend modes. See Rendering_Mode.

18.3. Composer Items

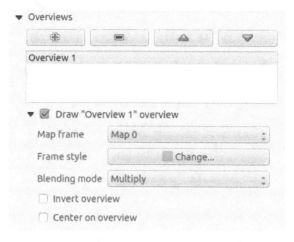

Figure 18.10: Map Overviews Dialog

- The *Invert overview* creates a mask around the extents when activated: the referenced map extents are shown clearly, whereas everything else is blended with the frame color.

- The *Center on overview* puts the extent of the overview frame in the center of the overview map. You can only activate one overview item to center, when you have added several overviews.

18.3.2 The Label item

To add a label, click the ![Add label] *Add label* icon, place the element with the left mouse button on the Print Composer canvas and position and customize its appearance in the label *Item Properties* tab.

The *Item Properties* tab of a label item provides the following functionality for the label item (see Figure_composer_label):

Figure 18.11: Label Item properties Tab

Main properties

- The main properties dialog is where the text (HTML or not) or the expression needed to fill the label is added to the Composer canvas.

- Labels can be interpreted as HTML code: check ☑ *Render as HTML*. You can now insert a URL, a clickable image that links to a web page or something more complex.

- You can also insert an expression. Click on **[Insert an expression]** to open a new dialog. Build an expression by clicking the functions available in the left side of the panel. Two special categories can be useful, particularly associated with the atlas functionality: geometry functions and records functions. At the bottom, a preview of the expression is shown.

Appearance

- Define *Font* by clicking on the **[Font...]** button or a *Font color* selecting a color using the color selection tool.

- You can specify different horizontal and vertical margins in mm. This is the margin from the edge of the composer item. The label can be positioned outside the bounds of the label e.g. to align label items with other items. In this case you have to use negative values for the margin.

- Using the *Alignment* is another way to position your label. Note that when e.g. using the *Horizontal alignment* in ◉ *Center* Position the *Horizontal margin* feature is disabled.

18.3.3 The Image item

To add an image, click the ▣ Add image icon, place the element with the left mouse button on the Print Composer canvas and position and customize its appearance in the image *Item Properties* tab.

The picture *Item Properties* tab provides the following functionalities (see figure_composer_image_1):

You first have to select the image you want to display. There are several ways to set the *image source* in the **Main properties** area.

1. Use the browse button ▣ of *image source* to select a file on your computer using the browse dialog. The browser will start in the SVG-libraries provided with QGIS. Besides SVG, you can also select other image formats like .png or .jpg.

2. You can enter the source directly in the *image source* text field. You can even provide a remote URL-address to an image.

3. From the **Search directories** area you can also select an image from *loading previews ...* to set the image source.

4. Use the data defined button ▣ to set the image source from a record or using a regular expression.

With the *Resize mode* option, you can set how the image is displayed when the frame is changed, or choose to resize the frame of the image item so it matches the original size of the image.

You can select one of the following modes:

- Zoom: Enlarges the image to the frame while maintaining aspect ratio of picture.

- Stretch: Stretches image to fit inside the frame, ignores aspect ratio.

- Clip: Use this mode for raster images only, it sets the size of the image to original image size without scaling and the frame is used to clip the image, so only the part of the image inside the frame is visible.

- Zoom and resize frame: Enlarges image to fit frame, then resizes frame to fit resultant image.

- Resize frame to image size: Sets size of frame to match original size of image without scaling.

Figure 18.12: Image Item properties Tab 🐧

Selected resize mode can disable the item options 'Placement' and 'Image rotation'. The *Image rotation* is active for the resize mode 'Zoom' and 'Clip'.

With *Placement* you can select the position of the image inside it's frame. The **Search directories** area allows you to add and remove directories with images in SVG format to the picture database. A preview of the pictures found in the selected directories is shown in a pane and can be used to select and set the image source.

Images can be rotated with the *Image rotation* field. Activating the ☑ *Sync with map* checkbox synchronizes the rotation of a picture in the QGIS map canvas (i.e., a rotated north arrow) with the appropriate Print Composer image.

It is also possible to select a north arrow directly. If you first select a north arrow image from **Search directories** and then use the browse button ⬚⬚⬚ of the field *Image source*, you can now select one of the north arrow from the list as displayed in figure_composer_image_2.

Note: Many of the north arrows do not have an 'N' added in the north arrow, this is done on purpose for languages that do not use an 'N' for North, so they can use another letter.

18.3.4 The Legend item

To add a map legend, click the ▦ *Add new legend* icon, place the element with the left mouse button on the Print Composer canvas and position and customize the appearance in the legend *Item Properties* tab.

The *Item properties* of a legend item tab provides the following functionalities (see figure_composer_legend_1):

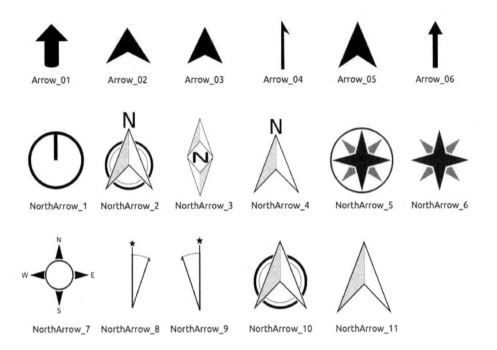

Figure 18.13: North arrows available for selection in provided SVG library

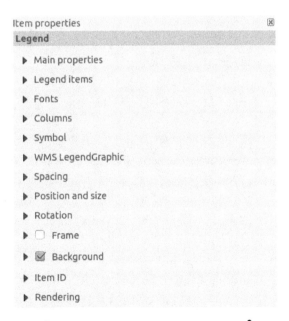

Figure 18.14: Legend Item properties Tab

Main properties

The *Main properties* dialog of the legend *Item Properties* tab provides the following functionalities (see figure_composer_legend_2):

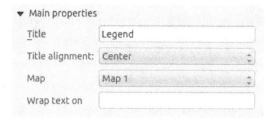

Figure 18.15: Legend Main properties Dialog ⚇

In Main properties you can:

- Change the title of the legend.
- Set the title alignment to Left, Center or Right.
- You can choose which *Map* item the current legend will refer to in the select list.
- You can wrap the text of the legend title on a given character.

Legend items

The *Legend items* dialog of the legend *Item Properties* tab provides the following functionalities (see figure_composer_legend_3):

Figure 18.16: Legend Legend Items Dialog ⚇

- The legend will be updated automatically if ✔ *Auto-update* is checked. When *Auto-update* is unchecked this will give you more control over the legend items. The icons below the legend items list will be activated.

- The legend items window lists all legend items and allows you to change item order, group layers, remove and restore items in the list, edit layer names and add a filter.

  - The item order can be changed using the **[Up]** and **[Down]** buttons or with 'drag-and-drop' functionality. The order can not be changed for WMS legend graphics.

  - Use the **[Add group]** button to add a legend group.

  - Use the **[plus]** and **[minus]** button to add or remove layers.

  - The **[Edit]** button is used to edit the layer-, groupname or title, first you need to select the legend item.

  - The **[Sigma]** button adds a feature count for each vector layer.

  - Use the **[filter]** button to filter the legend by map content, only the legend items visible in the map will be listed in the legend.

After changing the symbology in the QGIS main window, you can click on [**Update All**] to adapt the changes in the legend element of the Print Composer.

Fonts, Columns, Symbol

The *Fonts*, *Columns* and *Symbol* dialogs of the legend *Item Properties* tab provide the following functionalities (see figure_composer_legend_4):

Figure 18.17: Legend Fonts, Columns, Symbol and Spacing Dialogs 🐧

• You can change the font of the legend title, group, subgroup and item (layer) in the legend item. Click on a category button to open a **Select font** dialog.

• You provide the labels with a **Color** using the advanced color picker, however the selected color will be given to all font items in the legend..

• Legend items can be arranged over several columns. Set the number of columns in the *Count* 1.00 ◇ field.

 – 🗹 *Equal column widths* sets how legend columns should be adjusted.

 – The 🗹 *Split layers* option allows a categorized or a graduated layer legend to be divided between columns.

• You can change the width and height of the legend symbol in this dialog.

WMS LegendGraphic and Spacing

The *WMS LegendGraphic* and *Spacing* dialogs of the legend *Item Properties* tab provide the following functionalities (see figure_composer_legend_5):

When you have added a WMS layer and you insert a legend composer item, a request will be send to the WMS server to provide a WMS legend. This Legend will only be shown if the WMS server provides the GetLegend-Graphic capability. The WMS legend content will be provided as a raster image.

WMS LegendGraphic is used to be able to adjust the *Legend width* and the *Legend height* of the WMS legend raster image.

Spacing around title, group, subgroup, symbol, icon label, box space or column space can be customized through this dialog.

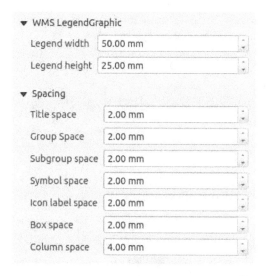

Figure 18.18: WMS LegendGraphic Dialogs △

18.3.5 The Scale Bar item

To add a scale bar, click the ⊞ Add new scalebar icon, place the element with the left mouse button on the Print Composer canvas and position and customize the appearance in the scale bar *Item Properties* tab.

The *Item properties* of a scale bar item tab provides the following functionalities (see figure_composer_scalebar_1):

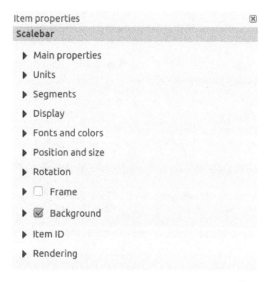

Figure 18.19: Scale Bar Item properties Tab △

Main properties

The *Main properties* dialog of the scale bar *Item Properties* tab provides the following functionalities (see figure_composer_scalebar_2):

- First, choose the map the scale bar will be attached to.

- Then, choose the style of the scale bar. Six styles are available:

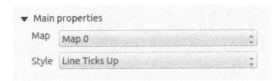

Figure 18.20: Scale Bar Main properties Dialog ⌂

– **Single box** and **Double box** styles, which contain one or two lines of boxes alternating colors.

– **Middle**, **Up** or **Down** line ticks.

– **Numeric**, where the scale ratio is printed (i.e., 1:50000).

Units and Segments

The *Units* and *Segments* dialogs of the scale bar *Item Properties* tab provide the following functionalities (see figure_composer_scalebar_3):

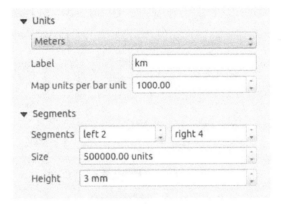

Figure 18.21: Scale Bar Units and Segments Dialogs ⌂

In these two dialogs, you can set how the scale bar will be represented.

- Select the map units used. There are four possible choices: **Map Units** is the automated unit selection; **Meters**, **Feet** or **Nautical Miles** force unit conversions.

- The *Label* field defines the text used to describe the units of the scale bar.

- The *Map units per bar unit* allows you to fix the ratio between a map unit and its representation in the scale bar.

- You can define how many *Segments* will be drawn on the left and on the right side of the scale bar, and how long each segment will be (*Size* field). *Height* can also be defined.

Display

The *Display* dialog of the scale bar *Item Properties* tab provide the following functionalities (see figure_composer_scalebar_4):

You can define how the scale bar will be displayed in its frame.

- *Box margin* : space between text and frame borders

- *Labels margin* : space between text and scale bar drawing

- *Line width* : line widht of the scale bar drawing

Figure 18.22: Scale Bar Display 🐧

- *Join style* : Corners at the end of scalebar in style Bevel, Rounded or Square (only available for Scale bar style Single Box & Double Box)

- *Cap style* : End of all lines in style Square, Round or Flat (only available for Scale bar style Line Ticks Up, Down and Middle)

- *Alignment* : Puts text on the left, middle or right side of the frame (works only for Scale bar style Numeric)

Fonts and colors

The *Fonts and colors* dialog of the scale bar *Item Properties* tab provide the following functionalities (see figure_composer_scalebar_5):

Figure 18.23: Scale Bar Fonts and colors Dialogs 🐧

You can define the fonts and colors used for the scale bar.

- Use the **[Font]** button to set the font

- *Font color*: set the font color

- *Fill color*: set the first fill color

- *Secondary fill color*: set the second fill color

- *Stroke color*: set the color of the lines of the Scale Bar

Fill colors are only used for scale box styles Single Box and Double Box. To select a color you can use the list option using the dropdown arrow to open a simple color selection option or the more advanced color selection option, that is started when you click in the colored box in the dialog.

18.3.6 The Basic Shape Items

To add a basic shape (ellipse, rectangle, triangle), click the ⬠ Add basic shape icon or the ╱ Add Arrow icon, place the element holding down the left mouse. Customize the appearance in the *Item Properties* tab.

When you also hold down the Shift key while placing the basic shape you can create a perfect square, circle or triangle.

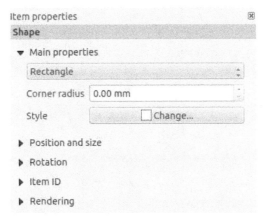

Figure 18.24: Shape Item properties Tab

The *Shape* item properties tab allows you to select if you want to draw an ellipse, rectangle or triangle inside the given frame.

You can set the style of the shape using the advanced symbol style dialog with which you can define its outline and fill color, fill pattern, use markers etcetera.

For the rectangle shape, you can set the value of the corner radius to round of the corners.

Note: Unlike other items, you can not style the frame or the background color of the frame.

18.3.7 The Arrow item

To add an arrow, click the ✐ Add Arrow icon, place the element holding down the left mouse button and drag a line to draw the arrow on the Print Composer canvas and position and customize the appearance in the scale bar *Item Properties* tab.

When you also hold down the Shift key while placing the arrow, it is placed in an angle of exactly 45° .

The arrow item can be used to add a line or a simple arrow that can be used, for example, to show the relation between other print composer items. To create a north arrow, the image item should be considered first. QGIS has a set of North arrows in SVG format. Furthermore you can connect an image item with a map so it can rotate automatically with the map (see the_image_item).

Item Properties

The *Arrow* item properties tab allows you to configure an arrow item.

The [**Line style ...**] button can be used to set the line style using the line style symbol editor.

In *Arrows markers* you can select one of three radio buttons.

- *Default* : To draw a regular arrow, gives you options to style the arrow head

- *None* : To draw a line without arrow head

- *SVG Marker* : To draw a line with an SVG *Start marker* and/or *End marker*

For *Default* Arrow marker you can use following options to style the arrow head.

- *Arrow outline color* : Set the outline color of the arrow head

---

Figure 18.25: Arrow Item properties Tab 🐧

- *Arrow fill color* : Set the fill color of the arrow head
- *Arrow outline width* : Set the outline width of the arrow head
- *Arrow head width*: Set the size of the arrow head

For *SVG Marker* you can use following options.

- *Start marker* : Choose an SVG image to draw at the beginning of the line
- *End marker* : Choose an SVG image to draw at the end of the line
- *Arrow head width*: Sets the size of Start and/or End marker

SVG images are automatically rotated with the line. The color of the SVG image can not be changed.

18.3.8 The Attribute Table item

It is possible to add parts of a vector attribute table to the Print Composer canvas: Click the ▦ Add attribute table icon, place the element with the left mouse button on the Print Composer canvas, and position and customize the appearance in the *Item Properties* tab.

The *Item properties* of an attribute table item tab provides the following functionalities (see figure_composer_table_1):

Main properties

The *Main properties* dialogs of the attribute table *Item Properties* tab provide the following functionalities (see figure_composer_table_2):

- For *Source* you can normally select only 'Layer features'.
- With *Layer* you can choose from the vector layers loaded in the project.
- The button **[Refresh table data]** can be used to refresh the table when the actual contents of the table has changed.
- In case you activated the ☑ *Generate an atlas* option in the *Atlas generation* tab, there are two additional *Source* possible: 'Current atlas feature' (see figure_composer_table_2b) and 'Relation children' (see figure_composer_table_2c). Choosing the 'Current atlas feature' you won't see any option to choose the layer, and the table item will only show a row with the attributes from the current feature of the atlas coverage

Figure 18.26: Attribute table Item properties Tab 🐧

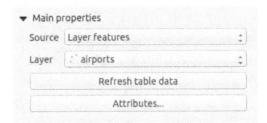

Figure 18.27: Attribute table Main properties Dialog 🐧

layer. Choosing 'Relation children', an option with the relation name will show up. The 'Relation children' option can only be used if you have defined a relation using your atlas coverage layer as parent, and it will show the children rows of the atlas coverage layer's current feature (for further information about the atlas generation see atlasgeneration).

Figure 18.28: Attribute table Main properties for 'Current atlas feature' △

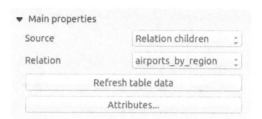

Figure 18.29: Attribute table Main properties for 'Relation children' △

- The button [**Attributes...**] starts the *Select attributes* menu, see figure_composer_table_3, that can be used to change the visible contents of the table. After making changes use the [**OK**] button to apply changes to the table.

In the *Columns* section you can:

   – Remove an attribute, just select an attribute row by clicking anywhere in a row and press the minus button to remove the selected attribute.

   – Add a new attribute use the plus button. At the end a new empty row appears and you can select empty cell of the column *Attribute*. You can select a field attribute from the list or you can select to build a new attribute using a regular expression (ε button). Of course you can modify every already existing attribute by means of a regular expression.

   – Use the up and down arrows to change the order of the attributes in the table.

   – Select a cel in the Headings column to change the Heading, just type in a new name.

   – Select a cel in the Alignment column and you can choose between Left, Center or Right alignment.

   – Select a cel in the Width column and you can change it from Automatic to a width in mm, just type a number. When you want to change it back to Automatic, use the cross.

   – The [**Reset**] button can always be used to restore it to the original attribute settings.

In the *Sorting* section you can:

   – Add an attribute to sort the table with. Select an attribute and set the sorting order to 'Ascending' or 'Descending' and press the plus button. A new line is added to the sort order list.

   – select a row in the list and use the up and down button to change the sort priority on attribute level.

   – use the minus button to remove an attribute from the sort order list.

Feature filtering

The *Feature filtering* dialogs of the attribute table *Item Properties* tab provide the following functionalities (see figure_composer_table_4):

Figure 18.30: Attribute table Select attributes Dialog △

Figure 18.31: Attribute table Feature filtering Dialog △

You can:

- Define the *Maximum rows* to be displayed.

- Activate ☑ *Remove duplicate rows from table* to show unique records only.

- Activate ☑ *Show only visible features within a map* and select the corresponding *Composer map* to display the attributes of features only visible on selected map.

- Activate ☑ *Show only features intersecting Atlas feature* is only available when ☑ *Generate an atlas* is activated. When activated it will show a table with only the features shown on the map of that particular page of the atlas.

- Activate ☑ *Filter with* and provide a filter by typing in the input line or insert a regular expression using the given ε expression button. A few examples of filtering statements you can use when you have loaded the airports layer from the Sample dataset:

  – ELEV > 500

  – NAME = 'ANIAK'

  – NAME NOT LIKE 'AN%

  – regexp_match(attribute($currentfeature, 'USE') , '[i]')

  The last regular expression will include only the arpoirts that have a letter 'i' in the attribute field 'USE'.

Appearance

The *Appearance* dialogs of the attribute table *Item Properties* tab provide the following functionalities (see figure_composer_table_5):

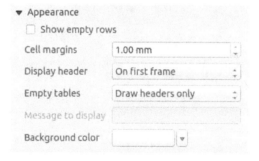

Figure 18.32: Attribute table appearance Dialog 🐧

- Click ☑ *Show empty rows* to make empty entries in the attribute table visible.

- With *Cell margins* you can define the margin around text in each cell of the table.

- With *Display header* you can select from a list one of 'On first frame', 'On all frames' default option, or 'No header'.

- The option *Empty table* controls what will be displayed when the result selection is empty.

  – **Draw headers only**, will only draw the header except if you have choosen 'No header' for *Display header*.

  – **Hide entire table**, will only draw the background of the table. You can activate ☑ *Don't draw background if frame is empty* in *Frames* to completely hide the table.

  – **Draw empty cells**, will fill the attribute table with empty cells, this option can also be used to provide additional empty cells when you have a result to show!

– **Show set message**, will draw the header and adds a cell spanning all columns and display a message like 'No result' that can be provided in the option *Message to display*

- The option *Message to display* is only activated when you have selected **Show set message** for *Empty table*. The message provided will be shown in the table in the first row, when the result is an empty table.

- With *Background color* you can set the background color of the table.

Show grid

The *Show grid* dialog of the attribute table *Item Properties* tab provide the following functionalities (see figure_composer_table_6):

Figure 18.33: Attribute table Show grid Dialog

- Activate *Show grid* when you want to display the grid, the outlines of the table cells.

- With *Stroke width* you can set the thickness of the lines used in the grid.

- The *Color* of the grid can be set using the color selection dialog.

Fonts and text styling

The *Fonts and text styling* dialog of the attribute table *Item Properties* tab provide the following functionalities (see figure_composer_table_7):

Figure 18.34: Attribute table Fonts and text styling Dialog

- You can define *Font* and *Color* for *Table heading* and *Table contents*.

- For *Table heading* you can additionally set the *Alignment* and choose from *Follow column alignment*, *Left*, *Center* or *Right*. The column alignment is set using the *Select Attributes* dialog (see Figure_composer_table_3).

Frames

The *Frames* dialog of the attribute table *Item Properties* tab provide the following functionalities (see figure_composer_table_8):

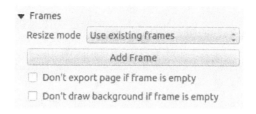

Figure 18.35: Attribute table Frames Dialog ⌂

- With *Resize mode* you can select how to render the attribute table contents:

    - *Use existing frames* displays the result in the first frame and added frames only.

    - *Extent to next page* will create as many frames (and corresponding pages) as necessary to display the full selection of attribute table. Each frame can be moved around on the layout. If you resize a frame, the resulting table will be divided up between the other frames. The last frame will be trimmed to fit the table.

    - *Repeat until finished* will also create as many frames as the *Extend to next page* option, except all frames will have the same size.

- Use the **[Add Frame]** button to add another frame with the same size as selected frame. The result of the table that will not fit in the first frame will continue in the next frame when you use the Resize mode *Use existing frames*.

- Activate ☑ *Don't export page if frame is empty* prevents the page to be exported when the table frame has no contents. This means all other composer items, maps, scalebars, legends etc. will not be visible in the result.

- Activate ☑ *Don't draw background if frame is empty* prevents the background to be drawn when the table frame has no contents.

18.3.9 The HTML frame item

It is possible to add a frame that displays the contents of a website or even create and style your own HTML page and display it!

Click the [icon] Add HTML frame icon, place the element by dragging a rectangle holding down the left mouse button on the Print Composer canvas and position and customize the appearance in the *Item Properties* tab (see figure_composer_html_1).

HTML Source

As an HTML source, you can either set a URL and activate the URL radiobutton or enter the HTML source directly in the textbox provided and activate the Source radiobutton.

The *HTML Source* dialog of the HTML frame *Item Properties* tab provides the following functionalities (see figure_composer_html_2):

- In *URL* you can enter the URL of a webpage you copied from your internet browser or select an HTML file using the browse button [...]. There is also the option to use the Data defined override button, to provide an URL from the contents of an attribute field of a table or using a regular expression.

- In *Source* you can enter text in the textbox with some HTML tags or provide a full HTML page.

- The **[insert an expression]** button can be used to insert an expression like [%Year($now)%] in the Source textbox to display the current year. This button is only activated when radiobutton *Source* is selected.

Figure 18.36: HTML frame, the item properties Tab

Figure 18.37: HTML frame, the HTML Source properties

After inserting the expression click somewhere in the textbox before refreshing the HTML frame, otherwise you will lose the expression.

- Activate ☑ *Evaluate QGIS expressions in HTML code* to see the result of the expression you have included, otherwise you will see the expression instead.

- Use the **[Refresh HTML]** button to refresh the HTML frame(s) to see the result of changes.

Frames

The *Frames* dialog of the HTML frame *Item Properties* tab provides the following functionalities (see figure_composer_html_3):

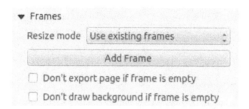

Figure 18.38: HTML frame, the Frames properties 🐧

- With *Resize mode* you can select how to render the HTML contents:

  - *Use existing frames* displays the result in the first frame and added frames only.

  - *Extent to next page* will create as many frames (and corresponding pages) as necessary to render the height of the web page. Each frame can be moved around on the layout. If you resize a frame, the webpage will be divided up between the other frames. The last frame will be trimmed to fit the web page.

  - *Repeat on every page* will repeat the upper left of the web page on every page in frames of the same size.

  - *Repeat until finished* will also create as many frames as the *Extend to next page* option, except all frames will have the same size.

- Use the **[Add Frame]** button to add another frame with the same size as selected frame. If the HTML page that will not fit in the first frame it will continue in the next frame when you use *Resize mode* or *Use existing frames*.

- Activate ☑ *Don't export page if frame is empty* prevents the map layout from being exported when the frame has no HTML contents. This means all other composer items, maps, scalebars, legends etc. will not be visible in the result.

- Activate ☑ *Don't draw background if frame is empty* prevents the HTML frame being drawn if the frame is empty.

Use smart page breaks and User style sheet

The *Use smart page breaks* dialog and *Use style sheet* dialog of the HTML frame *Item Properties* tab provides the following functionalities (see figure_composer_html_4):

- Activate ☑ *Use smart page breaks* to prevent the html frame contents from breaking mid-way a line of text so it continues nice and smooth in the next frame.

- Set the *Maximum distance* allowed when calculating where to place page breaks in the html. This distance is the maximum amount of empty space allowed at the bottom of a frame after calculating the optimum break location. Setting a larger value will result in better choice of page break location, but more wasted space at the bottom of frames. This is only used when *Use smart page breaks* is activated.

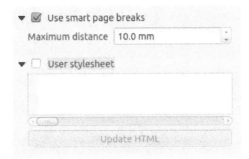

Figure 18.39: HTML frame, Use smart page breaks and User stylesheet properties △

- Activate ☑ *User stylesheet* to apply HTML styles that often is provided in cascading style sheets. An example of style code is provide below to set the color of <h1> header tag to green and set the font and fontsize of text included in paragraph tags <p>.

```
h1 {color: #00ff00;
}
p {font-family: "Times New Roman", Times, serif;
    font-size: 20px;
}
```

- Use the **[Update HTML]** button to see the result of the stylesheet settings.

18.4 Manage items

18.4.1 Size and position

Each item inside the Composer can be moved/resized to create a perfect layout. For both operations the first step is to activate the ⌖ Select/Move item tool and to click on the item; you can then move it using the mouse while holding the left button. If you need to constrain the movements to the horizontal or the vertical axis, just hold the Shift while moving the mouse. If you need a better precision, you can move a selected item using the Arrow keys on the keyboard; if the movement is too slow, you can speed up it by holding Shift.

A selected item will show squares on its boundaries; moving one of them with the mouse, will resize the item in the corresponding direction. While resizing, holding Shift will maintain the aspect ratio. Holding Alt will resize from the item center.

The correct position for an item can be obtained using snapping to grid or smart guides. Guides are set by clicking and dragging in the rulers. Guides are moved by clicking in the ruler, level with the guide and dragging to a new place. To delete a guide move it off the canvas. If you need to disable the snap on the fly just hold Ctrl while moving the mouse.

You can choose multiple items with the ⌖ Select/Move item button. Just hold the Shift button and click on all the items you need. You can then resize/move this group just like a single item.

Once you have found the correct position for an item, you can lock it by using the items on the toolbar or ticking the box next to the item in the *Items* tab. Locked items are **not** selectable on the canvas.

Locked items can be unlocked by selecting the item in the *Items* tab and unchecking the tickbox or you can use the icons on the toolbar.

To unselect an item, just click on it holding the Shift button.

Inside the *Edit* menu, you can find actions to select all the items, to clear all selections or to invert the current selection.

18.4.2 Alignment

Raising or lowering functionalities for elements are inside the 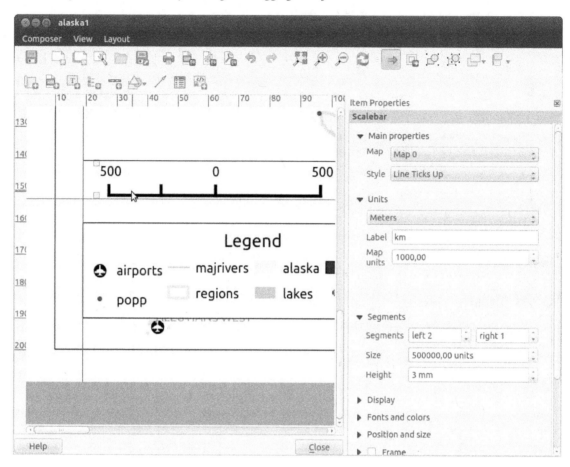 Raise selected items pull-down menu. Choose an element on the Print Composer canvas and select the matching functionality to raise or lower the selected element compared to the other elements (see table_composer_1). This order is shown in the *Items* tab. You can also raise or lower objects in the *Items* tab by clicking and dragging an object's label in this list.

Figure 18.40: Alignment helper lines in the Print Composer

There are several alignment functionalities available within the Align selected items pull-down menu (see table_composer_1). To use an alignment functionality, you first select some elements and then click on the matching alignment icon. All selected elements will then be aligned within to their common bounding box. When moving items on the Composer canvas, alignment helper lines appear when borders, centers or corners are aligned.

18.4.3 Copy/Cut and Paste items

The print composer includes actions to use the common Copy/Cut/Paste functionality for the items in the layout. As usual first you need to select the items using one of the options seen above; at this point the actions can be found in the *Edit* menu. When using the Paste action, the elements will be pasted according to the current mouse position.

Note: HTML items can not be copied in this way. As a workaround, use the **[Add Frame]** button in the *Item Properties* tab.

18.5 Revert and Restore tools

During the layout process, it is possible to revert and restore changes. This can be done with the revert and restore tools:

- Revert last change

- Restore last change

This can also be done by mouse click within the *Command history* tab (see figure_composer_29).

Figure 18.41: Command history in the Print Composer

18.6 Atlas generation

The Print Composer includes generation functions that allow you to create map books in an automated way. The concept is to use a coverage layer, which contains geometries and fields. For each geometry in the coverage layer, a new output will be generated where the content of some canvas maps will be moved to highlight the current geometry. Fields associated with this geometry can be used within text labels.

Every page will be generated with each feature. To enable the generation of an atlas and access generation parameters, refer to the *Atlas generation* tab. This tab contains the following widgets (see Figure_composer_atlas):

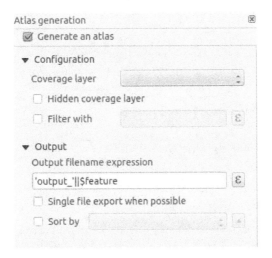

Figure 18.42: Atlas generation tab

- ☑ *Generate an atlas*, which enables or disables the atlas generation.

- A *Coverage layer* combo box that allows you to choose the (vector) layer containing the geometries on which to iterate over.

- An optional ☑ *Hidden coverage layer* that, if checked, will hide the coverage layer (but not the other ones) during the generation.

- An optional *Filter with* text area that allows you to specify an expression for filtering features from the coverage layer. If the expression is not empty, only features that evaluate to `True` will be selected. The button on the right allows you to display the expression builder.

- An *Output filename expression* textbox that is used to generate a filename for each geometry if needed. It is based on expressions. This field is meaningful only for rendering to multiple files.

- A ☑ *Single file export when possible* that allows you to force the generation of a single file if this is possible with the chosen output format (PDF, for instance). If this field is checked, the value of the *Output filename expression* field is meaningless.

- An optional ☑ *Sort by* that, if checked, allows you to sort features of the coverage layer. The associated combo box allows you to choose which column will be used as the sorting key. Sort order (either ascending or descending) is set by a two-state button that displays an up or a down arrow.

You can use multiple map items with the atlas generation; each map will be rendered according to the coverage features. To enable atlas generation for a specific map item, you need to check ☑ *Controlled by Atlas* under the item properties of the map item. Once checked, you can set:

- A radiobutton ◉ *Margin around feature* that allows you to select the amount of space added around each geometry within the allocated map. Its value is meaningful only when using the auto-scaling mode.

- A ◯ *Predefined scale* (best fit). It will use the best fitting option from the list of predefined scales in your project properties settings (see *Project –> Project Properties –> General –> Project Scales* to configure these predefined scales).

- A ◯ *Fixed scale* that allows you to toggle between auto-scale and fixed-scale mode. In fixed-scale mode, the map will only be translated for each geometry to be centered. In auto-scale mode, the map's extents are computed in such a way that each geometry will appear in its entirety.

18.6.1 Labels

In order to adapt labels to the feature the atlas plugin iterates over, you can include expressions. For example, for a city layer with fields CITY_NAME and ZIPCODE, you could insert this:

```
The area of [% upper(CITY_NAME) || ',' || ZIPCODE || ' is ' format_number($area/1000000,2) %] km2
```

The information *[% upper(CITY_NAME) || ',' || ZIPCODE || ' is ' format_number($area/1000000,2) %]* is an expression used inside the label. That would result in the generated atlas as:

The area of PARIS,75001 is 1.94 km2

18.6.2 Data Defined Override Buttons

There are several places where you can use a ⬜ Data Defined Override button to override the selected setting. These options are particularly usefull with Atlas Generation.

For the following examples the *Regions* layer of the QGIS sample dataset is used and selected for Atlas Generation. We also assume the paper format *A4 (210X297)* is selected in the *Composition* tab for field *Presets*.

With a *Data Defined Override* button you can dynamically set the paper orientation. When the height (north-south) of the extents of a region is greater than it's width (east-west), you rather want to use *portrait* instead of *landscape* orientation to optimize the use of paper.

In the *Composition* you can set the field *Orientation* and select *Landscape* or *Portrait*. We want to set the orientation dynamically using an expression depending on the region geometry. press the ⬜ button of field *Orientation*, select *Edit ...* so the *Expression string builder* dialog opens. Give following expression:

```
CASE WHEN bounds_width($atlasgeometry) > bounds_height($atlasgeometry) THEN 'Landscape' ELSE 'Portrait'
```

Now the paper orients itself automatically for each Region you need to reposition the location of the composer item as well. For the map item you can use the ⬅ button of field *Width* to set it dynamically using following expression:

```
(CASE WHEN bounds_width($atlasgeometry) > bounds_height($atlasgeometry) THEN 297 ELSE 210 END) - 20
```

Use the ⬅ button of field *Heigth* to provide following expression:

```
(CASE WHEN bounds_width($atlasgeometry) > bounds_height($atlasgeometry) THEN 210 ELSE 297 END) - 20
```

When you want to give a title above map in the center of the page, insert a label item above the map. First use the item properties of the label item to set the horizontal alignment to ⦿ *Center*. Next activate from *Reference point* the upper middle checkbox. You can provide following expression for field *X* :

```
(CASE WHEN bounds_width($atlasgeometry) > bounds_height($atlasgeometry) THEN 297 ELSE 210 END) / 2
```

For all other composer items you can set the position in a similar way so they are correctly positioned when page is automatically rotated in portrait or landscape.

Information provided is derived from the excellent blog (in english and portugese) on the Data Defined Override options Multiple_format_map_series_using_QGIS_2.6 .

This is just one example of how you can use Data Defined Overrides.

18.6.3 Preview

Once the atlas settings have been configured and map items selected, you can create a preview of all the pages by clicking on *Atlas → Preview Atlas* and using the arrows, in the same menu, to navigate through all the features.

18.6.4 Generation

The atlas generation can be done in different ways. For example, with *Atlas → Print Atlas*, you can directly print it. You can also create a PDF using *Atlas → Export Atlas as PDF*: The user will be asked for a directory for saving all the generated PDF files (except if the ☑ *Single file export when possible* has been selected). If you need to print just a page of the atlas, simply start the preview function, select the page you need and click on *Composer → Print* (or create a PDF).

18.7 Hide and show panels

To maximise the space available to interact with a composition you can use *View –>* ☑ *Hide panels* or press F10.

:: note:

```
It's also possible to switch to a full screen mode to have more space to interact by pressing
:kbd:`F11` or using :guilabel:`View --> |checkbox| :guilabel:`Toggle full screen`.
```

18.8 Creating Output

Figure_composer_output shows the Print Composer with an example print layout, including each type of map item described in the sections above.

Before printing a layout you have the possibility to view your composition without bounding boxes. This can be enabled by deactivating *View –>* ☑ *Show bounding boxes* or pressing the shortcut Ctrl+Shift+B.

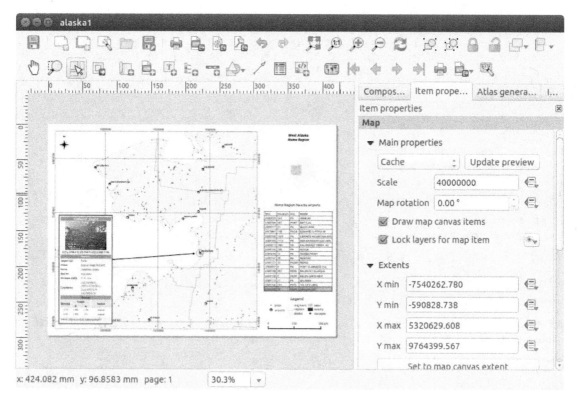

Figure 18.43: Print Composer with map view, legend, image, scale bar, coordinates, text and HTML frame added

The Print Composer allows you to create several output formats, and it is possible to define the resolution (print quality) and paper size:

- The ⎙ Print icon allows you to print the layout to a connected printer or a PostScript file, depending on installed printer drivers.

- The 🖼 Export as image icon exports the Composer canvas in several image formats, such as PNG, BPM, TIF, JPG,...

- 📄 Export as PDF saves the defined Print Composer canvas directly as a PDF.

- The 🖼 Export as SVG icon saves the Print Composer canvas as an SVG (Scalable Vector Graphic).

If you need to export your layout as a **georeferenced image** (i.e., to load back inside QGIS), you need to enable this feature under the Composition tab. Check ☑ *World file on* and choose the map item to use. With this option, the 'Export as image' action will also create a world file.

Note:

- Currently, the SVG output is very basic. This is not a QGIS problem, but a problem with the underlying Qt library. This will hopefully be sorted out in future versions.

- Exporting big rasters can sometimes fail, even if there seems to be enough memory. This is also a problem with the underlying Qt management of rasters.

18.9 Manage the Composer

With the 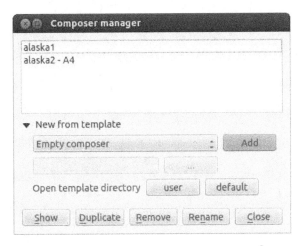 Save as template and Add items from template icons, you can save the current state of a Print Composer session as a `.qpt` template and load the template again in another session.

The Composer Manager button in the QGIS toolbar and in *Composer → Composer Manager* allows you to add a new Composer template, create a new composition based on a previously saved template or to manage already existing templates.

Figure 18.44: The Print Composer Manager

By default, the Composer manager searches for user templates in ~/.qgis2/composer_template.

The New Composer and Duplicate Composer buttons in the QGIS toolbar and in *Composer → New Composer* and *Composer → Duplicate Composer* allow you to open a new Composer dialog, or to duplicate an existing composition from a previously created one.

Finally, you can save your print composition with the Save Project button. This is the same feature as in the QGIS main window. All changes will be saved in a QGIS project file.

## CHAPTER 19

Plugins

19.1 QGIS Plugins

QGIS has been designed with a plugin architecture. This allows many new features and functions to be easily added to the application. Many of the features in QGIS are actually implemented as plugins.

You can manage your plugins in the plugin dialog which can be opened with *Plugins > Manage and install plugins* ....

When a plugin needs to be updated, and if plugins settings have been set up accordingly, QGIS main interface could display a blue link in the status bar to tell you that there are some updates for plugins waiting to be applied.

19.1.1 The Plugins Dialog

The menus in the Plugins dialog allow the user to install, uninstall and upgrade plugins in different ways. Each plugin have some metadatas displayed in the right panel:

- information if the plugin is experimental
- description
- rating vote(s) (you can vote for your prefered plugin!)
- tags
- some useful links as the home page, tracker and code repository
- author(s)
- version available

You can use the filter to find a specific plugin.

 All

Here, all the available plugins are listed, including both core and external plugins. Use [**Upgrade all**] to look for new versions of the plugins. Furthermore, you can use [**Install plugin**], if a plugin is listed but not installed, and [**Uninstall plugin**] as well as [**Reinstall plugin**], if a plugin is installed. If a plugin is installed, it can be de/activated using the checkbox.

 Installed

In this menu, you can find only the installed plugins. The external plugins can be uninstalled and reinstalled using the [**Uninstall plugin**] and [**Reinstall plugin**] buttons. You can [**Upgrade all**] here as well.

 Not installed

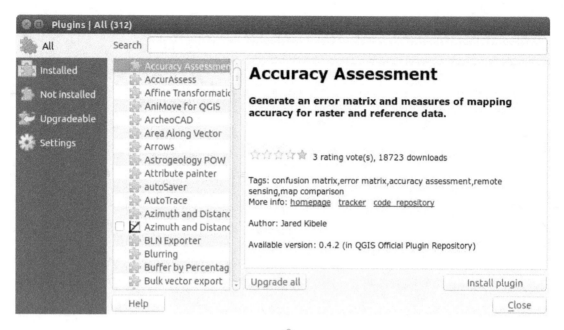

Figure 19.1: The 🌼 *All* menu 🐧

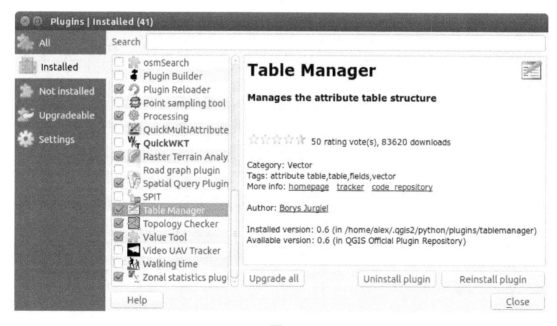

Figure 19.2: The 🏠 *Installed* menu 🐧

This menu lists all plugins available that are not installed. You can use the [**Install plugin**] button to implement a plugin into QGIS.

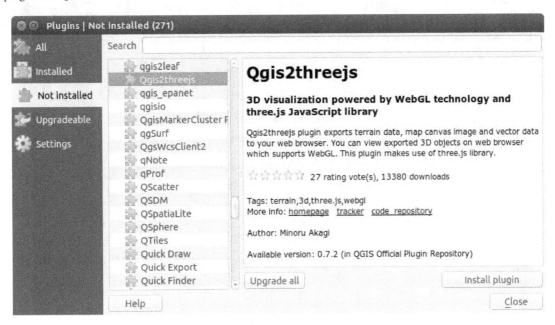

Figure 19.3: The *Not installed* menu △

 Upgradeable

If you activated ✅ *Show also experimental plugins* in the ⚙️ *Settings* menu, you can use this menu to look for more recent plugin versions. This can be done with the [**Upgrade plugin**] or [**Upgrade all**] buttons.

⚙️ *Settings*

In this menu, you can use the following options:

- ✅ *Check for updates on startup*. Whenever a new plugin or a plugin update is available, QGIS will inform you 'every time QGIS starts', 'once a day', 'every 3 days', 'every week', 'every 2 weeks' or 'every month'.

- ✅ *Show also experimental plugins*. QGIS will show you plugins in early stages of development, which are generally unsuitable for production use.

- ✅ *Show also deprecated plugins*. These plugins are deprecated and generally unsuitable for production use.

To add external author repositories, click [**Add...**] in the *Plugin repositories* section. If you do not want one or more of the added repositories, they can be disabled via the [**Edit...**] button, or completely removed with the [**Delete**] button.

The *Search* function is available in nearly every menu (except ⚙️ *Settings*). Here, you can look for specific plugins.

Tip: Core and external plugins

QGIS plugins are implemented either as **Core Plugins** or **External Plugins**. **Core Plugins** are maintained by the QGIS Development Team and are automatically part of every QGIS distribution. They are written in one of two languages: C++ or Python. **External Plugins** are currently all written in Python. They are stored in external repositories and are maintained by the individual authors.

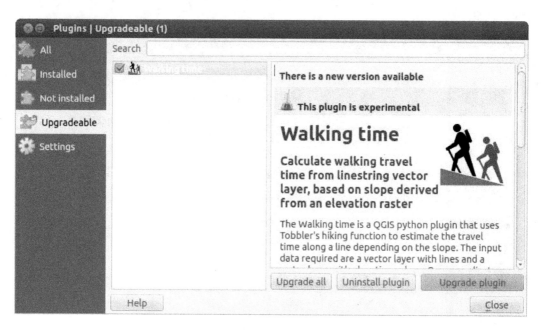

Figure 19.4: The *Upgradeable* menu

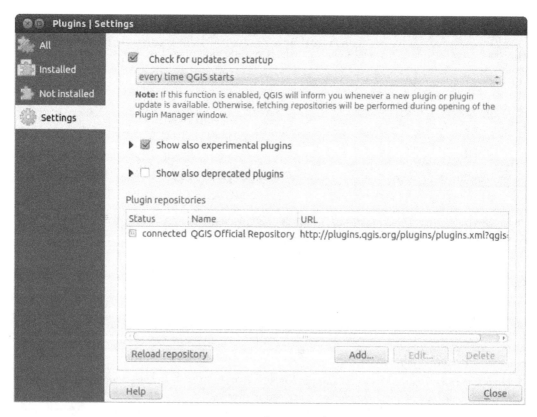

Figure 19.5: The *Settings* menu

Detailed documentation about the usage, minimum QGIS version, home page, authors, and other important information are provided for the 'Official' QGIS Repository at http://plugins.qgis.org/plugins/. For other external repositories, documentation might be available with the external plugins themselves. In general, it is not included in this manual.

.

19.2 Using QGIS Core Plugins

Icon	Plugin	Description	Manual Reference
	Accuracy Assessment	Generate an error matrix	*accuracy*
	CadTools	Perform CAD-like functions in QGIS	*cadtools*
	Coordinate Capture	Capture mouse coordinate in different CRS	*Coordinate Capture Plugin*
	DB Manager	Manage your databases within QGIS	*DB Manager Plugin*
	DXF2Shape Converter	Converts from DXF to SHP file format	*Dxf2Shp Converter Plugin*
	eVis	Event Visualization Tool	*eVis Plugin*
	fTools	A suite of vector tools	*fTools Plugin*
	GPS Tools	Tools for loading and importing GPS data	*GPS Plugin*
	GRASS	GRASS functionality	*GRASS GIS Integration*
	GDAL Tools	GDAL raster functionality	*GDAL Tools Plugin*
	Georeferencer GDAL	Georeference rasters with GDAL	*Georeferencer Plugin*
	Heatmap	Create heatmap rasters from input vector points	*Heatmap Plugin*
	Interpolation plugin	Interpolation on base of vertices of a vector layer	*Interpolation Plugin*
	Offline Editing	Offline editing and synchronizing with database	*Offline Editing Plugin*
	Oracle Spatial Georaster	Access Oracle Spatial GeoRasters	*Oracle Spatial GeoRaster Plugin*
	Plugin Manager	Manage core and external plugins	*The Plugins Dialog*
	Raster Terrain Analysis	Compute geomorphological features from DEMs	*Raster Terrain Analysis Plugin*
	Road Graph plugin	Shortest path analysis	*Road Graph Plugin*
	SQL Anywhere plugin	Access SQL anywhere DB	*sqlanywhere*
	Spatial Query	Spatial queries on vectors	*Spatial Query Plugin*
	SPIT	Shapefile to PostgreSQL/PostGIS Import Tool	*SPIT Plugin*
	Zonal Statistics	Calculate raster statistics for vector polygons	*Zonal Statistics Plugin*
CSW	MetaSearch	Interact with metadata catalogue services (CSW)	*MetaSearch Catalogue Client*

.

19.3 Coordinate Capture Plugin

The coordinate capture plugin is easy to use and provides the ability to display coordinates on the map canvas for two selected coordinate reference systems (CRS).

1. Start QGIS, select ✎ *Project Properties* from the *Settings* (KDE, Windows) or *File* (Gnome, OSX) menu and click on the *Projection* tab. As an alternative, you can also click on the ⊕ CRS status icon in the lower right-hand corner of the status bar.

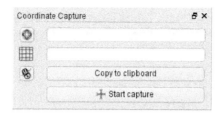

Figure 19.6: Coordinate Capture Plugin

2. Click on the ☑ *Enable on the fly projection* checkbox and select a projected coordinate system of your choice (see also *Working with Projections*).

3. Activate the coordinate capture plugin in the Plugin Manager (see *The Plugins Dialog*) and ensure that the dialog is visible by going to *View → Panels* and ensuring that ☑ *Coordinate Capture* is enabled. The coordinate capture dialog appears as shown in Figure figure_coordinate_capture_1. Alternatively, you can also go to *Vector → Coordinate Capture* and see if ☑ *Coordinate Capture* is enabled.

4. Click on the ^(Click to the select the CRS to use for coordinate display) icon and select a different CRS from the one you selected above.

5. To start capturing coordinates, click on **[Start capture]**. You can now click anywhere on the map canvas and the plugin will show the coordinates for both of your selected CRS.

6. To enable mouse coordinate tracking, click the ^(mouse tracking) icon.

7. You can also copy selected coordinates to the clipboard.

19.4 DB Manager Plugin

The DB Manager Plugin is officially part of the QGIS core and is intended to replace the SPIT Plugin and, additionally, to integrate all other database formats supported by QGIS in one user interface. The 🗄 DB Manager Plugin provides several features. You can drag layers from the QGIS Browser into the DB Manager, and it will import your layer into your spatial database. You can drag and drop tables between spatial databases and they will get imported. .. _figure_db_manager:

The *Database* menu allows you to connect to an existing database, to start the SQL window and to exit the DB Manager Plugin. Once you are connected to an existing database, the menus *Schema* and *Table* additionally appear.

The *Schema* menu includes tools to create and delete (empty) schemas and, if topology is available (e.g., PostGIS 2), to start a *TopoViewer*.

The *Table* menu allows you to create and edit tables and to delete tables and views. It is also possible to empty tables and to move tables from one schema to another. As further functionality, you can perform a VACUUM and then an ANALYZE for each selected table. Plain VACUUM simply reclaims space and makes it available for reuse. ANALYZE updates statistics to determine the most efficient way to execute a query. Finally, you can import layers/files, if they are loaded in QGIS or exist in the file system. And you can export database tables to shape with the Export File feature.

The *Tree* window lists all existing databases supported by QGIS. With a double-click, you can connect to the database. With the right mouse button, you can rename and delete existing schemas and tables. Tables can also be added to the QGIS canvas with the context menu.

If connected to a database, the **main** window of the DB Manager offers three tabs. The *Info* tab provides information about the table and its geometry, as well as about existing fields, constraints and indexes. It also allows you

Figure 19.7: DB Manager dialog

to run Vacuum Analyze and to create a spatial index on a selected table, if not already done. The *Table* tab shows all attributes, and the *Preview* tab renders the geometries as preview.

19.4.1 Working with the SQL Window

You can also use the DB Manager to execute SQL queries against your spatial database and then view the spatial output for queries by adding the results to QGIS as a query layer. It is possible to highlight a portion of the SQL and only that portion will be executed when you press F5 or click the *Execute (F5)* button.

19.5 Dxf2Shp Converter Plugin

The dxf2shape converter plugin can be used to convert vector data from DXF to shapefile format. It requires the following parameters to be specified before running:

- **Input DXF file**: Enter the path to the DXF file to be converted.
- **Output Shp file**: Enter desired name of the shapefile to be created.
- **Output file type**: Specify the geometry type of the output shapefile. Currently supported types are polyline, polygon, and point.
- **Export text labels**: When this checkbox is enabled, an additional shapefile point layer will be created, and the associated DBF table will contain information about the "TEXT" fields found in the DXF file, and the text strings themselves.

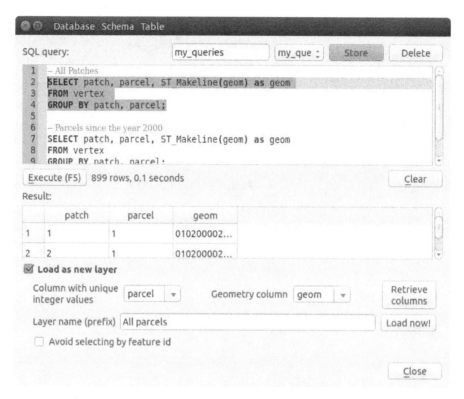

Figure 19.8: Executing SQL queries in the DB Manager SQL window

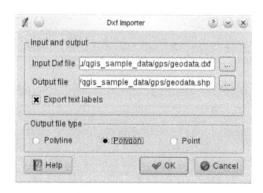

Figure 19.9: Dxf2Shape Converter Plugin

19.5.1 Using the Plugin

1. Start QGIS, load the Dxf2Shape plugin in the Plugin Manager (see *The Plugins Dialog*) and click on the
   ⬚ Dxf2Shape Converter icon, which appears in the QGIS toolbar menu. The Dxf2Shape plugin dialog appears, as shown in Figure_dxf2shape_1.

2. Enter the input DXF file, a name for the output shapefile and the shapefile type.

3. Enable the ☑ *Export text labels* checkbox if you want to create an extra point layer with labels.

4. Click [**OK**].

19.6 eVis Plugin

(This section is derived from Horning, N., K. Koy, P. Ersts. 2009. eVis (v1.1.0) User's Guide. American Museum of Natural History, Center for Biodiversity and Conservation. Available from http://biodiversityinformatics.amnh.org/, and released under the GNU FDL.)

The Biodiversity Informatics Facility at the American Museum of Natural History's (AMNH) Center for Biodiversity and Conservation (CBC) has developed the Event Visualization Tool (eVis), another software tool to add to the suite of conservation monitoring and decision support tools for guiding protected area and landscape planning. This plugin enables users to easily link geocoded (i.e., referenced with latitude and longitude or X and Y coordinates) photographs, and other supporting documents, to vector data in QGIS.

eVis is now automatically installed and enabled in new versions of QGIS, and as with all plugins, it can be disabled and enabled using the Plugin Manager (see *The Plugins Dialog*).

The eVis plugin is made up of three modules: the 'Database Connection tool', 'Event ID tool', and the 'Event Browser'. These work together to allow viewing of geocoded photographs and other documents that are linked to features stored in vector files, databases, or spreadsheets.

19.6.1 Event Browser

The Event Browser module provides the functionality to display geocoded photographs that are linked to vector features displayed in the QGIS map window. Point data, for example, can be from a vector file that can be input using QGIS or it can be from the result of a database query. The vector feature must have attribute information associated with it to describe the location and name of the file containing the photograph and, optionally, the compass direction the camera was pointed when the image was acquired. Your vector layer must be loaded into QGIS before running the Event Browser.

Launch the Event Browser module

To launch the Event Browser module, click on *Database → eVis → eVis Event Browser*. This will open the *Generic Event Browser* window.

The *Event Browser* window has three tabs displayed at the top of the window. The *Display* tab is used to view the photograph and its associated attribute data. The *Options* tab provides a number of settings that can be adjusted to control the behavior of the eVis plugin. Lastly, the *Configure External Applications* tab is used to maintain a table of file extensions and their associated application to allow eVis to display documents other than images.

Understanding the Display window

To see the *Display* window, click on the *Display* tab in the *Event Browser* window. The *Display* window is used to view geocoded photographs and their associated attribute data.

1. **Display window**: A window where the photograph will appear.

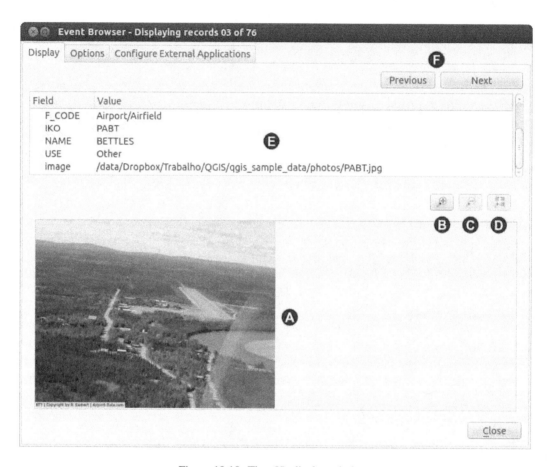

Figure 19.10: The *eVis* display window

2. **Zoom in button**: Zoom in to see more detail. If the entire image cannot be displayed in the display window, scroll bars will appear on the left and bottom sides of the window to allow you to pan around the image.

3. **Zoom out button**: Zoom out to see more area.

4. **Zoom to full extent** button: Displays the full extent of the photograph.

5. **Attribute information window**: All of the attribute information for the point associated with the photograph being viewed is displayed here. If the file type being referenced in the displayed record is not an image but is of a file type defined in the *Configure External Applications* tab, then when you double-click on the value of the field containing the path to the file, the application to open the file will be launched to view or hear the contents of the file. If the file extension is recognized, the attribute data will be displayed in green.

6. **Navigation buttons**: Use the Previous and Next buttons to load the previous or next feature when more than one feature is selected.

Understanding the Options window

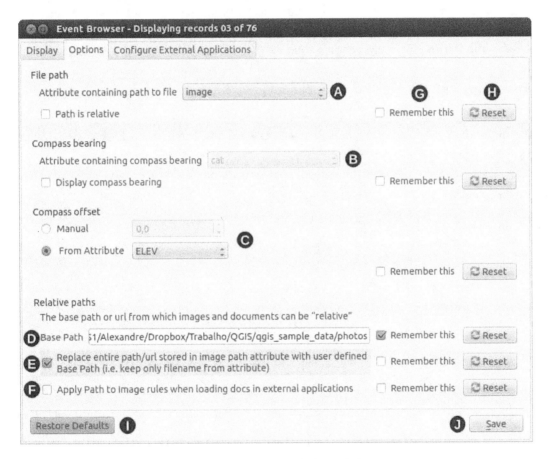

Figure 19.11: The *eVis* Options window

1. **File path**: A drop-down list to specify the attribute field that contains the directory path or URL for the photographs or other documents being displayed. If the location is a relative path, then the checkbox must be clicked. The base path for a relative path can be entered in the *Base Path* text box below. Information about the different options for specifying the file location are noted in the section *Specifying the location and name of a photograph* below.

2. **Compass bearing**: A drop-down list to specify the attribute field that contains the compass bearing associated with the photograph being displayed. If compass bearing information is available, it is necessary to click the checkbox below the drop-down menu title.

---

3. **Compass offset**: Compass offsets can be used to compensate for declination (to adjust bearings collected using magnetic bearings to true north bearings). Click the ⊙ *Manual* radio button to enter the offset in the text box or click the ⊙ *From Attribute* radio button to select the attribute field containing the offsets. For both of these options, east declinations should be entered using positive values, and west declinations should use negative values.

4. **Directory base path**: The base path onto which the relative path defined in Figure_eVis_2 (A) will be appended.

5. **Replace path**: If this checkbox is checked, only the file name from A will be appended to the base path.

6. **Apply rule to all documents**: If checked, the same path rules that are defined for photographs will be used for non-image documents such as movies, text documents, and sound files. If not checked, the path rules will only apply to photographs, and other documents will ignore the base path parameter.

7. **Remember settings**: If the checkbox is checked, the values for the associated parameters will be saved for the next session when the window is closed or when the [**Save**] button below is pressed.

8. **Reset values**: Resets the values on this line to the default setting.

9. **Restore defaults**: This will reset all of the fields to their default settings. It has the same effect as clicking all of the [**Reset**] buttons.

10. **Save**: This will save the settings without closing the *Options* pane.

Understanding the Configure External Applications window

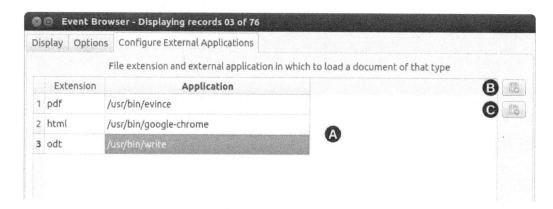

Figure 19.12: The *eVis* External Applications window

1. **File reference table**: A table containing file types that can be opened using eVis. Each file type needs a file extension and the path to an application that can open that type of file. This provides the capability of opening a broad range of files such as movies, sound recordings, and text documents instead of only images.

2. **Add new file type**: Add a new file type with a unique extension and the path for the application that can open the file.

3. **Delete current row**: Delete the file type highlighted in the table and defined by a file extension and a path to an associated application.

19.6.2 Specifying the location and name of a photograph

The location and name of the photograph can be stored using an absolute or relative path, or a URL if the photograph is available on a web server. Examples of the different approaches are listed in Table evis_examples.

```
X          Y          FILE                                                          BEARING
780596     1784017    C:\Workshop\eVis_Data\groundphotos\DSC_0168.JPG               275
780596     1784017    /groundphotos/DSC_0169.JPG                                    80
780819     1784015    http://biodiversityinformatics.amnh.org/\
                      evis_testdata/DSC_0170.JPG                                     10
780596     1784017    pdf:http://www.testsite.com/attachments.php?\
                      attachment_id-12                                              76
```

19.6.3 Specifying the location and name of other supporting documents

Supporting documents such as text documents, videos, and sound clips can also be displayed or played by eVis. To do this, it is necessary to add an entry in the file reference table that can be accessed from the *Configure External Applications* window in the *Generic Event Browser* that matches the file extension to an application that can be used to open the file. It is also necessary to have the path or URL to the file in the attribute table for the vector layer. One additional rule that can be used for URLs that don't contain a file extension for the document you want to open is to specify the file extension before the URL. The format is — file extension:URL. The URL is preceded by the file extension and a colon; this is particularly useful for accessing documents from wikis and other web sites that use a database to manage the web pages (see Table evis_examples).

19.6.4 Using the Event Browser

When the *Event Browser* window opens, a photograph will appear in the display window if the document referenced in the vector file attribute table is an image and if the file location information in the *Options* window is properly set. If a photograph is expected and it does not appear, it will be necessary to adjust the parameters in the *Options* window.

If a supporting document (or an image that does not have a file extension recognized by eVis) is referenced in the attribute table, the field containing the file path will be highlighted in green in the attribute information window if that file extension is defined in the file reference table located in the *Configure External Applications* window. To open the document, double-click on the green-highlighted line in the attribute information window. If a supporting document is referenced in the attribute information window and the file path is not highlighted in green, then it will be necessary to add an entry for the file's filename extension in the *Configure External Applications* window. If the file path is highlighted in green but does not open when double-clicked, it will be necessary to adjust the parameters in the *Options* window so the file can be located by eVis.

If no compass bearing is provided in the *Options* window, a red asterisk will be displayed on top of the vector feature that is associated with the photograph being displayed. If a compass bearing is provided, then an arrow will appear pointing in the direction indicated by the value in the compass bearing display field in the *Event Browser* window. The arrow will be centered over the point that is associated with the photograph or other document.

To close the *Event Browser* window, click on the [**Close**] button from the *Display* window.

19.6.5 Event ID Tool

The 'Event ID' module allows you to display a photograph by clicking on a feature displayed in the QGIS map window. The vector feature must have attribute information associated with it to describe the location and name of the file containing the photograph and, optionally, the compass direction the camera was pointed when the image was acquired. This layer must be loaded into QGIS before running the 'Event ID' tool.

Launch the Event ID module

To launch the 'Event ID' module, either click on the ![Event ID] Event ID icon or click on *Database* → *eVis* → *Event ID Tool*. This will cause the cursor to change to an arrow with an 'i' on top of it signifying that the ID tool is active.

To view the photographs linked to vector features in the active vector layer displayed in the QGIS map window, move the Event ID cursor over the feature and then click the mouse. After clicking on the feature, the *Event*

Browser window is opened and the photographs on or near the clicked locality are available for display in the browser. If more than one photograph is available, you can cycle through the different features using the **[Previous]** and **[Next]** buttons. The other controls are described in the ref:*evis_browser* section of this guide.

19.6.6 Database connection

The 'Database Connection' module provides tools to connect to and query a database or other ODBC resource, such as a spreadsheet.

eVis can directly connect to the following types of databases: PostgreSQL, MySQL, and SQLite; it can also read from ODBC connections (e.g., MS Access). When reading from an ODBC database (such as an Excel spreadsheet), it is necessary to configure your ODBC driver for the operating system you are using.

Launch the Database Connection module

To launch the 'Database Connection' module, either click on the appropriate icon [icon] eVis Database Connection or click on *Database → eVis → Database Connection*. This will launch the *Database Connection* window. The window has three tabs: *Predefined Queries*, *Database Connection*, and *SQL Query*. The *Output Console* window at the bottom of the window displays the status of actions initiated by the different sections of this module.

Connect to a database

Click on the *Database Connection* tab to open the database connection interface. Next, use the *Database Type* [icon] combo box to select the type of database that you want to connect to. If a password or username is required, that information can be entered in the *Username* and *Password* textboxes.

Enter the database host in the *Database Host* textbox. This option is not available if you selected 'MS Access' as the database type. If the database resides on your desktop, you should enter "localhost".

Enter the name of the database in the *Database Name* textbox. If you selected 'ODBC' as the database type, you need to enter the data source name.

When all of the parameters are filled in, click on the **[Connect]** button. If the connection is successful, a message will be written in the *Output Console* window stating that the connection was established. If a connection was not established, you will need to check that the correct parameters were entered above.

1. **Database Type**: A drop-down list to specify the type of database that will be used.
2. **Database Host**: The name of the database host.
3. **Port**: The port number if a MySQL or PostgreSQL database type is selected.
4. **Database Name**: The name of the database.
5. **Connect**: A button to connect to the database using the parameters defined above.
6. **Output Console**: The console window where messages related to processing are displayed.
7. **Username**: Username for use when a database is password protected.
8. **Password**: Password for use when a database is password protected.
9. **Predefined Queries**: Tab to open the "Predefined Queries" window.
10. **Database Connection**: Tab to open the "Database Connection" window.
11. **SQL Query**: Tab to open the "SQL Query" window.
12. **Help**: Displays the online help.
13. **OK**: Closes the main "Database Connection" window.

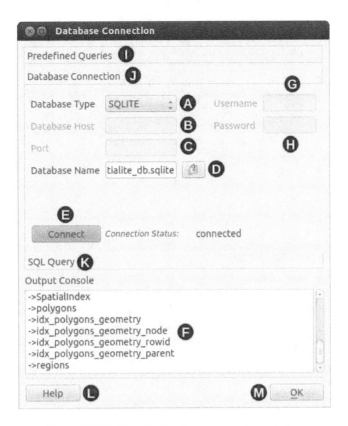

Figure 19.13: The *eVis* Database connection window

Running SQL queries

SQL queries are used to extract information from a database or ODBC resource. In eVis, the output from these queries is a vector layer added to the QGIS map window. Click on the *SQL Query* tab to display the SQL query interface. SQL commands can be entered in this text window. A helpful tutorial on SQL commands is available at http://www.w3schools.com/sql. For example, to extract all of the data from a worksheet in an Excel file, `select * from [sheet1$]` where `sheet1` is the name of the worksheet.

Click on the **[Run Query]** button to execute the command. If the query is successful, a *Database File Selection* window will be displayed. If the query is not successful, an error message will appear in the *Output Console* window.

In the *Database File Selection* window, enter the name of the layer that will be created from the results of the query in the *Name of New Layer* textbox.

1. **SQL Query Text Window**: A screen to type SQL queries.

2. **Run Query**: Button to execute the query entered in the *SQL Query Window*.

3. **Console Window**: The console window where messages related to processing are displayed.

4. **Help**: Displays the online help.

5. **OK**: Closes the main *Database Connection* window.

Use the *X Coordinate* [...▼] and *Y Coordinate* [...▼] combo boxes to select the fields from the database that stores the X (or longitude) and Y (or latitude) coordinates. Clicking on the **[OK]** button causes the vector layer created from the SQL query to be displayed in the QGIS map window.

To save this vector file for future use, you can use the QGIS 'Save as...' command that is accessed by right-clicking on the layer name in the QGIS map legend and then selecting 'Save as...'

Tip: Creating a vector layer from a Microsoft Excel Worksheet

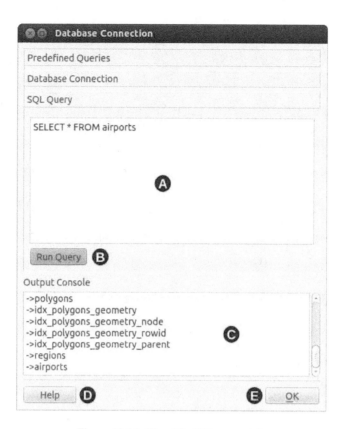

Figure 19.14: The eVis SQL query tab

When creating a vector layer from a Microsoft Excel Worksheet, you might see that unwanted zeros ("0") have been inserted in the attribute table rows beneath valid data. This can be caused by deleting the values for these cells in Excel using the `Backspace` key. To correct this problem, you need to open the Excel file (you'll need to close QGIS if you are connected to the file, to allow you to edit the file) and then use *Edit* → *Delete* to remove the blank rows from the file. To avoid this problem, you can simply delete several rows in the Excel Worksheet using *Edit* → *Delete* before saving the file.

Running predefined queries

With predefined queries, you can select previously written queries stored in XML format in a file. This is particularly helpful if you are not familiar with SQL commands. Click on the *Predefined Queries* tab to display the predefined query interface.

To load a set of predefined queries, click on the ▣ Open File icon. This opens the *Open File* window, which is used to locate the file containing the SQL queries. When the queries are loaded, their titles as defined in the XML file will appear in the drop-down menu located just below the ▣ Open File icon. The full description of the query is displayed in the text window under the drop-down menu.

Select the query you want to run from the drop-down menu and then click on the *SQL Query* tab to see that the query has been loaded into the query window. If it is the first time you are running a predefined query or are switching databases, you need to be sure to connect to the database.

Click on the **[Run Query]** button in the *SQL Query* tab to execute the command. If the query is successful, a *Database File Selection* window will be displayed. If the query is not successful, an error message will appear in the *Output Console* window.

1. **Open File**: Launches the "Open File" file browser to search for the XML file holding the predefined queries.

2. **Predefined Queries**: A drop-down list with all of the queries defined by the predefined queries XML file.

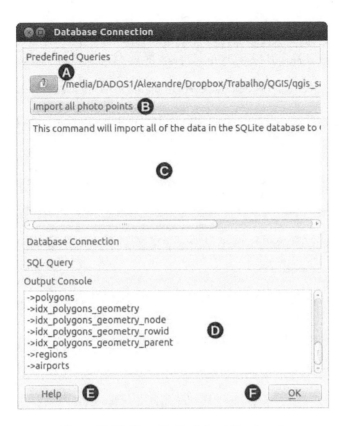

Figure 19.15: The *eVis* Predefined Queries tab

3. **Query description**: A short description of the query. This description is from the predefined queries XML file.

4. **Console Window**: The console window where messages related to processing are displayed.

5. **Help**: Displays the online help.

6. **OK**: Closes the main "Database Connection" window.

XML format for eVis predefined queries

The XML tags read by eVis

Tag	Description
query	Defines the beginning and end of a query statement.
shortde-scription	A short description of the query that appears in the eVis drop-down menu.
descrip-tion	A more detailed description of the query displayed in the Predefined Query text window.
database-type	The database type, defined in the Database Type drop-down menu in the Database Connection tab.
database-port	The port as defined in the Port text box in the Database Connection tab.
database-name	The database name as defined in the Database Name text box in the Database Connection tab.
databaseuser-name	The database username as defined in the Username text box in the Database Connection tab.
databasep-assword	The database password as defined in the Password text box in the Database Connection tab.
sqlstate-ment	The SQL command.
autocon-nect	A flag ("true"" or "false") to specify if the above tags should be used to automatically connect to the database without running the database connection routine in the Database Connection tab.

A complete sample XML file with three queries is displayed below:

```xml
<?xml version="1.0"?>
<doc>
 <query>
   <shortdescription>Import all photograph points</shortdescription>
   <description>This command will import all of the data in the SQLite database to QGIS
       </description>
   <databasetype>SQLITE</databasetype>
   <databasehost />
   <databaseport />
   <databasename>C:\textbackslash Workshop/textbackslash
eVis\_Data\textbackslash PhotoPoints.db</databasename>
   <databaseusername />
   <databasepassword />
   <sqlstatement>SELECT Attributes.*, Points.x, Points.y FROM Attributes LEFT JOIN
       Points ON Points.rec_id=Attributes.point_ID</sqlstatement>
   <autoconnect>false</autoconnect>
 </query>
  <query>
   <shortdescription>Import photograph points "looking across Valley"</shortdescription>
   <description>This command will import only points that have photographs "looking across
       a valley" to QGIS</description>
   <databasetype>SQLITE</databasetype>
   <databasehost />
   <databaseport />
   <databasename>C:\Workshop\eVis_Data\PhotoPoints.db</databasename>
   <databaseusername />
   <databasepassword />
   <sqlstatement>SELECT Attributes.*, Points.x, Points.y FROM Attributes LEFT JOIN
       Points ON Points.rec_id=Attributes.point_ID where COMMENTS='Looking across
       valley'</sqlstatement>
   <autoconnect>false</autoconnect>
 </query>
 <query>
   <shortdescription>Import photograph points that mention "limestone"</shortdescription>
   <description>This command will import only points that have photographs that mention
       "limestone" to QGIS</description>
   <databasetype>SQLITE</databasetype>
   <databasehost />
   <databaseport />
```

```
<databasename>C:\Workshop\eVis_Data\PhotoPoints.db</databasename>
<databaseusername />
<databasepassword />
<sqlstatement>SELECT Attributes.*, Points.x, Points.y FROM Attributes LEFT JOIN
    Points ON Points.rec_id=Attributes.point_ID where COMMENTS like '%limestone%'
    </sqlstatement>
<autoconnect>false</autoconnect>
</query>
</doc>
```

19.7 fTools Plugin

The goal of the fTools Python plugin is to provide a one-stop resource for many common vector-based GIS tasks, without the need for additional software, libraries, or complex work-arounds. It provides a growing suite of spatial data management and analysis functions that are both fast and functional.

fTools is now automatically installed and enabled in new versions of QGIS, and as with all plugins, it can be disabled and enabled using the Plugin Manager (see *The Plugins Dialog*). When enabled, the fTools plugin adds a *Vector* menu to QGIS, providing functions ranging from Analysis and Research Tools to Geometry and Geoprocessing Tools, as well as several useful Data Management Tools.

19.7.1 Analysis tools

Icon	Tool	Purpose
	Distance matrix	Measure distances between two point layers, and output results as a) Square distance matrix, b) Linear distance matrix, or c) Summary of distances. Can limit distances to the k nearest features.
	Sum line length	Calculate the total sum of line lengths for each polygon of a polygon vector layer.
	Points in polygon	Count the number of points that occur in each polygon of an input polygon vector layer.
	List unique values	List all unique values in an input vector layer field.
	Basic statistics	Compute basic statistics (mean, std dev, N, sum, CV) on an input field.
	Nearest neighbor analysis	Compute nearest neighbor statistics to assess the level of clustering in a point vector layer.
	Mean coordinate(s)	Compute either the normal or weighted mean center of an entire vector layer, or multiple features based on a unique ID field.
	Line intersections	Locate intersections between lines, and output results as a point shapefile. Useful for locating road or stream intersections, ignores line intersections with length > 0.

Table Ftools 1: fTools Analysis tools

19.7.2 Research tools

Icon	Tool	Purpose
	Random selection	Randomly select n number of features, or n percentage of features.
	Random selection within subsets	Randomly select features within subsets based on a unique ID field.
	Random points	Generate pseudo-random points over a given input layer.
	Regular points	Generate a regular grid of points over a specified region and export them as a point shapefile.
	Vector grid	Generate a line or polygon grid based on user-specified grid spacing.
	Select by location	Select features based on their location relative to another layer to form a new selection, or add or subtract from the current selection.
	Polygon from layer extent	Create a single rectangular polygon layer from the extent of an input raster or vector layer.

Table Ftools 2: fTools Research tools

19.7.3 Geoprocessing tools

Icon	Tool	Purpose
	Convex hull(s)	Create minimum convex hull(s) for an input layer, or based on an ID field.
	Buffer(s)	Create buffer(s) around features based on distance, or distance field.
	Intersect	Overlay layers such that output contains areas where both layers intersect.
	Union	Overlay layers such that output contains intersecting and non-intersecting areas.
	Symmetrical difference	Overlay layers such that output contains those areas of the input and difference layers that do not intersect.
	Clip	Overlay layers such that output contains areas that intersect the clip layer.
	Difference	Overlay layers such that output contains areas not intersecting the clip layer.
	Dissolve	Merge features based on input field. All features with identical input values are combined to form one single feature.
	Eliminate sliver polygons	Merges selected features with the neighbouring polygon with the largest area or largest common boundary.

Table Ftools 3: fTools Geoprocessing tools

19.7.4 Geometry tools

Icon	Tool	Purpose
	Check geometry validity	Check polygons for intersections, closed holes, and fix node ordering. You can choose the engine used by the in the options dialog, digitizing tab Change the Validate geometries value. There is two engines: QGIS and GEOS which have pretty different behaviour. Another tools exists which shows different result as well: Topology Checker plugin and 'must not have invalid geometries' rule.
	Export/Add geometry columns	Add vector layer geometry info to point (XCOORD, YCOORD), line (LENGTH), or polygon (AREA, PERIMETER) layer.
	Polygon centroids	Calculate the true centroids for each polygon in an input polygon layer.
	Delaunay triangulation	Calculate and output (as polygons) the Delaunay triangulation of an input point vector layer.
	Voronoi polygons	Calculate Voronoi polygons of an input point vector layer.
	Simplify geometry	Generalize lines or polygons with a modified Douglas-Peucker algorithm.
	Densify geometry	Densify lines or polygons by adding vertices.
	Multipart to singleparts	Convert multipart features to multiple singlepart features. Creates simple polygons and lines.
	Singleparts to multipart	Merge multiple features to a single multipart feature based on a unique ID field.
	Polygons to lines	Convert polygons to lines, multipart polygons to multiple singlepart lines.
	Lines to polygons	Convert lines to polygons, multipart lines to multiple singlepart polygons.
	Extract nodes	Extract nodes from line and polygon layers and output them as points.

Table Ftools 4: fTools Geometry tools

Note: The *Simplify geometry* tool can be used to remove duplicate nodes in line and polygon geometries. Just set the *Simplify tolerance* parameter to 0 and this will do the trick.

19.7.5 Data management tools

Icon	Tool	Purpose
	Define current projection	Specify the CRS for shapefiles whose CRS has not been defined.
	Join attributes by location	Join additional attributes to vector layer based on spatial relationship. Attributes from one vector layer are appended to the attribute table of another layer and exported as a shapefile.
	Split vector layer	Split input layer into multiple separate layers based on input field.
	Merge shapefiles to one	Merge several shapefiles within a folder into a new shapefile based on the layer type (point, line, area).
	Create spatial index	Create a spatial index for OGR- supported formats.

Table Ftools 5: fTools Data management tools

.

19.8 GDAL Tools Plugin

19.8.1 What is GDAL Tools?

The GDAL Tools plugin offers a GUI to the collection of tools in the Geospatial Data Abstraction Library, http://gdal.osgeo.org . These are raster management tools to query, re-project, warp and merge a wide variety of raster formats. Also included are tools to create a contour (vector) layer, or a shaded relief from a raster DEM, and to make a VRT (Virtual Raster Tile in XML format) from a collection of one or more raster files. These tools are available when the plugin is installed and activated.

The GDAL Library

The GDAL library consists of a set of command line programs, each with a large list of options. Users comfortable with running commands from a terminal may prefer the command line, with access to the full set of options. The GDALTools plugin offers an easy interface to the tools, exposing only the most popular options.

19.8.2 List of GDAL tools

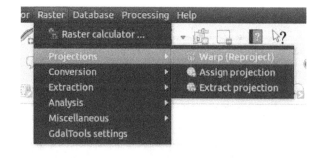

Figure 19.16: The *GDALTools* menu list

Projections

Warp (Reproject)	This utility is an image mosaicing, reprojection and warping utility. The program can reproject to any supported projection, and can also apply GCPs stored with the image if the image is "raw" with control information. For more information, you can read on the GDAL website http://www.gdal.org/gdalwarp.html.
Assign projection	This tool allows you to assign projection to rasters that are already georeferenced but miss projection information. Also with its help, it is possible to alter existing projection definitions. Both single file and batch mode are supported. For more information, please visit the utility page at the GDAL site, http://www.gdal.org/gdalwarp.html.
Extract projection	This utility helps you to extract projection information from an input file. If you want to extract projection information from a whole directory, you can use the batch mode. It creates both .prj and .wld files.

Conversion

Rasterize	This program burns vector geometries (points, lines and polygons) into the raster band(s) of a raster image. Vectors are read from OGR-supported vector formats. Note that the vector data must in the same coordinate system as the raster data; on the fly reprojection is not provided. For more information see http://www.gdal.org/gdal_rasterize.html.
Poly-gonize	This utility creates vector polygons for all connected regions of pixels in the raster sharing a common pixel value. Each polygon is created with an attribute indicating the pixel value of that polygon. The utility will create the output vector datasource if it does not already exist, defaulting to ESRI shapefile format. See also http://www.gdal.org/gdal_polygonize.html.
Translate	This utility can be used to convert raster data between different formats, potentially performing some operations like subsetting, resampling, and rescaling pixels in the process. For more information you can read on http://www.gdal.org/gdal_translate.html.
RGB to PCT	This utility will compute an optimal pseudocolor table for a given RGB image using a median cut algorithm on a downsampled RGB histogram. Then it converts the image into a pseudocolored image using the color table. This conversion utilizes Floyd-Steinberg dithering (error diffusion) to maximize output image visual quality. The utility is also described at http://www.gdal.org/rgb2pct.html.
PCT to RGB	This utility will convert a pseudocolor band on the input file into an output RGB file of the desired format. For more information, see http://www.gdal.org/pct2rgb.html.

Extraction

Con-tour	This program generates a vector contour file from the input raster elevation model (DEM). On http://www.gdal.org/gdal_contour.html, you can find more information.
Clip-per	This utility allows you to clip (extract subset) rasters using selected extent or based on mask layer bounds. More information can be found at http://www.gdal.org/gdal_translate.html.

Analysis

Sieve	This utility removes raster polygons smaller than a provided threshold size (in pixels) and replaces them with the pixel value of the largest neighbor polygon. The result can be written back to the existing raster band, or copied into a new file. For more information, see http://www.gdal.org/gdal_sieve.html.
Near Black	This utility will scan an image and try to set all pixels that are nearly black (or nearly white) around the edge to exactly black (or white). This is often used to "fix up" lossy compressed aerial photos so that color pixels can be treated as transparent when mosaicing. See also http://www.gdal.org/nearblack.html.
Fill nodata	This utility fills selected raster regions (usually nodata areas) by interpolation from valid pixels around the edges of the areas. On http://www.gdal.org/gdal_fillnodata.html, you can find more information.
Proximity	This utility generates a raster proximity map indicating the distance from the center of each pixel to the center of the nearest pixel identified as a target pixel. Target pixels are those in the source raster for which the raster pixel value is in the set of target pixel values. For more information see http://www.gdal.org/gdal_proximity.html.
Grid (Interpolation)	This utility creates a regular grid (raster) from the scattered data read from the OGR datasource. Input data will be interpolated to fill grid nodes with values, and you can choose from various interpolation methods. The utility is also described on the GDAL website, http://www.gdal.org/gdal_grid.html.
DEM (Terrain models)	Tools to analyze and visualize DEMs. It can create a shaded relief, a slope, an aspect, a color relief, a Terrain Ruggedness Index, a Topographic Position Index and a roughness map from any GDAL-supported elevation raster. For more information, see http://www.gdal.org/gdaldem.html.

Miscellaneous

Build Virtual Raster (Catalog)	This program builds a VRT (Virtual Dataset) that is a mosaic of the list of input GDAL datasets. See also http://www.gdal.org/gdalbuildvrt.html.
Merge	This utility will automatically mosaic a set of images. All the images must be in the same coordinate system and have a matching number of bands, but they may be overlapping, and at different resolutions. In areas of overlap, the last image will be copied over earlier ones. The utility is also described at http://www.gdal.org/gdal_merge.html.
Information	This utility lists various information about a GDAL-supported raster dataset. On http://www.gdal.org/gdalinfo.html, you can find more information.
Build Overviews	The gdaladdo utility can be used to build or rebuild overview images for most supported file formats with one of several downsampling algorithms. For more information, see http://www.gdal.org/gdaladdo.html.
Tile Index	This utility builds a shapefile with a record for each input raster file, an attribute containing the filename, and a polygon geometry outlining the raster. See also http://www.gdal.org/gdaltindex.html.

GDAL Tools Settings

Use this dialog to embed your GDAL variables.

.

19.9 Georeferencer Plugin

The Georeferencer Plugin is a tool for generating world files for rasters. It allows you to reference rasters to geographic or projected coordinate systems by creating a new GeoTiff or by adding a world file to the existing image. The basic approach to georeferencing a raster is to locate points on the raster for which you can accurately determine coordinates.

Features

Icon	Purpose	Icon	Purpose
	Open raster		Start georeferencing
	Generate GDAL Script		Load GCP Points
	Save GCP Points As		Transformation settings
	Add Point		Delete Point
	Move GCP Point		Pan
	Zoom In		Zoom Out
	Zoom To Layer		Zoom Last
	Zoom Next		Link Georeferencer to QGIS
	Link QGIS to Georeferencer		Full histogram stretch
	Local histogram stretch		

Table Georeferencer 1: Georeferencer Tools

19.9.1 Usual procedure

As X and Y coordinates (DMS (dd mm ss.ss), DD (dd.dd) or projected coordinates (mmmm.mm)), which correspond with the selected point on the image, two alternative procedures can be used:

- The raster itself sometimes provides crosses with coordinates "written" on the image. In this case, you can enter the coordinates manually.

- Using already georeferenced layers. This can be either vector or raster data that contain the same objects/features that you have on the image that you want to georeference and with the projection that you want for your image. In this case, you can enter the coordinates by clicking on the reference dataset loaded in the QGIS map canvas.

The usual procedure for georeferencing an image involves selecting multiple points on the raster, specifying their coordinates, and choosing a relevant transformation type. Based on the input parameters and data, the plugin will compute the world file parameters. The more coordinates you provide, the better the result will be.

The first step is to start QGIS, load the Georeferencer Plugin (see *The Plugins Dialog*) and click on *Raster → Georeferencer* , which appears in the QGIS menu bar. The Georeferencer Plugin dialog appears as shown in figure_georeferencer_1.

For this example, we are using a topo sheet of South Dakota from SDGS. It can later be visualized together with the data from the GRASS `spearfish60` location. You can download the topo sheet here: http://grass.osgeo.org/sampledata/spearfish_toposheet.tar.gz.

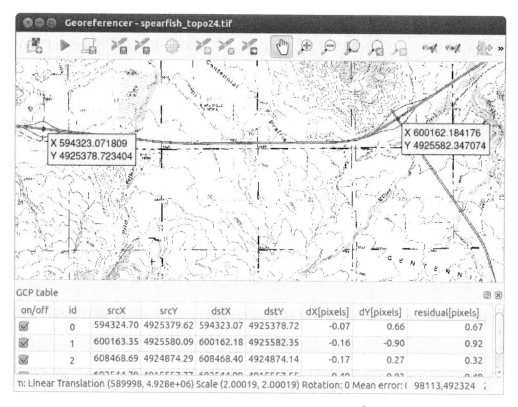

Figure 19.17: Georeferencer Plugin Dialog △

Entering ground control points (GCPs)

1. To start georeferencing an unreferenced raster, we must load it using the ▣ button. The raster will show up in the main working area of the dialog. Once the raster is loaded, we can start to enter reference points.

2. Using the ▣ Add Point button, add points to the main working area and enter their coordinates (see Figure figure_georeferencer_2). For this procedure you have three options:

   - Click on a point in the raster image and enter the X and Y coordinates manually.

   - Click on a point in the raster image and choose the ✎ From map canvas button to add the X and Y coordinates with the help of a georeferenced map already loaded in the QGIS map canvas.

   - With the ▣ button, you can move the GCPs in both windows, if they are at the wrong place.

3. Continue entering points. You should have at least four points, and the more coordinates you can provide, the better the result will be. There are additional tools on the plugin dialog to zoom and pan the working area in order to locate a relevant set of GCP points.

The points that are added to the map will be stored in a separate text file (`[filename].points`) usually together with the raster image. This allows us to reopen the Georeferencer plugin at a later date and add new points or delete existing ones to optimize the result. The points file contains values of the form: `mapX, mapY, pixelX, pixelY`. You can use the ▣ Load GCP points and ▣ Save GCP points as buttons to manage the files.

Defining the transformation settings

After you have added your GCPs to the raster image, you need to define the transformation settings for the georeferencing process.

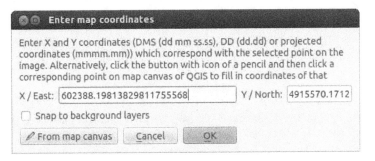

Figure 19.18: Add points to the raster image 🐧

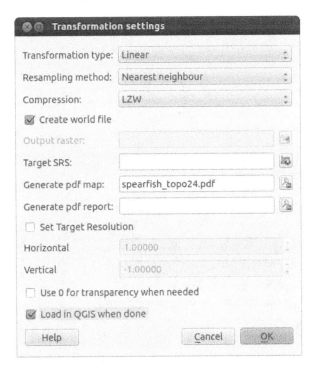

Figure 19.19: Defining the georeferencer transformation settings 🐧

Available Transformation algorithms

Depending on how many ground control points you have captured, you may want to use different transformation algorithms. Choice of transformation algorithm is also dependent on the type and quality of input data and the amount of geometric distortion that you are willing to introduce to the final result.

Currently, the following *Transformation types* are available:

- The **Linear** algorithm is used to create a world file and is different from the other algorithms, as it does not actually transform the raster. This algorithm likely won't be sufficient if you are dealing with scanned material.

- The **Helmert** transformation performs simple scaling and rotation transformations.

- The **Polynomial** algorithms 1-3 are among the most widely used algorithms introduced to match source and destination ground control points. The most widely used polynomial algorithm is the second-order polynomial transformation, which allows some curvature. First-order polynomial transformation (affine) preserves colliniarity and allows scaling, translation and rotation only.

- The **Thin Plate Spline** (TPS) algorithm is a more modern georeferencing method, which is able to introduce local deformations in the data. This algorithm is useful when very low quality originals are being georeferenced.

- The **Projective** transformation is a linear rotation and translation of coordinates.

Define the Resampling method

The type of resampling you choose will likely depending on your input data and the ultimate objective of the exercise. If you don't want to change statistics of the image, you might want to choose 'Nearest neighbour', whereas a 'Cubic resampling' will likely provide a more smoothed result.

It is possible to choose between five different resampling methods:

1. Nearest neighbour
2. Linear
3. Cubic
4. Cubic Spline
5. Lanczos

Define the transformation settings

There are several options that need to be defined for the georeferenced output raster.

- The ☑ *Create world file* checkbox is only available if you decide to use the linear transformation type, because this means that the raster image actually won't be transformed. In this case, the *Output raster* field is not activated, because only a new world file will be created.

- For all other transformation types, you have to define an *Output raster*. As default, a new file ([filename]_modified) will be created in the same folder together with the original raster image.

- As a next step, you have to define the *Target SRS* (Spatial Reference System) for the georeferenced raster (see *Working with Projections*).

- If you like, you can **generate a pdf map** and also **a pdf report**. The report includes information about the used transformation parameters, an image of the residuals and a list with all GCPs and their RMS errors.

- Furthermore, you can activate the ☑ *Set Target Resolution* checkbox and define the pixel resolution of the output raster. Default horizontal and vertical resolution is 1.

- The ☑ *Use 0 for transparency when needed* can be activated, if pixels with the value 0 shall be visualized transparent. In our example toposheet, all white areas would be transparent.

- Finally, ☑ *Load in QGIS when done* loads the output raster automatically into the QGIS map canvas when the transformation is done.

Show and adapt raster properties

Clicking on the *Raster properties* dialog in the *Settings* menu opens the raster properties of the layer that you want to georeference.

Configure the georeferencer

- You can define whether you want to show GCP coordiniates and/or IDs.

- As residual units, pixels and map units can be chosen.

- For the PDF report, a left and right margin can be defined and you can also set the paper size for the PDF map.

- Finally, you can activate to ☑ *Show Georeferencer window docked*.

Running the transformation

After all GCPs have been collected and all transformation settings are defined, just press the ▶ Start georeferencing button to create the new georeferenced raster.

19.10 Heatmap Plugin

The *Heatmap* plugin uses Kernel Density Estimation to create a density (heatmap) raster of an input point vector layer. The density is calculated based on the number of points in a location, with larger numbers of clustered points resulting in larger values. Heatmaps allow easy identification of "hotspots" and clustering of points.

19.10.1 Activate the Heatmap plugin

First this core plugin needs to be activated using the Plugin Manager (see *The Plugins Dialog*). After activation, the heatmap icon ⚬ can be found in the Raster Toolbar, and under the *Raster → Heatmap* menu.

Select the menu *View → Toolbars → Raster* to show the Raster Toolbar if it is not visible.

19.10.2 Using the Heatmap plugin

Clicking the ⚬ *Heatmap* tool button opens the Heatmap plugin dialog (see figure_heatmap_2).

The dialog has the following options:

- **Input point layer**: Lists all the vector point layers in the current project and is used to select the layer to be analysed.

- **Output raster**: Allows you to use the ⬚ button to select the folder and filename for the output raster the Heatmap plugin generates. A file extension is not required.

- **Output format**: Selects the output format. Although all formats supported by GDAL can be choosen, in most cases GeoTIFF is the best format to choose.

- **Radius**: Is used to specify the heatmap search radius (or kernel bandwidth) in meters or map units. The radius specifies the distance around a point at which the influence of the point will be felt. Larger values result in greater smoothing, but smaller values may show finer details and variation in point density.

When the ☑ *Advanced* checkbox is checked, additional options will be available:

- **Rows** and **Columns**: Used to change the dimensions of the output raster. These values are also linked to the **Cell size X** and **Cell size Y** values. Increasing the number of rows or columns will decrease the cell size and increase the file size of the output file. The values in Rows and Columns are also linked, so doubling the number of rows will automatically double the number of columns and the cell sizes will also be halved. The geographical area of the output raster will remain the same!

- **Cell size X** and **Cell size Y**: Control the geographic size of each pixel in the output raster. Changing these values will also change the number of Rows and Columns in the output raster.

- **Kernel shape**: The kernel shape controls the rate at which the influence of a point decreases as the distance from the point increases. Different kernels decay at different rates, so a triweight kernel gives features greater weight for distances closer to the point then the Epanechnikov kernel does. Consequently, triweight results in "sharper" hotspots, and Epanechnikov results in "smoother" hotspots. A number of standard kernel functions are available in QGIS, which are described and illustrated on Wikipedia.

- **Decay ratio**: Can be used with Triangular kernels to further control how heat from a feature decreases with distance from the feature.

  – A value of 0 (=minimum) indicates that the heat will be concentrated in the centre of the given radius and completely extinguished at the edge.

  – A value of 0.5 indicates that pixels at the edge of the radius will be given half the heat as pixels at the centre of the search radius.

  – A value of 1 means the heat is spread evenly over the whole search radius circle. (This is equivalent to the 'Uniform' kernel.)

  – A value greater than 1 indicates that the heat is higher towards the edge of the search radius than at the centre.

The input point layer may also have attribute fields which can affect how they influence the heatmap:

- **Use radius from field**: Sets the search radius for each feature from an attribute field in the input layer.

- **Use weight from field**: Allows input features to be weighted by an attribute field. This can be used to increase the influence certain features have on the resultant heatmap.

When an output raster file name is specified, the **[OK]** button can be used to create the heatmap.

19.10.3 Tutorial: Creating a Heatmap

For the following example, we will use the `airports` vector point layer from the QGIS sample dataset (see *Sample Data*). Another exellent QGIS tutorial on making heatmaps can be found at http://qgis.spatialthoughts.com.

In Figure_Heatmap_1, the airports of Alaska are shown.

1. Select the *Heatmap* tool button to open the Heatmap dialog (see Figure_Heatmap_2).

2. In the *Input point layer* field, select `airports` from the list of point layers loaded in the current project.

3. Specify an output filename by clicking the button next to the *Output raster* field. Enter the filename `heatmap_airports` (no file extension is necessary).

4. Leave the *Output format* as the default format, `GeoTIFF`.

5. Change the *Radius* to `1000000` meters.

6. Click on **[OK]** to create and load the airports heatmap (see Figure_Heatmap_3).

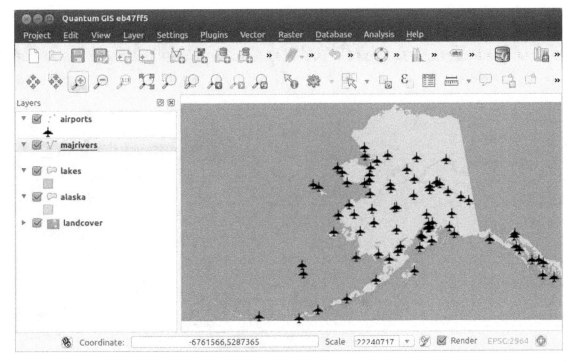

Figure 19.20: Airports of Alaska

Figure 19.21: The Heatmap Dialog

QGIS will generate the heatmap and add the results to your map window. By default, the heatmap is shaded in greyscale, with lighter areas showing higher concentrations of airports. The heatmap can now be styled in QGIS to improve its appearance.

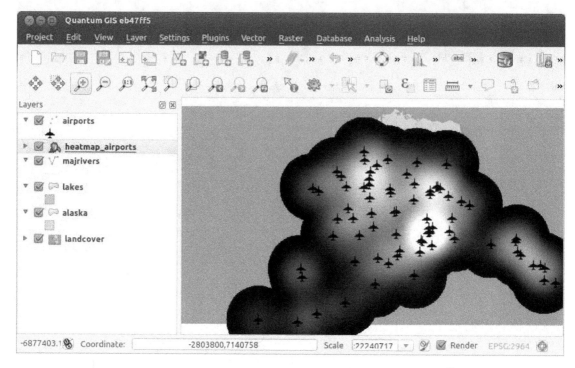

Figure 19.22: The heatmap after loading looks like a grey surface

1. Open the properties dialog of the `heatmap_airports` layer (select the layer `heatmap_airports`, open the context menu with the right mouse button and select *Properties*).

2. Select the *Style* tab.

3. Change the *Render type* to 'Singleband pseudocolor'.

4. Select a suitable *Color map* , for instance `YlOrRed`.

5. Click the **[Load]** button to fetch the minimum and maximum values from the raster, then click the **[Classify]** button.

6. Press **[OK]** to update the layer.

The final result is shown in Figure_Heatmap_4.

19.11 Interpolation Plugin

The Interplation plugin can be used to generate a TIN or IDW interpolation of a point vector layer. It is very simple to handle and provides an intuitive graphical user interface for creating interpolated raster layers (see Figure_interpolation_1). The plugin requires the following parameters to be specified before running:

- Input **Vector layers**: Specify the input point vector layer(s) from a list of loaded point layers. If several layers are specified, then data from all layers is used for interpolation. Note: It is possible to insert lines or polygons as constraints for the triangulation, by specifying either "points", "structure lines" or "break lines" in the *Type* combo box.

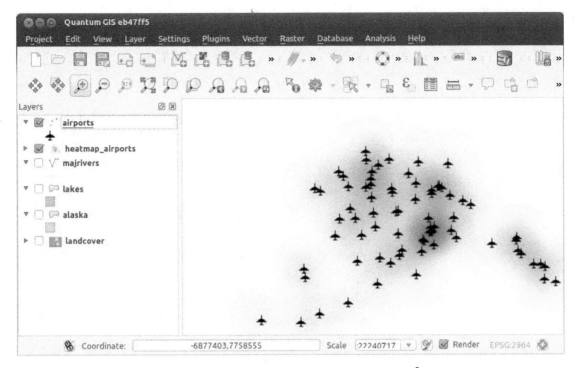

Figure 19.23: Styled heatmap of airports of Alaska 🐧

- **Interpolation attribute**: Select the attribute column to be used for interpolation or enable the ☑ *Use Z-Coordinate* checkbox to use the layer's stored Z values.

- **Interpolation Method**: Select the interpolation method. This can be either 'Triangulated Irregular Network (TIN)' or 'Inverse Distance Weighted (IDW)'. With the TIN method you can create a surface formed by triangles of nearest neighbour points. To do this, circumcircles around selected sample points are created and their intersections are connected to a network of non overlapping and as compact as possible triangles. The resulting surfaces are not smooth. When using the IDW method the sample points are weighted during interpolation such that the influence of one point relative to another declines with distance from the unknown point you want to create. The IDW interpolation method also has some disadvantages: the quality of the interpolation result can decrease, if the distribution of sample data points is uneven. Furthermore, maximum and minimum values in the interpolated surface can only occur at sample data points. This often results in small peaks and pits around the sample data points.

- **Number of columns/rows**: Specify the number of rows and columns for the output raster file.

- **Output file**: Specify a name for the output raster file.

- ☑ *Add result to project* to load the result into the map canvas.

Note that using lines as constraints for the interpolation the triangulation (TIN method) you can either use 'structure lines' or 'break lines'. When using 'break lines' you produce sharp breaks in the surface while using 'structure lines' you produce continous breaks. The triangulation is modified by both methods such that no edge crosses a breakline or structure line.

19.11.1 Using the plugin

1. Start QGIS and load a point vector layer (e.g., `elevp.csv`).

2. Load the Interpolation plugin in the Plugin Manager (see *The Plugins Dialog*) and click on the *Raster* → *Interpolation* → 🔲 *Interpolation* , which appears in the QGIS menu bar. The Interpolation plugin dialog appears as shown in Figure_interpolation_1.

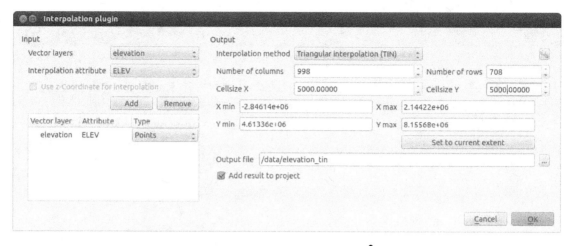

Figure 19.24: Interpolation Plugin

3. Select an input layer (e.g., *elevp*) and column (e.g., ELEV) for interpolation.

4. Select an interpolation method (e.g., 'Triangulated Irregular Network (TIN)'), and specify a cell size of 5000 as well as the raster output filename (e.g., elevation_tin).

5. Click **[OK]**.

19.12 MetaSearch Catalogue Client

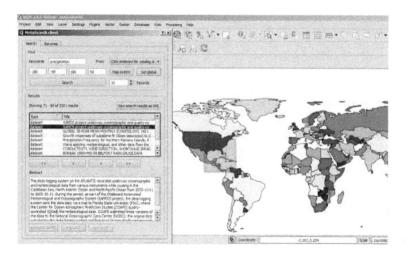

19.12.1 Introduction

MetaSearch is a QGIS plugin to interact with metadata catalogue services, supporting the OGC Catalogue Service for the Web (CSW) standard.

MetaSearch provides an easy and intuitive approach and user-friendly interface to searching metadata catalogues within QGIS.

19.12.2 Installation

MetaSearch is included by default with QGIS 2.0 and higher. All dependencies are included within MetaSearch.

Install MetaSearch from the QGIS plugin manager, or manually from http://plugins.qgis.org/plugins/MetaSearch.

19.12.3 Working with Metadata Catalogues in QGIS

CSW (Catalogue Service for the Web)

CSW (Catalogue Service for the Web) is an OGC (Open Geospatial Consortium) specification, that defines common interfaces to discover, browse, and query metadata about data, services, and other potential resources.

Startup

To start MetaSearch, click the MetaSearch icon or select Web / MetaSearch / MetaSearch via the QGIS main menu. The MetaSearch dialog will appear. The main GUI consists of two tabs: 'Services' and 'Search'.

Managing Catalogue Services

The 'Services' tab allows the user to manage all available catalogue services. MetaSearch provides a default list of Catalogue Services, which can be added by pressing 'Add default services' button.

To all listed Catalogue Service entries, click the dropdown select box.

To add a Catalogue Service entry, click the 'New' button, and enter a Name for the service, as well as the URL/endpoint. Note that only the base URL is required (not a full GetCapabilities URL). Clicking ok will add the service to the list of entries.

To edit an existing Catalogue Service entry, select the entry you would like to edit and click the 'Edit' button, and modify the Name or URL values, then click ok.

To delete a Catalogue Service entry, select the entry you would like to delete and click the 'Delete' button. You will be asked to confirm deleting the entry.

MetaSearch allows for loading and saving connections to an XML file. This is useful when you need to share settings between applications. Below is an example of the XML file format.

```
<?xml version="1.0" encoding="UTF-8"?>
<qgsCSWConnections version="1.0">
    <csw name="Data.gov CSW" url="http://catalog.data.gov/csw-all"/>
    <csw name="Geonorge - National CSW service for Norway" url="http://www.geonorge.no/geonetwork/srv/
    <csw name="Geoportale Nazionale - Servizio di ricerca Italiano" url="http://www.pcn.minambiente.it
    <csw name="LINZ Data Service" url="http://data.linz.govt.nz/feeds/csw"/>
```

```
    <csw name="Nationaal Georegister (Nederland)" url="http://www.nationaalgeoregister.nl/geonetw
    <csw name="RNDT - Repertorio Nazionale dei Dati Territoriali - Servizio di ricerca" url="http
    <csw name="UK Location Catalogue Publishing Service" url="http://csw.data.gov.uk/geonetwork/s
    <csw name="UNEP/GRID-Geneva Metadata Catalog" url="http://metadata.grid.unep.ch:8080/geonetwo
</qgsCSWConnections>
```

To load a list of entries, click the 'Load' button. A new window will appear; click the 'Browse' button and navigate to the XML file of entries you wish to load and click 'Open'. The list of entries will be displayed. Select the entries you wish to add from the list and click 'Load'.

The 'Service info' button displays information about the selected Catalogue Service such as service identification, service provider and contact information. If you would like to view the raw XML response, click the 'GetCapabilities response' button. A separate window will open displaying Capabilities XML.

Searching Catalogue Services

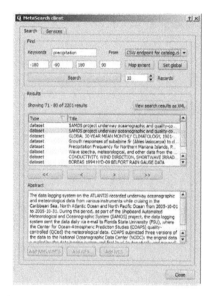

The 'Search' tab allows the user to query Catalogue Services for data and services, set various search parameters and view results.

The following search parameters are available:

- **Keywords**: free text search keywords

- **From**: the Catalogue Service to perform the query against

- **Bounding box**: the spatial area of interest to filter on. The default bounding box is the map view / canvas. Click 'Set global' to do a global search, or enter custom values as desired

- **Records**: the number of records to return when searching. Default is 10 records

Clicking the 'Search' button will search the selected Metadata Catalogue. Search results are displayed in a list and are sortable by clicking on the column title. You can navigate through search results with the directional buttons below the search results. Clicking the 'View search results as XML' button opens a window with the service response in raw XML format.

Clicking a result will show the record's abstract in the 'Abstract' window and provides the following options:

- if the metadata record has an associated bounding box, a footprint of the bounding box will be displayed on the map

- double-clicking the record displays the record metadata with any associated access links. Clicking the links opens the link in the user's web browser

- if the record is an OGC web service (WMS/WMTS, WFS, WCS), the appropriate 'Add to WMS/WMTS|WFS|WCS' buttons will be enabled for the user to add to QGIS. When clicking this button, MetaSearch will verify if this is a valid OWS. The OWS will then be added to the appropriate QGIS connection list, and the appropriate WMS/WMTS|WFS|WCS connection dialogue will then appear

Settings

You can fine tune MetaSearch with the following settings:

- **Connection naming**: when adding an OWS connection (WMS/WMTS|WFS|WCS), the connection is stored with the various QGIS layer provider. Use this setting to set whether to use the name provided from MetaSearch, whether to overwrite or to use a temporary name

- **Results paging**: when searching metadata catalogues, the number of results to show per page

- **Timeout**: when searching metadata catalogues, the number of seconds for blocking connection attempt. Default value is 10

19.13 Offline Editing Plugin

For data collection, it is a common situation to work with a laptop or a cell phone offline in the field. Upon returning to the network, the changes need to be synchronized with the master datasource (e.g., a PostGIS database). If several persons are working simultaneously on the same datasets, it is difficult to merge the edits by hand, even if people don't change the same features.

The ![Offline Editing] Plugin automates the synchronisation by copying the content of a datasource (usually PostGIS or WFS-T) to a SpatiaLite database and storing the offline edits to dedicated tables. After being connected to the network again, it is possible to apply the offline edits to the master dataset.

19.13.1 Using the plugin

- Open some vector layers (e.g., from a PostGIS or WFS-T datasource).

- Save it as a project.

- Go to *Database* → *Offline Editing* → ![icon] *Convert to offline project* and select the layers to save. The content of the layers is saved to SpatiaLite tables.

- Edit the layers offline.

- After being connected again, upload the changes using *Database → Offline Editing →* 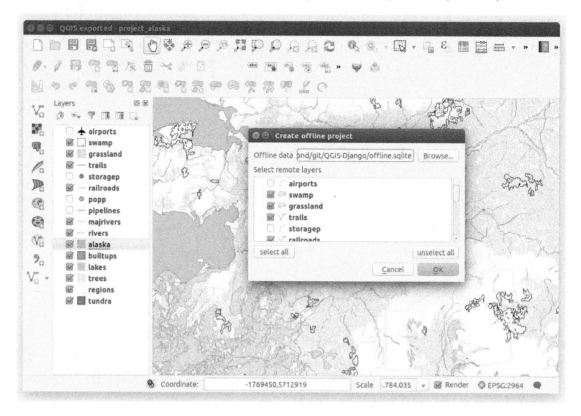 *Synchronize.*

Figure 19.25: Create an offline project from PostGIS or WFS layers

.

19.14 Oracle Spatial GeoRaster Plugin

In Oracle databases, raster data can be stored in SDO_GEORASTER objects available with the Oracle Spatial extension. In QGIS, the Oracle Spatial GeoRaster plugin is supported by GDAL and depends on Oracle's database product being installed and working on your machine. While Oracle is proprietary software, they provide their software free for development and testing purposes. Here is one simple example of how to load raster images to GeoRaster:

```
$ gdal_translate -of georaster input_file.tif geor:scott/tiger@orcl
```

This will load the raster into the default GDAL_IMPORT table, as a column named RASTER.

19.14.1 Managing connections

Firstly, the Oracle GeoRaster Plugin must be enabled using the Plugin Manager (see *The Plugins Dialog*). The first time you load a GeoRaster in QGIS, you must create a connection to the Oracle database that contains the data. To do this, begin by clicking on the Add Oracle GeoRaster Layer toolbar button – this will open the *Select Oracle Spatial GeoRaster* dialog window. Click on **[New]** to open the dialog window, and specify the connection parameters (See Figure_oracle_raster_1):

- **Name**: Enter a name for the database connection.

- **Database instance**: Enter the name of the database that you will connect to.
- **Username**: Specify your own username that you will use to access the database.
- **Password**: Provide the password associated with your username that is required to access the database.

Figure 19.26: Create Oracle connection dialog

Now, back on the main *Oracle Spatial GeoRaster* dialog window (see Figure_oracle_raster_2), use the drop-down list to choose one connection, and use the **[Connect]** button to establish a connection. You may also **[Edit]** the connection by opening the previous dialog and making changes to the connection information, or use the **[Delete]** button to remove the connection from the drop-down list.

19.14.2 Selecting a GeoRaster

Once a connection has been established, the subdatasets window will show the names of all the tables that contain GeoRaster columns in that database in the format of a GDAL subdataset name.

Click on one of the listed subdatasets and then click on **[Select]** to choose the table name. Now another list of subdatasets will show with the names of GeoRaster columns on that table. This is usually a short list, since most users will not have more than one or two GeoRaster columns on the same table.

Click on one of the listed subdatasets and then click on **[Select]** to choose one of the table/column combinations. The dialog will now show all the rows that contain GeoRaster objects. Note that the subdataset list will now show the Raster Data Table and Raster Id pairs.

At any time, the selection entry can be edited in order to go directly to a known GeoRaster or to go back to the beginning and select another table name.

The selection data entry can also be used to enter a `WHERE` clause at the end of the identification string (e.g., `geor:scott/tiger@orcl,gdal_import,raster,geoid=`). See http://www.gdal.org/frmt_georaster.html for more information.

19.14.3 Displaying GeoRaster

Finally, by selecting a GeoRaster from the list of Raster Data Tables and Raster Ids, the raster image will be loaded into QGIS.

The *Select Oracle Spatial GeoRaster* dialog can be closed now and the next time it opens, it will keep the same connection and will show the same previous list of subdatasets, making it very easy to open up another image from the same context.

Note: GeoRasters that contain pyramids will display much faster, but the pyramids need to be generated outside of QGIS using Oracle PL/SQL or gdaladdo.

The following is an example using `gdaladdo`:

Figure 19.27: Select Oracle GeoRaster dialog

```
gdaladdo georaster:scott/tiger@orcl,georaster\_table,georaster,georid=6 -r
nearest 2 4 6 8 16 32
```

This is an example using PL/SQL:

```
$ sqlplus scott/tiger
SQL> DECLARE
 gr sdo_georaster;
BEGIN
    SELECT image INTO gr FROM cities WHERE id = 1 FOR UPDATE;
    sdo_geor.generatePyramid(gr, 'rLevel=5, resampling=NN');
    UPDATE cities SET image = gr WHERE id = 1;
    COMMIT;
END;
```
.

19.15 Raster Terrain Analysis Plugin

The Raster Terrain Analysis Plugin can be used to calculate the slope, aspect, hillshade, ruggedness index and relief for digital elevation models (DEM). It is very simple to handle and provides an intuitive graphical user interface for creating new raster layers (see Figure_raster_terrain_1).

Description of the analysis:

- **Slope**: Calculates the slope angle for each cell in degrees (based on first- order derivative estimation).

- **Aspect**: Exposition (starting with 0 for north direction, in degrees counterclockwise).

- **Hillshade**: Creates a shaded map using light and shadow to provide a more three-dimensional appearance for a shaded relief map. The output map is a Single band gray reflecting the gray value of the pixels.

- **Ruggedness Index**: A quantitative measurement of terrain heterogeneity as described by Riley et al. (1999). It is calculated for every location by summarizing the change in elevation within the 3x3 pixel grid.

- **Relief**: Creates a shaded relief map from digital elevation data. Implemented is a method to choose the elevation colors by analysing the frequency distribution. The output map is a multiband color with three bands reflecting the RGB values of the shaded relief.

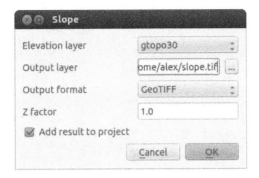

Figure 19.28: Raster Terrain Modelling Plugin (slope calculation)

19.15.1 Using the plugin

1. Start QGIS and load the `gtopo30` raster layer from the GRASS sample location.

2. Load the Raster Terrain Analysis plugin in the Plugin Manager (see *The Plugins Dialog*).

3. Select an analysis method from the menu (e.g., *Raster → Terrain Analysis → Slope*). The *Slope* dialog appears as shown in Figure_raster_terrain_1.

4. Specify an output file path, and an output file type.

5. Click [**OK**].

19.16 Road Graph Plugin

The Road Graph Plugin is a C++ plugin for QGIS that calculates the shortest path between two points on any polyline layer and plots this path over the road network.

Main features:

- Calculates path, as well as length and travel time.

- Optimizes by length or by travel time.

- Exports path to a vector layer.

- Highlights roads directions (this is slow and used mainly for debug purposes and for the settings testing).

As a roads layer, you can use any polyline vector layer in any QGIS-supported format. Two lines with a common point are considered connected. Please note, it is required to use layer CRS as project CRS while editing a roads layer. This is due to the fact that recalculation of the coordinates between different CRSs introduces some errors that can result in discontinuities, even when 'snapping' is used.

In the layer attribute table, the following fields can be used:

- Speed on road section (numeric field).

- Direction (any type that can be cast to string). Forward and reverse directions correspond to a one-way road, both directions indicate a two-way road.

If some fields don't have any value or do not exist, default values are used. You can change defaults and some plugin settings in the plugin settings dialog.

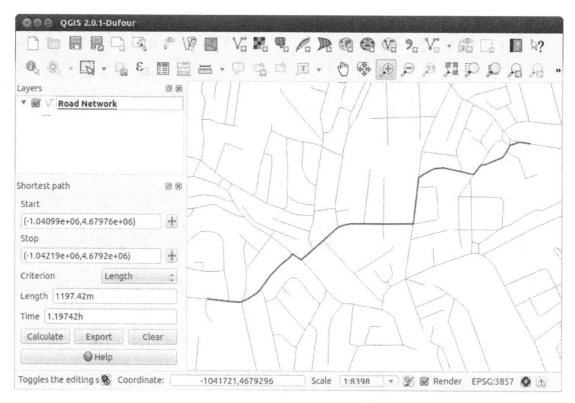

Figure 19.29: Road Graph Plugin ⬡

19.16.1 Using the plugin

After plugin activation, you will see an additional panel on the left side of the main QGIS window. Now, enter some parameters into the *Road graph plugin settings* dialog in the *Vector → Road Graph* menu (see figure_road_graph_2).

After setting the *Time unit*, *Distance unit* and *Topology tolerance*, you can choose the vector layer in the *Transportation layer* tab. Here you can also choose the *Direction field* and *Speed field*. In the *Default settings* tab, you can set the *Direction* for the calculation.

Finally, in the *Shortest Path* panel, select a Start and a Stop point in the road network layer and click on [**Calculate**].

.

19.17 Spatial Query Plugin

The Spatial Query Plugin allows you to make a spatial query (i.e., select features) in a target layer with reference to another layer. The functionality is based on the GEOS library and depends on the selected source feature layer.

Possible operators are:

- Contains
- Equals
- Overlap
- Crosses
- Intersects

Figure 19.30: Road graph plugin settings

- Is disjoint
- Touches
- Within

19.17.1 Using the plugin

As an example, we want to find regions in the Alaska dataset that contain airports. The following steps are necessary:

1. Start QGIS and load the vector layers `regions.shp` and `airports.shp`.

2. Load the Spatial Query plugin in the Plugin Manager (see *The Plugins Dialog*) and click on the Spatial Query icon, which appears in the QGIS toolbar menu. The plugin dialog appears.

3. Select the layer `regions` as the source layer and `airports` as the reference feature layer.

4. Select 'Contains' as the operator and click **[Apply]**.

Now you get a list of feature IDs from the query and you have several options, as shown in figure_spatial_query_1.

- Click on Create layer with list of items.
- Select an ID from the list and click on Create layer with selected.
- Select 'Remove from current selection' in the field *And use the result to*.
- You can Zoom to item or display Log messages.
- Additionally in *Result Feature ID's* with the options 'Invalid source' and 'Invalid reference' you can have a look at features with geometries errors. These features aren't used for the query.

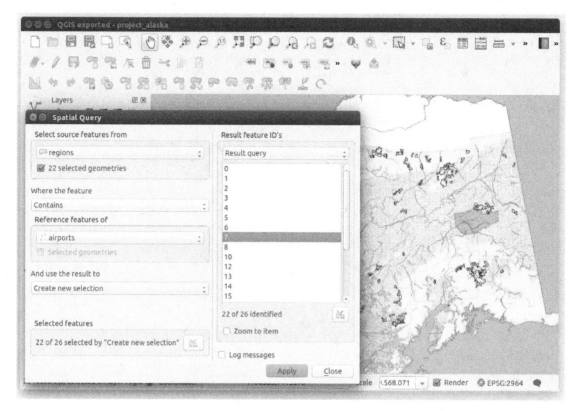

Figure 19.31: Spatial Query analysis - regions contain airports ⌂

19.18 SPIT Plugin

QGIS comes with a plugin named SPIT (Shapefile to PostGIS Import Tool). SPIT can be used to load multiple shapefiles at one time and includes support for schemas. To use SPIT, open the Plugin Manager from the *Plugins* menu, in the 🧩 *Installed* menu check the box next to the ✅ *SPIT* and click **[OK]**.

To import a shapefile, use *Database → Spit → Import Shapefiles to PostgreSQL* from the menu bar to open the *SPIT - Shapefile to PostGIS Import Tool* dialog. Select the PostGIS database you want to connect to and click on **[Connect]**. If you want, you can define or change some import options. Now you can add one or more files to the queue by clicking on the **[Add]** button. To process the files, click on the **[OK]** button. The progress of the import as well as any errors/warnings will be displayed as each shapefile is processed.   .

19.19 Topology Checker Plugin

Topology describes the relationships between points, lines and polygons that represent the features of a geographic region. With the Topology Checker plugin, you can look over your vector files and check the topology with several topology rules. These rules check with spatial relations whether your features 'Equal', 'Contain', 'Cover', are 'CoveredBy', 'Cross', are 'Disjoint', 'Intersect', 'Overlap', 'Touch' or are 'Within' each other. It depends on your individual questions which topology rules you apply to your vector data (e.g., normally you won't accept overshoots in line layers, but if they depict dead-end streets you won't remove them from your vector layer).

QGIS has a built-in topological editing feature, which is great for creating new features without errors. But existing data errors and user-induced errors are hard to find. This plugin helps you find such errors through a list of rules.

It is very simple to create topology rules with the Topology Checker plugin.

On **point layers** the following rules are available:

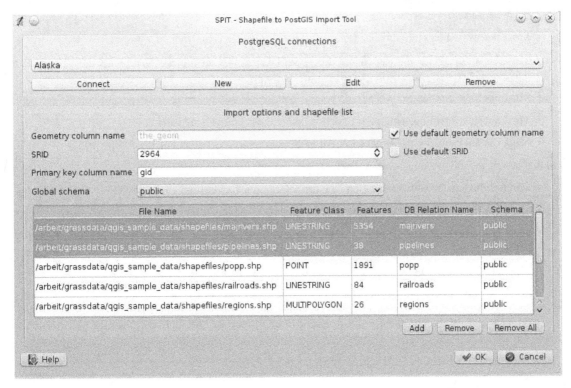

Figure 19.32: Using SPIT Plugin to import Shape files to PostGIS

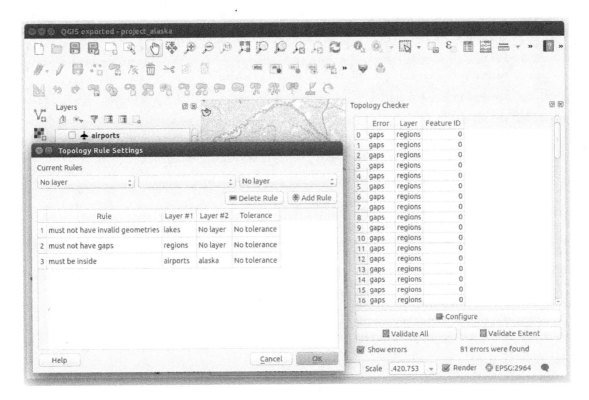

Figure 19.33: The Topology Checker Plugin

- **Must be covered by**: Here you can choose a vector layer from your project. Points that aren't covered by the given vector layer occur in the 'Error' field.

- **Must be covered by endpoints of**: Here you can choose a line layer from your project.

- **Must be inside**: Here you can choose a polygon layer from your project. The points must be inside a polygon. Otherwise, QGIS writes an 'Error' for the point.

- **Must not have duplicates**: Whenever a point is represented twice or more, it will occur in the 'Error' field.

- **Must not have invalid geometries**: Checks whether the geometries are valid.

- **Must not have multi-part-geometries**: All multi-part points are written into the 'Error' field.

On **line layers**, the following rules are available:

- **End points must be covered by**: Here you can select a point layer from your project.

- **Must not have dangles**: This will show the overshoots in the line layer.

- **Must not have duplicates**: Whenever a line feature is represented twice or more, it will occur in the 'Error' field.

- **Must not have invalid geometries**: Checks whether the geometries are valid.

- **Must not have multi-part geometries**: Sometimes, a geometry is actually a collection of simple (single-part) geometries. Such a geometry is called multi-part geometry. If it contains just one type of simple geometry, we call it multi-point, multi-linestring or multi-polygon. All multi-part lines are written into the 'Error' field.

- **Must not have pseudos**: A line geometry's endpoint should be connected to the endpoints of two other geometries. If the endpoint is connected to only one other geometry's endpoint, the endpoint is called a psuedo node.

On **polygon layers**, the following rules are available:

- **Must contain**: Polygon layer must contain at least one point geometry from the second layer.

- **Must not have duplicates**: Polygons from the same layer must not have identical geometries. Whenever a polygon feature is represented twice or more it will occur in the 'Error' field.

- **Must not have gaps**: Adjacent polygons should not form gaps between them. Administrative boundaries could be mentioned as an example (US state polygons do not have any gaps between them...).

- **Must not have invalid geometries**: Checks whether the geometries are valid. Some of the rules that define a valid geometry are:

  - Polygon rings must close.

  - Rings that define holes should be inside rings that define exterior boundaries.

  - Rings may not self-intersect (they may neither touch nor cross one another).

  - Rings may not touch other rings, except at a point.

- **Must not have multi-part geometries**: Sometimes, a geometry is actually a collection of simple (single-part) geometries. Such a geometry is called multi-part geometry. If it contains just one type of simple geometry, we call it multi-point, multi-linestring or multi-polygon. For example, a country consisting of multiple islands can be represented as a multi-polygon.

- **Must not overlap**: Adjacent polygons should not share common area.

- **Must not overlap with**: Adjacent polygons from one layer should not share common area with polygons from another layer.

19.20 Zonal Statistics Plugin

With the Σ *Zonal statistics* plugin, you can analyze the results of a thematic classification. It allows you to calculate several values of the pixels of a raster layer with the help of a polygonal vector layer (see figure_zonal_statistics). You can calculate the sum, the mean value and the total count of the pixels that are within a polygon. The plugin generates output columns in the vector layer with a user-defined prefix.

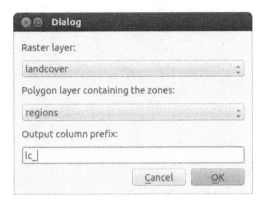

Figure 19.34: Zonal statistics dialog (KDE)

## CHAPTER 20

Help and Support

20.1 Mailing lists

QGIS is under active development and as such it won't always work like you expect it to. The preferred way to get help is by joining the qgis-users mailing list. Your questions will reach a broader audience and answers will benefit others.

20.1.1 qgis-users

This mailing list is used for discussion of QGIS in general, as well as specific questions regarding its installation and use.   You can subscribe to the qgis-users mailing list by visiting the following URL: http://lists.osgeo.org/mailman/listinfo/qgis-user

20.1.2 fossgis-talk-liste

For the German-speaking audience, the German FOSSGIS e.V. provides the fossgis-talk-liste mailing list. This mailing list is used for discussion of open-source GIS in general, including QGIS. You can subscribe to the fossgis-talk-liste mailing list by visiting the following URL: https://lists.fossgis.de/mailman/listinfo/fossgis-talk-liste

20.1.3 qgis-developer

If you are a developer facing problems of a more technical nature, you may want to join the qgis-developer mailing list here: http://lists.osgeo.org/mailman/listinfo/qgis-developer

20.1.4 qgis-commit

Each time a commit is made to the QGIS code repository, an email is posted to this list.   If you want to be up-to-date with every change to the current code base, you can subscribe to this list at: http://lists.osgeo.org/mailman/listinfo/qgis-commit

20.1.5 qgis-trac

This list provides email notification related to project management, including bug reports, tasks, and feature requests. You can subscribe to this list at: http://lists.osgeo.org/mailman/listinfo/qgis-trac

20.1.6 qgis-community-team

This list deals with topics like documentation, context help, user guide, web sites, blog, mailing lists, forums, and translation efforts. If you would like to work on the user guide as well, this list is a good starting point to ask your questions. You can subscribe to this list at: http://lists.osgeo.org/mailman/listinfo/qgis-community-team

20.1.7 qgis-release-team

This list deals with topics like the release process, packaging binaries for various OSs and announcing new releases to the world at large. You can subscribe to this list at: http://lists.osgeo.org/mailman/listinfo/qgis-release-team

20.1.8 qgis-tr

This list deals with the translation efforts. If you like to work on the translation of the manuals or the graphical user interface (GUI), this list is a good starting point to ask your questions. You can subscribe to this list at: http://lists.osgeo.org/mailman/listinfo/qgis-tr

20.1.9 qgis-edu

This list deals with QGIS education efforts. If you would like to work on QGIS education materials, this list is a good starting point to ask your questions. You can subscribe to this list at: http://lists.osgeo.org/mailman/listinfo/qgis-edu

20.1.10 qgis-psc

This list is used to discuss Steering Committee issues related to overall management and direction of QGIS. You can subscribe to this list at: http://lists.osgeo.org/mailman/listinfo/qgis-psc

You are welcome to subscribe to any of the lists. Please remember to contribute to the list by answering questions and sharing your experiences. Note that the qgis-commit and qgis-trac lists are designed for notification only and are not meant for user postings.

20.2 IRC

We also maintain a presence on IRC - visit us by joining the #qgis channel on irc.freenode.net. Please wait for a response to your question, as many folks on the channel are doing other things and it may take a while for them to notice your question. If you missed a discussion on IRC, not a problem! We log all discussion, so you can easily catch up. Just go to http://qgis.org/irclogs and read the IRC-logs.

Commercial support for QGIS is also available. Check the website http://qgis.org/en/commercial-support.html for more information.

20.3 BugTracker

While the qgis-users mailing list is useful for general 'How do I do XYZ in QGIS?'-type questions, you may wish to notify us about bugs in QGIS. You can submit bug reports using the QGIS bug tracker at http://hub.qgis.org/projects/quantum-gis/issues. When creating a new ticket for a bug, please provide an email address where we can contact you for additional information.

Please bear in mind that your bug may not always enjoy the priority you might hope for (depending on its severity). Some bugs may require significant developer effort to remedy, and the manpower is not always available for this.

Feature requests can be submitted as well using the same ticket system as for bugs. Please make sure to select the type `Feature`.

If you have found a bug and fixed it yourself, you can submit this patch also. Again, the lovely redmine ticketsystem at http://hub.qgis.org/wiki/quantum-gis/issues has this type as well. Check the `Patch supplied` checkbox and attach your patch before submitting your bug. One of the developers will review it and apply it to QGIS. Please don't be alarmed if your patch is not applied straight away – developers may be tied up with other commitments.

20.4 Blog

The QGIS community also runs a weblog at http://planet.qgis.org/planet/, which has some interesting articles for users and developers as well provided by other blogs in the community. You are invited to contribute your own QGIS blog!

20.5 Plugins

The website http://plugins.qgis.org provides the official QGIS plugins web portal. Here, you find a list of all stable and experimental QGIS plugins available via the 'Official QGIS Plugin Repository'.

20.6 Wiki

Lastly, we maintain a WIKI web site at http://hub.qgis.org/projects/quantum-gis/wiki where you can find a variety of useful information relating to QGIS development, release plans, links to download sites, message-translation hints and more. Check it out, there are some goodies inside!

## CHAPTER 21

Appendix

21.1 GNU General Public License

Version 2, June 1991

Copyright (C) 1989, 1991 Free Software Foundation, Inc. 59 Temple Place - Suite 330, Boston, MA 02111-1307, USA

Everyone is permitted to copy and distribute verbatim copies of this license document, but changing it is not allowed.

Preamble

The licenses for most software are designed to take away your freedom to share and change it. By contrast, the GNU General Public License is intended to guarantee your freedom to share and change free software–to make sure the software is free for all its users. This General Public License applies to most of the Free Software Foundation's software and to any other program whose authors commit to using it. (Some other Free Software Foundation software is covered by the GNU Library General Public License instead.) You can apply it to your programs, too.

When we speak of free software, we are referring to freedom, not price. Our General Public Licenses are designed to make sure that you have the freedom to distribute copies of free software (and charge for this service if you wish), that you receive source code or can get it if you want it, that you can change the software or use pieces of it in new free programs; and that you know you can do these things.

To protect your rights, we need to make restrictions that forbid anyone to deny you these rights or to ask you to surrender the rights. These restrictions translate to certain responsibilities for you if you distribute copies of the software, or if you modify it.

For example, if you distribute copies of such a program, whether gratis or for a fee, you must give the recipients all the rights that you have. You must make sure that they, too, receive or can get the source code. And you must show them these terms so they know their rights.

We protect your rights with two steps: (1) copyright the software, and (2) offer you this license which gives you legal permission to copy, distribute and/or modify the software.

Also, for each author's protection and ours, we want to make certain that everyone understands that there is no warranty for this free software. If the software is modified by someone else and passed on, we want its recipients to know that what they have is not the original, so that any problems introduced by others will not reflect on the original authors' reputations.

Finally, any free program is threatened constantly by software patents. We wish to avoid the danger that redistributors of a free program will individually obtain patent licenses, in effect making the program proprietary. To prevent this, we have made it clear that any patent must be licensed for everyone's free use or not licensed at all.

The precise terms and conditions for copying, distribution and modification follow. TERMS AND CONDITIONS FOR COPYING, DISTRIBUTION AND MODIFICATION

    0. This License applies to any program or other work which contains a notice placed by the copyright holder saying it may be distributed under the terms of this General Public License. The "Program", below, refers to

any such program or work, and a "work based on the Program" means either the Program or any derivative work under copyright law: that is to say, a work containing the Program or a portion of it, either verbatim or with modifications and/or translated into another language. (Hereinafter, translation is included without limitation in the term "modification".) Each licensee is addressed as "you".

Activities other than copying, distribution and modification are not covered by this License; they are outside its scope. The act of running the Program is not restricted, and the output from the Program is covered only if its contents constitute a work based on the Program (independent of having been made by running the Program). Whether that is true depends on what the Program does.

1. You may copy and distribute verbatim copies of the Program's source code as you receive it, in any medium, provided that you conspicuously and appropriately publish on each copy an appropriate copyright notice and disclaimer of warranty; keep intact all the notices that refer to this License and to the absence of any warranty; and give any other recipients of the Program a copy of this License along with the Program.

   You may charge a fee for the physical act of transferring a copy, and you may at your option offer warranty protection in exchange for a fee.

2. You may modify your copy or copies of the Program or any portion of it, thus forming a work based on the Program, and copy and distribute such modifications or work under the terms of Section 1 above, provided that you also meet all of these conditions:

   (a) You must cause the modified files to carry prominent notices stating that you changed the files and the date of any change.

   (b) You must cause any work that you distribute or publish, that in whole or in part contains or is derived from the Program or any part thereof, to be licensed as a whole at no charge to all third parties under the terms of this License.

   (c) If the modified program normally reads commands interactively when run, you must cause it, when started running for such interactive use in the most ordinary way, to print or display an announcement including an appropriate copyright notice and a notice that there is no warranty (or else, saying that you provide a warranty) and that users may redistribute the program under these conditions, and telling the user how to view a copy of this License. (Exception: if the Program itself is interactive but does not normally print such an announcement, your work based on the Program is not required to print an announcement.)

   These requirements apply to the modified work as a whole. If identifiable sections of that work are not derived from the Program, and can be reasonably considered independent and separate works in themselves, then this License, and its terms, do not apply to those sections when you distribute them as separate works. But when you distribute the same sections as part of a whole which is a work based on the Program, the distribution of the whole must be on the terms of this License, whose permissions for other licensees extend to the entire whole, and thus to each and every part regardless of who wrote it.

   Thus, it is not the intent of this section to claim rights or contest your rights to work written entirely by you; rather, the intent is to exercise the right to control the distribution of derivative or collective works based on the Program.

   In addition, mere aggregation of another work not based on the Program with the Program (or with a work based on the Program) on a volume of a storage or distribution medium does not bring the other work under the scope of this License.

3. You may copy and distribute the Program (or a work based on it, under Section 2) in object code or executable form under the terms of Sections 1 and 2 above provided that you also do one of the following:

   (a) Accompany it with the complete corresponding machine-readable source code, which must be distributed under the terms of Sections 1 and 2 above on a medium customarily used for software interchange; or,

   (b) Accompany it with a written offer, valid for at least three years, to give any third party, for a charge no more than your cost of physically performing source distribution, a complete machine-readable copy of the corresponding source code, to be distributed under the terms of Sections 1 and 2 above on a medium customarily used for software interchange; or,

(c) Accompany it with the information you received as to the offer to distribute corresponding source code. (This alternative is allowed only for noncommercial distribution and only if you received the program in object code or executable form with such an offer, in accord with Subsection b above.)

The source code for a work means the preferred form of the work for making modifications to it. For an executable work, complete source code means all the source code for all modules it contains, plus any associated interface definition files, plus the scripts used to control compilation and installation of the executable. However, as a special exception, the source code distributed need not include anything that is normally distributed (in either source or binary form) with the major components (compiler, kernel, and so on) of the operating system on which the executable runs, unless that component itself accompanies the executable.

If distribution of executable or object code is made by offering access to copy from a designated place, then offering equivalent access to copy the source code from the same place counts as distribution of the source code, even though third parties are not compelled to copy the source along with the object code.

4. You may not copy, modify, sublicense, or distribute the Program except as expressly provided under this License. Any attempt otherwise to copy, modify, sublicense or distribute the Program is void, and will automatically terminate your rights under this License. However, parties who have received copies, or rights, from you under this License will not have their licenses terminated so long as such parties remain in full compliance.

5. You are not required to accept this License, since you have not signed it. However, nothing else grants you permission to modify or distribute the Program or its derivative works. These actions are prohibited by law if you do not accept this License. Therefore, by modifying or distributing the Program (or any work based on the Program), you indicate your acceptance of this License to do so, and all its terms and conditions for copying, distributing or modifying the Program or works based on it.

6. Each time you redistribute the Program (or any work based on the Program), the recipient automatically receives a license from the original licensor to copy, distribute or modify the Program subject to these terms and conditions. You may not impose any further restrictions on the recipients' exercise of the rights granted herein. You are not responsible for enforcing compliance by third parties to this License.

7. If, as a consequence of a court judgment or allegation of patent infringement or for any other reason (not limited to patent issues), conditions are imposed on you (whether by court order, agreement or otherwise) that contradict the conditions of this License, they do not excuse you from the conditions of this License. If you cannot distribute so as to satisfy simultaneously your obligations under this License and any other pertinent obligations, then as a consequence you may not distribute the Program at all. For example, if a patent license would not permit royalty-free redistribution of the Program by all those who receive copies directly or indirectly through you, then the only way you could satisfy both it and this License would be to refrain entirely from distribution of the Program.

If any portion of this section is held invalid or unenforceable under any particular circumstance, the balance of the section is intended to apply and the section as a whole is intended to apply in other circumstances.

It is not the purpose of this section to induce you to infringe any patents or other property right claims or to contest validity of any such claims; this section has the sole purpose of protecting the integrity of the free software distribution system, which is implemented by public license practices. Many people have made generous contributions to the wide range of software distributed through that system in reliance on consistent application of that system; it is up to the author/donor to decide if he or she is willing to distribute software through any other system and a licensee cannot impose that choice.

This section is intended to make thoroughly clear what is believed to be a consequence of the rest of this License.

8. If the distribution and/or use of the Program is restricted in certain countries either by patents or by copyrighted interfaces, the original copyright holder who places the Program under this License may add an explicit geographical distribution limitation excluding those countries, so that distribution is permitted only in or among countries not thus excluded. In such case, this License incorporates the limitation as if written in the body of this License.

9. The Free Software Foundation may publish revised and/or new versions of the General Public License from time to time. Such new versions will be similar in spirit to the present version, but may differ in detail to address new problems or concerns.

Each version is given a distinguishing version number. If the Program specifies a version number of this License which applies to it and "any later version", you have the option of following the terms and conditions either of that version or of any later version published by the Free Software Foundation. If the Program does not specify a version number of this License, you may choose any version ever published by the Free Software Foundation.

10. If you wish to incorporate parts of the Program into other free programs whose distribution conditions are different, write to the author to ask for permission. For software which is copyrighted by the Free Software Foundation, write to the Free Software Foundation; we sometimes make exceptions for this. Our decision will be guided by the two goals of preserving the free status of all derivatives of our free software and of promoting the sharing and reuse of software generally.

NO WARRANTY

11. BECAUSE THE PROGRAM IS LICENSED FREE OF CHARGE, THERE IS NO WARRANTY FOR THE PROGRAM, TO THE EXTENT PERMITTED BY APPLICABLE LAW. EXCEPT WHEN OTHERWISE STATED IN WRITING THE COPYRIGHT HOLDERS AND/OR OTHER PARTIES PROVIDE THE PROGRAM "AS IS" WITHOUT WARRANTY OF ANY KIND, EITHER EXPRESSED OR IMPLIED, INCLUDING, BUT NOT LIMITED TO, THE IMPLIED WARRANTIES OF MERCHANTABILITY AND FITNESS FOR A PARTICULAR PURPOSE. THE ENTIRE RISK AS TO THE QUALITY AND PERFORMANCE OF THE PROGRAM IS WITH YOU. SHOULD THE PROGRAM PROVE DEFECTIVE, YOU ASSUME THE COST OF ALL NECESSARY SERVICING, REPAIR OR CORRECTION.

12. IN NO EVENT UNLESS REQUIRED BY APPLICABLE LAW OR AGREED TO IN WRITING WILL ANY COPYRIGHT HOLDER, OR ANY OTHER PARTY WHO MAY MODIFY AND/OR REDISTRIBUTE THE PROGRAM AS PERMITTED ABOVE, BE LIABLE TO YOU FOR DAMAGES, INCLUDING ANY GENERAL, SPECIAL, INCIDENTAL OR CONSEQUENTIAL DAMAGES ARISING OUT OF THE USE OR INABILITY TO USE THE PROGRAM (INCLUDING BUT NOT LIMITED TO LOSS OF DATA OR DATA BEING RENDERED INACCURATE OR LOSSES SUSTAINED BY YOU OR THIRD PARTIES OR A FAILURE OF THE PROGRAM TO OPERATE WITH ANY OTHER PROGRAMS), EVEN IF SUCH HOLDER OR OTHER PARTY HAS BEEN ADVISED OF THE POSSIBILITY OF SUCH DAMAGES.

QGIS Qt exception for GPL

In addition, as a special exception, the QGIS Development Team gives permission to link the code of this program with the Qt library, including but not limited to the following versions (both free and commercial): Qt/Non-commerical Windows, Qt/Windows, Qt/X11, Qt/Mac, and Qt/Embedded (or with modified versions of Qt that use the same license as Qt), and distribute linked combinations including the two. You must obey the GNU General Public License in all respects for all of the code used other than Qt. If you modify this file, you may extend this exception to your version of the file, but you are not obligated to do so. If you do not wish to do so, delete this exception statement from your version.

21.2 GNU Free Documentation License

Version 1.3, 3 November 2008

Copyright 2000, 2001, 2002, 2007, 2008 Free Software Foundation, Inc

<http://fsf.org/>

Everyone is permitted to copy and distribute verbatim copies of this license document, but changing it is not allowed.

Preamble

The purpose of this License is to make a manual, textbook, or other functional and useful document "free" in the sense of freedom: to assure everyone the effective freedom to copy and redistribute it, with or without modifying it, either commercially or noncommercially. Secondarily, this License preserves for the author and publisher a way to get credit for their work, while not being considered responsible for modifications made by others.

This License is a kind of "copyleft", which means that derivative works of the document must themselves be free in the same sense. It complements the GNU General Public License, which is a copyleft license designed for free software.

We have designed this License in order to use it for manuals for free software, because free software needs free documentation: a free program should come with manuals providing the same freedoms that the software does. But this License is not limited to software manuals; it can be used for any textual work, regardless of subject matter or whether it is published as a printed book. We recommend this License principally for works whose purpose is instruction or reference.

1. APPLICABILITY AND DEFINITIONS

This License applies to any manual or other work, in any medium, that contains a notice placed by the copyright holder saying it can be distributed under the terms of this License. Such a notice grants a world-wide, royalty-free license, unlimited in duration, to use that work under the conditions stated herein. The **Document**, below, refers to any such manual or work. Any member of the public is a licensee, and is addressed as "**you**". You accept the license if you copy, modify or distribute the work in a way requiring permission under copyright law.

A "**Modified Version**" of the Document means any work containing the Document or a portion of it, either copied verbatim, or with modifications and/or translated into another language.

A "**Secondary Section**" is a named appendix or a front-matter section of the Document that deals exclusively with the relationship of the publishers or authors of the Document to the Document's overall subject (or to related matters) and contains nothing that could fall directly within that overall subject. (Thus, if the Document is in part a textbook of mathematics, a Secondary Section may not explain any mathematics.) The relationship could be a matter of historical connection with the subject or with related matters, or of legal, commercial, philosophical, ethical or political position regarding them.

The "**Invariant Sections**" are certain Secondary Sections whose titles are designated, as being those of Invariant Sections, in the notice that says that the Document is released under this License. If a section does not fit the above definition of Secondary then it is not allowed to be designated as Invariant. The Document may contain zero Invariant Sections. If the Document does not identify any Invariant Sections then there are none.

The "**Cover Texts**" are certain short passages of text that are listed, as Front-Cover Texts or Back-Cover Texts, in the notice that says that the Document is released under this License. A Front-Cover Text may be at most 5 words, and a Back-Cover Text may be at most 25 words.

A "**Transparent**" copy of the Document means a machine-readable copy, represented in a format whose specification is available to the general public, that is suitable for revising the document straightforwardly with generic text editors or (for images composed of pixels) generic paint programs or (for drawings) some widely available drawing editor, and that is suitable for input to text formatters or for automatic translation to a variety of formats suitable for input to text formatters. A copy made in an otherwise Transparent file format whose markup, or absence of markup, has been arranged to thwart or discourage subsequent modification by readers is not Transparent. An image format is not Transparent if used for any substantial amount of text. A copy that is not "Transparent" is called **Opaque**.

Examples of suitable formats for Transparent copies include plain ASCII without markup, Texinfo input format, LaTeX input format, SGML or XML using a publicly available DTD, and standard-conforming simple HTML, PostScript or PDF designed for human modification. Examples of transparent image formats include PNG, XCF and JPG. Opaque formats include proprietary formats that can be read and edited only by proprietary word processors, SGML or XML for which the DTD and/or processing tools are not generally available, and the machine-generated HTML, PostScript or PDF produced by some word processors for output purposes only.

The "**Title Page**" means, for a printed book, the title page itself, plus such following pages as are needed to hold, legibly, the material this License requires to appear in the title page. For works in formats which do not have any title page as such, "Title Page" means the text near the most prominent appearance of the work's title, preceding the beginning of the body of the text.

The "**publisher**" means any person or entity that distributes copies of the Document to the public.

A section "**Entitled XYZ**" means a named subunit of the Document whose title either is precisely XYZ or contains XYZ in parentheses following text that translates XYZ in another language. (Here XYZ stands for a specific section name mentioned below, such as "**Acknowledgements**", "**Dedications**", "**Endorsements**", or "**History**".)

To "**Preserve the Title**" of such a section when you modify the Document means that it remains a section "Entitled XYZ" according to this definition.

The Document may include Warranty Disclaimers next to the notice which states that this License applies to the Document. These Warranty Disclaimers are considered to be included by reference in this License, but only as regards disclaiming warranties: any other implication that these Warranty Disclaimers may have is void and has no effect on the meaning of this License.

2. VERBATIM COPYING

You may copy and distribute the Document in any medium, either commercially or noncommercially, provided that this License, the copyright notices, and the license notice saying this License applies to the Document are reproduced in all copies, and that you add no other conditions whatsoever to those of this License. You may not use technical measures to obstruct or control the reading or further copying of the copies you make or distribute. However, you may accept compensation in exchange for copies. If you distribute a large enough number of copies you must also follow the conditions in section 3.

You may also lend copies, under the same conditions stated above, and you may publicly display copies.

3. COPYING IN QUANTITY

If you publish printed copies (or copies in media that commonly have printed covers) of the Document, numbering more than 100, and the Document's license notice requires Cover Texts, you must enclose the copies in covers that carry, clearly and legibly, all these Cover Texts: Front-Cover Texts on the front cover, and Back-Cover Texts on the back cover. Both covers must also clearly and legibly identify you as the publisher of these copies. The front cover must present the full title with all words of the title equally prominent and visible. You may add other material on the covers in addition. Copying with changes limited to the covers, as long as they preserve the title of the Document and satisfy these conditions, can be treated as verbatim copying in other respects.

If the required texts for either cover are too voluminous to fit legibly, you should put the first ones listed (as many as fit reasonably) on the actual cover, and continue the rest onto adjacent pages.

If you publish or distribute Opaque copies of the Document numbering more than 100, you must either include a machine-readable Transparent copy along with each Opaque copy, or state in or with each Opaque copy a computer-network location from which the general network-using public has access to download using public-standard network protocols a complete Transparent copy of the Document, free of added material. If you use the latter option, you must take reasonably prudent steps, when you begin distribution of Opaque copies in quantity, to ensure that this Transparent copy will remain thus accessible at the stated location until at least one year after the last time you distribute an Opaque copy (directly or through your agents or retailers) of that edition to the public.

It is requested, but not required, that you contact the authors of the Document well before redistributing any large number of copies, to give them a chance to provide you with an updated version of the Document.

4. MODIFICATIONS

You may copy and distribute a Modified Version of the Document under the conditions of sections 2 and 3 above, provided that you release the Modified Version under precisely this License, with the Modified Version filling the role of the Document, thus licensing distribution and modification of the Modified Version to whoever possesses a copy of it. In addition, you must do these things in the Modified Version:

1. Use in the Title Page (and on the covers, if any) a title distinct from that of the Document, and from those of previous versions (which should, if there were any, be listed in the History section of the Document). You may use the same title as a previous version if the original publisher of that version gives permission.

2. List on the Title Page, as authors, one or more persons or entities responsible for authorship of the modifications in the Modified Version, together with at least five of the principal authors of the Document (all of its principal authors, if it has fewer than five), unless they release you from this requirement.

3. State on the Title page the name of the publisher of the Modified Version, as the publisher.

4. Preserve all the copyright notices of the Document.

5. Add an appropriate copyright notice for your modifications adjacent to the other copyright notices.

6. Include, immediately after the copyright notices, a license notice giving the public permission to use the Modified Version under the terms of this License, in the form shown in the Addendum below.

7. Preserve in that license notice the full lists of Invariant Sections and required Cover Texts given in the Document's license notice.

8. Include an unaltered copy of this License.

9. Preserve the section Entitled "History", Preserve its Title, and add to it an item stating at least the title, year, new authors, and publisher of the Modified Version as given on the Title Page. If there is no section Entitled "History" in the Document, create one stating the title, year, authors, and publisher of the Document as given on its Title Page, then add an item describing the Modified Version as stated in the previous sentence.

10. Preserve the network location, if any, given in the Document for public access to a Transparent copy of the Document, and likewise the network locations given in the Document for previous versions it was based on. These may be placed in the "History" section. You may omit a network location for a work that was published at least four years before the Document itself, or if the original publisher of the version it refers to gives permission.

11. For any section Entitled "Acknowledgements" or "Dedications", Preserve the Title of the section, and preserve in the section all the substance and tone of each of the contributor acknowledgements and/or dedications given therein.

12. Preserve all the Invariant Sections of the Document, unaltered in their text and in their titles. Section numbers or the equivalent are not considered part of the section titles.

13. Delete any section Entitled "Endorsements". Such a section may not be included in the Modified Version.

14. Do not retitle any existing section to be Entitled "Endorsements" or to conflict in title with any Invariant Section.

15. Preserve any Warranty Disclaimers.

If the Modified Version includes new front-matter sections or appendices that qualify as Secondary Sections and contain no material copied from the Document, you may at your option designate some or all of these sections as invariant. To do this, add their titles to the list of Invariant Sections in the Modified Version's license notice. These titles must be distinct from any other section titles.

You may add a section Entitled "Endorsements", provided it contains nothing but endorsements of your Modified Version by various parties—for example, statements of peer review or that the text has been approved by an organization as the authoritative definition of a standard.

You may add a passage of up to five words as a Front-Cover Text, and a passage of up to 25 words as a Back-Cover Text, to the end of the list of Cover Texts in the Modified Version. Only one passage of Front-Cover Text and one of Back-Cover Text may be added by (or through arrangements made by) any one entity. If the Document already includes a cover text for the same cover, previously added by you or by arrangement made by the same entity you are acting on behalf of, you may not add another; but you may replace the old one, on explicit permission from the previous publisher that added the old one.

The author(s) and publisher(s) of the Document do not by this License give permission to use their names for publicity for or to assert or imply endorsement of any Modified Version.

5. COMBINING DOCUMENTS

You may combine the Document with other documents released under this License, under the terms defined in section 4 above for modified versions, provided that you include in the combination all of the Invariant Sections of all of the original documents, unmodified, and list them all as Invariant Sections of your combined work in its license notice, and that you preserve all their Warranty Disclaimers.

The combined work need only contain one copy of this License, and multiple identical Invariant Sections may be replaced with a single copy. If there are multiple Invariant Sections with the same name but different contents, make the title of each such section unique by adding at the end of it, in parentheses, the name of the original author or publisher of that section if known, or else a unique number. Make the same adjustment to the section titles in the list of Invariant Sections in the license notice of the combined work.

In the combination, you must combine any sections Entitled "History" in the various original documents, forming one section Entitled "History"; likewise combine any sections Entitled "Acknowledgements", and any sections Entitled "Dedications". You must delete all sections Entitled "Endorsements".

6. COLLECTIONS OF DOCUMENTS

You may make a collection consisting of the Document and other documents released under this License, and replace the individual copies of this License in the various documents with a single copy that is included in the collection, provided that you follow the rules of this License for verbatim copying of each of the documents in all other respects.

You may extract a single document from such a collection, and distribute it individually under this License, provided you insert a copy of this License into the extracted document, and follow this License in all other respects regarding verbatim copying of that document.

7. AGGREGATION WITH INDEPENDENT WORKS

A compilation of the Document or its derivatives with other separate and independent documents or works, in or on a volume of a storage or distribution medium, is called an "aggregate" if the copyright resulting from the compilation is not used to limit the legal rights of the compilation's users beyond what the individual works permit. When the Document is included in an aggregate, this License does not apply to the other works in the aggregate which are not themselves derivative works of the Document.

If the Cover Text requirement of section 3 is applicable to these copies of the Document, then if the Document is less than one half of the entire aggregate, the Document's Cover Texts may be placed on covers that bracket the Document within the aggregate, or the electronic equivalent of covers if the Document is in electronic form. Otherwise they must appear on printed covers that bracket the whole aggregate.

8. TRANSLATION

Translation is considered a kind of modification, so you may distribute translations of the Document under the terms of section 4. Replacing Invariant Sections with translations requires special permission from their copyright holders, but you may include translations of some or all Invariant Sections in addition to the original versions of these Invariant Sections. You may include a translation of this License, and all the license notices in the Document, and any Warranty Disclaimers, provided that you also include the original English version of this License and the original versions of those notices and disclaimers. In case of a disagreement between the translation and the original version of this License or a notice or disclaimer, the original version will prevail.

If a section in the Document is Entitled "Acknowledgements", "Dedications", or "History", the requirement (section 4) to Preserve its Title (section 1) will typically require changing the actual title.

9. TERMINATION

You may not copy, modify, sublicense, or distribute the Document except as expressly provided under this License. Any attempt otherwise to copy, modify, sublicense, or distribute it is void, and will automatically terminate your rights under this License.

However, if you cease all violation of this License, then your license from a particular copyright holder is reinstated (a) provisionally, unless and until the copyright holder explicitly and finally terminates your license, and (b) permanently, if the copyright holder fails to notify you of the violation by some reasonable means prior to 60 days after the cessation.

Moreover, your license from a particular copyright holder is reinstated permanently if the copyright holder notifies you of the violation by some reasonable means, this is the first time you have received notice of violation of this License (for any work) from that copyright holder, and you cure the violation prior to 30 days after your receipt of the notice.

Termination of your rights under this section does not terminate the licenses of parties who have received copies or rights from you under this License. If your rights have been terminated and not permanently reinstated, receipt of a copy of some or all of the same material does not give you any rights to use it.

10. FUTURE REVISIONS OF THIS LICENSE

The Free Software Foundation may publish new, revised versions of the GNU Free Documentation License from time to time. Such new versions will be similar in spirit to the present version, but may differ in detail to address new problems or concerns. See http://www.gnu.org/copyleft/.

Each version of the License is given a distinguishing version number. If the Document specifies that a particular numbered version of this License "or any later version" applies to it, you have the option of following the terms and conditions either of that specified version or of any later version that has been published (not as a draft) by the Free Software Foundation. If the Document does not specify a version number of this License, you may choose any version ever published (not as a draft) by the Free Software Foundation. If the Document specifies that a proxy can decide which future versions of this License can be used, that proxy's public statement of acceptance of a version permanently authorizes you to choose that version for the Document.

11. RELICENSING

"Massive Multiauthor Collaboration Site" (or "MMC Site") means any World Wide Web server that publishes copyrightable works and also provides prominent facilities for anybody to edit those works. A public wiki that anybody can edit is an example of such a server. A "Massive Multiauthor Collaboration" (or "MMC") contained in the site means any set of copyrightable works thus published on the MMC site.

"CC-BY-SA" means the Creative Commons Attribution-Share Alike 3.0 license published by Creative Commons Corporation, a not-for-profit corporation with a principal place of business in San Francisco, California, as well as future copyleft versions of that license published by that same organization.

"Incorporate" means to publish or republish a Document, in whole or in part, as part of another Document.

An MMC is "eligible for relicensing" if it is licensed under this License, and if all works that were first published under this License somewhere other than this MMC, and subsequently incorporated in whole or in part into the MMC, (1) had no cover texts or invariant sections, and (2) were thus incorporated prior to November 1, 2008.

The operator of an MMC Site may republish an MMC contained in the site under CC-BY-SA on the same site at any time before August 1, 2009, provided the MMC is eligible for relicensing.

ADDENDUM: How to use this License for your documents

To use this License in a document you have written, include a copy of the License in the document and put the following copyright and license notices just after the title page:

> Copyright © YEAR YOUR NAME. Permission is granted to copy, distribute and/or modify this document under the terms of the GNU Free Documentation License, Version 1.3 or any later version published by the Free Software Foundation; with no Invariant Sections, no Front-Cover Texts, and no Back-Cover Texts. A copy of the license is included in the section entitled "GNU Free Documentation License".

If you have Invariant Sections, Front-Cover Texts and Back-Cover Texts, replace the "with ... Texts." line with this:

> with the Invariant Sections being LIST THEIR TITLES, with the Front-Cover Texts being LIST, and with the Back-Cover Texts being LIST.

If you have Invariant Sections without Cover Texts, or some other combination of the three, merge those two alternatives to suit the situation.

If your document contains nontrivial examples of program code, we recommend releasing these examples in parallel under your choice of free software license, such as the GNU General Public License, to permit their use in free software.

## CHAPTER 22

Literature and Web References

GDAL-SOFTWARE-SUITE. Geospatial data abstraction library. http://www.gdal.org, 2013.

GRASS-PROJECT. Geographic ressource analysis support system. http://grass.osgeo.org , 2013.

NETELER, M., AND MITASOVA, H. Open source gis: A grass gis approach, 2008.

OGR-SOFTWARE-SUITE. Geospatial data abstraction library. http://www.gdal.org/ogr , 2013.

OPEN-GEOSPATIAL-CONSORTIUM.   Web   map   service   (1.1.1)   implementation   specification. http://portal.opengeospatial.org, 2002.

OPEN-GEOSPATIAL-CONSORTIUM.   Web   map   service   (1.3.0)   implementation   specification. http://portal.opengeospatial.org, 2004.

POSTGIS-PROJECT. Spatial support for postgresql. http://postgis.refractions.net/ , 2013.

www.ingramcontent.com/pod-product-compliance
Lightning Source LLC
LaVergne TN
LVHW060135070326
832902LV00018B/2808